MANAGEMENT
A Basic Handbook

W. F. COVENTRY is officially retired but continues to be active in British academic and business circles. He has served as course director of business policy with the Polytechnic of Central London, general director of the third largest building society in the United Kingdom, and president of the Building Society's Institute of Great Britain. He still plays an active consulting role with the BBC and as the Building Society's honorary vice president.

IRVING BURSTINER received his Ph.D. from St. John's University and is currently a professor of marketing at Baruch College of Business and Public Administration, the City University of New York. In addition to teaching and research, he conducts seminars for administrators, both in public education and in industry. He has served in a number of management positions, has published in professional journals, is active in the field of creative problem-solving, and owns the Creative Management Institute, a New York consulting firm.

MANAGEMENT
A Basic Handbook

W. F. COVENTRY
and Irving Burstiner

A SPECTRUM BOOK

Prentice-Hall, Inc., *Englewood Cliffs, New Jersey 07632*

Library of Congress Cataloging in Publication Data

COVENTRY, WILLIAM F
    Management: a basic handbook.

    (A Spectrum Book)
    Original ed. published in 1970 under title:
Management made simple.
    Includes bibliographies and index.
    1. Industrial management. 2. Management.
I. Burstiner, Irving, joint author. II. Title.
HD31.C627 1977   658.4   77-2931
ISBN 0-13-549188-6
ISBN 0-13-549170-3 pbk.

© 1977 by Prentice-Hall, Inc.
Englewood Cliffs, New Jersey 07632

A SPECTRUM BOOK

10 9 8 7 6 5 4 3 2 1

Printed in the United States of America

PRENTICE-HALL INTERNATIONAL, INC., *London*

PRENTICE-HALL OF AUSTRALIA PTY. LIMITED, *Sydney*

PRENTICE-HALL OF CANADA, LTD., *Toronto*

PRENTICE-HALL OF INDIA PRIVATE LIMITED, *New Delhi*

PRENTICE-HALL OF JAPAN, INC., *Tokyo*

PRENTICE-HALL OF SOUTHEAST ASIA PTE. LTD., *Singapore*

WHITEHALL BOOKS LIMITED, *Wellington, New Zealand*

Contents

Preface

It is axiomatic that the success of any enterprise largely depends upon the caliber and efficacy of the people who staff its managerial slots. In turn, efficient executive performance (given a sufficiently high level of self-motivation) can be linked to a thorough grounding in the fundamentals of management and to the development of requisite human and conceptual skills, as well as those demonstrating technical and communicative proficiency.

Given the rapidly changing world environment, the mechanics and intricacies of managing an enterprise—whether it be within the private or the public sector of a modern economy—grow increasingly complex and varied with each succeeding year. Consequently, this work, which was originally published in Great Britain in 1970, has since been updated and revised twice (1973, 1975). Because of its intrinsic value for present and would-be managers everywhere, I have attempted, in coauthoring this present text, to extract Professor Coventry's material from its original cultural framework and apply it, with studied care, to the United States politico-socio-economic environment that so sharply diverges from its British counterpart. I hope that this process of "Americanizing" an English basic work will be helpful to American readers.

As Professor Coventry wrote in his introductory remarks to the 1975 edition, "Most people today have some interest in management, from the captains of industry, commerce and finance, public administrators, and the like, right down to the ambitious rank and file. Even the unambitious are concerned to the point of tilting at management and the way it allegedly works. Between are the middle managers, supervisors, and foremen. There are also the small business owners—for whom a special chapter has been written—voluntary workers running a variety of concerns, and housewives managing the affairs of the home."

Management: A Basic Handbook can serve admirably as a basic textbook for a one-semester introductory course at either junior- or senior-college level; as meaningful supplementary reading for the graduate business student in specializations ranging from accounting to marketing and law; as a refresher or "brush-up" reference work for senior managerial personnel; as a concise, informative foundation for executives-to-be in industrial training programs; or simply as a self-study text for all those who aspire to a working knowledge of management.

Unnecessary business jargon has been deliberately avoided. Although both management theory and practice are presented in a simple, straightforward, and logical way, the emphasis has been most decidedly placed on the latter in the hope that this will enable the reader to gain a realistic view of management, from the top. For further, in-depth treatment of each subject area in the book, a list of *Suggested Further Reading* appears at the end of each chapter.

Entire chapters are devoted to current areas of interest, such as *mergers and acquisitions, long-range planning, decision-making,* and *management and the small firm.* There is detailed, intensive treatment of the four major policy areas in business management: *marketing/sales, production, finance,* and *personnel.*

—IRVING BURSTINER

MANAGEMENT
A Basic Handbook

ONE

A Practical Approach to Management

During the past several decades, the "managerial revolution" has changed the status of management from amateur to professional. Consequently, there is much that is old hat to be forgotten and much that is new to be learned. A forward-looking, more exact philosophy is in the air. Management can no longer fly by the seat of its pants; it must use instead more accurate instruments and vastly improved techniques.

A fresh emphasis is placed on corporate growth with mergers and acquisitions, on long-range planning, on management by objectives, and on computer and other mathematical services; there are a new vocabulary and an unsatisfied demand for further education. "Profits" is no longer a dirty word; it rightfully measures the use made by management of all available resources. Quantitative techniques are, therefore, much in vogue.

Nevertheless, there is still room for the inspired hunch, though backed today by probability-theory decision-making. Happily, too, most managers still regard people as more important than things. A place exists for the social or behavioral specialist as well as for the accountant.

Sooner or later, the old generation of managers will have to be replaced by today's youth. As yet, however, there do not seem to be enough recruits of the right caliber joining the ranks, perhaps because the incentives for a managerial career are somewhat blunted by taxation. For all that, however, the challenge of the 1970s is exciting, dynamic, and full of opportunities; there is ample room for the best brains.

It is with this thought in mind that we begin our outline of the latest developments in management practice. Although limits of space have made it necessary to concentrate on the private sector of the economy, most of the text is equally valid for management in the public sector. Today, a goodly number of institutions of higher education offer degrees in public administration and/or public policy to prepare substantial numbers of young people to enter the public sector as managers-to-be. Government departments and agencies such as the Post Office and other state and local authorities are seeking managerial competence and accenting "productivity" as never before. Often, such agencies enlist the aid of local universities and top businessmen in helping to introduce advanced management techniques developed in the private sector.

Similarly, in the running of local governments and municipalities, it is becoming increasingly recognized that each one should be treated as if it were a large corporation, again using every relevant management technique. The only difference would appear to be the lack of a profit incentive, the usual criterion for measuring success.

MANAGEMENT DEFINED

Management has as many definitions as there are managers; so much depends on the viewpoint, or background, of the speaker or writer concerned. Some, like a personnel manager, have a natural bias towards the sociological approach, being concerned mainly with human activities. Others, such as a financial tycoon, can just as easily show a preference for the quantitative aspects.

Somewhere in between is the president, or general manager, with an integrated and balanced viewpoint—a bird's-eye view—taking in the whole scene at once. That at least is the theory. Yet all too often, despite promotion to general management, the former accountant, for example, still remains an accountant. For one of the problems of any specialist in this context is learning how to stand back from his profession in order to look at the business objectively, as a whole, instead of from one side or the other.

Disciplines and Integration

In the academic teaching of management, the first few terms are usually devoted to basic concepts allied to separate disciplines (i.e., human, quantitative, financial, and commercial aspects), after which increasing emphasis is placed on integration. The task is then related to identifying and understanding the common core of top-management problems, the subject being taught as a developing and practical contribution to general management skills.

Reference has already been made to "top" and "general" management, and reference will also be made to "central" management. For the moment, however, these can all be considered as being one and the same thing, and would normally include the board of directors, in particular the chief executive officer or president, a general manager, and any other "generalists" of similar rank and responsibilities, whatever the actual titles they might be given in real life.

A Broad Definition

Basically, there are few problems of definition, as most of them have a common thread. This is to the effect that a manager is one who is responsible for getting things done through other people, instead of doing the job himself (we will conveniently assume that the masculine includes the feminine). With stated objectives to achieve, i.e., to produce certain goods or services, he directs human activities, with the help of the other resources available, towards those ends. As a positive way of life, the ambitious junior clerk could well think of himself as being on a management ladder the day he delegates some of his work to a new junior clerk, keeping a watchful eye on what he is doing in the process. There is nothing like having the right idea and starting young.

Popular Considerations

Textbooks tend to devote valuable space to the thoughts and concepts of pioneers and to the history of management generally. Our intention, however, is to study the present and look ahead. Some textbooks are also keen to debate whether management is an art or a science and whether managers are born or made. From a sociological point of view management would seem to be mainly an art (for example, how to motivate people to give of their best), whereas from a quantitative point of view it appears to be far more scientific. But even on the sociological side we are now becoming familiar with behavioral scientists. This is dangerous ground for debate anyway, as it is a major philosophical study in itself to distinguish between "art" and "science," whether related to management or not.

As to whether managers are born or made, there must, of course, be certain minimal innate qualities (i.e., potential) which can be added to effectively by proper training and planned experience. Fortunately, or unfortunately, we have already been created; but at least we can build on nature, such as it is in our case, by adopting the right management attitudes and using every possible means to come to grips with a fascinating career. The personal satisfaction arising from even modest managerial achievements usually makes such efforts well worthwhile.

BASIC CONCEPTS AND THE MANAGERIAL REVOLUTION

Each company, or similar body, may be quite different from others of the same genus, but for *any* organization a common core of problems exists at the top, to be dealt with by its management. These basic problems may be classified as follows:

(a) Objectives and Policies   As a first step there is a need to establish corporate objectives (where the company is aiming to go) and determine the major policies (how it intends to get there) to be followed. These and other terms will be defined and illustrated later, but for the

moment they should not be difficult to understand. Fundamentally, it is important to focus attention on the activities to be undertaken, to establish guidelines for the way ahead, and to ensure that everyone concerned knows clearly what is going on.

(b) Tailor-made Organization   A purpose-built structure should be set up to determine responsibilities for the various jobs that must be done (in order to achieve the objectives) and the formal relationships between these jobs.

(c) Resources.   Then, of course, there must be a building or buildings to work in (factory, warehouse, office, shop, etc.), machines and other technical equipment, furniture, stock, managers, supervisors, and supporting staff. These we talk about as "resources."

(d) Planning the Activities.   Finally, there must be long-term and short-term programs of work; also appropriate techniques for getting the operations carried out, making sure at all times that they conform effectively to the objectives and policies that have been laid down.

All this is fairly obvious, but needs to be stated. Usually, of course, a manager grows up in, or takes over, an established concern, but even so a "grass-roots" approach to a new responsibility is always worthwhile. For sometimes the obvious is overlooked. How many firms, for example, know exactly what are their *real* objectives, as opposed to assumed objectives?

Mechanics and Dynamics

A traditional (surely a dangerous word to use in a book on management!) approach to concepts connotes a list of functions under two main headings: the "mechanics" of management and the "dynamics." These are given in Fig. 1, each function being dealt with in detail later. It may be noted in passing, however, that the principal functions are Planning, Organizing and Controlling and that Leadership is essentially the motivating force.

Paid to Solve Problems

As management is largely concerned with identifying, analyzing, and solving problems, top managers are likely to have a difficult time.

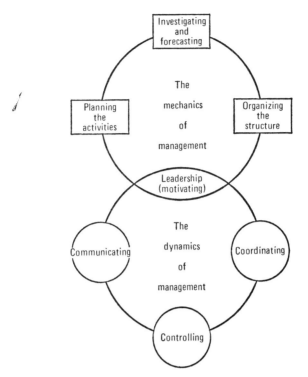

FIGURE 1. The traditional functions of management

This is, of course, exactly why they are paid top salaries. In dealing with awkward people and tackling tough problems each day, they clearly require above-average intelligence, tact, patience, and resourcefulness; also firmness and a modicum of ruthlessness. It is necessary, too, that their judgment, as reflected in decisions, should be far more often right than wrong. These, then, are some of the qualities of management implied in its basic definition.

Through the 1970s

With an expanding economy, management has needed to become even more vital and demanding. The market is now worldwide in scope, with a tendency towards larger and more complex corporate units. Mergers and acquisitions add to the many problems of scale

—for, regrettably, size and efficiency do not always go together. The computer and other scientific aids to management have already made their mark, with new "generations" of equipment still on the drawing-board. In a moon-landing age, even space, let alone the sky, is no longer a limit. Hence the so-called "managerial revolution," which makes some of our older textbooks read like *Alice in Wonderland.*

Basically, the main turnaround has been for management to start *actively* to manage and not be managed. Environmental influences may seem overpowering at times, but there can be no room today for passive drifting. Nor is there room for "ad-lib" manufacturing likely to embarrass even a top-flight sales force. Instead, the initial emphasis should be placed fairly and squarely on marketing, while production is effectively planned to match up with demand.

Such a logical approach implies setting realistic (but exacting) targets, making top-level judgments based on *all* the information obtainable, and, whenever possible, allowing local managers (who are nearer the market) to make working decisions on the spot. This means delegating responsibility and authority well down the line, training throughout for more effective personal contribution, and converting complacency into planned and positive performance. In this sophisticated era of the 1970s, management must be improving skills and more mature philosophies if consistent and continued success is to be assured. The overall question then remaining is whether the managerial revolution, dynamic and dramatic though its achievements may have been to date, is as yet proceeding fast enough. Fortunately, the reader may be one of those who can help it on its way, not only through the 1970s, but towards the next century as well.

THE CHALLENGE OF MANAGEMENT

Currently there is a shortage of top-flight managers. Yet so many of the old guard, and the not-so-old, have been terminated for a variety of reasons, including mergers and reorganization. Certainly the incompetents should be weeded out to make way for the best of the up-and-coming, not kicked upstairs or promoted sideways where they can do no harm. For, in a computer world, today is the age of youth. But despite that, there should still be room for *seasoned* youth, in their fifties or early sixties, who over the years have conscientiously achieved invaluable experience and contemporary sophistication.

Opportunities for Youth

In modern business it is the quality of management, and of leadership in particular, that determines in the end whether a corporate body will succeed, exist, or fail. For even in the largest companies, the major decisions are normally taken by a small number at the top, with wide-ranging consequences. There is surely an opportunity, and a challenge, here for youth, at a time when what a man should earn is becoming less dependent on his age. Yet, as mentioned earlier, the right kind of professionally qualified new management talent seems to be in short supply. Fortunately, looking into the future, there is increasing evidence of a growing interest in management technology, backed by every medium for management studies, and of a healthy desire to find out what modern management is all about and why. But this improving trend still has a long way to go.

The growth of large-scale enterprises, including national and multinational corporations, connotes exciting opportunities for future management. These should, in time, be able to attract most of the "high fliers" required to meet the challenge of the approaching 2000s. Fiscal and other disincentives there may be, but true motivation goes well beyond take-home pay. In the meantime, companies and other organizations must make the best use of the human resources they already have, which, however obvious to the outside observer, all too often tend to be overlooked internally—for the budding prophet in his own country is seldom accorded honor.

The Protest of Youth

Youth today is not prepared to accept the "establishment" at its face value, without asking a great many questions. The new generation of students, of all political persuasions, suspect the concentrated power of government in big business, the economic strain of the defense effort, the industrial giants, the old-school tie, boardroom networks, the alleged lack of social responsibility, the sordid profit motive, and the emotive gap between management and worker.

The new generation talks instead of "industrial democracy" and "worker participation"; they see a case for equality of the sexes; they dislike "depersonalization" and argue for "human rights." Whereas youth once served its years of apprenticeship, graduating to management, if at all, only in old age, it now becomes impatient for experience in management almost from the start. So far as *qualified* youth is concerned, this has its points, which the old guard in management would do well to appreciate. For the record of youth in management studies, illustrated by its display of keenness, application to hard work, imagination and forward-looking executive qualities, augur well for the future.

Nevertheless, youth can still learn something from the past. It cannot effect revolutionary change overnight, but must proceed to build a bridge between the best of the old and the new industrial revolution ahead.

Industry in the past tended to be concentrated in family hands, but with mergers and acquisitions and complex organizations, many such firms have now become large national concerns with near-monopoly power. How far the ideals of youth, with special reference to "democracy in business management," can be successfully infiltrated into the established way of life is a matter for the future. The tremendous energy being expended in political demonstrations against this and that, if directed towards the industrial scene instead, could go a long way towards Utopia. But there is a vast gap between criticizing and destroying the *status quo* and making a constructive success of the resources that would be left. Fortunately this is the very challenge that, given the chance, youth would have the courage to accept.

It is highly significant and encouraging in this context that so many thousands of young people are currently matriculated in part-time or full-time business management programs at our colleges and universities.

THE MOTIVATION OF MANAGEMENT

It is important, with the space-age future in mind, to assess the main factors which motivate managers today. At first sight, it might appear that high salaries would be the main attraction, but financial incentives in business have their limits net of tax. Fringe benefits (special pension plans, stock options, company cars, executive dining-rooms, foreign travel, expense accounts, etc.) are also subject to fiscal control.

Nevertheless, with promotion through the hierarchy, it is possible to achieve an increasing standard of living, inflation notwithstanding. Once certain acceptable standards have been achieved every effort will usually be made to keep them.

Disincentives

Yet, in any questionnaire completed by top or other levels of management on the subject of motivation, financial incentives tend to be well down the list in order of importance. At any point, too, managers could well be expected to stop and weigh the time, effort, and risk involved in taking on more arduous responsibilities, against the satisfactions that they, and their families, would be likely to gain from extra pay. Promotions within the firm, or by joining another firm, usually cause domestic disturbance, perhaps more travel, and increased expenses, to say nothing of additional worry. Money alone then seems hardly the best way to stimulate managerial performance or motivate mobility.

Nonfinancial Aspects

The answer can usually be found in nonfinancial incentives. Top rating in questionnaire assessments is often given to personal achievements, measured against mutually acceptable company targets, and the recognition given to those achievements. Then there is the interest of the job itself, the satisfaction derived from doing it well, and of sharing in the firm's successes—usually measured by rate of growth and increased profitability. Allied factors usually mentioned are promotion prospects, opportunities for taking on increased responsibilities, the nature of the work itself, job security, and the climate of work. In the successful firm there is usually managerial drive, excitement, a sense of urgency, and a feeling of power. Yet, fortunately, few managers seek such power merely for the sake of power.

Public recognition, too, attaches to the top jobs; and social satisfactions can often be felt through the impact on the man in the street of decisions made concerning goods or services offered. High office usually provides ancillary opportunities for public service outside the firm, but for most managers the sheer weight of responsibility tends to concentrate their efforts on the job itself.

Rewards and Penalties

Reference is often made to the "carrot and the stick." Recognitions of achievement, at all managerial levels, should be genuinely related to efforts made; but at a time of no growth, or no profit, there is hardly likely to be much recognition given even to the successful. In such a context, a case could well be made out for demotion, inspired resignation, or straight dismissal, to weed out costly passengers; or, to put it in modern terms, to have a "productivity shake-out." In general, however, it is unlikely, with mature management personalities each operating at a reasonable standard, that there would be much long-term reaction to either carrots or sticks.

By the very nature of the pyramid of promotion there can be only a few top jobs in management. Motivation, to be effective at other managerial levels, depends on a clear line of command so that everyone knows to whom he must account for his results and who could be expected (it is devoutly hoped) to recognize his achievements.

Motivating Future Managers

With the 1970s and beyond in mind, industry and other sections of the economy requiring professional managers must do everything possible to attract the new recruits wherever and whenever they become available. In this way companies can continue to improve the quality of their management team and be able to cope with developing techniques in a rapidly changing world. But, having hired the graduates, perhaps as trainee managers, it is essential that they should not be disenchanted through imperfect motivation. To avoid this they must be trusted, used, and given at least some responsibility as soon as possible. They need stretching mentally and encouragement to learn what *real* management is all about.

HOW TO STUDY MANAGEMENT

Assuming a sound basic education, and some experience of business life, the next step for the budding manager is obviously to study management. In the Armed Forces, suitable officer material is selected on potential and then trained specifically in the arts and crafts of defense. So it should be with a management career, but there are still those from the old school, the school of experience only, who consider that management cannot be taught. Yet experience alone cannot be sufficient; for, in extreme cases, 30 years' experience simply means one year's experience repeated 30 times.

Facilities for Further Education

Ideally, the best way to study management is to enroll in a postgraduate/post-experience program at a polytechnic institute, graduate school of business, or university management center, either full-time or part-time. A master's degree in business management or a Certificate in Management Studies (the latter offered at a small number of universities around the country) is a valuable objective. In the certificate program, for example, the participant has a continuing opportunity to sharpen his wits on relatively youthful contemporaries, to pool his knowledge and ideas, take part in business games, help to "solve" case studies, and listen to, and discuss, the experiences of specialists and generalists from the academic and business worlds.

Unfortunately, some of the old-timers are still resisting change. Where this is so a gap exists between the new generation of management recruits, with the latest techniques at their fingertips, and their experienced seniors who do not understand and perhaps even distrust what they are talking about. But this will solve itself in time, and the young trainees, given wisdom and having gained respect, should help to leaven the whole process of future management. Meanwhile, the experienced seniors can still take advantage of management-appreciation courses and of the many top-level conferences and seminars organized for their benefit. By this, and similar means, the managerial generation gap can at least be partly closed. Professional examinations (accounting, insurance, engineering, etc.) are tending more and more to include the subject of management, in some form or another, in the syllabus. For it is becoming increasingly recognized that the specialist of today may well become the chief executive officer of tomorrow.

In-company training, including special courses and learning by doing the job, has clear practical value, too, and will be dealt with in Chapter Fourteen, coupled with a few thoughts on management training in general.

Self-help Today

The purpose of this section, however, is to introduce a note of self-help; for, whether or not the reader has the kind of opportunities mentioned above, he can still take a lively and intelligent interest in the business world around him. He can start, for example, by reading a few basic up-to-date books on management and then branching out into more detailed accounts of specific ideas and techniques. In support, there are now some excellent management and business periodicals on the market, with pertinent and informed comment on current developments. Both the *New York Times* and the *Wall Street Journal* provide their quotas of management information, with appropriate articles and special supplements. Reading widely in this way, dovetailing everything into an understanding of the business world at large, links new knowledge to daily work, and adds both purpose and color to the daily routine.

Keeping "With It"

A loose-leaf notebook or card system, for jotting down notes, and/or folders of carefully selected articles worth further thought can be built up as a personalized aid to progress. But, obviously, to be of any *real* value, such notes and articles must be conscientiously read, thoroughly digested, and weeded out continuously. In addition, it may be considered worthwhile to study autobiographies and biographies of outstanding captains of industry and case histories of selected industries and firms to illustrate the successes and setbacks of top management in action.

A Working Philosophy

It may be useful also to build up a comprehensive account (perhaps in chart form) of one's own experience of corporate business activity and attempt to trace the theoretical concepts and techniques of management learned as seen to exist (or not exist) in practice. By this method the reader would soon become accustomed to thinking constructively, in terms of higher management, thereby acquiring a working philosophy at the right level. Knowledge for the sake of knowledge has a limited use, as it can so soon become out of date. But today the modern concept of teaching is one of educating for change, which clearly is far more positive in outlook and implies the achievement of creative and flexible thinking on the part of the student. It is within this spirit of teaching oneself how to continue to learn that the above suggestions have been made. This then is the practical and personal approach to management.

Professionals versus Amateurs

Knowing all the latest management techniques is not sufficient in and of itself. The important factor is understanding when and how to apply them and being able to appreciate their limitations. The whole process of professionalism lies in having a fund of expertise that goes well beyond the present problem or situation. The effective manager is then able to select from the range of alternatives available to him and is not confined to a makeshift solution or half-baked technique. This means extensive training, as well as experience, and it is here that the management schools are making such a material contribution and becoming, deservedly, a growth industry in their own right.

The amateur, on the other hand, may be full of enthusiasm and "off-the-cuff" effort, but sooner or later he is going to find himself unable to cope with the increasing complexities of the years ahead. Only by having a top layer of professionalism can industry today, with all its environmental problems, hope to prosper toward the challenging world of tomorrow.

Nor is there much room for those who constantly look backward over their shoulder. Tradition, history, and precedents all have their residual value in management, but survival means creativity with the accent on innovation. This connotes new products, new processes, new approaches to problems, and new structures, and anticipated adjustment to dynamic environment in an era of rapid technological change. It is an exciting and stimulating world, but one that needs the informed professional rather than the inspired amateur, whatever may have been the experience in the past. There is, of course, still room for the inspired amateur, but not, it is contended, at the top.

THE PLAN OF THIS BOOK

With the reader in mind, the aim has been to deal with management theory and practice in a simple, straightforward, and logical way; modern concepts have accordingly been reduced to essentials for better understanding. The text, too, has been kept as free as possible from unnecessary jargon, but at the same time, all important terms and techniques have been mentioned by their fashionable name. For, jargon or not, the potential manager would be unwise (particularly in these days of one-upmanship) not to have at least a working knowledge of managerial matters currently in vogue.

Similarly, for space reasons, there has not been the usual indulgence in an academic spate of references and footnotes about this or that writer, theory, or point of view. Nevertheless, a personal debt is fully acknowledged to all management writers and practitioners who have, in any way, influenced the setting down of concept or practice in the following pages.

There is a danger, of course, in attempting to simplify and condense, but it is hoped that the younger reader will regard this book as a first approximation only, and make full use of the lists of "Suggested Further Reading" given at the end of each chapter. Management in all its forms is a fascinating subject, and the volume of literature, from both sides of the Atlantic, is by now overwhelming. Hence the selections concluding each chapter are of necessity arbitrary.

Accent on the Practical

Emphasis has been placed on management practice, as opposed to pure theory, in the hope that this will enable the reader to gain a realistic view of a business or other enterprise from the top. Admittedly many readers will still be on their way up the management ladder, but even so this overall view should enable them to see their present jobs better, both in perspective and in depth. To start with, it is necessary to look at the company, or other business organization, as a whole in its total dynamic environment. Specialized topics can then be dealt with in logical sequence later.

Still on a practical note, brief mention must be made of the "power game" or "playing politics," which merits no elaboration here. Sufficient to say, by way of warning, that a great deal can happen in business, and does, which seems a far cry from the theories of textbook management. With this in mind the embryo manager would be well advised to watch events if only in self-defense.

Summary

1. The Managerial Revolution
   a. Management has changed from amateur to professional.
   b. Managers must *actively* manage.
   c. Marketing today comes before production.
   d. More sophisticated skills are needed.
2. Definition
   a. Management means achieving stated objectives (usually to produce certain goods or services) by directing human and other resources towards those ends.
   b. Management must be positive.
3. Basic Concepts
   a. Objectives and policies are the corporate guidelines.
   b. The functions of management are seen as "mechanics" and "dynamics."

   c. Management is concerned with the identification, analysis, and solution of problems.

4. *Today's Challenge to Youth*

   a. Management opportunities abound, but new talent is in short supply.

   b. Plenty of qualified recruits are equal to the challenge, but they tend to be impatient.

5. *Motivation of Management*

   a. Besides financial reward, nonfinancial incentives ranging from job satisfaction to public recognition are important considerations.

   b. Interest of management trainees must be sustained.

6. *Preparing for Management*

   a. The requirements are practical experience plus management courses.

   b. Managers and graduate recruits can learn from each other.

   c. Vital preparation includes self-help and acquiring the right working philosophy.

Suggested Further Reading

     As recommended, many readers will want to widen their knowledge of management principles and practice. To help them, a short list of books for specific reading or reference has been added to each chapter. The following, however, are necessarily of a more general nature:

ALBERS, H.H. *Principles of Management: A Modern Approach.* 4th ed. New York: Wiley, 1974.

ALLEN, L.A. *Professional Management: New Concepts and Proven Practices.* New York: McGraw-Hill, 1973.

CLELAND, D.I., AND W.R. KING. *Management: A Systems Approach.* New York: McGraw-Hill, 1972.

DALE, E. *Management: Theory and Practice.* 3d ed. New York: McGraw-Hill, 1973.

DRUCKER, P.F. *Management: Tasks, Responsibilities, Practices.* New York: Harper & Row, 1974.

LUTHANS, F. *Introduction to Management: A Contingency Approach.* New York: McGraw-Hill, 1976.

MCFARLAND, E. *Management Principles and Practices.* 4th ed. New York: Macmillan, 1974.

WEBBER, R.A. *Management: Basic Elements of Managing Organizations.* Homewood, Ill.: Irwin, 1975.

WORTMAN, M.S., AND F. LUTHANS. *Emerging Concepts in Management.* 2d ed. New York: Macmillan, 1975.

Various publications of the American Management Association.

TWO

The Dynamic Setting
of a Company

For most people, the word "dynamic" implies something vital, energetic, and powerful, as in a context such as "dynamic personality" or the "dynamics of management." But the basic meaning is movement, or change, as opposed to "static," and it is with the changing scene that this chapter is concerned.

On the Alert for Change

These are certainly vital, energetic, and powerful days, for it is only necessary to read the newspapers, watch television, or listen to the radio to be reminded constantly of the tremendous impact on everyday life of international and national stress and strife. Wars (hot and cold), strikes, crimes of violence, student unrest, religious controversy, massive shortages, political by-play, and a variety of other comparable topics all jostle daily for individual attention. Then, there are the all-too-familiar (and depressing) economic problems, ranging the gamut from prolonged inflationary pressures that contribute towards an ever-mounting cost-of-living level through retrenchment in industry and government services at all levels to the diligent hunt for alternate sources of energy other than oil, and so on *ad nauseam*. But it is with the impact of change on the business community that we are mainly concerned here. For the overall environment is seen to be constantly on the move, sometimes at a slow pace but mostly these days at a much more rapid tempo. Many years ago the average manager could contentedly jog along, more or less successfully, serenely expecting the mixture as before, but today's manager has to be continually on the alert for the unexpected.

At any given moment he must be ready and able to adapt himself and the operations of his company to the opportunities and challenges that come along with change. It is perhaps in this latter sense that the word "dynamic" can be given its more exciting meaning.

Psychological Aspects

In business, as in other walks of life, few people are really very happy about change; for the majority it produces stresses and strains and releases fears and frustrations. But for the firm, or similar organization, it can bring new life and vitality, the other side of the coin entirely from complacency and slow corporate death.

Hence, there are two opposing forces which it is the duty of management to try to reconcile. As well as adapting the firm to make the best use of opportunities arising from change, it must, at the same time, endeavor to preserve an atmosphere of stability and continuity for the rank and file. In practice, however, such a reconciliation is not always possible to achieve.

Forecasting Change

To take full advantage of change (i.e., to become more effective, more profitable, etc.) management must be able to anticipate change. There is obvious merit in being a step ahead of competitors, of being prepared for a breakthrough, or ready to meet an emergency when it arises, but forecasting business conditions of this order is a complex operation. Fortunately, there are modern techniques to help with forecasting; these will be dealt with later.

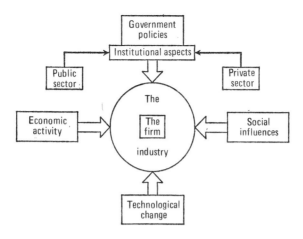

FIGURE 2. The firm in its national environment

Environment Vital to Management

It is of little use, therefore, to study any kind of management without first giving full weight to the environment in which it has to conduct its business. The extreme case, perhaps, is the international or multinational company with separate organizations in different countries, making it even more difficult to be able to adapt itself to a variety of changing circumstances. In fact, *any* company, or other organization, wishing to make an effective environmental study must start with the international scene and then narrow it down to the country or countries in which it operates and has its being. For the world gets effectively smaller every day and the individual firm must increasingly think internationally. Similarly it must look at the industrial setting as a whole before facing up to its own performance within that industry. By starting with a world-wide canvas it can finish up with a clearer picture of its own local sphere of influence, seen now in true perspective, and with top management better prepared to forecast and deal with change.

Although in practice the setting of a company has to be considered as a whole, it is convenient for our present purpose to confine discussion to our own society and to break down the total environment into the usual constituent parts shown in Figure 2.

GOVERNMENT POLICIES AND
THEIR EFFECTS

It used to be argued by supporters of the *laissez-faire* principle that the economy of a country was best left alone and should be allowed to work itself out, eventually, through the natural laws of supply and demand. This approach, of course, had its roots in the ideals of "pure" capitalism, a hypothetical economic structure designed to provide a nation's requisite goods and services, at a profit for the makers and sellers of such goods and services, in the most efficient manner. This idealized version of capitalism evidenced certain characteristics, the most important of which included private ownership of all property, free and unrestricted competition, and the complete absence of governmental interference in business and industry. Today's reality, however, has been labeled "limited" or "modified" capitalism, since not all property is privately owned, competition is not so free as consumers would prefer it to be, and government involvement and activity—at federal, state, and local levels—is considerable in scope within the private sector. In practice, one extreme (i.e., for the government to do nothing) can be as bad as the other (i.e., government dominating the industrial scene), but in the United States, at any rate, there tends to be a middle course. This compromise varies in bias from time to time between too much government interference and too little. In recent years, the realization has been growing that more government involvement in business can mitigate against free enterprise and a higher standard of living; consequently, the pendulum has been swinging back the other way—at least in political circles.

Politics and Economics

It is difficult to determine today where the influence of politics ends and that of economics starts, or the other way around. But, whatever the order, it is clear to everyone that government policies can, and do, vitally affect the trend of business activity. Most managers contrive to keep abreast of major policy changes, with special reference to those which directly affect their own sphere of industry, but other political influences exert an indirect effect and must first be identified and analyzed. The following more general examples are largely relevant to business as a whole.

Main Areas for Intervention

(a) Balance-of-payments measures, including import quotas and tariffs, trade expansion and development plans, and financial credit.

(b) Environmental protection policies to clean up our atmosphere and waterways, combat various forms of pollution, and avoid other ecological threats.

(c) Taxation changes in such areas as corporate income taxes, capital gains tax, and general sales and excise taxes.

(d) Legislation to control corporations, monopolies, mergers and acquisitions, fraudulent advertising, restrictive practices, and the like.

(e) "Security" legislation designed to protect the safety and well-being of consumers in many areas, including product information and reliability, credit protection, and old age and retirement.

(f) "Affirmative action" policies designed to guarantee the right of employment to minorities of all types.

Making Management Decisions Difficult

Fundamentally, of course, the federal government has the task of keeping the economy in balance, internally and externally; of making the most efficient use of resources; of protecting industry and the consumer; and of providing special services for industry, even intervening where essential for the common good. It is also responsible for monitoring the annual growth rate of total output, commensurate with productive capacity, bearing in mind that unused capacity produces unemployment.

With regard to the political and legal environment, it is essential to keep abreast of new developments and impending changes, in order to be able to make positive policy decisions for future action.

Even when using the latest planning techniques, there must be at least a reasonable element of certainty about the future before any lasting forecasts can be attempted. Industry could, however, face the future with more confidence if the government were to consult it more effectively. Government departments would then be able to appreciate more readily the full, practical repercussions likely to follow from intended policies and, where applicable, amend such policies at the embryo stage.

Probabilities Probed

Political statements, proposed new legislation, and the setting up of special bodies such as government committees and commissions can all be indications of the way the winds of fortune are likely to blow. Presidential speeches before Congress and the nation, "state of the union" messages, budget statements, and other major political addresses are cases in point. The shrewd businessman, however, must sort out the possible from the political (particularly just before national elections), the intentions from the words, and the likely timescale of achievement in practice. It must not be forgotten either that policies can change with each new administration.

Random examples of the aims of the federal government can be quoted as:

(a) To regard increases in industrial investment as an overriding priority in economic strategy.

(b) To build and maintain a strong surplus in the balance of payments, by encouraging manufacturers to take full advantage of opportunities in exports and to seek to reduce imports, consistent with overall trends in world trade.

(c) To cut back the spiraling growth in government spending through the exercise of greater control.

(d) To maintain a (high interest rate) monetary squeeze while this appears to be necessary to the best interests of the economy.

(e) To attempt, if needed, control of inflationary pressures by "jawboning" or even by temporary price freezes and wage restrictions.

(f) To improve industrial relations through mediation and arbitration, direct intervention where necessary, and legislation.

(g) To achieve a satisfactory annual growth rate in the gross national product by encouraging industry (through favorable tax incentives or other facilitating initiatives) to increase output, productivity, and employment. In this context (as against (b) above), balance-of-payments problems are not to stand in the way of sustained growth.

In the process, the managerial problem becomes that of identifying and balancing the aims as a whole, geared to the needs of the economy.

Whatever the trends may be at any given time, however, the probabilities and repercussions of further government initiative and other political aspects must be given their full weight when deciding on any managerial program for "the way ahead." Similarly, reverse adjustments to forecasting would be needed if the political winds of fortune were felt to be blowing towards lessened government involvement in the free enterprise system.

INSTITUTIONAL ASPECTS OF THE ENVIRONMENT

Having briefly mentioned government policies, it is convenient to include here such assorted matters as the effects of government institutions and government-regulated industries, trade associations, and unions.

Public and Private Sectors

Ours is a mixed economy, partly public sector (operated/controlled by government) and partly private enterprise; indeed, it is difficult to separate these, even for study purposes, because they are so intricately interwoven within the very fabric of our society. In and of itself, government is an enormous contributor to the other side;

government purchases at federal, state, and local levels have been increasing steadily over the years. Even setting aside the billions annually expended in the military budget, the innumerable departments and sections of government at all levels must be supplied each year with the wherewithal to continue operating. Highway, bridge, and tunnel construction; law enforcement, public education, and other services; the stockpiling of goods; subsidies and price support programs—all such activities combine to support the economy and provide, in cooperation with the private sector, a high standard of living. (As one indicator, it should be noted that the discretionary income of American consumers doubled in the decade from 1960 to 1970.)

At the same time, of course, government is itself partially supported by industry, through taxation. Yet, government also acts to monitor and even restrain the private sector. Its effects range from the maintenance of minimal wage and living standards as well as fair employment practices for the nation's workers through watchful controls on public utilities, transportation, banking, and the securities markets to the diligent fostering of free competition, fair business practices and tactics, and "social conscience" in the private sector.

Unions today are well established, and their place in the environment needs little comment. The main successes of the A.F.L.-C.I.O. for American labor in general have been in achieving improvements in wage levels and in working conditions, mainly through collective bargaining, joint negotiation, and strikes. (Industrial relations are covered more fully in Chapter Twelve.) Trade associations exist today in just about every segment of industry; each is supported by its own segment, the firms of which constitute its members. Their purpose in life is to represent and safeguard that industry as a whole, to supply up-to-date facts and figures, and to provide an information service for the benefit of members.

Social Responsibility

Over the past several decades, the American culture appears to have undergone significant change, attributable perhaps to a variety of causes besides the continuing knowledge explosion and technological advances. Our cities are slowly stifling and decaying; large numbers of families continue to leave the North for relocation in southern states and the West; the growth of suburbs continues. In addition to this extensive "geographical mobility," substantial shifts in values, mores, and attitudes can be discerned. Our long-established institutions are being challenged. Attitudes toward religion, government, family life, the woman's role, and even business and government appear to be more skeptical, more open, and more challenging at the same time. There is a new orientation to having things now instead of in the future, on personal appearance and on living life to the fullest, on youthfulness and on the simple life. People today are better educated than ever and live in a state of comparative affluence as against yesteryear; hence, the rise of consumerism and the concurrent responsiveness of government with policy-making and legislation designed to meet consumers' needs.

In response to these sociocultural patterns, business today reflects a growing awareness of the fact that its place in the economy is no longer simply earning profits and thereby satisfying stockholders, but that its very existence and growth depends, in the final analysis, on helping to keep the society which it serves and upon which it depends in a healthy state. Today, industry accepts not only the responsibilities of its position within the economy but also its obligations—for public service and consumer education, for product safety and reliability, for the ethics of its marketing efforts, and for the well-being of the communities it serves. Aided by a number of important pieces of legislation, business today seeks to protect the environment: the air, the water, and the dwindling stocks of essential reserves.

ECONOMIC ACTIVITY AND THE FUTURE

A balanced and informed view has to be taken of the future with regard to economic activity. Forecasting business conditions is no easy matter, by any token, but it can conveniently start with the overall economic situation.

A working knowledge of economics is a valuable introduction to the study of management, but this topic is largely outside the scope of the present volume. Suffice it to say that the subject is currently studied in two parts:

(a) *Macro economics*, which attempts to cover the whole field of the economy looked at comprehensively and to show how it works, and

(b) *Micro economics*, which narrows down the study into the role played by the firm and the family household within that economy.

Econometric Models

Modern scientific method is becoming increasingly quantitative, based on model-building, using simulation or mathematical analysis, with equations expressing the performances of different constituent elements and the relationships which exist between them. Such econometric forecasting models, computerized wholly or partly, can be statistically constructed for the American economy, for industries, or for large firms and often indicate which elements can be controlled by management and which cannot. Although there are still certain drawbacks to model-building, because of the necessary assumptions and complications, suitable safeguards can be imposed from other sources, by way of checking. To facilitate effective comparison, adjustments may prove to be essential to eliminate any seasonal influences and take into account currency depreciation.

Gross National Product

In overall economic forecasting, the analysis usually starts with the statistical "gross national product" for the period (year, half-year, etc.) in question, indicating the percentage change in the nation's output over the previous comparable period. Commonly referred to as the GNP, it represents the sum total of all expenditures for goods and services by consumers and government, together with gross private investments; in short, the total value of all goods and services produced by the economy. From the other side of the coin, it can be considered as the aggregate sum of all salaries, wages, rents, interest, company profits, and the like. Yearly GNP totals for comparison purposes are expressed in "current and constant" dollars, based on the value of the American dollar in 1958. The energetic growth of the

U.S. gross national product in recent decades can be seen below:

Year	GNP (in billions)
1940	$ 99.7
1950	284.8
1960	503.7
1970	977.1
1973	1,294.9

GNP trends are particularly valuable as they enable long-term and short-term projections of prosperity or otherwise to be built into corporate plans.

The selection of published statistics available for detailed study naturally depends on the industry and purpose in mind; it could include, for example, such items as durable and nondurable consumer spending, fixed private investment in new plants and equipment, inventories, housing, and the like, as well as imports and exports of goods and services.

In the context of economic forecasting, brief reference must be made to "input-output analysis." Theoretically, this consists of a large grid system (often called a "matrix") demonstrating the impact of each industry in turn on all other industries. The system is based on the premise that the input of one industry must be the output of another. For example, the input of steel for the automobile industry is a corresponding output for the steel industry. If, therefore, car manufacturing seems likely to slow down at some point in the future, steel output will be adversely affected, unless compensated by the likely inputs of some other industry during the same period.

Given up-to-date quantified statistical information (an expensive business with a dynamic environment to deal with), input-output analysis can be a useful forecasting tool, particularly if the simple grid is replaced by a sophisticated computer model. Such an analysis can help a company, as well as an industry, to work out the total demand, direct or indirect.

Published Information

It may be asked where official statistics such as the gross national product can be found. The answer is relatively simple, for a wealth of government publications exist today, containing much basic information relative to economic activity. For a fairly comprehensive review of the economy's operations each year, the businessman can consult (at his local public library) the Department of Commerce's annual "Statistical Abstract of the United States." A monthly report emanating from the same department will keep him abreast of current trends; it is the "Survey of Current Business."

It would appear that the Bureau of the Census is the most active federal agency in this regard, in that it continually accumulates huge quantities of data on the economy (and on the population itself), issuing every few years a number of comprehensive, multivolumed "censuses." Among these are the:

(a) *Census of Population*, which not only tallies "head counts" across the country each decade but also characterizes individuals according to any number of variables, including educational levels attained, income, sex, race, and other "demographics" so useful to marketing analysts.

(b) *Census of Manufactures*, which provides information on the product lines, sales, and capital expenditures and the like of American manufacturing firms.

(c) *Census of Business*, which supplements that of *Manufactures* by supplying details about the retail and wholesale trades and service businesses.

(d) *Census of Agriculture*.

(e) *Census of Housing*, of value to home-builders and the construction industry.

(f) *Census of Governments*, which details the revenues and the expenditures of state and local governments.

For firms involved in foreign trade, there is the "Foreign Trade Report" as well as the biweekly "Commerce Today." Close contact with the Bureau of International Commerce would be profitable for companies involved in importing and exporting. In a similar vein, a query to the Superintendent of Documents will bring a catalog of the many thousands (if not more) of government publications available at very modest cost. Unfortunately, much of the information is descriptive or historical (though nonetheless interesting and useful); and even the latest statistics are often subject to subsequent, and appreciable, adjustment.

Other departments of the federal government publish substantial amounts of usable information for business. Reports issued by the Federal Reserve banks include up-to-date indexes of sales and of inventories; a monthly "Bulletin" provides details on banking and credit—and on how money is circulating within the economy. Statistical reports in series are issued by the Bureau of Labor Statistics (Department of Labor), as well as occasional reports of studies. Research publications are issued by the Department of Agriculture, the Department of Health, Education, and Welfare, and others. Special reports are put out from time to time by such agencies as the Federal Communications Commission, the Securities and Exchange Commission, and the Federal Trade Commission.

There are many other sources of published economic information, as well as general business information. Newspapers such as the *Wall Street Journal,* the *New York Times,* and *Barron's* enable the businessman to keep up with current fluctuations; such general business publications as *Duns',* *Forbes,* and *Fortune* provide the depth and insights for business planning; economic and business journals such as the *Journal of Business,* the *American Economic Review,* the *Harvard Business Review,* and the *Journal of Marketing* help to shape the long-range view for upper management. Other sources include the trade associations and trade papers, Chambers of Commerce (on a more local level), and any number of reference works. Reference should be made here to the various indexes useful in locating information, such as the *Business Periodicals Index,* the *New York Times Index,* the *Wall Street Journal Index,* and the *Readers' Guide to Periodical Literature.*

Checking for Accuracy

The businessman using published forecasts, or any other economic information, must test for accuracy. Whether taken from official sources or from independent outside observers, a real problem exists as to how much should be taken at face value and how much treated skeptically. This may well be where the hunch comes in. The businessman must check where possible on the reasoning or facts behind the forecasts, on any assumptions made, and on the likely margin of error. Only then can he make up his mind as to what the future holds for the firm or industry in which he is interested. Nor should he fail to take inflationary tendencies fully into account.

Income and Productivity

Finally, it can be said that, while discussions of long-term changes take the growth of total income into account, a more potent factor has been the change in the distribution of income. For instead of the pyramidal picture of the 1930s, with a few very rich at the top of the pyramid and the remainder well down the slopes, with the poor forming the enormous base, we have seen the emergence of a middle-income majority exerting powerful effects on total consumer demand.

There has been a corresponding growth in total output, as already mentioned, and a consistent increase in productivity (not yet nearly enough) resulting from technological change. Indeed, more effective adaptation to technological change still remains a major problem in its own right.

SOCIAL INFLUENCES ASSESSED

In trying to assess social influences, again it is difficult to draw firm boundary lines, in this case between the economic and the social environments; hence the current use of the embracing term "socioeconomic."

Population Trends

Social changes are similarly important to forecasting, and reference should be made first of all to the future growth of the population (representing more workers and more consumers). This growth, of course, is basically a function of the netting-out process between two statistical trends, the birth rate and the death rate. Although our national death rate has reflected a comparatively static picture in recent years (approximately 9-plus deaths per 1,000 population), there has been a rather sharp decline in the birth rate. Sociologists have attributed this decline to an extensive list of possible causes, ranging the gamut from worries about the population explosion and the depletion of natural resources to more effective birth control, changing family patterns, higher education levels, and economic trends. Whatever the reasons, the number of births per 1,000 Americans in 1960 was estimated at nearly 24; by 1974, this rate had dropped to slightly below 15. Traditionally, population growth estimates computed by the Bureau of the Census involve the use of a number of differing assumptions as to expected birth rates, yet even the lowest rate employed yields the likelihood of some 250 million people in this country by the year 1980—and nearly 300 million just one decade after that. It would be illuminating, for purposes of comparison, to reflect on the fact that our population reached only the 50 million mark in 1880; hence, the forecasted figure for 1980 would represent a quintupling of the population in a single century.

The full statistical information, dealing with various forms of distribution (by age, sex, marital status, and the like) can be studied in detail as a guide to likely future trends. Such distributions are expected to change substantially over the long term, as will occupations and income distribution throughout the population. As an example, by 1980, it is expected that some 15% of the total population—or some 37 million individuals—will be in the age group from 25 to 34, making this the largest segment of the population. People of age 65 and over will then number over 23 million. Such facts pose enormous challenge (and opportunity) for today's businessmen and may transform consumer marketing and production patterns accordingly.

Sophisticated simulation models of the American economy are capable of producing long-range, industry-by-industry forecasts for management—with built-in provisions for the effects of social, political, and economic change.

Other relevant factors to be kept in mind include the number of households (63 million in 1970; a projected 84 million by 1985), the occupations of heads of households (and of other earning members), family income and spending patterns, and so on.

Educational Changes

Better education is essential to the improved future skills of management and workers; with such higher levels of education, however, many more workers than at present will want to be managers, and proportionately fewer will remain satisfied for long with monotonous, soul-destroying run-of-the-mill tasks. In the year 1950, slightly over one million young people graduated from our nation's high schools; by 1972, the annual graduating class size reached nearly three times that figure. Full-time attendance at four-year colleges has also nearly tripled since 1950. Moreover, the numbers of two-year, "junior" colleges have similarly burgeoned.

Significantly, both compulsory public education and better opportunities in higher education mean for the future a more discriminating and less gullible public. The public will need to be convinced of value before becoming consumers of this or that advertised product or service and will seek to obtain maximum satisfaction from any given household expenditure.

Note also the educational and broadening influences of television, radio, the theater, the movies, and foreign travel, which are now well within the range of the middle-income majority. All these factors contribute effectively towards social change. Even exposure to imported merchandise and publications will tend to widen horizons and introduce new thoughts on fashions and taste. Coupled with improved education, too, is the natural desire for increased leisure and, what is more important, a new ability to make the best use of it.

THE IMPACT OF
TECHNOLOGICAL CHANGE

Looking back over the past decade or so, let alone back to the beginning of the century, there are innumerable instances of revolutionary technological change to which industry has had to adjust itself.

For example, the invention of the integrated circuit in electronics has enabled even small electronics firms to compete effectively with far more powerful firms. For a single large-scale integrated circuit, held comfortably in one hand, can contain as many parts as some 50 color television sets; and an ordinary electronic circuit need be no bigger than a pinhead. The application of complex integrated circuits to a wide range of industrial products has obvious advantages: the electronics firms themselves enjoy greatly reduced overhead expenses and, in the process, enhanced profits.

The successful landing of men on the moon, the Concorde,

Jumbo jets, hovercraft, and the Arab embargo on oil are similar matters of recent history with varying repercussions on industrial growth; many other examples can be listed at random.

Concern for the Future

But the concern of industry should be with the future, and it is here that research comes into its own under the grandiose title of "technological forecasting." The large organization with a long-range planning section can "brainstorm" its way into future changes in technology. This ranges from a free flow of imagination over the whole gamut of industry, probably best left to pure researchers working independently, to the more concentrated search for possible changes relevant to a particular industry. Either way, large lists of potential changes, however much they may resemble science fiction at the outset, can be drawn up and examined for feasibility, probability, and time-scale. The problem then remaining is to find ways and means of achieving the selected innovations, forecasting their impact, and integrating them environmentally with marketing, production, and finance.

Basically this is the province of research and development (R & D), an aspect developed further in Chapter Ten. The important factor at the moment is to become aware at an early date of the trend and impact of technological advance. Managerial action can then be taken, in good time, to contain it.

LOOKING AT AN INDUSTRY

Having absorbed the background of the country as a whole, the next step within that environment (i.e., political, institutional, economic, social, and technological change) is to study the outlook for a particular industry.

The Entrepreneur

In any industry there must initially have been someone who could see a need for goods or services not already being produced, someone who promoted that industry by setting up the first individual firm within it. This pioneer, in economic parlance an "entrepreneur," literally an undertaker(!) who initiates new ventures and takes the risks, would most likely have been guided at the time solely by his own ideas and instincts. But a later entrepreneur, creating a new firm within an established industry, would have precedents to follow or avoid. For there are managerial patterns, good, bad, and indifferent, from which any innovator can learn; and the mistakes of others can be the starting-point for successful strategy in the future.

A Questioning Approach

It is relevant here to have a look at some of the more important factors that should be taken into account; the following questions must not only be asked, but answered satisfactorily:

(a) What does an integrated study of the constituent aspect of environment suggest as to the immediate and longer-term future of the industry concerned? What facts and figures relevant to that industry are available, from which proper judgments can be made? What further information should be sought?

(b) What *exactly* is the nature of the industry? What place does it fill in the country's economy?

(c) What is the significant demand for its products or services, the word "demand" implying usefulness, desire, stability of desire, and the ability of the customers to pay for the products or services offered now and in the future?

(d) What is the pattern of competition within the industry? Are there, for instance, a few dominating firms and many smaller ones, or many small companies each having a relatively small share of the market? How is the industry organized? Is it possible for any "substitutes" to arise from outside the industry?

(e) What is the industry's capacity, need for labor and materials, and operating costs? Are there any heavy expenses to be taken into account, for example, a basic requirement for large and expensive plant and machinery right from the outset?

These are general questions and need to be amended in the context of the particular industry concerned. In practice there would be many more such questions, all of them requiring to be dealt with in detail and in depth.

ASSESSING THE PROSPECTS OF A FIRM

Having obtained a clear picture of an industry, it is then important to study the individual firm existing or planned, in the context of that industry.

Questions about the Firm

Here again, certain basic questions suggest themselves and need effective answers:

(a) What is its market position? In particular, how well is the firm doing in relation to its competitors in the same industry? How does the standing and reputation of its goods or services compare with those of the other firms in the market?

(b) What is its comparative cost position with regard to geographical location (raw materials, local labor and market), efficiency of plant and equipment, and any special advantages (long-term contracts, patents, etc.)?

(c) Are there any production problems? Are the operations satisfactory in terms of skills and resources?

(d) Are there any financial problems? Is the firm making or losing money? What is its relative financial strength? Does it have adequate capital, for example, or access to new capital, or sufficient liquid resources?

(e) Are there any personnel problems? In particular, what are the strengths and weaknesses of its management?

Management the Key Factor

The last question is, of course, the critical one; for a firm can only be as good as its management will allow it to be. To take extremes, a company with everything but good management will most likely fail, whereas one with good management but little else will most probably succeed. Hence there is a vital need to have at the top men with the ability to think creatively and produce the right answers to questions such as those above.

Questions of this kind are necessarily general at this stage, but as the book proceeds additional background to managerial policies and problems will be introduced systematically. For the moment, then, it is sufficient to emphasize that the casualty rate of even the largest firms is historically high and that in most cases the underlying blame could be laid fairly and squarely at the door of management. This is not necessarily because of technical inefficiency in the job itself, but possibly because that job was carried out in isolation and in blinders. In such a context, three further important questions require continual investigation:

(f) What, at any given time, are the crucial factors likely to determine which of the firms in a particular industry will be highly successful and which will become casualties?

(g) How do the strengths and weaknesses of the individual firm under consideration match up against these crucial factors?

(h) What managerial action may be taken to boost the strengths and eliminate the weaknesses?

Bearing in mind the importance of good management to the achievement of success, it is appropriate to look next at the organization and viewpoint of the people at the top. For it is they who make the major decisions guiding the destinies of individual firms and thereby of industry in general.

Summary

1. The Impact of Change
   a. Change arises from the dynamic environment.

    b. Management must be on the alert for the unexpected; it can then take advantage of opportunities and meet challenges.

    c. The ability to anticipate events is an essential quality of management.

2. Government Policies

    a. Government intervention affects business decisions.

    b. Forecasting probes politics for probabilities.

3. Economic Activities

    a. Study should start with the gross national product.

    b. Official statistics should be tested for validity and relevance.

    c. The distribution of incomes has been changing.

4. Social Influences

    a. Management needs to consider such social factors as population growth, including birth and death rates, number of households, and family income and spending habits—as well as other demographics.

    b. Better education improves skills.

5. Technological Change

    a. Revolutionary progress has occurred over the past few decades.

    b. Forecasting takes research into account.

6. Looking at an Industry or Firm

    a. The entrepreneur is the one who takes initial risks.

    b. Certain basic questions need satisfactory answers.

    c. Strengths and weaknesses need to be assessed.

    d. Good management remains the key factor.

Suggested Further Reading

BETHEL, L.L., *et al. Industrial Organization and Management.* 5th ed. New York: McGraw-Hill, 1971.

CHISHOLM, R.K., AND G.R. WHITAKER, JR. *Forecasting Methods.* Homewood, Ill.: Irwin, 1971.

COOPER-JONES, D. *Business Planning and Forecasting.* New York: Wiley, 1974.

CURWEN, P.J. *Managerial Economics.* New York: Crane-Russak, 1975.

HAYNES, W.W., AND W.R. HENRY. *Managerial Economics: Analysis and Cases.* Dallas: Business Publications, 1974.

SIMON, J.L. *Applied Managerial Economics.* Englewood Cliffs, N.J.: Prentice-Hall, 1975.

WEBB, S.C. *Managerial Economics.* Boston: Houghton Mifflin, 1976.

WESTON, J.F., AND E.F. BRIGHAM. *Managerial Finance.* 4th ed. New York: Holt, Rinehart and Winston, 1972.

THREE

The Board of Directors

To become a director is to get to the top, the board of directors being in the key position from which to guide the activities of a business enterprise toward its objectives. Although usually only a small group in practice, a board of directors can exert immense influence on a company's prospects. For our present purpose, therefore, it seems a good idea to start at the top.

CREATING THE GOVERNING BODY

For the most part, we are concerned with publicly owned corporations and perhaps those that are privately held. The main difference between these two types is that the former offers its shares to the general public, whereas the latter is basically a "closed shop." We should bear in mind that there are other institutions, also concerned with management, where the governing body is given some other title such as board of governors, council, or management committee. The general approach is, however, basically the same.

Election by Stockholders

Theoretically, the directors are elected by the stockholders to run the business on their behalf in such a way that satisfactory (not necessarily maximum) profits are achieved. At one time, it was quite usual for a board to be dominated by one or more proprietary families, which controlled the capital; but shares now tend to be widely spread over the country. In the process, many of our corporations have grown considerably; business life on the whole has become increasingly complicated; and today's decisions seem to be much more difficult and complex.

The election of directors is normally carried out at the corporation's first meeting, generally a personal selection from among the entrepreneurs and their supporters. Usually, directors are elected for one-year terms; subsequent elections and re-elections take place at annual general meetings. In a small number of cases, as for example with some insurance firms, directors may serve for three years, generally on a staggered basis.

Self-perpetuation

Whether through inertia, satisfaction with past performance, or sheer indifference, a board of directors is normally a self-appointed, self-perpetuating body. When vacancies arise, they tend to be filled by the board to please itself. Rightly or wrongly, a board is usually able to go its own way, virtually unchecked by the stockholders, unless something appears to be radically wrong. With a widely based shareholding, it is difficult for the stockholders to get together as an effective body to oppose the directors; nor is it easy to challenge incompetence, as distinct from obvious fraud. In fact, apart from cases of fraud, there is no effective way to sue the directors in order to recover any losses resulting from bad policy decisions and/or ineffectual performance. Directors are charged with exercising their authority with "due care"; a challenge in this area is quite difficult to sustain in court. Of course, directors do bear a fiduciary relationship to their corporations and cannot take undue advantage of their position; hence conflicts of interest may constitute another area open to litigation.

Corporations are obliged to provide an increasing amount of

information to government and state agencies as well as for the guidance of stockholders. In the case of corporations registered on any of the stock exchanges, directors (as well as officers and large stockholders) must file reports regularly with the Securities and Exchange Commission.

It has been suggested that annual reports should include forecasts for the current year of sales, profits, and the like so that results achieved can be measured against intention. However, given the difficulties of accurate forecasting in a changing world, it is easy to appreciate the natural reluctance of directors to be accused, perhaps unfairly, of incompetence. Although boards are hard to topple from their peak, for reasons already given the ultimate power remains with the stockholders, and on occasion a whole board has been made to resign. Normally, capital is divorced from direction, but where the board itself holds a majority of the shares the position becomes rather different. This is a limiting situation, however, as such a position inhibits further growth.

Also to be considered in this connection is the power of the financial press. Any suspicion that all is not well with a given company, or other organization, will tend to reflect itself in print. The same applies to any defensive statements made, for example, by the chairman on behalf of the board. Carefully weighed comment by the press will at least put the stockholders on the alert; whether they do anything about it collectively, with regard to the board, is another matter.

One final thought can be devoted to the few "lone-wolf" stockholders who always make a point, even a hobby, of challenging vague phrases or figures in company statements, possibly concealing awkward facts, attacking the way in which information is supplied, or seeking further information. On occasion, such active, often eccentric, protagonists can cause considerable consternation at an annual general meeting.

Optimum Size and Composition

Whereas two or three directors usually constitute the basic minimum in most states, in practice the leading corporations tend on average to have about twelve directors on the board. Obviously, having too few directors places a heavy burden on them individually, fails to provide for emergencies, and denies the company a wide enough range of experience and wisdom. Having too many directors, on the other hand, tends to slow down decisions through too much debate. But these are generalizations, and each company must work out its own optimum size in the light of growth prospects, territory covered, and type of activity undertaken.

Of greater importance is the overall quality of the board. Instead of the old family director, the trend today is towards a mixture of subjective expertise and objective wisdom. These two extremes, taken in isolation, can be illustrated by a board composed entirely of executives of the company (a management—or "inside"—board) and a directorate made up entirely of non-executives (a nonmanagement—or "outside"—board). The former could result, of course, in a dictatorship, the president probably being the board chairman as well. The latter could possibly lead to a frustrated general manager, depending upon the power of his personality *vis-à-vis* that of the chairman and the other members of the board. Nevertheless, a nonmanagement board is good in theory in that it separates policy making from policy execution.

From time to time suggestions have been made for a two-tier board for large corporations, on continental lines. The two tiers would be:

(a) *A supervisory board,* mainly concerned with general policy and forward planning, but with power to appoint and dismiss management directors, thereby exercising control on behalf of the shareholders;

(b) *A management (executive) board,* with delegated authority to manage current performance within that general policy and planning laid down by the supervisory board.

The right composition of a normal board can be achieved, however, by the inclusion of nonmanagement or outside directors, as already indicated. This arrangement usually provides sufficient supervision and, at the same time, enables management directors to participate more fully in the policy determination.

MANAGEMENT AND NONMANAGEMENT DIRECTORS

In a corporation, there are three basic management levels:

(a) The board of directors.

(b) General management.

(c) Specialist management.

This is an oversimplification, but one that will suit our present purpose. In some firms (for example, banks and insurance companies), it is usual for the three levels to be maintained separately as distinct strata; but in most other commercial organizations and in nearly all manufacturing concerns there is a varying degree of overlapping.

As the study of management has grown up with rather loose terminology, we use such words as director, manager, administrator, and executive as taken indiscriminately from our everyday vocabulary. Strictly speaking, though, a director is concerned with the determination of policy and a manager with carrying out or executing that policy. But as we shall see later, the ends and the means often become interwoven in practice. Hence, we get a "managing director" (president) and "management directors" with two capacities, wearing both a directorial hat and a managing hat.

In this context there are dangers, outside the boardroom, of "two-hatted" directors pulling their rank not only on subordinates but on managers of equal status who are not directors.

The Management (Inside) Board

The president is the chief executive, as well as being a member of the board; the other executives who are directors represent major operational aspects such as marketing, production, finance, and research and development. Where the chief executive is not a director, as in certain commercial firms already mentioned, he is generally known as a general manager. It is difficult to classify titles, however, as a general manager could be a board member without having adopted the usual tag of "managing director."

Inside directors work on a full-time basis and are accordingly well informed about day-to-day departmental activities. They bring their expert knowledge to the board table. The company is their working life, and they are always available for discussion and consultation. Being so close to the job, however, they may find it difficult to take an objective, long-term view of the company's future. They may also have partisan, perhaps biased, interests in their own areas of specialization, with which they could become emotionally involved in board-meeting deliberations. Yet, once they don their directors' hats, they must do their best to be objective and forget their partisan viewpoints.

A further fundamental problem is that an ordinary management director is junior in status to the president outside the boardroom, which again may influence his strength and attitudes in debate. He would tend to be conscious of possible repercussions after a board meeting in which he took, for example, too hard or too independent a line on certain items. He has to live with his boss and his colleagues outside the boardroom; any other interpretation of the facts of life would tend to be unreal. Much, of course, depends on the general atmosphere in which members of top management normally work together. For the executive environment can be friendly or hostile, or both in turn.

Management directors do, of course, leave their jobs to gain better pay and prospects or perhaps to get away from an unhealthy climate. They can also be "encouraged" to leave for incompetence, not producing satisfactory results, becoming excess (as through a merger), or failing to keep sufficiently in line with modern management developments. In the case of fraud, discharge becomes obvious.

The Nonmanagement (Outside) Board

Part-time or nonmanagement directors are a different, more independent species. As such they bring to bear their own expertise, for example as professional men, with wide background knowledge and experience from other interests and contacts. An outside director could be a practicing accountant, lawyer, banker, architect, engineer, surveyor, or management consultant, as relevant to the particular business. He could have special knowledge of other countries or regions. He could represent spheres of influence, political or otherwise. He could hold directorships in other companies, preferably noncompeting. He could be on the board simply to watch over a particular interest on behalf of a large creditor, major customer, or supplier. In fact, the combinations are legion and as often haphazard as they are logical. Whatever their background, some companies allocate specific functions to nonmanagement directors either through appointment to standing committees or as individuals in oversight capacities.

The advantages of outside directors lie in their independence from domination, their objective judgment, including matters affecting their full-time colleagues on the board, and their ability to take a long-term view of the company's progress freed from undue concern for daily problems. It is maintained, too, that they tend to look more closely after the interests of the shareholders. Often they have personal experience of modern management thinking and techniques, as applied to other spheres of activity in the public and/or private sectors of the economy. Clearly, the more points of view that can be brought together around the boardroom table, the better are the chances of effective discussion. Even a director who is perhaps too much of a specialist, and therefore unable to make a major contribution at every meeting, could prove invaluable at times when his specialty was under active debate.

As against these virtues, nonmanagement directors tend to be insufficiently informed concerning the company's operations, to have limited time to spare for acquiring background information and perhaps a less committed approach to the company's future. Nor is it unknown for the boardroom to be virtually the last resting-place of formerly competent personalities now well past their best. Not being on the staff, as in the case of inside directors, it may be a difficult matter to remove them, if unsatisfactory. One way to minimize such risk is obviously to make a better selection in the first place, not through the "old-boy network" so often heard about, but by careful choice made objectively in the best interests of the company and its future. This in turn suggests a need for offering higher financial rewards.

Achieving a Proper Balance

Management and nonmanagement directors each have offsetting advantages and disadvantages, so that the most successful type of board would appear to be a combination of the two kinds, taking the best from both worlds. This is a matter, however, for each company to decide for itself, some boards preferring not to have any inside directors, or outside directors, as the case may be. The practical answer lies in having the right balance of ability, experience, and range of viewpoint, with perhaps the occasional rough diamond contributing an earthy wisdom and basic common sense to boardroom discussion. It is, of course, essential that full advantage should be taken of all the qualities represented on the board, in every way possible.

Whatever the type of director, however, no distinction exists in law, and all directors have the same fiduciary responsibilities.

Given the right selection, there is a valuable control element in the appointment of outside directors. Apart from acting as a check on the management directors as a body, likely to be influenced and led by the president, there can be complementary checks on individuals. An enthusiastic marketing director, for instance, would be all the more effective if liable to be subjected at board meetings to discerning questions from an outside director having special marketing skills and experience elsewhere.

Worker-Directors

Some attention has been given at various times to the concept of worker-directors, the essence of their participation being to increase industrial efficiency. As none of these has executive power, each would tend to become more inhibited, in the continual presence of higher authority, than those directors who are company executives. Nevertheless, there could be practical value in having such representation from the shop floor, if only to keep directional feet more firmly on the ground. The danger seems to be that, over the course of time, worker-directors tend to get out of touch with the men.

THE CHAIRMAN

A company can be only as good as its president; a president can be only as good as the board of directors will allow him to be; and a board can be only as good as its chairman.

Positive Leadership

Unless the chairman can stimulate the board to have vision, new ideas, and enthusiasm he is, in effect, putting a dead hand on the wheel and should accordingly be replaced. Admittedly, on occasion, there is room for caution and restraint, but by and large the emphasis should be firmly placed on a positive and constructive approach. In other words, it takes a dynamic board to cope with a dynamic environment. Therefore, although the view is often held that in order to be more objective the chairman should be an outside director, in general the main quality required is the philosophical wisdom of the man himself.

Organizational Aspects

It will be seen later that there must be a good relationship, and working partnership, between the chairman and the president. The chairman may, in fact, be the president as well. The chairman would be wise to ensure that there exists an effective organizational pyramid, with a properly balanced board at the top, composed of directors specifically selected for the valuable contributions they could be expected to make.

Being elected, at least theoretically, by the directors as a whole, the chairman is subject to the board and continues in office at its pleasure. He may, of course, be the principal stockholder, or have strong family stockholder connections, and take the chair automatically as a matter of "divine right." It may be customary, too, for the president to occupy that position, or for the chair to be held on a rotating basis with a new chairman being elected perhaps after each annual general meeting. This latter variety brings in fresh blood at the top and gives experience of the chairmanship to individual directors in turn, but it could also be argued that it occasions a regrettable loss of continuity, always assuming that the chairman was already felt to be the best man for the job. In more ordinary circumstances, the election result is likely to be the outcome of natural leadership, popularity, seniority, or some other distinguishing feature, or even the outcome of power politics.

Presiding at Meetings

At annual general meetings, board meetings, and other statutory events, press conferences, and the like the chairman takes the chair by right and controls the formal proceedings. He would normally initiate *(a)* the setting up of any board committees required, whether standing (permanent) or *ad hoc* (special purpose), to facilitate detailed consideration of such functional aspects as finance; *(b)* the preparation of reports, with recommendations, on delegated topics; *(c)* the giving of effect to board decisions; and *(d)* the handling of special matters best dealt with outside the boardroom.

He would also be primarily concerned with the conduct of the board and its legal and community responsibilities to shareholders and other interested parties.

RESPONSIBILITIES OF THE BOARD

Although the board is an important part of top management, it cannot be expected to perform all the functions of top management unless it is entirely composed of inside directors. For much of the daily drive, initiative, and business vitality must essentially come from the president and his team. This is particularly true when there is an outside board, which of necessity has to leave most of the administrative duties to the executives. It is useful, therefore, at this stage, to enumerate the essential responsibilities of a board of directors and then fill in the remaining top-management functions in the chapter that follows.

The Directors' Role.

In summary form, it can be stated that the main responsibilities of a board of directors include the following:

(a) Approving or initiating the objectives, major policies, long-range planning, and strategies (all defined in Chapters Seven and Eight) in the light of the overall total environment.

(b) Complying with all legal requirements.

(c) Ensuring that sufficient capital is always available for effective operations.

(d) Authorizing large capital expenditures, including major contracts and other commitments; granting mandates, where appropriate, to the executives; maintaining the physical assets.

(e) Engaging, and selecting, top executives, including the president or chief executive officer, and approving promotions of key managers and salary scales; ensuring management succession and effective executive development.

(f) Maintaining a suitable organizational structure and satisfactory relationships from the president downwards.

(g) Providing leadership to the company as a whole, e.g., through the chairman, in liaison with the president.

(h) Ensuring that the shareholders, whom they represent, are dealt with fairly with regard to dividend policy, changes in capital structure, and other matters affecting their financial interests.

(i) Evaluating results achieved and maintaining control, with special reference to regular reports and statements from the president, coupled with the technique of asking discerning questions.

(j) Initiating, defending, or encouraging mergers and acquisitions, as appropriate, including takeover bids made or received, keeping the shareholders adequately advised of such developments.

(k) Giving professional advice to executives, when consulted formally or informally.

In brief, the board of directors has special responsibilities towards the stockholders, customers, employees, and the community at large. Only when the board has won the confidence of all four groups can it exercise its full authority effectively.

Stockholders, customers, and employees are dealt with in later chapters, but passing reference to the board's community responsibilities is appropriate here. Although some organizations have little or no social conscience, the majority are prepared to go well beyond their legal obligations with regard to public welfare in general. There are indeed many corporate examples of helping to build up local communities, with attractive housing, coupled with allied leisure facilities for workers and other residents; contributions to disaster funds, for example, earthquake, famine, and flood relief; donations to the arts; the establishment of university chairs; and so on, quite apart from voluntary participation by directors and officials in local affairs. With multinational and international companies generally, the extension of social responsibilities to other communities provides further examples, including the export of "know-how" to underdeveloped countries.

While we are considering the directors' role we should note that the outside directors are in a suitably detached position to give impartial help to the chairman, and the board generally, on any board responsibility needing wise judgment free from any element of self-interest. As examples we may cite such items as directors' salaries, fringe benefits, and the process of succession to the presidency.

Keeping Informed

With the extensive delegation of boardroom power to lower levels in the hierarchy, there is a danger of blind spots at the top. Directors must, therefore, ensure that they are kept adequately informed as to what is going on in the company as well as being up to date on background information concerning the overall environment. In the presentation of key information, outside directors can often tighten up the service by requesting revised formats to help their understanding of vital issues.

Presented with effective statements and reports, including the right kind of relevant data, today's directors should be able to keep abreast of events. If not satisfied, they can always demand more facts and figures, providing that such requests (which can result in much time-absorbing efforts by executives) are kept within reasonable bounds. Given the basic information, an outline of likely results from alternative courses of action, and a firm recommendation by the president, the scene is then properly set in advance for boardroom deliberations. The art and techniques of decision-making are dealt with in Chapter Eight.

Motivation of Directors

The motivational influences, as seen in a previous context, are mainly nonfinancial. Directors welcome, for example, the prestige, the challenge, the sense of contributing to a worthwhile venture, and the opportunities for meeting a much wider circle of business associates. Individual directors may derive other, and perhaps more personal, satisfactions from active participation of this kind. Certainly outside directors tend to have insufficient rewards financially. So far as management directors are concerned, the status of being directors as well as managers gives them a sense of equality in the boardroom. This can be lacking when, as executives only, they are merely "in attendance" at board meetings in an administrative capacity.

BOARDROOM TECHNIQUES

As the focal point for so much vital decision, it is essential that meetings in the boardroom should be well planned and conducted. The main responsibility clearly lies with the chairman, whose task it is to see that the directors, individually and collectively, discharge their duties efficiently. Even with the right kind of leadership, however, much will depend on the composition of the board as a whole. In small companies nominal meetings are often considered to be sufficient; but, with growth, properly organized meetings, with full discussion, soon become a necessity.

Essential Preparation

Effective policy formulation is a joint product of the directors and the executive organization, although the final responsibility for success rests with the board as a whole. The contributions of the chief executive officer and his team must be thoroughly thought out in advance, either as an attempt to initiate policy or as a report on policy matters referred to it by the board, usually at a previous meeting.

Agendas can be tailor-made for each meeting, which may be weekly, fortnightly, or monthly, as appropriate, or they can be based on a consistent but flexible format. A well-devised comprehensive agenda is a valuable asset in the running of an effective meeting, and this is usually agreed upon in advance by the chairman, president, and company secretary. The structuring of the agenda is important from the point of view of making sure that the business of the meeting is dealt with efficiently and in the best order. This order may be to place the routine matters first, to get them out of the way quickly, thus leaving the remainder of the time free to deal with items of policy; or the other way around, i.e., to deal with the policy matters first, leaving routine items to take their chances.

It has been known, too, for the agenda order to be used as a factor in power politics, by the chairman or president anxious to get his own way, but that is another subject. A controversial item, for example, dealt with early in the day, with time for debate, could have a different reception from one introduced towards the end of the morning, when directors were anxious to get the meeting over before lunch and therefore less inclined to argue. Similarly, a short agenda tends to produce too much discussion, and a long agenda a sense of urgency.

A formal agenda for board meetings could usefully be based on a logical order of standard main headings, under which detailed items could be dealt with as appropriate. Not all such headings would necessarily be applicable every meeting, but they would at least serve as a checklist covering the whole field. One established method is to build the agenda around the company's financial accounts. In practice, some matters might be regular weekly items, others monthly, quarterly, semi-annual, or annual.

In sending out the agenda in advance of the board meeting, the major items would be supported by an overall president's report, by separate reports from executives dealing with issues in their particular areas, or by a combination of both. The main requirement is that the paperwork, diligently prepared by the executive team, should give all the necessary information, set out the pros and cons, and make appropriate recommendations. The directors than have a properly documented opportunity to consider each agenda item before arriving at the meeting. In addition, there must be systematically planned reports on progress, covering all aspects of the business—marketing and sales, production, finance, and personnel.

The accent, however, must be on the way ahead, through corporate planning, and this should be clearly reflected in the board agenda. By this means, too, the directors become informed of developments and topical issues automatically. Directors are, of course, mainly concerned with matters of policy and should not, in general, be burdened with much, if any, administrative detail.

From time to time the president should submit overriding reports, projected, say, five years ahead, showing how it is proposed to carry out agreed-upon and recommended company policies. The financial implications should be included as far as they could reasonably be forecast at this early stage.

At the Board

Given a properly structured agenda and a board with clearly defined functions, the chairman should make sure that the time available is allocated effectively with due emphasis on important items. In this context, much more time should be spent on policies for company growth and the like, focused on the way ahead, than on matters of historical or passing interest only. The formal practice of continually looking forward has great value in a dynamic environment.

Directors failing to put in sufficient attendance or relying on inspiration at the meeting, having failed to read the circulated board papers, should be disciplined, where possible, by the chairman.

The chairman has an overriding responsiblity to ensure free and fair discussion for all board members and to arrive at effective policy decisions only after all relevant points of view have been sufficiently ventilated. This aspect is developed further in Chapter Five. There are also many textbooks on established formal procedure at meetings, including the duties of the chairman, and some of these are included in the reading lists at the end of this chapter and of Chapter Five.

Directors' Contributions

It has been seen that an effective board meeting can be organized and run so that no time is wasted on irrelevant discussion. Such a meeting, even in a large company can, given sufficient delegation, be held within a single morning with concentration on decision-making rather than too much debate. Unfortunately, there are some (usually outside) directors who regard meetings as concert platforms for their own solo performance, who use each occasion to "impress" fellow board members with their expertise and experience, whether relevant to the item concerned or not. Others are less loquacious and tend to take a back seat even though they may in fact have a great deal of value to contribute; these need encouragement.

A good chairman conducts his board as an orchestra and makes sure that every instrument comes in at the right time and plays at the right volume and tempo. His job is to keep a sense of urgency and importance, stimulate creative thought and ensure that all new ideas are given a proper hearing, and refrain from importing prejudice by airing his own opinions before all present have had a chance to speak.

Among the more voluble offenders likely to waste precious time is the former chief executive officer, on the board still in his retirement years, who likes to seize every opportunity to dwell on past glories. Tact from the chair is required here, as well as in the handling of young up-and-coming directors, with their sights set on the future, who are liable to become impatient with the restraining wisdom of their more experienced colleagues. Once again the emphasis must be on the achievement of a proper balance so that all concerned can make effective contributions to the end result.

The president, as the chief executive responsible to the board, must play his full part, but theoretically at least it is the chairman (he could, of course, also be the president) who actually leads the board. The right kind of chairman/president boardroom relationship is important and will be dealt with in Chapter Four.

Decisions into Action.

Top executives who have been present at a board meeting, either as directors or in attendance, are better able to translate that meeting's policy decisions into everyday practice.

All decisions taken at a board meeting are formally recorded in the "minutes," which are usually prepared by the company secretary and reviewed with the chairman. They are ratified at the next meeting, preferably having been circulated with the new agenda, and form the official basis for executive action through the president and his team.

Even with a well-thought-out and fully documented report, covering an agenda item presented, for example, by the president, the board as a whole may have doubts as to the wisdom of the recommendations, or require further information, or wish to know the outcome of some imminent event, before coming to a firm decision. In these circumstances, the report would be taken back by the president, if necessary for further reflection, and re-presented with any amendments to a subsequent board meeting. Alternatively, it could be referred by the board to a committee for detailed consideration, to come back to the board again with firm recommendations.

DIVISIONAL BOARDS

So far, we have been concerned only with a company having one board of directors. It will be seen later that there are large companies that are broken up into separate, more or less self-contained divisions, each responsible for an important aspect of the business and having its own board of directors. There are in addition what are called "holding" companies, exercising control over a number of subsidiary operating companies each of which has a separate board of directors. Holding companies and operating companies are often deliberately created from one large company to facilitate business organization at a time of rapid growth.

Secondary Boards

Each division, or subsidiary, operates on powers delegated by the main board and may be controlled with a loose rein or kept tightly in check according to the overall management philosophy of the particular company or group of companies. For the moment, however, we are concerned only with the board structure. One method is for each divisional or subsidiary board to be made up of management directors with a full-time inside chairman.

There is a legal difference, of course, between divisions of a company each with, say, an executive board for administrative convenience and subsidiary companies each with a statutory board. But in either case it is possible in practice to use inside and/or outside directors according to the needs of the situation. Given a territorial coverage, for example, there may be an argument for including a proportion of local directors, with special knowledge or influence, on a nonmanagement basis.

Interlocking Boards

There is a vital need for an effective relationship to be built up, and a workable channel of communication, between the main board and other boards. To facilitate liaison, in part at least, it is normal practice for divisional or subsidiary chairmen to be *ex-officio* members of the main board. In this way, the secondary boards can make their presence felt at the top, through their chairmen, who can in turn bring back the latest information on main-board policy and group progress.

An alternative is for the main board to allocate certain of its members to specific divisions, or to specialize on subsidiaries, either as chairmen or as liaison directors under local chairmen. In this latter event, the local chairmen may not be required to attend main-board meetings, as this would tend to be unnecessary duplication. Questions of this kind, however, boil down to matters of judgment as to what, in any given set of circumstances, constitutes the best form of organization to get the desired results. There are cases, for example, where every company in a group has exactly the same board of directors as the others. There should be no hard-and-fast rules in management.

Summary

1. *The Governing Body*
   a. Board of directors, although elected by stockholders, is self-perpetuating.
   b. Stockholders cannot easily control a board.
   c. A corporation may have as few as two or three directors.
   d. The board should be well balanced.
   e. The board may be organized as a two-tier structure.
   f. There may be divisional boards interlocking with the main board.

2. *Types of Board*
   a. Inside or management directors are familiar with detailed operations.
   b. Nonmanagement directors bring in outside experience.
   c. A mixture of (a) and (b) provides the best of both worlds.

3. The Chairman
   a. The chairman must provide positive leadership.
   b. He must get along with the president.
   c. He takes the chair at meetings and is responsible for the board in action.
4. Duties of the Board
   a. The board is concerned with objectives, major policies, long-range planning, and strategies.
   b. Board members must see that they are kept informed.
5. Boardroom Procedure
   a. Board papers should be well prepared and circulated in advance.
   b. Agenda order is significant.
   c. The chairman allows full discussion but no time-wasting.
   d. The president has an important role to play.
   e. The minutes of the meeting should be translated into executive action.

Suggested Further Reading

BACON, J., AND J.K. BROWN. *Corporate Directorship Practices: Role, Selection and Legal Status of the Board.* New York: The Conference Board, 1975.

BROWN, C.C. *Putting the Corporate Board to Work.* New York: Macmillan, 1976.

BULL, G. (ed.). *The Director's Handbook.* New York: McGraw-Hill, 1969.

FEUER, M. *Handbook for Corporate Directors.* Englewood Cliffs, N.J.: Prentice-Hall, 1965.

LOUDEN, J.K. *The Effective Director in Action.* New York: American Management Association, 1975.

MACE, M.L. *Directors: Myth and Reality.* Boston: Graduate School of Business Administration, Harvard Univeristy, 1971.

MUELLER, R.K. *Board Life: Realities of Being a Corporate Director.* New York: American Management Association, 1974.

NICHOLSON, M.S. *Duties and Liabilities of Corporate Officers and Directors.* Englewood Cliffs, N.J.: Prentice-Hall, 1972.

VANCE, S.C. *The Corporate Director: A Critical Evaluation* Homewood, Ill.: Dow Jones-Irwin, 1968.

FOUR

Top Executives and Administrative Organization

Among the responsibilities of a board of directors (set out in Chapter Three) is the engaging and selecting of top executives, including the chief executive officer (CEO)—usually, the company president. The president, like all other executive directors, has to wear two different hats: one as a director making policy, the other as a manager carrying out that policy. It could be argued that the function of a board of directors should be kept quite separate from the function of the top-executive group, and this is indeed the practice in certain firms. But by far the majority of companies mix up the two functions in a variety of ways to suit their individual requirements.

Confusion at the Top

Many firms, for example, have a chairman who is also the chief executive, with or without the support of one or more operating officers. Others have a chairman who is not an operating head at all. In fact the real power at the top can range from a one-man dictatorship to group rule by committee. Such a dictatorship could be a chairman cum chief executive, answerable only to the shareholders, or a strong CEO with a weak non-executive chairman and a "rubber-stamping" board. Whatever the situation, however, it is advisable that there should be unity at the top. Without unity there can only be conflict and frustration, with a natural tendency for the power game to be in full play, to the obvious disadvantage of the firm as a whole.

THE PRESIDENT

For the present purpose it can be assumed that the chairman has confined himself to the formulation of policy, as the elected head of the directors, leaving the president to run the executive side of the business within the intention and scope of that policy. In theory, at any rate, it is wise for everyone to keep the directional side quite distinct from the managerial side. In practice, there is often board-room confusion, particularly on borderline issues, requiring guidance from the chair. Directors are ever prone to discuss the more interesting daily, domestic, and detailed affairs of the company to the detriment of dealing with difficult abstract policy matters having a much longer time span and considerably more corporate importance.

As a Focal Point

The main burden of everyday administration should therefore fall on the president, who serves as the main link between the board and the remainder of the organization. Figure 3 illustrates this concept of the president as a focal point.

The importance of good communications throughout a company is dealt with later. It will be shown how information should be processed upward through the organization into the boardroom and how, following the making of decisions, instruction should be filtered downward. Either way, up or down, the focal point is the president, the words "focal point" being deliberately chosen. It would be disastrous, for instance, in any firm, if the applicable word happened to be "bottleneck."

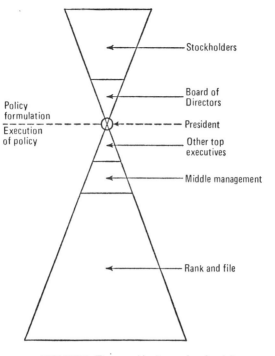

Policy
formulation
- - - - - - - -
Execution
of policy

Stockholders

Board of
Directors

President

Other top
executives

Middle management

Rank and file

FIGURE 3. The president as a focal point

Selection and Appointment

Where a new chief executive is appointed from existing staff, he may be selected from among the middle-management specialists. Usually there is an intermediate step, such as becoming a vice president, but the main promotional factor for the individual concerned is the change-over from being a specialist to being a generalist. For many executives this is no easy transition; having become accustomed, almost wedded, to departmental bias, they now find it difficult to look objectively at the business *as a whole.* In the interests of integration and control, however, no firm can allow a specialist promoted to general management to hold this elevated position in name only. His new responsibilities obviously require much broader treatment than the old, and, in any case, his former duties should by now be in the hands of a capable successor.

The position of a vice president, particularly where there is only one, may be invidious. It is sometimes hard for subordinates to know who is responsible for what and who can make which decisions. Although this is mainly a matter for clear definition of duties and effective communication, problems can still arise in practice. For some vice presidents tend to assume more duties than they should, while others try to evade their responsibilities. In either case, the remedy lies in the chief executive officer.

Fashions change with regard to the route to the top; at any given time the favored specialists may be the engineers or the accountants, the marketing men or the legal experts, or indeed some other class. Much depends, however, on the type of business, the qualities of the candidates, and perhaps the latest trends in management thought.

Where a top appointment is being made from outside the firm, a great deal may depend on whether the candidate has had relevant and successful previous experience in a similar managerial capacity, either within the same industry or in some comparable industry. In the light of this kind of outside competition, it is sometimes held to be unfortunate that the handicap of a first-class *specialist* may simply be that, so far, he has never been in *general* management. Yet the ambitious executive, with the right potential, must cross this bridge somewhere.

Basic Qualities

Although advertisements for chief-executive appointments often refer to the need for drive and initiative, to having a broad outlook, vision, ability to plan ahead, qualities of leadership and so on, in the event a compromise may have to be accepted. Few top men possess all the theoretical virtues; but they should know how to make the best of what they have, possibly with the help of subordinates displaying abilities complementary to their own. In this context, it may be a mistake for, say a qualified engineer, promoted to company president, to appoint another qualified engineer to be his executive vice president; it might be better to have, for example, a former marketing manager in second place. There is a similar argument for an extrovert to be offset by an introvert, or an optimist by a pessimist—or perhaps, in either case, the other way around.

Responsibilities

As the focal point between the board and the executive, the president is clearly at the apex of the staff/worker pyramid as their leader. He is also at the bottom of the reversed board pyramid (Figure 3) as the "servant" of the board. His responsibilities are indeed wide; some of the more important are set out below:

(a) Making sure that the objectives, as laid down by the board, are kept well in mind by the whole organization and, where necessary, recommending to the board revisions in those objectives to keep pace with change.

(b) Being actively concerned with long-range planning and strategy, based on a thorough understanding of the main trends in the dynamic environment of the firm. Supervising any changes, e.g., in production, considered necessary.

(c) Ensuring the financial soundness of the company as a whole, with each department, branch or operation making its proper contribution.

(d) Maintaining an effective organizational structure, with the practical effects of growth, including likely changes in key personnel, kept firmly in mind. Building up a strong management team.

(e) Coordinating all activities, e.g., through a management committee (to be defined later).

(f) Being available, whenever possible, to all important contacts of the company, e.g., principal stockholders, customers, and suppliers.

(g) Keeping control over the business so that it conforms to the plans laid down.

(h) Providing a high standard of personal leadership and motivating all concerned to give continually of their best.

It can be seen that much of this ties up logically with the traditional functions of management, set out earlier, and with the directors' role outlined in Chapter Three. Any differences thought to exist are mainly a matter of emphasis. Even when the chief executive is not a member of the board, it is only to be expected that his influence on policy and planning will be considerable. The CEO, as the key figure in general management, therefore has the widest possible range of responsibilities. How he copes with these duties, given the limited time at his disposal, is described later.

RELATIONSHIP WITH THE CHAIRMAN

Where the chairman and the chief executive are one and the same person, unity prevails, but not necessarily harmony; for everything depends on that person's caliber and character, holding as he does such a prominent and powerful position. It has already been intimated that it is usually better to keep these two jobs separated.

It is said to be lonely—for a company president or other chief executive—at the top. This situation is eased by having two complementary leaders, a board chairman and a chief executive, who can sharpen their wits on each other, maintain effective coordination between board and executive, and keep each other informed and in check. Similar valuable top-level contacts, free from protocol restraint, would be with the chairmen or presidents, respectively, of other firms operating in the same industry.

The Chief Executive Officer Kept in Check

This near "equality" in status means that each leader can discourage the other, by the timely word, from developing the wrong kind of board or managerial habits. In particular, it should prevent a CEO from becoming too much of a dictator over the other executives and staff; for the chairman, being constitutionally above him in rank, can exert pressure on him whenever the occasion appears to demand it.

From a business angle, it is a valuable routine for both men to get together regularly, perhaps the day before each board meeting, to discuss such matters as future policy, current affairs, and happenings within the industry and company. There must be at least a modicum of mutual respect, however, for such meetings to have full practical effect.

Given the right kind of individual personalities, the chairman will usually concern himself with looking after the formal occasions and will develop the important external relationships, leaving the CEO to deal with the administration, with the help of his team, in the most effective way possible.

Harmony or Frustration

When a bad relationship develops with a chairman, there could ensue a clash for power, a breakdown in communications at the top, boardroom arguments, and divided loyalties. The effect on company morale can be disastrous. The ability to get on with the chairman, and with the remainder of the board, is often a test of personality for the CEO. On occasion, unfortunately, success becomes virtually impossible to achieve—perhaps because the chairman insists on maintaining a rigid independence or stands firmly on his dignity at all times. In such circumstances, the company president can only rationalize the situation philosophically and hope for attitudes to change—or seek an executive position with some other company!

Where general harmony prevails, the chairman and the CEO can usually resolve any differences of opinion frankly and objectively at their regular meetings. In the boardroom and elsewhere, the chairman should create the right atmosphere for the president to be fully effective as the company's chief executive and should protect or support him whenever necessary, for example, in the face of concerted personal attack from the other directors.

THE EXECUTIVE TEAM IN ACTION

The dictum that fundamentally there should be only one effective leader clearly applies to having a sole executive officer, not *joint* executive officers. In the latter situation, the chairman has an opportunity to divide and rule; and senior executives near the top may seek to play one executive officer off against the other. There is, however, a possible case for dual executives at the top, but only when the responsibilities and duties are mutually exclusive: for example, one executive officer could concentrate on external development, growth, and the like, and the other could devote his time to finance, accounting, and internal administration. In broad terms, one would be looking ahead, while the other would be dealing mainly with the present. There are other logical divisions, too, such as products, functions, or territory. But again there must be a final coordinating executive voice, preferably not that of the chairman, which in a large enough concern could be a *chief* executive officer.

In a relatively small firm, however, the president would have a second line of executives such as sales manager, production manager, comptroller, and company secretary. This falls in line with the logic of a simple industrial breakdown in marketing, production, finance, and personnel. Each of these top jobs could be at board level, in which case there might be, for example, a marketing (or sales) director, a production director, a financial director and, less likely, a personnel director.

The company secretary is often described as the "servant of the board" and has statutory responsibilities, but in a line capacity he is answerable to the chief executive, namely the president. There is nothing to stop the president from also being the secretary, but in that case he would be wise to have an assistant secretary to do most of the work. In a small firm the secretary would probably look after the general administration and deal with the personnel side as well.

There are no really typical organizational structures, and even titles given to particular functions vary from firm to firm. Some companies, for instance, prefer to emphasize that the directorial side should be clearly distinguished from the managerial side, in which case the duality can be demonstrated by a title such as "marketing manager and director." In the boardroom, of course, the marketing man will be concerned with policy generally; outside the boardroom he reverts to his specialist role.

At a further stage of growth there could be a wider range of specialists needing, say, two of their number to be promoted to general-management level to help the president. They could be titled vice presidents or, if not on the board, general managers. Each of these top executives would be responsible for a group of the remaining specialists, including their own replacements, such divisions, if possible, being mutually exclusive as indicated above. These third-line (formerly second-line) executives could, in effect, be reclassified as "middle" management.

Top-level Meetings

Whatever the structure at the top, there must be some coordinating executive organization, so that all in command can speak officially with the same managerial voice. This organization may take several forms, the simplest and most usual being the holding of a daily (or weekly) meeting—preferably short—between the president and his top executives. Such regular meetings could be used as a clearing-house for all general management problems, external and internal, of current significance. To have several minds on such matters as the impact of change, daily trends, special correspondence, personnel problems, and future developments could be a useful corrective to any tendency towards a one-man partisan opinion. Plans, ideas, and action can be discussed on policy lines, leaving the details to be worked out in the normal course of the ordinary day's work. The CEO, being kept informed, then knows what is going on; and his lieutenants, having aired embryo lines of approach to their own prob-lems, can proceed with renewed confidence or, if necessary, make a fresh start.

The words "preferably short" must be underlined when organiz-ing daily (or weekly) meetings, often conveniently timed to take place over the morning coffee. For busy executives carrying a heavy load of time-consuming responsibilities find it a frustrating business if any meeting of this kind should develop into a vehicle for the CEO's ego, whether related to business or his week-end golf. Occasionally, special matters demand a more lengthy get-together, but the crisper the con-ference the better for managerial efficiency. The final answer obvi-ously lies with the president himself.

There is a useful technique, however, for getting to the root of complicated problems, by using rather lengthier management meet-ings than normal, as a vehicle for debate. Here, the president, acting as a one-man jury or judge, deliberately arranges for his top execu-tives to argue out the pros and cons of thorny questions by taking opposing sides, whether or not their personal beliefs happen to be different. This type of approach enables all the facts to be properly considered, weighted, and evaluated, as a practical prelude to more realistic decision-making.

Management Coordination

At such informal top-level conferences, it is not unusual for specialists to be brought in to advise on matters needing urgent man-agerial consideration. Controlled first-hand contact of this kind can be a useful time-saver in the end and therefore has practical value. There is a strong case in fact for having regular more formal management meetings, whether weekly, monthly, or quarterly, attended by all key executives above a certain status level. Those qualified to attend would constitute a management committee or conference at which all important aspects of the organization would be represented by responsible specialists.

Such a committee would be concerned with carrying out the objectives and policies, developing long-range plans, evaluating progress, reviewing budgeting and so on, under the chairmanship of the CEO himself or as delegated to one of his top team, possibly on a rotation basis. Given a clearly defined comprehensive agenda, high-level conferences of this kind can be a valuable vehicle for achieving coordination, initiating action, renewing enthusiasm, and dealing with doubt and despondency.

Again it is essential that no time should be wasted, an ideal even more difficult to achieve because of the larger numbers likely to be present. It is important, of course, that all those present should have proper deputies to run their specialist side of the business while they are away at meetings. Regular exposure to general-management problems broadens the viewpoint of specialists and enhances their potential for subsequent promotion.

Meetings with Subordinates

The CEO and his top team, as the key personalities, have a profound effect on the organization as a whole and set the tone for managerial conferences and discussions throughout. These can be conducted in an atmosphere of rigid formality, in a completely casual way, or in the happy compromise of a close relationship based on mutual respect. Some formality is usually essential to the achievement of results, but not to the point of inhibiting the participants and frustrating communication. Proper communication up and down, across the structure, and in between oils the wheels of cooperation, ensuring maximum participation by all concerned in discussions likely to affect them and their responsibilities.

One aspect of formality particularly relevant here is the right of access permitted by a superior to his subordinates. At one extreme is the "open-door" principle and at the other the "wait-until-you-are-sent-for" attitude. The open-door method enables a specialist, for example, to consult his immediate superior, perhaps a vice president, without formally requesting an audience. This ensures continuous and frank liaison, of lasting benefit to both sides, subject as always to the reasonable exercise of discretion.

In such a context a superior must always be approachable and be prepared to give instant attention to the needs of his subordinates; but there are times, of course, when he is engaged with other people, or particularly busy with some urgent report, or preparing for a meeting, or otherwise not currently wishing to be available. This situation should be made known to his secretary, and any subordinate would be wise to check first to see whether his presence would be welcomed. Nevertheless, knowing that direct access is an accepted way of executive life has an appreciable psychological benefit.

A superior interrupted at an awkward time by a less imaginative subordinate has the simple choice of inviting that subordinate to stay, taking a rest from his own duties in the meanwhile, or of asking him to come back at a specified time, or wait to be advised.

Coupled with this less formal approach is the further step of getting away from the conventional inhibitions of sitting on either side of an executive desk, one side being less important than the other! The key factor here is not really a matter of furniture, but the development of an attitude of mind that removes emotive barriers and welcomes two-way communication.

Where there are regular opportunities, such as the daily (or weekly) informal conference or the setting aside of specified times for direct access, the need for unstructured contact becomes correspondingly less.

ORGANIZATIONAL FRAMEWORKS

An efficient management must "get organized," and it is useful at this point to consider the general principles of organization and their practical application to the successful running of a business.

Basic Concepts

Usually a corporate structure evolves haphazardly over the years, or a newly appointed president inherits an existing organization created by his predecessors; it is seldom feasible to begin again with a blank sheet of paper. Nevertheless, in theory at any rate, it is possible to design an optimum structure in detail and then see how the existing organization matches up to it, or can be adjusted to fit into it, preferably without losing the goodwill of interested parties.

The exercise conveniently starts by listing all the many activities to be covered, deciding on their logical classification into divisions, departments, sections, and so on, these normally being grouped by product, function, or territory, as appropriate. Next, it must be decided which grades of people are to be in charge of others, conceiving this as being so many layers of authority, progressively built up on superior/subordinate relationships. It is then necessary to determine how much and how far authority and responsibility should be delegated downwards through these layers. Finally, the need for committees must be looked at as a coordinating factor, bearing in mind the nature of the work to be performed by each classified group.

In the end it must be seen that every piece in the organizational jigsaw puzzle has been fitted neatly into the picture as a whole. There must be no pieces missing and no pieces left over. Throughout the exercise it remains essential, as usual, to keep faith with the overall objectives, the corporate plans, and the major policies that have already been agreed upon.

Successful organization, in a corporate sense, requires a structural form in which all these gainfully employed by a firm can be enabled to attain maximum efficiency, individually and collectively, in the achievement of a common purpose. Top management must, as always, be the motivating force here and create the right pattern of relationships, based on sound human principles, properly coordinated and controlled. Organization then becomes a management art in its own right, increasing in practical difficulty with the growing importance and complexities of large-scale enterprise.

Organization Charts

Most executives, when asked to describe the structure of their firm, find the easiest way of answering it to rough out some sort of chart of the main features, even if only drawn crudely on the back of an envelope. The management theorist is ever ready to produce colorful and impressive-looking charts, of all sorts and sizes, purporting to show how an organization works, or could work, but in the hands of a practical manager their construction and use becomes a more controversial issue. The following points, for and against, summarize the main arguments put forward.

Advantages of Charts:

(a) In order to produce an organization chart, it is first necessary to make a full-scale structural study of the firm itself. This is a good objective discipline.

(b) Once it has been prepared, a chart serves as an informative blueprint of the organization for easy reference by executives and staff generally, including newcomers. In the latter context, it can be a useful visual aid for staff-training purposes at induction level.

(c) Where a chart accurately sets out the current framework in diagrammatic form, it serves as a practical starting-point for discussing the structural effects of any proposed plans for reorganization, including mergers and acquisitions.

(d) Planning effects can be followed through in sequence by having a series of charts, based on forecasts, at regular intervals (say, every third year), each chart demonstrating progressively the organizational effects of growth from small/medium size to large-scale enterprise. This evolution in visual form should highlight the forecasting implications of growth with special reference to management succession, manpower planning, and training needs.

Disadvantages of Charts:

(a) As charts tend to be static, often described as snapshots taken at a fixed point of time, they quickly become out of date. This is certainly true when copied and issued, but if retained by management for its own use they can be easily updated by any of the flexible modern methods available for visual aid.

(b) Taken too literally, a chart, as drawn up, can encourage some managers to become hidebound in their outlook, seeing themselves neatly placed in watertight boxes, linked together by formal channels of communication. In practice, a much more flexible relationship needs to be fostered.

(c) Although most charts add a cautionary note to the effect that no status significance is to be attached to the levels of various boxes and their relationships as drawn in, human nature tends to disregard this caveat. In the very process of dealing with superior/subordinate strata, some importance must be given to certain positions and less to others. For whether top management is itself shown at the top, or by an alternative convention at the center of a circle, this must still be the focal point to which other personalities have to be attached in less exalted roles. The real trouble starts when necessarily placing a number of individuals on the same relationship level, or concentric circle, when these may not have anything like the same status. In any case, a chart cannot show degrees of responsibility and authority, except by inference, which can itself be misinterpreted.

Hence there may be tactical resistance to the publication of detailed organization charts, which may be locked up in the president's desk and not displayed at all. There may even be, for example, a deliberate "haze" about the position of certain executives. Naturally, the main lines of organization must be known to everyone concerned, and a streamlined noncontroversial edition could perhaps be issued instead. There is always the danger of having too rigid an administration, resulting in such attitudes as "it's not my job" even though a colleague might be away ill, instead of a more fluid organization backed by a flexible and enthusiastic team.

Examples of highly simplified charts are given in Fig. 4, but ideally readers should construct their own tailor-made charts. In attempting to do so, the top-management structure, if not already known, can usually be taken from the directors' statutory annual report and the remaining relationships from personal observation and by asking discreet questions.

A full-scale chart, as used in a large firm, can be very complicated indeed if all the main jobs are indicated and the appropriate types of relationship drawn in with distinctive kinds of line. Names of key personalities would normally be included, as well as their titles. It is important that any organization, and therefore chart, should be appropriate to the objectives and strategy of the firm concerned; it must also be sufficiently flexible to keep pace with, or anticipate, change. For there may be new markets or new products to be taken into account, environmental developments, and perhaps mergers and acquisitions, all increasing the chart problem in trying to cope with the effects of size and the growing complexity of operations.

(a) Traditional pyramid chart

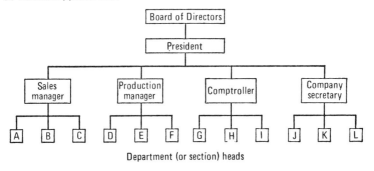

Department (or section) heads

(b) Circle Chart

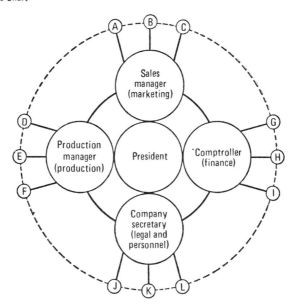

FIGURE 4. Simple organization charts

Formal Relationships

In drawing up a chart there are certain relationships to watch which are fundamental. These are briefly summarized below:

(a) "Line" Relationship. This implies authority to take action and make decisions. In essence there should be an unbroken line from the top of the organization to the bottom showing how this authority is exercised through each level from the president down to the newest junior clerk or worker. An army parallel, much favored by theorists, shows how this authority starts with the commanding officer of the regiment and passes downward from rank to rank until it necessarily finishes at the corporal with sectional authority over his quota of privates.

With such a line there must be no conflict or confusion; that is to say, the superior must be certain who his subordinates are and the subordinates must be clear as to who is their boss. This may seem obvious, but in practice many problems arise through just such a lack of clear definition. As a result, a person may, for instance, find himself answerable to two superiors and therefore tempted to play one off against the other. Nor should any specific duty be the responsibility of more than one person, as otherwise each will tend, deliberately or by wrong assumption, to leave it to the others.

(b) "Functional" Relationship. This exists where a specialist is responsible to a superior for particular activities grouped on a basis of functional similarity, such as marketing, production, or finance. In a large company, a personnel manager, for example, could be responsible for all staff matters through its organization, but the staff themselves (except in his own department) would be under the line command of other executives. In the army parallel he could be compared with the chief paymaster at headquarters functionally responsible for all unit paymasters. These latter would be under local operation line authority for discipline and the like, but would be in a liaison relationship, so far as the work itself was concerned, with the chief paymaster.

(c) "Staff" Relationship. This connotes the provision of special services to assist the line managers in achieving optimum results. There is no question here of exercising any authority or of making any decisions. The use of the word "staff" in this context can be mislead-

ing, as it does not specifically relate to personnel matters. Continuing the army example, this relationship can be well illustrated by the use of chairborne "staff officers" at the Department of Defense, or as attached to operational commanders, with the important job of advising on specific aspects of army tactics, organization, or techniques. In business, this relationship covers all personnel allocated the duties of assisting, or advising, line management; they may be executives in their own right, or merely acting as personal assistants, such as "assistant to" the president, helping him to think and acting as his general factotum. Normally, a staff officer has no authority of his own, but operates entirely on the authority of his superior.

(d) Practical Aspects. The three terms—line, functional, and staff —are sometimes loosely used and can be misleading in practice, but there should be no difficulty in appreciating the logic of the differences between them. Often, too, there is a combination of relationships such as the well-known "line and staff" illustrated in Figure 5(b). It will be appreciated also that there is a world of difference between an executive vice president, with considerable authority, and a "assistant to the president," with no authority. The former has arrived at senior office and the latter is still being initiated into its many mysteries.

Spreading the Administrative Load

As a firm expands from its original one-man business, or partnership, into a medium-sized and then large-scale corporation, with directors, it inevitably grows to a point of impersonality. It is no longer possible for top management to know every one in the firm and exactly what they are doing or should be doing. Nor is it possible any more to oversee the whole of the now extensive activities personally. Instead, various organizational techniques must be brought in to "spread the load" or "break down the bulk." The following concepts are particularly relevant:

(a) Span of Control. There are many views on this, but basically it means that a company president or other chief executive cannot personally control more than a given number of subordinates whose work interlocks. In the simple charts given in Figure 4 there is a span of four: the sales manager, production manager, comptroller, and

company secretary, each having a direct line relationship with the president. In Figure 5(a) the span of control has increased to eight.

The limits to a span of control cannot really be laid down by any exact numbers, for management structure must be organized dynamically, not constrained by mathematical formulas. Nevertheless, at a point of growth, it is likely to become necessary to reduce the span of control, the specialists by then having become too many for the CEO to deal with directly and still have sufficient time left for his more important duties. In so doing, it may be advisable to promote two of the specialists, as indicated earlier, to share the load between them as

(a) Wide span of control

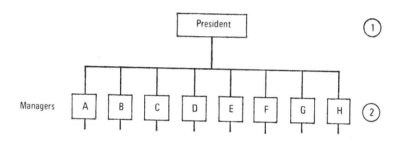

(b) The problem of third place

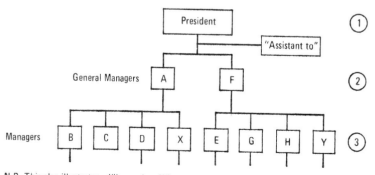

N.B. This also illustrates a "line and staff" organization

FIGURE 5. Spreading the administrative load

vice presidents or general managers. The "demotion" of the remaining executives comprising the original span to third place, as shown in Figure 5(b), clearly needs tact and diplomacy, but this would possibly be helped by their continued inclusion as members of the management committee.

Where people are doing basically the same job, as in the same department, it is relatively easy at this lower level of management to control a considerably larger number. But again there comes a critical point at which it is obviously necessary to bring in supervisors, foremen, section leaders and so on to ease the strain.

Too wide a span of control means lack of control; too narrow a span tends to be wasteful and costly, unless, as in the case of the CEO himself, this releases his energies for more essential responsibilities likely to take up most of his time. Also, too narrow a span may cause an increase in the levels of management, which, as well as being costly, renders communication more complex. There are no hard-and-fast rules, however, as in each case the practical answer depends on the nature of the work, the capacity of the particular manager concerned, the efficiency of the system employed, and the extent to which use is made of "staff" assistance.

(b) Delegation.   This is simply the concept of handing over to a subordinate some part of the job that a superior is expected to carry out. On the face of it this seems to be an easy way to reduce the administrative burden, but unfortunately some managers are constitutionally incapable of passing on work for others to perform. Among the usual reasons to be found are lethargy, undue concern for supposed loss of prestige, fear of being superseded, personal interest in doing the job, and lack of confidence in subordinates. Often enough the main reason is simply that the manager, in his view, is indispensable! Yet the only way by which managers can hope to concentrate effectively on their major responsibilities is by unloading as much of the remaining work as possible.

An established guideline here is to delegate work down through the organization to the point where it is just being done well enough without too many mistakes; at this point the staff concerned would be doing the utmost of which they are capable, costs thereby being kept to a minimum. Usually, too, there is an increase in morale through enhanced job satisfaction. In addition, the work itself may be done much better than before, simply because of the opportunity afforded for specialization.

It goes without saying that delegation also requires someone suitable to whom the work can be handed over; this involves good staff selection, training, and the like, a subject developed in Chapter Twelve. It is fundamental, of course, that corresponding authority should be delegated with responsibility, and that there should be full accountability to a superior for the actions that are taken.

It may be asked whether there can be too much delegation, and the answer here is "yes." Apart from major executive responsibilities, including policy matters, that should be retained, it is feasible to pass on only work that will not continually overburden those immediately below. But this is a bottleneck that can be eliminated by providing additional help or pushing the less essential work of such subordinates still further down the line.

Work having been delegated, it is wrong to interfere with how the job is being done, provided always that it is being done well enough; but delegation does not mean abdication. There is still a shared responsibility, even though the authority has been properly delegated, with a need for control to match accountability.

(c) Decentralization. This is a form of maximum delegation spread throughout a large organization and consists of taking away administrative bulk from the headquarters establishment and allocating it to regions or branches, each mounting its own functions as appropriate. There will be structural evolution with growth. Overall responsibilities for policy determination, planning, and control are still retained centrally, together with the allocation of physical and human resources. Local mandates are granted, however, to the regions or branches to enable decisions to be made on the spot, this being where production takes place and/or where the customers are situated. It remains a matter of judgment, in any given business, as to which functions or services should remain centralized and which should be decentralized: and opinions here can change with events. The important factor is that top management ("central" management may be more appropriate in this context) should so organize itself as to be able to concentrate at all times on its retained functions, including integration.

In order to ease the load of the president in a very large complicated undertaking, various forms of organization have come into being. One technique used has been the concept of the "office" of the president, in which a number of top managers have shared the chief executive task by undertaking specific duties such as the supervision of individual regions from the home office. These executives have been at general manager or vice president level only, so that the final burden has still remained fairly and squarely on the shoulders of the president himself. Splitting the chief executive job is no answer, by orthodox standards, and there are limits to the weight that can be thrown on the next level of executive responsibility, while still retaining the overall control of a large corporate body. Thus it is a more realistic step to break the administrative unit as a whole into a strategic number of separate divisions, each with almost complete autonomy, as shown in Figure 6. These divisions would have their own separate organizational structures, as necessary.

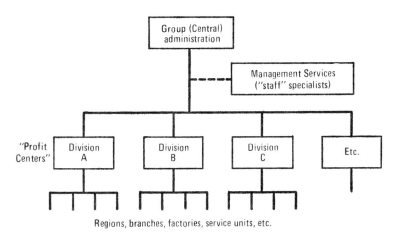

FIGURE 6. Organization into divisions

(d) Divisionalization.   Divisionalization implies the separation and coordination of all the activities relating to a given product or market, with consequent accountability to the group central administration for its operating performance as evidenced by profits made. Most of the usual supporting services are carried on within the division itself, but there is generally a small highly skilled "staff" organization at the central office to give help and advice as required locally. In return,

each division feeds back marketing and operating information to assist overall planning, policy formulation, and final control.

Structurally, each division within a group has its own chief executive, and usually its own local board, these boards being interlocked as explained in Chapter Three. Merged or acquired companies or wholly owned subsidiaries have separate legal status but, to the extent that they become divisions with allegiance to the group and some dependence on central services, part of their autonomy must be lost. This is more than balanced, however, by the greater strength of the group as a whole and the flexible allocation of resources, as between divisions, in response to special needs, emergencies, or opportunities.

There is a link here with decentralization through the splitting up of a large complex business into a number of virtually self-contained operating divisions, consisting of separate products, markets, or whole geographical regions. Each division may have its own network of factories, branches, and so on. Quite apart from easing the overall burden of administration, there is often a logic in grouping certain manufacturing activities together, or certain sales activities, or both.

The concept of "profit centers" is introduced here, each operating division working to financial targets laid down by the parent (group) board of directors. This aspect is covered in detail in Chapter Eleven. In the meantime, it may be stated that a different form of organization has started to emerge. Given the previously illustrated linear or pyramidal structures on the one hand and the "center periphery" model on the other, responsibility and authority have been seen to emanate from the top or center. In line with the developing evolution of "free-form" management, the emphasis is now being placed on centralized control (performance usually being evaluated by computer) and virtually autonomous decentralized divisions. Thus responsibility and authority flow downward, or outward, according to the convention chosen, subject to overriding rules for the group as a whole. But the application of these rules is then left to flexible local discretion in the light of opportunities in the prevailing environment. Operationally, and structurally, therefore, considerable scope exists (despite growth to large scale) for renewed entrepreneurial freedom.

In addition to "line and staff" organization, as further illustrated in Figure 6, there may also be some form of superimposed matrix with special reference to projects. For "matrix organization" basically consists of a vertical line of project managers and a horizontal line taken across the (usually functional) board, thereby banding together hand-picked specialists as required. The significance of such project teams, for "short-term programs," is developed in Chapter Thirteen. Under a divisionalized organization, the chief executive officer will concentrate his attention on the group as a whole. He will also keep in mind the possible need for regrouping his divisions to meet developments in technology, or changes in market areas or consumer demand, aiming to maintain at all times the optimum benefits flowing from divisionalization. In the same way he will review periodically the allocation of staff (service) units as between the home office and the product/regional divisions. Where these services, individually or collectively, can be better and more economically performed locally, rather than continue as a group service centrally, they should obviously be dealt with locally.

THE ROLE OF SPECIALISTS

Having given some attention to the board of directors, president, and general managers, and to their deputies and assistants—all of whom represent the generalist side of business activities—we must turn now to the role of specialists.

Central Office Departments

The creation of departments, under specialist managers, is a natural structural development. Top management requires specialized help over a wide range of activities including corporate planning, marketing, purchasing, manufacturing, research and development, distribution, finance, personnel, legal, and secretarial. Departments would be set up dealing with these matters as appropriate to the business concerned. In a large enough firm there would be two or more logical groups of such departments, each under a general executive responsible to the chief executive.

With decentralization, or divisionalization, most departments would be token units only at the home office, the bulk of the departmental work being attached to the branches or divisions. Some departments, however, are essentially home office or group departments and it is a matter of judgment, convenience, and cost as to how much should be kept centralized. By retention, it is possible to maximize specialization and ensure that adequate attention is being given to the particular service aspect, consistently and effectively. It is not necessarily uneconomic to maintain even a relatively large staff centrally to provide essential common services, as this may be cheaper than having such services duplicated at each of the operational units. But there must be safeguards against any tendency towards empire-building.

In the context of the previous paragraph, it may be asked whether a central office, or group central administration, is necessary at all, bearing in mind that the action takes place in the divisions or branches. Sufficient has been indicated, however, to demonstrate the need for total planning, coordination, control, and the provision of certain central services. At the same time, it is clear that a central office, being nonoperational, earns no direct profits against which to offset its costs; these costs must therefore be kept to an absolute minimum. This statement is often in strange contrast to the expensive and opulent home offices in prestige locations enjoyed by many large enterprises in both the public and the private sectors of the economy. There may, of course, be excellent public relations reasons for having impressive central establishments of this kind, but even so the cost/benefit ratio must be thoroughly and objectively assessed.

Organization and Methods

For some years now it has been popular to set up O. & M. units, ostensibly to increase the efficiency of office work by improving organization, methods, and performance generally. Their effectiveness has varied considerably from firm to firm: in some there have been large-scale attempts at overhauling the whole organizational structure; in others the unit has been unable to do more than redesign a few forms and procedures. Basically, an O. & M. department or section is an internal consulting service making recommendations to central management; its success depends on how far that higher authority is prepared to authorize their implementation.

Usually, O. & M. work requires skilled staff with academic and/or professional standing, and such a unit often proves to be a useful training ground for future management. Apart from expertise, all O. & M. personnel must be highly diplomatic in their investigations and attempts at reorganization. Being so vitally concerned with change, any bull-in-a-china-shop tactics will meet with only frustration, if not open opposition. But if O. & M. staff consult and seek participation in their deliberations, by those likely to be affected by change, a much better chance of success will emerge.

Management Services

Developing O. & M. a stage further is the wider concept of a management-services unit covering such quantitative areas as data processing and operations research. This unit again should be answerable to higher authority, preferably direct to the president, and is ideally made up of top-flight specialists. An advanced unit of this kind could be costly, but with considerable financial savings in mind as an end product, it should be made to pay for itself in the course of time—or better still make a profit. Initial acceptance of a management-services unit is again critical, for a great deal depends on the way it is introduced to the organization at the outset. If it is considered to be a potential threat, and to some managers almost any change can appear to be a threat, then once again opposition and ineffectiveness may well result. The president would presumably be wise to introduce the unit himself, setting out the advantages and dealing tactfully with the psychological reaction to change.

An efficient management-services unit will cover the full gamut of managerial techniques from planning to performance; it should be far-seeing, practical, and sophisticated.

Organization and the Computer

The introduction of electronic data-processing, usually after an extensive feasibility study and exhaustive comparisons between competing systems, makes a fundamental change in the organizational structure. To start with, all relevant processes will come under the critical scrutiny of the systems analysts, whose job it is to translate the daily round of administrative work into computer terms and procedures. In most cases, this means a complete overhaul of existing organization and methods to match up to computer requirements; it may also mean bringing in additional expertise from outside.

Apart, however, from initial installation, usually a lengthy operation, a permanent team, including the systems analysts, must be recruited, selected, and trained for action. It is a matter of opinion how far such a team should be made up of computer specialists from outside the firm and how far it should consist of existing personnel having a detailed knowledge of the internal administration. A strategic mixture of both is probably the right answer, possibly with an inside specialist as manager.

On the administrative side, it can be seen that a computer takes over many of the routine jobs of all kinds previously performed by a myriad of clerks. This suggests less need for a middle manager to supervise and run any department where clerical work was formerly a major function: obvious examples are accounting, payroll, purchasing, stock, and shipping. Instead of routine information going through certain processes and being filtered upwards to top management, it can now jump from original entry direct to final printed form. By and large, middle management thus tends to be cut out of the hierarchy, and the organization pyramid thereby becomes flatter; responsibility and authority can be pushed further down the line.

Any middle managers displaced may be used as specialist "staff" advisers interpreting computer results, possibly without departments, or found other useful administrative work. Their redundant staff could be employed elsewhere, some perhaps helping with the routine computer tasks. But it is worth noting that during the lengthy transitional period of installation, more and more staff seem to become necessary, for, as well as the work involved in putting in the new system, the old routine has to be continued in parallel. Eventually, when the changeover is complete, it may be found that because of normal business growth and natural staff attrition in the meantime, the need for layoffs is minimal.

Having settled in with a computer, it is still wise for management to keep up to date with subsequent developments. At the time of writing, the so-called fourth generation of computers is awaited with interest, although it seems unlikely to produce such an electronic impact as the third generation, now several years old.

Using Management Consultants·

It is quite usual today to bring in external management consultants, often because, in addition to having wider experience to offer, they can make sufficient time available to concentrate on the organizational problems, time which the firm's top executives can hardly spare. There is particular value in looking at the organization of a company objectively, if necessary from top to bottom, by using experts with experience in other comparable fields. These experts have the advantage of bringing an open mind to bear on the problems and having no axes to grind in the process.

Success in using reputable management consultants calls initially for a clear idea of what particular help is required. The next step is to work out comprehensive terms of reference jointly. Thereafter it is important to keep in close touch with the consultants while they are carrying out the assignment. Consultants are employed to give advice, but they will also assist in bringing about, systematically and diplomatically, any changes agreed by the board. The consultants' function is to identify the problem, when it is not known, and suggest a solution that will achieve optimum results quickly, cheaply, and acceptably. The brief may, of course, be highly specific, such as dealing with a new factory or extension, organizing a move from one area to another, introducing a computer, or bringing out a new product, in any of which events it may pay to engage a specialist experienced in the field concerned.

It is sometimes considered that valuable staff time is taken up in briefing management consultants on the background and operations of the firm, but this must be weighed realistically when considering the net advantage to be gained from expert investigation. Most consultants will submit that, in view of the administrative savings they are able to achieve, their fees should be regarded as a valuable investment and not just an expense.

Whether the advice eventually submitted is acceptable or not is a matter entirely for the board of directors itself. Should it be considered necessary to take action in the field of organizational reform, and therefore be likely to affect people's jobs, the calling in of management consultants depersonalizes the investigation. It demonstrates at the same time that although the board means business, it is prepared initially at least to seek objective advice.

Purchasing Special Services

Instead of setting up expensive full-scale headquarter departments, some services may be engaged when required, possibly on a retainer basis. Typical examples are the occasional uses made of architects, lawyers, advertising agencies, market-research organizations, and printing and duplicating firms.

Mention may be made here of introducing a regular management audit to check up on the comparative effectiveness of the firm, as against the productivity and performance of other firms in the same industry, at home and abroad. The analogy of a company doctor, testing the health and strength of the firm, has often been used. This audit is a service that may be better purchased, probably from a leading consultancy firm, than left to the subjective attention of the firm's own management-services unit. There are no hard-and-fast rules; it is all a matter of managerial judgment not unrelated to comparative cost and convenience.

INFORMAL ORGANIZATION

Formal relationships, as seen earlier, are those which can easily be drawn in bold lines on an organization chart, looking clear cut and efficient. In support (or instead) of a chart, there are usually detailed procedure manuals, office instructions, and the like, putting these formalities into writing for the guidance of all concerned with the daily routine.

But in any business, large or small, there is always a tendency for an informal organization to grow up and operate concurrently. This may be to remedy inherent deficiencies in the organization as laid down, take advantage of a weak manager, anticipate natural changes eventually requiring the taking of formal action, or simply to cut through excessive red tape. It is essential, therefore, that top management should become aware of the strength of such informal relationships, encourage those which facilitate the firm's objectives and help morale, and deal with any irregularities likely to lead to damaging consequences.

All organizations have informal leaders, barracks-room lawyers and unofficial pressure groups, and it is important for management to identify these as accurately as possible. For it is imperative that these individualistic personalities should be motivated into effective channels, thereby rationalizing the formal and the informal.

THE BEST USE OF EXECUTIVE TIME

Even with maximum unloading of his work, through the various techniques discussed earlier, a top manager still remains consistently up against the problem of limited time. In fact his whole existence is one long round of problems, which continually need his skill and that of the other members of the executive team, in the search for satisfactory solution. For problem solving is the very essence of top jobs; and solving the problem of limited time is clearly related to all the other problems.

Constraints

A top manager is under constant pressure from a number of constraints. First of all, he must always know what is going on inside and outside the organization. He must make sure that his immediate subordinates are carrying out their responsibilities effectively; if they are not, he must find the time to deal with their problems and shortcomings. This kind of help must be carefully watched, however, as otherwise a subordinate may be encouraged to lean too heavily on his superior, waste valuable time, and fail to achieve initiative and confidence.

Second, a top manager is usually conditioned by past, present, and future board meetings, conferences, and committees of all kinds. Before each board meeting, in particular, he is vitally concerned with a variety of allied topics including the preparation and submission of reports. After each meeting he must deal with the policy decisions reached and with any new problems arising from them requiring attention before the next meeting. There may even be a feeling of living (perhaps "existing" is a better word) from board meeting to board meeting, with limited time for anything else.

Third, he is, or should be, always approachable for help, both internally and externally; he, in turn, will expect to make substantial demands on other people's time.

How Executive Time Is Spent

Arising from these occupational constraints, and other time-absorbing factors, the following aspects are worth special mention:

(a) Meetings and Interviews. Discussions of all kinds at meetings, conferences, interviews, through social contacts, on the telephone, and so on, whether formal or informal, can take up a considerable amount of executive time. It is, therefore, imperative that such time should be well spent, not frittered away.

(b) The Manager's Office. Generally speaking, a large proportion of the day's work is conducted in the manager's private office. Some executives have all their immediate subordinates visit them regularly, by request, by appointment, or on the open-door principle, singly or collectively. Others combine these contacts with tours of inspection to see what is going on in the office and workshop, and, it is hoped, help to build up morale in the process.

(c) Secretaries and Dictation. The amount of time spent on dictating to a secretary or machine varies with the type of job and the ability of the executive. Some managers write out their reports for typing, others dictate them, some pass out correspondence for subordinates to deal with, others handle everything that comes on to their desk. A good secretary can, of course, sort out priorities, deal with many matters on her own initiative, and act as a time-saving personal assistant, the so-called Girl Friday. The value of a good secretary in this context cannot be overrated; unfortunately, in practice, so many are allowed to be just shorthand typists cum filing clerks, with little else to do other than look attractive as a managerial status symbol.

(d) Reading and Paperwork. In the main, most executive reading is confined to the *Times* and/or *Wall Street Journal*, miscellaneous trade journals, the day's mail, and a variety of internal office documents,

many of which are of a time-wasting nature and possibly need not be read by top management at all. So far as the newspapers and technical information are concerned, it may be worthwhile to have a daily digest prepared by a small research unit or intelligence section. Official forms received should be passed down the line for completion, or other action, although even at the lower levels any excess form-filling can be a burdensome chore. It is always hoped, however, that there will be some compensating advantages forthcoming. Excess internal paperwork is often a symptom of increasing size and may need to be reviewed regularly and streamlined to essentials. Even so, many managers prefer to have too much information rather than take a chance or having too little. This again is a matter for personal judgment and decision as appropriate; not surprisingly, there are even status aspects with regard to information flow, whereby certain managers insist on receiving forms and reports that in fact they should not need. The alternative to any excessive paperwork at top levels is perhaps to have more face-to-face contact with senior colleagues and subordinates.

Brief mention may be made of the growing interest in courses available for speed reading, to deal with what is known as the "information explosion," the vast array of reading matter that continues to increase in volume. Practitioners mounting such courses aim at a progressive speeding up of the number of words, or lines, that can be read in a given time, a technique based on key phrases, with tests on comprehension. Remarkable results are claimed for this acquired ability, which has obvious merit for the busy executive. But, as stated above, much of his paperwork can be reduced to essentials or eliminated altogether.

(e) Traveling Time.   It is often held that time spent in traveling is not time wasted, for there are such dramatic luxuries as boardrooms or private offices in executive aircraft, or on board ship, and dictation by telephone in company cars. But, generally speaking, most executives find that the amount of effective work that they can do while traveling normally tends to be limited. The ability and energy to read and process official papers in the air or on boats or trains have their physical and mental limits, particularly when coupled with the effects of international time changes while going long distances east or west. There may be a better case instead for relaxation.

(f) Taking Work Home.   The bulging briefcase is as much a part of the executive image as the traditional bowler hat and rolled umbrella, but

it could also be a sign of not making the best use of available time. Although emergencies may well justify this practice on occasion, the taking of work home as a regular habit is another matter entirely.

(g) Social Activities. The entertaining of customers and other visitors tends to take up an increasing amount of managerial time, in club lunches, social evenings, executive golf or perhaps sailing, but this can usually be kept under reasonable control. Sometimes, however, important visitors, especially from overseas, tend to arrive unannounced, yet feel that they should be entertained forthwith as valuable contacts to be fostered even to the point of personal inconvenience. As always, tact and circumstances dictate the right action to be taken. The availability of an in-company executives' club provides not only a social meeting-place for management, helping internal coordination in the process, but also provides a built-in opportunity for official visitors to meet a range of executives informally.

(h) Time Left to Think. Given adequate organization of the day's work, a philosophical adjustment to necessary constraints, and the maximum use of help from subordinates, it should be possible to arrange to have at least some part of the day left free for constructive thought.

Maintaining the Initiative

The progressive manager, anxious not to waste time along the lines indicated above, can find out for himself how he is using each day in detail. The usual technique is to draw up and maintain a weekly time-sheet indicating how each half-hour throughout the day is actually spent. The manager can then go through the obvious steps of asking himself whether the amount of time used up on each of the jobs scheduled was in fact necessary at all; if so, whether someone else could have dealt with the job instead, possibly quicker or better; and whether other people were tending to waste his time by certain of the activities listed or whether he was guilty of wasting other people's time. A factual record of this kind will often convince one in concrete terms, sometimes dramatically, of the need for readjustment based on a stricter personal discipline. If appropriate action is taken, this extra chore will have proved to be worthwhile. It only remains then, having worked out a new approach, to guard against slipping back again into long-established habits.

Summary

1. The President
  a. The president should be a focal point; he must not be a bottleneck.
  b. He must have the right basic qualities.
  c. He has a wide range of executive responsibilities.
  d. His collaboration with the chairman is essential.

2. Executive Team in Action
  a. Sole command is fundamental.
  b. The team must have a strong second line in support.
  c. Regular meetings of top personnel help coordination.
  d. An "open-door" philosophy leads to good relationships with subordinates.

3. Organizational Frameworks
  a. Organization often becomes haphazard through growth.
  b. While optimum structure is being planned, the effect on personnel needs to be watched.
  c. Organization charts are a mixed blessing.
  d. The span of control should be kept within bounds.
  e. Delegation, decentralization, and divisionalization provide means of passing responsibility and authority down the line.
  f. Informal relationships should not be underestimated.

4. Role of Specialists
  a. Departmental structure may be functional.
  b. Central management services, computer facilities, and the like affect organization.
  c. Specialist services are often brought in.

5. Making the Best Use of Executive Time
  a. The executive must find out in detail how his day is spent.
  b. He can then attempt to regain initiative.
  c. It is necessary to have time available for constructive thought.

Suggested Further Reading

BABBITT, H.R., JR., ET AL. *Organizational Behavior: Understanding and Prediction*. Englewood Cliffs, N.J.: Prentice-Hall, 1974.

BEHLING, O., AND C.A. SCHRIESHEIM. *Organizational Behavior: Theory, Research, and Application*. Boston: Allyn and Bacon, 1976.

BRINK, V.Z. *Computers and Management: The Executive Viewpoint*. Englewood Cliffs, N.J.: Prentice-Hall, 1971.

DRUCKER, P.F. *The Effective Executive*. New York: Harper & Row, 1967.

HALL, R. *Organizations: Structure and Behavior*. Englewood Cliffs, N.J.: Prentice-Hall, 1972.

HODGE, B.J., AND H.J. JOHNSON. *Management and Organizational Behavior*. New York: Wiley, 1970.

HUSE, E.F., AND J.L. BOWDITCH. *Behavior in Organizations: A Systems Approach to Managing*. Reading, Mass.: Addison-Wesley, 1973.

LITTERER, J.A. *The Analysis of Organizations*. 2d ed. New York: Wiley, 1973.

SANDERS, D.H. *Computers and Management in a Changing Society*. 2d ed. New York: McGraw-Hill, 1974.

SCOTT, W.G., AND T. MITCHELL. *Organization Theory: A Behavioral Analysis for Management*. Rev. ed. Homewood, Ill.: Irwin, 1972.

SISK, H.L. *Management and Organization*. 2d ed. Cincinnati: South-Western, 1973.

VON HALLER GILMER, B., ET AL. *Industrial and Organizational Psychology*. New York: McGraw-Hill, 1971.

FIVE

Committees in Management

Committees are an accepted, if controversial, part of modern living, linked with meetings of all kinds and conferences. We have already seen that board meetings give rise to standing (permanent) and *ad hoc* (special-purpose) committees. Reference has also been made to management committees at top level. There are many committees, of course, in every walk of life—political, social, educational, sports—but we are particularly concerned here with the pros and cons of using committees in business. The extent to which use is made of committees by companies, divisions, or departments varies with overall corporate policy and with the attitude of directors and executives within that policy. Committees can be welcomed as a coordinating influence or disregarded as a waste of executive time.

Definition

A committee may be defined as a group of people formally appointed by another, usually larger, group (sometimes, groups) to meet with the intention of discussing certain matters laid down by stated terms of reference. The usual intention is to make decisions, given a mandate to do so on behalf of the parent body, or to make recommendations to that body. The term "committee" is often used loosely in practice and could refer to the parent body itself. The main aspect dealt with here, however, is that of being created by the parent body for a specific purpose.

It may be asked what the difference is between a meeting, a committee, and a conference. Broadly speaking, a meeting is a getting together of people for any purpose whatever, whether formalized or not; a committee has just been defined; and a conference is an infrequent, large gathering of people, usually with a common interest, to listen to papers read, take part in debate, discuss business, and receive the latest information on relevant issues.

In practice, these terms are often used synonymously; for example, a company president said to be "in conference" may simply be having a meeting in his office with an important customer.

THE PURPOSES OF COMMITTEES

For committees to succeed, there must be clear-cut terms of reference (preferably in writing), competent chairmanship, wise selection of committee members, and an efficient secretary. The main purpose of committees in business may be summarized as follows:

(a) Coordination. This aspect relates to liaison between groups of executives at much the same level in the hierarchy and to bridging the gap between adjacent levels. In particular, it is essential that the various functions should be systematically coordinated, for example, the production side with the marketing side, through properly constituted committees. Ideally, such committees should cover all functions needing integration into the corporate whole. In the process, all departmental managers are encouraged to obtain a better understanding of the work of other departments and to appreciate more realistically how they can and should link up with each other to achieve optimum results.

When executives from different divisions, branches, and the like are brought together in committee, centrally or regionally, this adds to the range of personal contact, cooperation, and understanding, quite apart from coordinating action on policy matters and the broadening of experience generally. In particular, it allows the introduction of problems containing a common interest and the discussion of local solutions found to be effective. This is a valuable method in itself of exchanging information, the important factor here being that everyone concerned with management, and participating in activities towards a common end, should be told not only what is going on but also why and how. It is clearly better to arrange to give a personal briefing to a group, all the members of which are present at the same time and in an atmosphere where questions can be asked and answered, than to rely on the alternative of sending out written instructions that can be misconstrued or go astray.

(b) Consultative and Advisory.   A similar opportunity is created whenever key personnel are brought together in committee to give specialized advice, help with decision-making, or air their views on particular issues referred to them by a superior. The superior is thereby provided with a regular channel for seeking the opinions of subordinates, using their special skills, local knowledge, experience, and judgment to the best effect.

This kind of approach implies that the superior is genuinely anxious to obtain the views of his team before coming to a point of view or making a decision. In many cases, however, the superior has already made up his mind and is only seeking approval, perhaps even on a "yes-man" basis, whereby subordinates are discouraged from intimating any contrary opinion. Such a committee approach is largely a waste of time. Nor is a "no-man" attitude any better, the obvious ideal being an atmosphere of frank discussion with each case being objectively decided on its merits.

By bringing together in committee people of varying types, drawn, for example, from the company strata concerned, it is possible to obtain a reasonably balanced point of view. Positive contributions will tend to offset more negative attitudes, highlighted by a natural optimist being matched with a confirmed pessimist; and practical operational experience will leaven backroom theory.

It often happens, too, that simply by being together, the members of such a committee can spark off more ideas and solve problems more easily than they could do if approached individually. This is one of those group benefits whereby 2 + 2 clearly equals more than 4. A management committee is a good example.

Special uses of the consultative-advisory approach include a policy-making body giving advice to a chief executive; in addition, there is joint consultation, relating to a series of meetings between management and workers, a valuable type of contact described in Chapter Twelve.

(c) Progress Review. This category refers to regular meetings held to discuss projects and targets in general or as related to specific items. Such committees would deal with problems arising from current plans, ensure that everyone is working efficiently to the desired end, review progress made, and "follow through" into the future all action taken to date.

(d) Development. Grouped together here are various unstructured meetings, including those of a training nature, of particular value in executive development. "Brainstorming" sessions and other free-thinking opportunities for constructive contribution give full scope to the imagination and ingenuity of those present.

Although these committee purposes have been listed here separately, for theoretical convenience, there will obviously be considerable overlapping in practice. For example, brainstorming used as a technique in a product-development meeting could also be classified under "Consultative and Advisory."

Reference has already been made to the importance of a committee having proper terms of reference; it is also essential that these terms should be kept continually in mind. It is by no means unknown for a committee, in existence for some time, to be operating with a purpose that has become substantially different from that originally intended—sometimes without the members realizing that a change has taken place. If such a change is seen to be the logical outcome of events, then revised terms of reference and appropriate authority should be initiated by or sought from the parent body. Similarly, a committee set up for one purpose only can have unexpected spin-off advantages in another direction as well.

TYPES OF COMMITTEES

There are no standard practices to be observed with regard to the types, number, and frequency of committees that should be set up in any particular company. Nevertheless, industry and business in general make great use of committees of many kinds. Although a few typical examples can be given here, each company will establish its own committee structure in the light of practical experience. To start with, some authorities believe that there are too many committees today; hence, this chapter sets out their main advantages and disadvantages to enable a balanced opinion to be made. Although selection is largely a matter of judgment in any given set of circumstances, certain committees have clearly stood the test of time.

Committees of the Board

To enable more concentration to be given to detailed specialized (perhaps, technical) issues, it is a useful practice to appoint one or more permanent or standing committees. Meeting at intervals, usually regularly, these committees consider relevant problems as they become important and make recommendations to the board. Examples found in practice are a finance committee, with important budgeting and capital-expenditure responsibilities; a marketing committee; a salaries and pensions committee; and a corporate planning committee. Each standing committee meets regularly, or, when necessary, under its own chairman. Appropriate executives attend either by right as directors or are invited as specialists. Formal records should normally be kept. Each committee chairman reports his committee's findings to the board, preferably supporting them with a written report that can be included with the papers circulated in advance of board meetings. Where a board meeting follows a committee meeting with insufficient time for the preparation of a written report, then a verbal report should be made seeking action on any matters of urgency, the formal report (committee minutes) following later. In any case, the board minutes would formalize any action taken on the committee's recommendations, as adopted.

The Executive Committee

A special and frequently used committee device is the formation of an executive committee with wide terms of reference and power to make decisions. This reports back periodically to the board, or other governing body, for "rubber-stamping" approval and/or new guidelines on general policy to be adopted for future activities. An executive committee may meet either regularly, which is usually the case in most large organizations, or occasionally.

Executive committees are an even more controversial subject than committees in general, for it is claimed that the board, or other governing body, is thereby evading its proper responsibilities. It is often held, too, that decisions reached can be the result of one committee member (perhaps the president) having overly-persuasive powers and exercising undue influence on the remainder. In that case, a committee decision really becomes a personal decision, in the absence of any contrary opinion being effectively expressed.

With recommendations emanating from a normal committee, it is within the province of a board to accept, amend, or reject; but with an executive committee, there is usually no reporting back until after action has been taken on the decisions made.

Nevertheless, there may be practical reasons, such as the directors being widely dispersed geographically, why it is difficult to hold a full board meeting except at long intervals of time. Or there may be a very large governing body of council members elected or appointed to a professional institution, for prestige reasons, many of whom, because of heavy normal managerial commitments, are unable to attend more than occasional policy meetings. In such cases, the appointment of a small executive committee enables the business to be properly carried on in the interim.

An *ad hoc* committee is simply a committee set up for a special purpose, often constituting a working party, usually with a succession of meetings but with its life limited to that purpose. Examples include committees appointed to deal with the practical implications to a firm of a major change in legislation, with new plant or branch locations, or with policy and plans for mergers and acquisitions.

Management Committees

It was shown in Chapter Four that management coordination could be enhanced by committees. Such committees have power to take and enforce executive action within overall board policy. Here would be included regular meetings of central managers with division heads, branch managers, or department managers, as appropriate to a given organization. Other examples are regular functional meetings such as the marketing director with the sales manager, advertising manager, and sales representatives or the production director with the production managers and their key personnel. Here again there can be standing committees or *ad hoc* committees, as determined by circumstances.

It must also be recognized that whenever executives get together for any informal purpose, even social purpose, there is a natural tendency for them to "talk shop." Consequently, there must be many unstructured committees of this kind meeting week by week and serving a valuable purpose with respect to information-passing, discussing problems, and helping communication generally.

Similarly, the procedure at the committees themselves can vary from the strictly formal to the informal. In some cases, strict rules of order are observed with structured agendas, properly presented reports, voting, and minutes, all according to the book; in other cases, scant attention is paid to any formalities, the committee members themselves ranging freely over a wide area of discussion. The choice largely depends on the purpose of the committee, the attitude of the chairman, the status of the members, and any constraints imposed by the appointing body. The venue, too, can range from the boardroom or the directors' committee room to the employees' cafeteria.

EFFECTIVENESS OF COMMITTEES

The list of main purposes of committees has already indicated some of their advantages such as achieving better coordination, securing advice, giving opportunities for consultation, stimulating cooperation in planning and progress, and helping with training. This section attempts to evaluate the effectiveness of committees in the use and development of group judgment, as opposed to individual thought and action taken in isolation.

Group Effectiveness

The following questions summarize the practical features most likely to be significant in the determination of group effectiveness:

(a) Is the chairman qualified as a chairman with approved ability to produce results representing the collective judgment of the committee members as a whole? Does he know how to keep the discussion free and relevant, but under control, without wasting time? Can he ensure at any given moment that members know clearly what matters are under consideration and what conclusions have so far been reached?

(b) Does every member understand the exact purpose for which the committee was set up, what it is attempting to achieve, and to what end he was appointed to add his individual contributions to the general pool?

(c) Is the committee large enough to include all the expertise and experience required for the purpose in hand, but small enough to enable the business to be concluded expeditiously? Is there, in fact, an optimum size that can be related to any given set of circumstances?

(d) Are the formalities of preparing agendas, reports, minutes, and the like being carried out as efficiently and accurately as the occasion demands?

(e) Is it fully appreciated that once a committee has ceased to serve a useful purpose it should be wound up, even though there are status advantages to members in continuing that committee?

COMMITTEES MISUSED

Much of the criticism of committees arises from their misuse. The keen businessman should therefore learn to appreciate both the practical value of committees that are properly and effectively used and the inherent dangers of committees that are misused.

Dangers to Be Avoided

Some of the following disadvantages become apparent when "wrong" answers are given to the basic questions suggested in the previous section; other problems appear to be equally frustrating.

(a) Ineffective Meetings.   Bad chairmanship, for example, can result in domination from the chair or by some other member; poorly controlled discussion; inept members holding up proceedings; overlong meetings; failure to sort out the important from the unimportant; and confusion as to the real issues in hand.

Too large a committee can itself be a material cause of ineffectiveness. Trying to extract a collective point of view from, say, fifty different people needs skillful and experienced chairmanship. This kind of situation gives rise to the often-expressed sentiment that the best committee is a committee of one. There is also the well-known cynical comment that a camel is simply a horse designed by a committee. One method of dealing with the problem of size is to appoint a small active working subcommittee, with a suitable mandate, reporting back to the full committee as necessary. This kind of approach has already been indicated in connection with an executive committee of a company board.

However, if the main purpose of the committee is information-passing, or for exchanging experiences with a common basis, then large size can be an advantage. Too small a committee can also be a problem; for instance, two people can arrive at a deadlock, and two out of a committee of three can easily exclude the third. The question of stalemate can arise, of course, with even numbers at any size, but this may be overcome where the chairman has an extra (casting) vote. But as a matter of practical politics, the chairman should not use this personal power to force through any controversial change, unless there are exceptional circumstances or he has strong convictions in the company's best interests. He may, of course, have vital information which he is not prepared, or able, to divulge for the time being.

(b) Time-wasting.   Having too many committees or overlong committee meetings can be costly in expensive executive time. It is a sobering exercise to total up the salaries, expenses, and administrative costs of time absorbed by committees in preparation, traveling, in session, and when dealing with the resultant paperwork, together with the cost of supporting services. This must be the subject of a cost-benefit analysis in realistic terms, not forgetting the opportunity-cost element of being unable to carry out some other important duty instead. Against this type of approach, it can be held that many of the more indirect benefits are valuable but intangible and therefore cannot be quantified and evaluated accurately.

(c) Avoiding Responsibility. Appointing a special committee or referring a particular matter to a standing committee can be used as a device to delay the making of difficult or unpalatable decisions, without justifiable reason. The existence of committees can also make it easy to avoid personal responsibility by substituting group judgment for individual judgment; similarly, it is possible for individuals to vote for a group decision they would not make themselves. In certain circumstances, too, perhaps simply to preserve committee harmony or to get through the agenda in time, a compromise solution may be reached that, by its very nature, is unlikely to be the best solution.

(d) Undermining Authority. A committee created for something better dealt with by the chief executive officer on his own would tend to undermine his authority. It would also tend to slow down operating efficiency through lack of proper delegation.

It can be seen, therefore, that committees are a mixed blessing, but, properly constituted and used, they serve a valuable purpose in modern democratic management. Nevertheless, although every member of a committee is jointly responsible for the recommendations or decisions of that committee, he cannot individually be held accountable. He could be, in fact, in minority opposition.

THE GOOD COMMITTEEMAN

Committee members combine all characteristics, shades of political opinion, knowledge, background, and temperament. They may be joined together by the same basic bonds or find themselves on opposing sides; they may be on the committee in their own right or simply as agents representing other interests; but, collectively, they represent a valuable mixture of different viewpoints, expertise, and experience.

Concerted and Contrary Opinion

In making a selection of committee members, where selection is possible and not dictated by controlling interests, it is important to

avoid appointing either domineering personalities or those too reserved to make any contribution at all. The latter type of person must
not be confused, however, with the good listener who, when necessary
or when encouraged to contribute, can produce a valuable and informed point of view.

Naturally, the members as a body need to cover all the technical
knowledge, experience, and so on required for the particular job in
hand, both academically and practically. Under an effective chairman, they should be blended to work harmoniously together, but not
to the point where other loyalties, such as separate interests represented on the committee, are not given their full weight if likely to
be in opposition.

There must always be room for a minority opinion, which
should be given fair play and a proper hearing. Where strong feelings
exist, this contrary opinion should be stated in writing or by oral
report when the situation is one of recommendations being made to a
parent body. If the minority committee member is also on the parent
body, he can reserve his right to speak at the meeting of that body and
vote against the majority recommendation. Without reserving such
rights, he would be duty-bound to support his committee's majority
verdict. There is a much stronger case, of course, where there is a
minority group of members all wishing to make themselves heard at
the higher level.

Points to Watch

Newly appointed committee members are usually anxious to
start off on the right foot, and therefore must make themselves aware
of well-established rules which can make all the difference between
becoming effective and being considered simply a passenger. The
following points are relevant in this context:

(a) There is more or less standard formal procedure for conducting business at meetings that should be understood by all those
taking part. Similarly, it is the committee member's responsibility to
find out the terms of reference, the nature of the committee and its
powers, the degree of formality expected, and allied matters, which
can usually be discovered by careful inquiry in advance. Committee

members should, of course, be given such essential information on appointment, but this may not happen in practice.

(b) Experience suggests that it usually pays to play a waiting game at the first few meetings, at least until the various personalities can be sized up, the pressure groups discovered, and the atmosphere thoroughly absorbed. In any case, too strong a contribution made too early could be along the wrong lines, through lack of background awareness, or could be resented by more serious members. Where the meeting is not one of a series, the position must be sized up quickly and contributions made as tactfully as possible. Even so, it often pays to draw the fire of the opposition first, if such exists, before expending any valuable ammunition of one's own.

(c) Making careful preparation for a meeting would seem to be obvious; but all too often, because of other time-absorbing interests and responsibilities, it is overlooked in practice. Such preparation should include coming to a point of view, by logical reasoning from the facts; finding the need for additional information; and deciding on which points it may be essential to stand firmly and on which, under pressure, it would do no real harm to give way.

(d) Tact, courtesy, patience, and good humor are likely to achieve more in the long run than riding roughshod over opponents. Participation should be cooperative, constructive, and a genuine attempt to help towards arriving at a "right" group decision; it could assist, on occasion, by building a bridge between opposing sides. On other occasions, it may become necessary to take a firm stand in support of strongly held principles found to be coming under attack. There can be no definite rules for such situations, only suggestions, as human relationships can be so diverse and unpredictable.

(e) There are, of course, innumerable tactics that can be employed, some acceptable, others more ethically dubious. A good committeeman, while knowing how to achieve effective participation, should at the same time be sophisticated enough to recognize any less reputable tactics adopted by other members, particularly when directed towards himself and his special interests.

(f) Chairmanship has already been dealt with in the context of a board of directors; a committee chairman requires much the same qualities. In particular, he has a choice of either holding back and aiming for full participation or holding forth and aiming at consent. In between, there is a flexible approach geared to the situation in hand, a happy medium whereby the chairman neither dominates his committee nor abstains from control.

Although, theoretically, a distinction has been made between boards of directors making policy and executives carrying out that policy, in practice there are wide variations. For example, taking extreme cases, a board can confine itself to pure policy or take a major part in the operational side, using an executive committee (in itself an indication of a dual role) to centralize managerial decision within its own membership. Where the directors are operating executives, the integration of policy making and executive action has a practical logic. However, it still remains necessary for the theoretical concept to be maintained, if only to ensure that proper attention is given to essential policy without too much time being wasted on less important executive action (which could be delegated down the managerial line).

Summary

1. *Committees*
    a. Committees are a feature of modern life.
    b. They can be a coordinating and informing influence, but they can also be a waste of time.
2. *Definition*
    A committee is a group of people formally appointed by another, larger group to meet and consider matters laid down by stated terms of reference.
3. *Essentials of a Committee*
    a. Any committee needs clear-cut terms of reference, preferably in writing.
    b. It should have a competent chairman, a wise selection of members, and an efficient secretary.
4. *Purpose of a Committee*
    a. A committee may be concerned with coordination.
    b. It may be consultative and advisory.
    c. It may conduct a progress review.
    d. It may administer development and training.

5. Types of Committees

    a. Committees of the board deal with special aspects.

    b. Executive committees have power to act at once and report back.

    c. *Ad hoc* committees are set up for particular temporary purposes.

    d. Management committees may take executive action within board policy.

6. Effectiveness of Committees

    a. Effectiveness depends on a good chairman.

    b. Members must know why they have been appointed.

    c. All the required expertise should be represented.

    d. Formal arrangements (e.g., circulation of material) must be efficient.

    e. A committee should wind up when its work is finished, disregarding status psychology.

7. Defects of Committees

    a. A committee may be inefficient.

    b. It may waste time.

    c. It may be used as a means of avoiding responsibility.

    d. It may undermine the authority of individuals.

8. Points for New Members

    a. A newly appointed member of a committee should read the background data, or ask around discretely.

    b. He should play himself in gently and carefully.

    c. He needs to arrive at the meeting prepared, knowing what is necessary, and with a point of view.

    d. He should be tactful, courteous, patient and good humored.

    e. In the last resort, he should never abandon his principles.

Suggested Further Reading

Auger, B.Y. *How to Run Better Business Meetings.* New York: American Management Association, 1973.

Lobingier, J. *Business Meetings That Make Business.* New York: Macmillan, 1969.

Zelko, H.P. *The Business Conference: Leadership and Participation.* New York: McGraw-Hill, 1969.

SIX

Looking at Leadership

Leadership has many facets, often far divorced from textbook analysis. It is easy enough to catalogue the many theoretical virtues attributed to leadership, but in practice, usually in dealing with an unexpected emergency, the most unlikely people can rise to a challenge while formal leaders can panic and prove ineffective. This statement is not intended to imply that formal leaders are unlikely to be the most effective when put to the extreme test; it is simply that some of them fail to match up to an established reputation.

Because of this type of approach, certain schools of thought argue for unstructured relationships leaving a natural leader to emerge, as necessary, whenever the occasion demands. For the present purpose, it is to the more usual, formal, approach that attention is directed. Nevertheless, the above aspects cannot be disregarded in any practical context. It may be helpful to know, for example, when and to what extent a nominal leader, even in normal circumstances, is not the real leader, but subject to some stronger power behind his managerial throne.

Managerial Types

Basically, any study of leadership must take into account not only the leader himself, his abilities, characteristics and general approach to his responsibilities, but the people he has to lead and their abilities and characteristics, coupled with the overriding dynamic environment. To put the situation on all fours with the managerial revolution outlined in Chapter One, the leader must effectively lead and not passively be led. If the latter situation obtains, he should certainly be replaced.

There have been many attempts to put name-tags on types of leadership or managerial style, and some highly sophisticated studies have been published with special reference to management training. Suitable reading along these lines is suggested at the end of the chapter. For our present purpose, a simple ABC version will serve as an illustration of such attempts to categorize management, bearing in mind that few leaders can be wholly contained in watertight compartments. There are many so-called characters, for instance, who defy any rigid classification.

However, looked at alphabetically, it is possible to list such varied descriptions as autocratic, benevolent, bureaucratic, charismatic, democratic, and dictatorial, without going any further than the letter D. All these explain themselves with the possible exception of charismatic, which literally translated means "favored of God." Each type or hybrid combination can work in the right kind of setting, but in today's environment the democratic approach would seem to be the most likely to prove successful.

It could be asked, in much the same context, whether there is any ideal type of leadership toward which future managers should aim when training for the top jobs. Probably there is no practical answer to this, except the age-old advice just to be oneself, but to strive at all times to make the best of oneself. Acting a character part is by its very nature artificial and needs a good actor to see it through, so that, generally speaking, only sincerity would seem to be a tenable approach acceptable to the rank and file.

However, as leadership starts at the top, it is essential that the chief executive officer should be in close touch and in harmony with his top-management team, for obviously his main executive function is to be their leader.

An Interest in People·

A successful leader must clearly spend a considerable amount of his time on "people" rather than "things." He should, for instance, take a special interest in his subordinates' careers and progress; he should hold his team sympathetically in check when their enthusiasm tends to step over the mark, encourage them when they are having personal doubts, and motivate them by any appropriate means to maximum effort.

Only when each member of the team has been stimulated to the point where he is giving the utmost of which he is capable, provided that it is directed towards the right ends, can it be claimed that the CEO has satisfactorily carried out his role as leader. Moreover the process of achieving the utmost must be carried out in an atmosphere of cooperation and goodwill.

PERSONALITY FOR LEADERSHIP

Like many terms in daily use, "personality" has different meanings for different people. Personality may suggest having acceptable qualities of individuality and self-expression, mainly evidenced by an ability to charm others through the exercise of a pleasant and persuasive manner. It savors of something extrovert and attractive in a social context. This is only one side of the picture, however, as "personality" refers to the whole person, taking into account *all* the qualities that are revealed by his general behavior and attitude toward life.

Personality for management is a study of great importance to the successful running of an enterprise, large or small. For the people at the top set the leadership tone for the whole business.

Extroverts and Introverts

It is generally held that an extrovert is a person who is most interested in the world around him and the people in it. Usually he is a cheerful, sociable, dynamic person, with many friends, who likes going out and about but who can be impulsive, excitable, and sometimes volatile.

The opposite, of course, is the introvert, generally defined as one who is most interested in his own thoughts and feelings. This type of person is usually of a retiring disposition, inward-looking, reliable, preferring to do things rather than meet people, one who seldom takes chances but tends to work out each move well ahead. As a result, he lives an ordered life, which he takes seriously, and is likely to be on an even keel temperamentally.

Broadly speaking, an extrovert is optimistic and an introvert pessimistic, the former state possibly being translated more accurately as blind faith and the latter as informed caution.

In a management setting there is room for both the "hail-fellow-well-met" and the "bookworm," but usually there are many shades of grey in between jet black and snow white. We are, therefore, more concerned in practice with tendencies than with extreme types.

Emotional Rating

The majority of failures among managers arise, not from lack of technical knowledge, but from inability to deal with people effectively. Part of the problem is related to feelings and emotions that can influence a manager's capacity to look at people and situations accurately and objectively. Emotional age can be very different from physical or mental age.

As before, there are black and white extremes with shades of grey in between, the emotional limits being a stable personality as opposed to an unstable personality. Emotion can be used as an asset, but only when kept firmly under control, well below the danger point of the near-neurotic. While a manager is entitled to have feelings, he must be careful not to exhibit undue emotional tendencies when under work-stress or personal attack: lack of poise tends to cloud logic, affect judgment, and weaken authority.

Achieving Poise

There are at least three ways whereby a manager can achieve emotional poise.

(a) First, he must learn to get the right mental picture of his job and to be able to see it in its true perspective. For example, with a great many pressures on hand, he can be forgiven for feeling that he has everything to do at once, a feeling that usually leads to panic. Yet, at any given moment, it is only physically or mentally possible to do one job; so this job should be done, quietly and efficiently, leaving the others to take their turn. Interruptions can be taken as physical or mental rest from the job in hand and so on.

(b) He should not make emotional demands on other people, whether above or below. In other words, he should not expect thanks or appreciation, and he should not feel hurt when such gestures fail to arrive.

(c) He should widen his horizon as much as possible, by extending his interests outwards, which in turn will help him to develop his perspective and maturity. This suggests, of course, some kind of midway point in the two extreme areas we have just considered above.

In this context, the chief executive, for example, might be slightly more extroverted than introverted, being more positive than negative, and perhaps be slightly more emotional rather than have no feelings at all. Other managers would probably range round this near-central position. A sales manager, for example, would by nature tend to be an extrovert, being mainly concerned with people, while an accountant could well tend towards the introvert, being mainly engrossed with figures. It is dangerous, however, to overgeneralize when dealing with human characteristics in a business context.

Summary of Attributes

To be successful as a leader, a company president or other executive should have certain innate and acquired qualities. Some of these qualities have been mentioned previously, including vision, drive, good judgment, initiative, poise, and maturity. In particular, a true leader usually has a personal magnetism that commands acceptability, enthusiasm, loyalty, and cooperation, plus natural sincerity, tact, courtesy, and a sense of humility. Leadership, to be effective, should radiate confidence, show ability to dominate circumstances when necessary to achieve given ends, keep up morale, and exercise control through inspiration rather than command.

Few managers possess all these qualities, but personal assets can be capitalized to the full and personal liabilities overhauled and improved. On occasion, however, a leader is found with completely opposite traits and yet is seen to "succeed"—perhaps riding roughshod over the rank and file. As already indicated, there are no magic formulas; each chief executive must work out his own salvation to match his special qualities and personality in the light of the particular environment concerned.

CREATING THE RIGHT ATMOSPHERE

Early in this chapter, reference was made to "an atmosphere of cooperation and goodwill." This was said to be a sign of effective leadership. Books on management often refer to atmosphere or the climate of work, on the analogy that most plants thrive in normal sunshine, some are killed by excessive heat or frost, but many survive the storms. Plants in a hothouse atmosphere will flourish while protected, but faced with adverse weather from outside they tend to curl up and die. Hardier plants, having had no protection at all, can face up to almost any conditions that come along.

Management's Responsibility

In a management setting, it is unfortunately true that many firms have failed through excessive kindness; this has been taken as weakness by all concerned and abused. At factory level, it is often found that workers prefer toughness from the bosses coupled with singlemindedness of purpose. This they can respect. Higher up the hierarchy, the situation can be less black and white, with more sophisticated interplay of mature personalities. Nevertheless, most people, at all levels, flourish better in a pleasant atmosphere and prove less effective, or become frustrated, in hostile conditions.

It is the job of top management to create the right atmosphere for the organization as a whole, giving, where necessary, special attention to problem areas. This right atmosphere may be tough or re-laxed, depending on the circumstances over any given period. There should, of course, be consistency, with no blowing hot and cold, for it is always a tragedy when subordinates have to "take the temperature" of their superiors day by day as a necessary precaution for their own safety.

The Power Game

It may be thought that because top management has done its best to create the right atmosphere, with varying degrees of success, other managers and staff will work together in harmony. They should do so, of course, but human nature being ever subject to hopes and fears, the ambitious will tend to play the power game and the lesser lights resort to self-defense. Most firms, especially large firms, are subject to some rivalries and jealousies; and, given a merger, there can be, for a time, near internal warfare. Top management should be continually aware of such basic characteristics and allow for office politics when dealing with all aspects of personnel policy.

This is no place for chapter and verse on the arts of intrigue, but a few examples may serve to illustrate the general theme. The first is the art of attracting favorable attention to oneself, whether by honest ambition or dark cunning. This includes taking the credit for all suc-cessful projects, even if only reporting success by someone else, and opting out of bad mistakes, perhaps by blaming others, or by sending letters of complaint with carbon copies to superiors. Then there is the old maxim of reporting only good news, leaving others to tell of misfortune and thereby attract the odium. Moral blackmail occasion-ally plays a part in securing freedom from sanctions, if not actually securing preferred treatment.

The second art is always to side with the potentially stronger elements in management. This implies negotiating to be as near to the seat of power as possible and building up strength by any means —including marrying the boss's daughter and aiming for the good opinions of his wife and/or secretary. The last favorable contact has particular value in securing cooperation by being told when it is the best time to see the boss, when he is in a good mood, and when it would be wise to keep away.

Then there is the subtle art of discrediting opponents. A professionally or academically qualified manager, for instance, may stress the lack of expertise in an unqualified rival. The rival, on the other hand, may well hint that his qualified colleague lacks judgment, practical ability, or common sense. Again, a top executive beginning to make a name for himself, perhaps with a trade association or in some other relevant field, may be denigrated by the suggestion being put around that he is allowing his real job (with the firm) to take only second place. Such insidious offenders are often identified by their colleagues, who act accordingly and, it is hoped, effectively. As mentioned earlier, a real leader will be well aware of such tendencies, dealing firmly with any bad feeling, jealousies, and rivalries, and will try to make sure that office politicians do not succeed.

It is worth recording here that the average company president usually knows far more about what is going on in the firm than those lower down may give him credit for. If, in fact, he does not know, then there is usually someone near at hand who will see that he does.

RELATIONSHIPS AT THE TOP

Probably the most important factor in establishing amicable relationships at the top is that of making sure that everyone above a certain rank is fully consulted and informed. The management committee is a good medium to start with; below that committee it is essential for middle management, supervisors, and the like to be brought into the picture in much the same way. Given reasonable understanding among the top and middle ranks, it should then follow that the rest of the organization will have a better chance also of enjoying a satisfactory climate of work. Team spirit is much sought after, and despite the friction of office politics, it can often be achieved in time, given strong and inspired leadership. Regular meetings at the different levels have been seen to provide a valuable clearinghouse for misunderstandings and complaints, and enable management's point of view to be restated *vis-à-vis* the future.

The Chief Executive Officer and Key Executives

It is a healthy sign for management succession to have a number of key executives in competition with each other for the top jobs. This inevitably tends towards office politics in some form or another, but, as always indicated, the CEO should know how to deal firmly with any hint of disharmony. He would need to maintain a detached point of view, develop a sixth sense for the true position, be fair in his judgments, and avoid creating favorites.

Many CEOs adopt a friendly attitude towards their immediate lieutenants; personal friendships are often built up in this way. At the same time, such lieutenants should not abuse managerial friendship, but maintain instead a genuine respect for their superior as a person, or for the position he holds, or ideally for both.

Stress must be laid on the unconscious power that a CEO or other top manager can exercise on all who come into contact with him, either directly or by hearsay. For it is not only what he says, or writes, but the attitudes he adopts, his cheerfulness (or lack of cheer), his known wishes, the decisions he makes, and the actions he takes. Whatever overall impression he may happen to give at any time, whether intended or not, the chances are that its influence will have company-wide repercussions. A cheerless, worried leader, for example, may well be reflected in a disturbed and dispirited staff.

With an approachable attitude, possibly coupled with open-door policy, a CEO is available to deal with any personal problems of his top team (and often further down the line) and offer sympathetic understanding at difficult times. Similarly, with such an attitude, he can correct mistakes and errors of judgment, and still secure cooperation, without those displays of temper so inherent and damaging in a near-apoplectic environment.

COMMUNICATION AND THE GRAPEVINE

In a good working atmosphere everyone in the firm knows what the plans are and how they are to be achieved. In fact, the full story that should be told goes even further, dealing with the many facets of who, what, how, when, and why.

The Value of Personal Contact

It has already been shown that meetings, formal and informal, are usually held at different managerial levels throughout the structure to facilitate integrated and effective communication. This starts with the board of directors followed by further meetings of a superior/subordinate relationship right down the line. Communication, as stated earlier, travels up as well as down, partly as vital information required by the board for policy decision and partly as feedback on policy implemented.

Managers at all levels should take every reasonable opportunity for face-to-face contact with their subordinates. This enables them to explain the background to new policy, consult all concerned about new jobs to be done, and generally to clear away problems, misunderstandings, and ambiguities. Failing such personal contact, appropriate telephone calls and letters can be made to serve the same ends, albeit at second best.

There is a particular problem concerning personal contact in a large firm with decentralized or autonomous units, national or international. Part of the solution comes from visits, both ways, of top personnel, specialists, and the like, and it is considered valuable in addition to set up annual, quarterly, or occasional conferences of directors, managers, and sales staff as appropriate at any given time. These provide an excellent clearinghouse for complaints; they facilitate better communication and recharge peripheral enthusiasm. Usually there is a social side as well as a business side. Because of size, conferences of this kind may have to be regionalized, for the most part, possibly with some interlocking centrally.

Written Instructions

In theory, it seems simple to suggest that good communication can be translated into a set of workable instructions, with copies to all concerned. In practice, all kinds of problems and misunderstandings arise from policy statements, manuals of procedure and office instructions: hence the need to supplement written communication with verbal communication. The main criteria for judging effective office instructions are that they should be complete in every relevant detail, within the scope and capability of recipients intended to take action on them, clear and free from ambiguity and, whenever important issues are involved, reduced to writing.

Opinions vary to how much board policy and management practice should be put in writing for the benefit of the rank and file. There is obvious value in having the main aspects available for constant reference, particularly when action is continuous or likely to take place in the future. Writing ensures that everyone concerned has the same information, although whether they all get the same message is another matter. One difficulty is the lack of standard terminology, coupled with the wider problem of semantics, in that words mean different things to different people with different backgrounds. In this book, for example, the word "staff" has been used; this can mean all the employees in the firm or it can be restricted to those with specialized advisory roles.

Another problem is whether to put everything into office instructions and kill initiative, or to put only the bare essentials into writing and chance different interpretations of detail arising in practice. There is, as always, a happy medium. What is certain is that written instructions alone are not enough.

Usually, there is a restricted circulation of confidential or highly technical documents, some to the board and top management only, others perhaps released as far down as middle management. There may be some mainly for specialists. It is a matter of judgment as to how much of all this should be regarded as being highly confidential; experience suggests that it is better to err a little on the side of releasing information down the line than suppressing it.

Important written instructions should be followed up, for example, by test checks, to ensure that all concerned have actually received them and that appropriate action has been taken. Instructions without follow-up tend to be ignored by busy or irresponsible members of staff; this is particularly so if, in their view, there are far too many instructions already.

Unofficial and Informal Communication

There are few firms, if any, that do not have a so-called grapevine or "bush telegraph," whether in the office or on the shop floor. A top-level conversation or telephone call overheard, a chance remark or meeting, an attitude, or even amateur detective work on boardroom blotting-paper can set in motion half-truths, rumors, and wild speculations. Insofar as these unofficial messages, which travel with extraordinary speed, may be inaccurate, confidential, or wrongly timed, there can be dangers.

This again comes back to having the right climate of work. In an atmosphere of near silence and mistrust, the only hope for information, which is often personally identified with advancement or survival, would seem to be the grapevine. The obvious managerial remedy is to have a strong channel of official communication so that everyone knows that they will be told as much as possible, and as soon as possible, what is going on. Good management has much to gain from well-informed personnel; it also has much to fear from ignorance.

It is not unknown for management itself to use the grapevine as a tactical device in special circumstances, as, for instance, by leaving vital information about for a rumor-monger to find and pass on, but such questionable actions would be exceptional. There are, of course, more reputable informal channels of communication used as a time-saving device, including advance news given out as conversation at the executive luncheon table.

In general, although organizational structures may seem efficient enough in theory, they are often only held together in practice, and made to work, by the sheer ability of people at all levels to talk with each other informally as well as formally. This is a sobering thought for the purists.

Leadership Aspects of Communication

The subject of communication is highly pertinent to any study of leadership. On a practical note, a chairman, president, or other top executive must always be able to communicate effectively whatever the occasion and whatever the demands made upon him.

Thus if called upon suddenly to appear on television to discuss a topical matter concerned with his organization—perhaps management's approach to controversial matters of public policy or its attitude toward a strike—the challenge must be met. For not only is his personal reputation at stake, but also that of the organization it is his responsibility and privilege to represent. Similarly, when presenting a paper at an industrial or specialist conference, as an afterdinner speaker in lighter vein, or taking part in open discussion, he must always remember that what he says and how he says it can have wide public relations repercussions.

In fact, the leadership of any large enterprise carries with it the implication that many impromptu speeches and statements will have to be made. It is therefore a matter of common sense for a top executive to have a few thoughts ready in case he is called upon to say a few words at any function attended. It has often been said that the good impromptu speech is always prepared in advance. Effective public speaking is an art or science that can be acquired professionally and should be part of the training for leadership. For the publicity power of public speaking has considerable value, even for the ambitious young tyro with his sights set firmly on a seat at the boardroom table.

Similarly with the written words, the hard-won ability to write effective reports, memoranda, and letters is a vital subject in itself, based on simple rules. But as with all communication, rules are deceptively easy to accept and hard to follow. For despite all the thousands of words written on communication, despite the many concepts and practical tips, the business world, no less than the world in general, finds complete understanding remarkably difficult to achieve.

MOTIVATION AND MORALE

In Chapter One consideration was given to the motivation of management, linked with financial and nonfinancial incentives and disincentives. Given a well-motivated management, the right kind of working atmosphere, effective communication, and other evidence of good leadership, it is likely that the rank and file will be well motivated, too, and that morale will be high. For harmony must come from the top; it can then permeate downwards through the organization. All concerned are encouraged thereby to do their best, if only out of respect or personal regard for those above. Failing such a lead, there will tend to be disharmony, discontent, frustration, and other negative aspects of working life, with likely repercussions on the quality and quantity of output.

In the motivation of subordinates, a manager is said to be influenced by his conscious or subconscious conception of their attitudes toward their work and of the nature of human behavior in general. Behavioral scientists talk of the late Douglas McGregor's "Theory X" and "Theory Y." The former suggests that the average worker, though he covets security, dislikes work and has to be coerced to perform his duties at an acceptable level. On the other hand, the

"Theory Y" attitude holds not only that work is as natural as play but that workers do accept responsibility and can learn to accept the objectives of the firm and exercise self-direction toward those objectives. "Theory Y" further suggests that the intellectual potentialities of the average human being are only partially utilized, thus presenting a challenge to management to make better use of its available manpower.

Monetary Incentives and Security

It goes without saying that there must be adequate financial reward for a fair day's work, possibly with extra pay for extra effort. This latter imposes the thorny problem of evaluation, but less so perhaps as related to quantifiable items such as production bonuses and commission on sales. There must be a recognizable, if rough, justice, in the setting of salary scales and wage structures, including merit additions where considered appropriate. An office employee, for example, well satisfied with his salary, could become discontented on finding out that someone he considered less important was receiving higher pay, or even the same amount. This raises the troublesome issue of salary scales and general personnel policy; for instance, should such scales and policy be published? Practice varies considerably; this again is a matter for managerial judgment in any given set of circumstances. Should there be scales at all, or should everyone be dealt with on individual merit? If the latter, how can merit be assessed objectively so that all concerned remain properly motivated? These and allied matters will be dealt with more fully in Chapter Twelve.

Coupled with salary or wages, there are usually other monetary attractions, such as pension rights, sickness benefits, extra holidays with pay, employee loans for those in financial difficulty, and perhaps help with housing. Taken together, insofar as they exist in a particular case, they add up to increased security for the individual. With this thought in mind it seems clear that more effective work will be forthcoming given freedom from financial worry; although some people welcome risk and change, the majority prefer to know where they are going and what the future is likely to hold in store for them. The psychological effects of change have been dealt with earlier, coupled with the need to preserve an appearance of stability or prepare workers for inevitable change well in advance. Security also comes from knowing that the job can be properly done, given existing knowledge or special training, and that the work is acceptable to those above.

Job Satisfaction

Most individuals work better if their job is a pleasant one, among friendly companions, and in a cheerful setting. The process starts, however, with the firm's products or services; if these appear to be worthwhile, perhaps making some contribution to the welfare of the community, personal pride can be taken in the firm and what it stands for. There can be pride, too, in individual creative ability and craftsmanship, but opportunities for work of this kind tend to grow ever less with increasing automation. If the job is standardized, monotonous, perhaps menial, it is important not only to seek ways of relieving boredom but to reassure the individual that his personal contribution to the firm's progress is both significant and appreciated.

While many workers prefer routine to promotion, and security to taking a risk, they still want to feel important, or at least acceptable. Where there are square pegs in round holes, or the job is too easy or too hard, obviously there is a need for rearrangement. Others, however, who have settled down perhaps resigned to routine work may seek their personal satisfaction elsewhere. This may be in the firm itself, perhaps in the softball team, dramatic society, bowling league, or company band, or outside through special interests and personal hobbies. With regard to music, it may be noted that the canned variety, played while workers work, may be appreciated by most, but certainly not by all!

When promotion takes place, or there are special rewards, any assessment of merit must be objective. Even more important is that it must be seen by all as being reasonable and just, for favoritism in any form is highly damaging to morale.

The Need for Discipline

The human resources of a firm must be channeled into the achievement of the common purpose, the set objectives. When this can be suitably accomplished by the exercise of positive incentives, a satisfactory atmosphere usually prevails. But ours is an imperfect world; and, even with good leadership, there can be personal problems best dealt with by the exercise of a tougher line. When there is an absolutely clear case for dismissal, demotion, or reprimand, for example, this must be carried out firmly but sensitively, with a proper regard for the other person's feelings. Whatever action is decided, it must be fully justified by the circumstances, after objective inquiry, fair to the individual and consistent with overall policy.

Strong action when taken has a sobering effect on the remaining employees, which is exactly as it should be. For when rules are broken it must be seen that sanctions automatically follow; if not, any respect for management will evaporate, and further infringements will become a matter of course.

There are other negative incentives based on fear. Acquisitions, mergers, and layoffs can be included here, but in modern life the consequences of these are mitigated by a reasonably low level of unemployment. In former days, by contrast, with excessive unemployment, fear and harsh discipline went hand in hand.

LEADERSHIP DOWN THE LINE

Key executives down the line should consistently act in accordance with the basic objectives and working policies of the company. They should be mature enough to rationalize their personal beliefs with such objectives and policies, entirely without emotional involvement. This should be possible, even when they have had no hand in policy decision-making, or when they took a different line when consulted but are now asked to accept the party line and implement it faithfully in the best interest of the firm.

While managers down the line of authority tend to take their cue from above, the usual exceptions can be found. There is, for instance, the newly promoted middle manager or supervisor who, for a time at least, feels his position and tends to use his recently acquired authority unwisely. Then there is the empire builder who believes that a counting of heads, or work, connotes importance. Fortunately, the former acquires wisdom and discretion with experience, sometimes painful experience; and the latter is, or should be, guided into a deeper understanding of cost constraints and the need for maximum productivity.

The Importance of Intermediate Command

Middle managers, following the lead of top management, usually exert considerable influence on the attitudes of subordinates and help to create the climate of work in which they operate. For it is largely the middle manager's personal attitudes towards those in authority above towards the firm, its products, services, other departments, and so on that influence or condition the attitudes of his own staff. In this context such a manager clearly represents top management to the workers below and must uphold the line of authority. But at the same time he also represents the workers to top management, either by direct access or through other levels of management above him. It is important, therefore, that this two-way contact should be properly understood and kept free from undue bias. On the one hand, he should not attempt to rule his team with the iron grip of supreme authority; nor, on the other hand, should he attempt to side with that team against superior authority. A middle manager must in fact consistently do his best to steer a middle course, swinging to the one side or the other only when justified by exceptional circumstances.

A paternal attitude (acting the heavy father or dutch uncle as and when necessary) usually results in the creation of a loyal team. The manager or supervisor must be sincerely dedicated to his men and be prepared to fight for them, secure maximum pay and good working conditions for them, deal with their problems and look after their welfare. He should also see that they are properly trained and give them opportunities to acquire wider knowledge and experience whenever this appears to be in the best interests of their development. Nor should he stand in the way of his staff gaining promotion, even though this may mean a transfer to another department or branch.

Encouraging Progress

Managers down the line should not be, and seldom are, passive about communication; those needing information to do their job more effectively will usually seek it out whenever and wherever it is to be found. Staff, in turn, should be actively encouraged to show equal initiative and should be properly fed with regular information as to what is going on and why. This may seem obvious at first sight, but it is not unknown for weak managers, seeking to acquire extra power, to be tempted to hold back policy documents and instructions that should be passed down the line; we can also include here publications or newspaper clippings sent to the department or section for information. Nor should staff-training facilities be bottlenecked; those selected or seeking to attend courses and similar activities should be encouraged to go, wherever possible, even at the risk of temporary departmental inconvenience. For, in the long run, the benefits of highly trained staff should more than offset any short-term problems of staff shortage on the way through.

So far as possible, top management should identify the ambitions of the workers with the progress of the firm; leadership down the line can add the further step of positive identification with a particular section of the firm. Given justified pride and job satisfaction under effective intermediate command, it can usually be expected that departmental loyalty will follow. Insofar as this can be built into the objectives and policies of the firm, it can prove to be a valuable contribution to productivity. In too many cases, however, there is little ambition, negative loyalty, and cynical indifference to the fate of the firm.

Summary

1. *Managerial Types*
   a. Natural leaders emerge.
   b. The real leader may not be the formal leader.
   c. As a manager, be yourself and be sincere.
   d. Managers must be interested in people.
2. *Personality for Leadership*
   a. A mixture of many qualities—innate and acquired—is called for.
   b. A leader may be an extrovert or an introvert.
   c. Emotional maturity is essential.
   d. Poise can be acquired.
   e. A leader makes the most of his personal assets.

f. There is no magic formula.
3. *The Right Climate of Work*
   a. The climate may be tough or relaxed, but it must be consistent.
   b. A pleasant atmosphere produces the best results.
   c. The "power game" undermines harmony.
4. *Relationships at the Top*
   a. All top executives need to be consulted and kept informed.
   b. Attitudes towards subordinates should be friendly but detached.
   c. Impressions given by top management spread down the line.
5. *Communication*
   a. Personal contact is essential: written instructions are not enough.
   b. Initiative should be encouraged and uncertainty eliminated.
   c. Too much information is better than too little.
   d. Good communication reduces the role of the "grapevine."
   e. Speaking and writing ability are essential for leadership.
6. *Motivation and Morale*
   a. Attitudes towards work are reflected in workers' behavior.
   b. Financial incentives should be adequate and equitable, but job satisfaction is of equal importance.
   c. Not all seek promotion, but all need to feel accepted.
   d. Disciplinary action must be taken when necessary.
7. *Leadership Down the Line*
   a. Tone is taken from the top, but not by all.
   b. Middle managers have an important role.
   c. A paternal attitude creates a loyal team.
   d. Middle managers must encourage subordinates and pass on information.
   e. The workers' interests should be identified with the firm's progress.

Suggested Further Reading

ADAIR, J. *Action-centered Leadership.* New York: McGraw-Hill, 1973.

ARGYRIS, C. *Executive Leadership.* New York: Harper & Row, 1967.

BITTEL, L.R. *What Every Supervisor Should Know.* 3d ed. New York: McGraw-Hill, 1974.

DOWLING, W.F., JR., AND L.R. SAYLES. *How Managers Motivate: The Imperatives of Supervision.* New York: McGraw-Hill, 1971.

FLEISHMAN, E.A., AND A.R. BRASS, eds. *Studies in Personnel and Industrial Psychology.* 3d ed. Homewood, Ill.: Dorsey Press, 1974.

GELLERMAN, S.W. *Management by Motivation.* New York: American Management Association, 1968.

SAYLES, L.R., AND M.K. CHANDLER. *Managing Large Systems: Organizations for the Future.* New York: Harper & Row, 1971.

————, AND G. STRAUSS. *Human Behavior in Organizations.* Englewood Cliffs, N.J.: Prentice-Hall, 1966.

THAYER, L.O. *Communication and Communication Systems in Organization, Management, and Interpersonal Relations.* Homewood, Ill.: Irwin, 1968.

TILLEY, K.W. *Leadership and Management Appraisal.* New York: Crane-Russak, 1973.

SEVEN

Objectives and
Long-range Planning

A clear understanding of the dynamic setting in which a company operates was shown, in Chapter Two, to be an important first step towards effective management. Having narrowed down the overall environment, international and national, to the key factors affecting the outlook for a particular industry, preliminary consideration could then be given to the prospects of a single firm within it. From that point onwards, it is now necessary to determine, with as much detail as possible, where such a firm intends to go and how it aims to get there.

THE IMPORTANCE OF OBJECTIVES

Although it might be thought that every firm would know exactly where it is going, there are in fact far too many firms with only a rough idea of direction and a vague sense of purpose.

Objectives Defined

In management terms, an "objective" can be defined as an end in view or a goal to be sought—the "where" of management as distinct from the "how." Objectives may be said to impart direction, purpose, and meaning to the operations of a firm. Being essentially long-term in character, the more distant the end or goal the broader will tend to be its scope. Within the long-range targets, set by objectives, there may be certain short-term and medium-term objectives as well. Where there is a collection or range of objectives, these should, of course, be consistent throughout. This is not to say, however, that a firm cannot operate in a number of different directions at the same time; but, in the last analysis, it should be possible to reconcile them all with long-range plans. This might imply, for example, having one or more main objectives, company-wide in character, with more limited objectives operating sectionally within them.

Although objectives may be broad in scope, it is not sufficient just to express them in general terms. It is not sufficient, for example, to have an objective declaring the simple intention to make as much profit as possible. Objectives must be quantified and stated with all relevant detail. In the example given, the objective might well be reworded to indicate an intention, say, to achieve a profit growth of a certain percentage per annum. Clearly, however, when looking more than, say, five years ahead, such detail must necessarily be kept as flexible as the changing scene is likely to demand.

Objectives should be written down, comprehensively, clearly, and logically. This is a worthwhile discipline in itself and may well substitute effective expression of purpose for pious hope only partly or inaccurately understood. As a start, there are certain fundamental objectives to be observed that any firm should consider carefully.

Fundamental Objectives

Arising out of its way of life, any firm may be said to have an "ethos," character, personality, or "image" reflected in, or from, the basic objectives it adopts. These can be briefly stated as follows:

(a) Relationships with the Environment. No firm can conduct its busi-

ness in a vacuum; it must deal with government and other institutions, customers, suppliers, competitors, its own personnel, and, where appropriate, shareholders. For each of these relationships, it should lay down clear, workable objectives. For example, will it collaborate with, or fight, government agencies, competitors, and the like? Will it exploit customers or give them effective credit and aftersales service? Will it be loyal to suppliers, or build them up and then exploit them, or play one off against another? Will it look after its stockholders and its staff? All these and similar issues are vital factors for success that must be carefully thought out, defined and communicated, directly or indirectly, to all concerned.

(b) Part Played within Industry.   Here the basic issues involved relate to such matters as specialization or diversification of products or services and their relative cost and quality. Also, they concern whether to aim at leadership, perhaps through the appropriate trade association, or just to jog along quietly and unnoticed as one of the crowd. The actual part played normally depends, of course, on the power that comes from size, but leadership can also come from outstanding innovation at any size.

(c) Growth Ambitions.   Linked with what has just been said is the choice between taking risks or playing for safety: being aggressive *vis-à-vis* competitors or aiming at a more conservative but cooperative existence; seeking mergers and acquisitions or remaining aloof. Taking undue risks has obvious dangers for any firm, but so, too, has any half-hearted development. It is often said that no organization can stand still; either it goes backward to extinction or progresses forward to success.

(d) Organization for Progress.   Each firm, or other enterprise, must define its management objectives within certain parameters. These boundaries extend between dictatorship on the one hand and the democratic rule on the other, between centralization and decentralization, and between management development internally and recruitment for management from outside. These, then, are examples of fundamental objectives that should be thrashed out before attempting to proceed with any detailed consideration of long-range planning as a whole.

OBJECTIVES IN PRACTICE

In the setting of objectives, the lead must obviously come from the top. The board of directors, in liaison with key executives, needs to determine the fundamental and other main objectives including those already indicated. Worthy of particular attention are the rate of growth, with or without acquisitions, mergers, and so on; the kind of risks the board would be willing to take; whether there would be specialization or diversification; and to what extent, if at all, short-term profits would be sacrificed to long-term gain.

The Managerial Role

Having settled these basic issues in principle, the next task of the executive team is to determine whether sufficient resources (such as buildings, plant and machinery, materials, and manpower) could be made available at each stage in order to achieve the proposed objectives. As already suggested, it is necessary to review the situation realistically from time to time. Given major changes in the environment or in the assumptions on which the original decisions were made, a strong case can then be made for revised objectives.

In the formulation of general, overall objectives, it may be good strategy to ensure maximum consultation and participation, preferably by a special meeting or meetings of the management committee. For managers, and others, are far more willing to comply with objectives if they have had a hand in their making. The same applies to subobjectives at lower managerial levels, with regard to section heads and supervisors.

In any superior/subordinate relationship, there is a balance to be struck between the excessive use of authority and the granting of excessive freedom. The section heads and supervisors, as subordinates, can be bluntly told of agreed objectives; they can be "sold" on the way ahead, which suggests manipulation; or they can be encouraged to understand and appreciate the background and commit themselves voluntarily along the right lines.

Secondly, there should be adequate publicity for objectives and plans at special meetings of management and staff in training courses, in the house organ, in printed memoranda, and in company procedure manuals. Similarly, there should be proper briefing with regard to changes in objectives. In this process, the key men are likely to be the departmental managers and supervisors whose job it is to interpret management goals to their subordinates; they must at all times, therefore, be "in the picture" well ahead of their subordinates.

Testing for Validity

Before finally adopting a set of objectives, it is worthwhile to test them for validity. In the first place, it can be asked whether they are sufficiently compatible with the objectives of the national economy; do they, for instance, fit into the current pattern of prices, incomes, and productivity? Bearing long-term issues in mind, however, to what extent is it reasonable for a given firm to be influenced by such current patterns as against "taking a view" of the future uncluttered by the past or present? Would the objectives ensure survival in the environments likely to be encountered ahead? Do they reflect, or balance, the possibly conflicting claims of stockholders, suppliers, customers, management, and staff? Are there sufficient incentives, with and without profit motivation, for all concerned?

Are the strengths of the firm likely to be maximized and the weaknesses either overcome or at least taken realistically into account? Given imposed or internal constraints on future progress, is it true to say that these would not unduly impair the chances of success? At no time, of course, can there be any guarantee of success, but at least by facing up to potential dangers the risk of failure can usually be minimized or discounted in advance. More positively, what are the key factors for success implied in the objectives themselves?

Management having guaranteed the necessary resources, would these be of the right quality, as well as available at the right time, to deal with quantified objectives? If not, would it be possible to recruit strength from outside or set up effective programs for training? Do the objectives give full consideration to the claims of marketing, production, finance, and personnel in the overall plan? Would the mangement structure stand the strain, or could it be changed progressively to match the development planned? Are the objectives sufficiently ambitious and challenging to stimulate personal effort and provide reasonable work satisfaction? Can it be inferred from the objectives, as written down, that misunderstandings, possibly culminating in abortive effort and loss of direction, are unlikely to arise?

These, and many other questions, could and should be asked at the outset. By this time it should be clear that the whole conception has become one of feasibility and directed effort, based on a cool, hard look into the long-term future.

It follows that a practical appreciation and willing acceptance of objectives is an important preliminary step to corporate planning. As signposts to the determination of policy, well-conceived objectives help to keep all company personnel on the right road; they provide regular progress checks along the way, and they ensure consistency of purpose throughout the journey.

Earlier reference was made to the preoccupation of management with difficult problems; by effective planning, many future problems can be avoided entirely.

PLANNING BY STAGES

It is fashionable today to talk of "corporate planning," and a great deal has been written recently on this vital subject. Nevertheless, the number of firms that have, in fact, installed effective long-range planning is still relatively small. All firms naturally have some planning, but often this is simply confined to a detailed annual accounting budget, with perhaps a few vague figures for a year or two beyond.

Corporate Planning

By contrast, corporate planning not only covers every functional aspect of a firm's business, but takes into account as well the full environment in which it has to operate. It is, or should be, a systematic assessment of a most comprehensive nature leading to realistic planning, stage by stage, towards a long-term and more profitable future.

To introduce corporate planning in its widest sense usually means at least three years' work before its full effectiveness can be properly experienced, judged, and appreciated. Full effectiveness goes well beyond mere forecasting, for planning involves creating change to overcome future conditions and achieve a different result from that likely to flow from *laissez-faire*. Bearing in mind the normally heavy daily pressures on top management, and this time-lag in operation, it can be easily understood why corporate planning, despite obvious advantages, would appear to be taking root so slowly in the economy.

Basically, the initial steps should cover the following aspects of corporate life:

(a) A trend assessment of the international, national, industry, and company environment (political, institutional, economic, social, and technological).

(b) The setting of quantified objectives for so many years ahead.

(c) An appraisal of company strengths and weaknesses.

(d) The determination of suitable strategies to achieve those objectives.

(e) The production of detailed plans, procedures, and schedules covering every aspect of the business, short-term and long-term, culminating in a master plan and work assignments for total administrative action.

Planning Categories

Planning problems may be classified into three main categories:

(a) Broad Strategic (Long-range) Planning.   This comes well within the province of top management since it is concerned with the determination of objectives and the consideration of alternative courses of action designed to attain those objectives. Such planning is principally concerned with the economic, financial, and technological aspects of the environment, with special reference to the problems of corporate growth.

(b) Year-to-year Tactical (Short-term) Planning.   This deals with the effective use of all resources that can be allocated to achieving any given objective; it is largely concerned with the problems of creating new facilities.

(c) Operational (Budget) Planning. This covers the numerous problems to be solved by top management in setting up a monitoring and control mechanism for running the business as a whole.

New techniques are developing in all three areas and it is the job of those concerned to make the best of them whenever they arise. Management science must always keep pace with planning needs or, better still, proceed ahead of them.

The Need for Planners

Everyone in management has a planning responsibility, the chief executive officer having the ultimate responsibility. However, as top management is normally under heavy day-to-day pressure, it is a logical step to create a long-range planning department to act in a "staff" capacity. This means being directly responsible to the CEO, but freed from "line" authority and any routine duties. Ideally, such a department should be small (possibly consisting of only one man as the corporate planner) and made up of top quality "generalists" trained to see the woods as well as the individual trees.

These planners would take into account all aspects of the dynamic environment, the size and complexity of the problems to be solved, and the critical part to be played by the profit factor in achieving the desired rate of growth, making whatever assumptions are vitally necessary. As staff advisers, the corporate planning department would cover the widest possible area of strategic and tactical planning, eventually indicating alternative courses of action, setting out the pros and cons, the risks involved, and making appropriate recommendations. For it still remains the final responsibility of the board of directors and top executives to determine the company-wide objectives and to lay down the operational plans necessary for their achievement. The task of the corporate planners does not stop at getting a system going; it is also their job to keep it going.

At this stage, it is worthwhile to pause and re-emphasize the vital contribution of all areas of management to the organization for, and process of, planning. This is no job for a corporate planner working alone in an ivory tower, supported on occasion by a few specialists. The practical philosophy with regard to this problem is that, at an early stage, an assessment of the strengths and weaknesses is made, as indicated earlier, for action to be taken on them as soon as possible. In the process, top management becomes essentially involved in long-range planning, thus helping to break down the "them-and-us" complex that can so easily arise between management and corporate planner.

In the case of holding companies, the objectives and plans would be determined centrally, the subsidiaries being conditioned and motivated to carry them out.

The corporate planning department would naturally make the maximum use of advanced techniques, seeking from other departments all the specialized help available and required. Mention may be made of the increasing use of operations research, in all its many forms, as discussed in Chapter Eight, and of the computer as a tool for providing total management information. This would include, it is to be hoped, the basic material for long-range planning. As used at present, however, few computers are exploited to the full extent of their operational ability. Total management information does not mean excessive information, a danger likely to be accelerated by the use of computers which tend to "print out" paper by the ton. Obviously, there is a need for all such data to be processed down to essentials.

The use of computers in the strategic and tactical planning areas invokes simulation and model-building techniques. Here the computer performs such services as cash-flow forecasting, financial analysis, and risk simulation, based on various assumptions made about the future course of events. These and other techniques are considered in Chapter Eleven.

The Time-scale

Long-range planning clearly means looking well ahead, but how far ahead will usually depend on the particular business concerned, and on its products and services, current and potential. Long and short are relative terms, but the former is generally used to denote planning of from two years upward, although in practice almost any organization would be wise to plan five or ten years ahead. Short-term planning is often thought of as being for one year, and, for many companies, this simply relates to the normal annual budget.

Taking a general approach, however, it is convenient to consider long-range periods of, say, three to five years, then up to ten years, and possibly beyond that to twenty or twenty-five years. The important factor is to be in position to recognize and anticipate problems well before they arise and to achieve satisfactory progress, having "cashed in" on every favorable opportunity seen well in advance. Whatever the time-scale used, there must be full provision for frequent and coordinated review of objectives and plans; also a constant reevaluation of plans against actual results achieved. In general policy terms, there are three main choices before management:

(a) No Planning at All. Figure 7 *(a)* indicates the likely trends of results in a situation where there is no planning at all. In this situation, the firm would tend to go steadily downhill.

(b) Planning, Using Existing Resources to Full Capacity. Given normal planning, aiming to make the best use of existing resources, the position would be improved, as shown in Figure 7 *(b)*, but again there is likely to be eventual decline.

(c) Corporate Planning Target. By flexible long-range corporate planning, anticipating problems and taking advantage of new and profitable opportunities, it could be expected that the firm would continue to prosper as demonstrated in Figure 7 *(c)*.

If Figure 7 *(c)* were superimposed on Figure 7 *(b)*, or better still on Figure 7 *(a)*, there would be a considerable profits gap over the years between the graph rising as a result of corporate planning and either of the two graphs trending downward. This gap measures the planning effort required to achieve the desired progress, and detailed consideration of its importance is usually referred to as "gap analysis." These illustrations refer to profits/time, but similar graphs are often drawn for sales/time, in which case the planning gap would represent the special sales effort to be made to achieve the long-range sales objectives.

MANAGEMENT BY OBJECTIVES

The setting of objectives is no new idea, but until recently there has been little evidence of companies making systematic and sustained attempts to relate objectives to performance as measured by quantified profits. Management by objectives (M.B.O.) goes a stage further in that it involves not only the establishment of realistic targets, but also the full support of management, at all levels, in the achievement

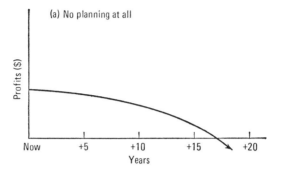

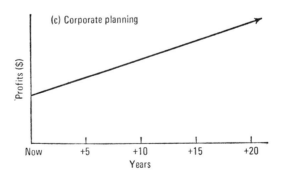

FIGURE 7. Progress through planning

of those targets. The whole process is thus one of active involvement from the board of directors downward.

Personal Involvement

We have already traced the formulation of profit-conscious planning for a given company and the many factors that have to be taken into account when fixing key objectives. The next stage, the essential stage of personal involvement, arises from the translation of company-wide objectives into detailed action. In the process every manager, supervisor, and foreman should become fully briefed as to what *he* has to achieve as *his* contribution to the master plan, and as to when (also possibly how) he has to achieve it. Given a policy of consultation in advance, while those details are still being evolved, it is likely that such personal involvement will result in efficient and willing service leading to successful company results throughout.

Critics of M.B.O., however, ask whether the system when installed will be seen as being imposed control rather than voluntary involvement and self-control. This means that the human aspects, or "behavioral consequences" as they have been called in this context, must be carefully thought out in advance. This includes the kind of approach to be adopted in setting the targets at the right (acceptable) levels. On balance, it would appear that the benefits of M.B.O. outweigh the disadvantages.

Planning for M.B.O.

From a practical angle, the actual processing of management by objectives can be tackled either from the top or from the bottom. In the former, as indicated above, the master plan is first written up as a whole and then translated into detailed subordinate plans, stage by stage, right down to office-desk/shop-floor supervision. This keeps in mind the "key areas" of a job, which have the greatest potential effect on profits, and the "key tasks," which pinpoint the action required to achieve the improved results. Ideally, these plans should be set out clearly, in the form of management guides demonstrating level by level how each key objective is to be attained in practice. Each manager must be helped to appreciate both the value of his own personal efforts and the way in which these efforts are expected to fit into the contributions to be made by those above and those below. Thus there should be a clear understanding of the various parts to be played, by whom they are to be played, and when, leading up to a fully integrated appreciation of the plan as a whole.

The alternative procedure is to build up management guides from the shop floor, starting with supervisors and foremen; every guide would become progressively more comprehensive as higher levels of management are reached, and covered, on the way to the top.

Whichever method is adopted in practice, the opportunity should be taken to rationalize endeavor and to produce improved performance through active and responsible participation by all concerned. This, in turn, brings us back to the functions of management, with special reference to the dynamics of motivating, coordinating, communicating, and controlling.

After the management guides, with key tasks and standards, have been agreed upon, it is essential for the various managers concerned to be allowed to get on with their jobs without too much day-to-day interference. At the end of, say, three months, however, it is useful for a superior to discuss progress with his subordinate managers, and supervisors, modifying the plans as necessary. This procedure is then repeated on a regular basis.

Suggestions for Improvements

An important by-product of management by objectives comes from the research that goes into every aspect of the work, including job or unit analysis. This by-product consists of the valuable suggestions usually made, at all levels, for improving performance in order to facilitate the desired results. These improvements may be initiated by the long-range planners themselves or, better still, encouraged to arise from their meetings with top management and managers in the various departments and sections. They may, in fact, emerge from any getting together of management, staff and workers where "brainstorming" can take place in a creative atmosphere.

Whatever the source, all such suggestions should be carefully evaluated, those considered to be worthy of adoption being agreed upon by general consent. Official job or unit improvement plans could then be issued periodically. These are normally of an *ad hoc* nature; for the best motivational results, however, "operation improvement" should be deliberate and continuous, quarterly, half-yearly, or at least annually. Arising from job improvement there must be room for personnel improvement, and this includes management development plans—which are sufficiently important to be given specialized treatment in Chapter Fourteen.

Publicizing Success

Involvement, improvement, and achievement are implicit in any scheme for management by objectives, but all this must be actively stimulated by carefully planned internal publicity geared to success.

It may be argued that having advertised success, one cannot then avoid admitting failure in times of difficulty. Even so, the emphasis should always be on positive (but realistic) thinking. This means, for instance, channelling the internal publicity temporarily into encouraging extra effort for earlier recovery.

Nevertheless, most people like to feel that they are on the winning side and to share success. Given satisfactory evidence of achievement, there should then be overall recognition by chart, bulletin, or letter, with appropriate attention to special efforts, needing perhaps a few strategic words of appreciation from those above. At the same time, every manager should periodically review individual, as well as unit, performance, to ensure that each job under his control is being carried out properly according to plan. It is to be hoped, of course, that sustained improvement would be suitably rewarded with increased pay.

KEEPING THE PLANNING FLUID

Much of corporate planning is necessarily still in the melting-pot, but any scheme must keep in mind the vital issue of flexibility. With a dynamic environment and problems of imperfect forecasting, internationally, nationally, and industrially, it is obvious that any long-range planning must be subject to a considerable margin of error.

It follows, therefore, that there must be full provision for frequent and effective review of objectives and plans; in fact it is hardly feasible to separate planning from controlling. It is no use making plans unless they are continually reviewed and kept in line. If it is found impossible to keep the plans in line, the time has clearly come for new plans to be made or the old ones adjusted. This realistic aspect of monitoring and controlling planning is elaborated further in Chapter Thirteen.

Where enthusiasm for management by objectives exists, with long-range planning permeating the whole fabric of the firm, a considerable improvement in marketing, production, and so on can usually be found. It is to be hoped, therefore, that corporate planning, with all its ramifications, will become more and more acceptable as a standard practice for industry in general.

Summary

1. *Definition*
   a. An objective is an end in view or goal to be sought: it gives direction to the operations of a firm.
   b. An objective should be a quantified purpose rather than a pious hope.
2. *Basic Objectives*
   a. These are laid down by the board, but executives should be consulted.
   b. Objectives reflect corporate attitudes towards external relationships.
   c. They determine the part to be played by the firm within its industry.
   d. They express the firm's growth ambitions and may determine the type of organization required.
3. *Corporate Planning*
   a. This is still the exception in practice.
   b. Although it takes time to organize, it is invaluable.
   c. Planning starts with forecasting.
   d. The main categories are strategic, tactical and operational.
   e. "Staff" corporate planners advise the company president, but all managers should be concerned with planning.

f. It is advisable for firms to plan for five to ten years ahead.
4. *Gap Analysis*
   a. Sales and profits decline if there is no planning, or if planning is limited to existing resources.
   b. Corporate planning aims at qualified growth by all means possible.
   c. The difference between (a) and (b) measures the effort required.
   d. Analysis follows, and resources are built up as required.
5. *Management by Objectives*
   a. M.B.O. means achieving mutually agreed targets, subject to a master plan.
   b. Active personal involvement of managers and the like is essential.
   c. Results should be monitored and discussed periodically.
   d. Positive recognition should be given to efforts made, and success should be publicized.
6. *Planning Kept Fluid*
   a. Dynamic environment connotes change.
   b. Objectives and plans must therefore be kept flexible.
   c. This implies regular review and revision.

Suggested Further Reading

ANSOFF, H.I. *Corporate Strategy: An Analytic Approach to Business Policy for Growth and Expansion*. New York: McGraw-Hill, 1965.

ANSOFF, I., ET AL., eds. *From Strategic Planning to Strategic Management*. New York: Wiley, 1975.

ARGENTI, J. *Systematic Corporate Planning*. New York: Wiley, 1974.

HUMBLE, J.W. *How to Manage by Objectives*. New York: American Management Association, 1973.

MALI, P. *Managing by Objectives: A Systems Approach*. New York: Wiley, 1972.

RAIA, A.P. *Managing by Objectives*. Glenview, Ill.: Scott, Foresman, 1974.

STEINER, G.A. *Top Management Planning*. New York: Macmillan, 1969.

EIGHT

Top-level Policy Decisions

In Chapter Seven an objective was defined as an end in view or a goal to be sought, i.e., the "where" of management as distinct from the "how." It is now appropriate to consider the "how," extended here to mean how to achieve that end in view or the goal being sought. It is important to emphasize the difference between objectives and policies, particularly as in everyday use (sometimes even management use) the two words are often regarded as synonymous. It is quite usual, for example, to use the term "business policy" to cover almost the whole range of management practice, including objectives.

"POLICY" FLOWS FROM "OBJECTIVES"

A dictionary definition of the word "policy" is "prudence, worldly wisdom, cunning or dexterity of management; the art or manner of governing." It is appropriate here, however, to attempt a purpose-built definition.

Policy Defined

In this chapter, "policy" will be regarded as the guidelines laid down, in general or specific terms, to enable a company or other organization to reach the long-range target, or targets, set by the objectives. It is a rule of action for the rank and file to show them how they are expected to attain the desired results.

From a practical standpoint, it has been mentioned previously that policy decisions emanate from the board of directors or other governing body and are communicated downward through a president or chief executive officer to enable action to be taken at every appropriate level of administration below. In the formulation of that policy, all relevant information and recommendations are usually passed upward; and even after a given policy has been promulgated there should be a regular feedback of results to confirm that policy as being right or to suggest a need for revised policy. Policy, therefore, flows from objectives; the ends are stated first and the means then follow as a matter of course.

Major Policies

In every company there are a number of important issues that require the attention of top management, in this context the board of directors. These are fundamental policies that emerge from the basic objectives and can be conveniently divided up into *(a)* marketing and sales policies, *(b)* production policies, *(c)* financial policies, and *(d)* personnel policies. Each of these justified a separate chapter in this book.

Policy decisions as laid down in statement form set out the standing answers to each of the main questions likely to be raised, so that all staff concerned are able to know exactly what is expected of them in any normal set of circumstances. Situations that arise regularly can be dealt with automatically by reference to the standard rules made in advance. This ensures that all action taken will be in accordance with the wishes of the board and a step nearer attaining the desired objectives.

The laying down of basic policy decisions clearly helps to achieve uniformity of action throughout the company and consistency as for one time to another. Furthermore, it helps with delegation, as all below can be reasonably expected to know the rules, and it helps coordination.

These rules can be put in writing as manuals of procedure, office instructions and memoranda, provided that adequate provision is made for them to be kept up-to-date and to be flexible enough to cope with special or local circumstances. There may even be unwritten rules well appreciated and observed by all concerned. The important factor is that all policy decisions should be understood throughout the organization as a vital part of its existence and as a means of achieving consistency in action.

Some policy decisions, of course, have to be made to deal with exceptional circumstances or emergencies, and these require special treatment, as described later.

MAKING THE RIGHT DECISIONS

Whatever policy is laid down, it must be the result of deliberation and decision. Hence the making of right decisions is fundamental to good management practice.

The Decision-makers

Although policy decisions emanate from the board of directors, they may originate from *any* level of management in the form of recommendations upwards to the board. Such policy decisions are usually broad in scope, the detailed interpretation of them, that is to say policy in action, being the responsibility of management at the point of impact. Thus the president, or other top executive, lays down guidelines for others to follow, in harmony with the objectives and board policy generally.

At top-management level the decisions to be taken are not usually numerous, but they may be far-reaching in effect and costly if based on an error of judgment. Problems arising at lower levels can be dealt with as and when they occur, provided that they are within the discretionary limits of responsibility and authority of those concerned. Problems of a wider nature are passed upwards for decision within the more extensive mandates of line management above. Thus there may be a series of filters with the mesh progressively narrowing as problems pass through for higher decision. Those which survive to the top are clearly of special importance or difficulty. At that level the critical factor is to determine the points of principle involved. If they are within the framework of the objectives and board policy, a firm decision can be made and communicated. Should new policy be invoked, however, then the matters concerned may need a special report, with appropriate recommendations, and a place on an early board agenda.

The decision-maker may be a single individual, but often enough there is added value in consultation and even in the collective wisdom of a formal or informal committee used judiciously. In this context it is important to have regard for the personality and temperament of the decision-maker. Is he, for instance, an incurable optimist or a cautious pessimist? Does he still prefer hunch to scientific method? Do his decisions suffer from inconsistency? It is here that, despite the usual arguments against committee decision, there is a chance of leveling out any undue bias.

It is conventional to talk of "real" judgments, based on facts, as against "value" judgments, where flair tends to be at a premium. All decisions require good judgment but not all executives, even those otherwise highly qualified, possess it. Fortunately, in today's sophisticated environment, there is a variety of techniques, described later, to increase the facts. But in the final analysis, sound judgment is still essential.

So far it has been assumed that the decision-maker, single or collective, actually makes decisions. It is a regrettable fact, however, that there is often a lack of decision-making. This takes such forms as appointing commissions at the national level, committees at the corporate level, or finding reasons for postponing decisions at any level. Granted that it may be unwise in many circumstances to make too hasty a decision, at some stage or other a decision must be made—if only to leave things as they are. It has even been said that a bad decision is better than no decision at all. There is yet another adage which goes "take counsel, consider well, decide and repent not."

Component Parts of Decision-making

Some decisions can be made easily, by precedent or from wide experience, but others demand a detailed investigation first. Viewed in its entirety, managerial decision-making is a process that involves problem definition, the gathering of pertinent facts, the generation of various alternative courses of action, and the selection of the "right" course, usually judged according to a number of evaluative criteria. The ability to make right decisions (more often than wrong ones, at least) depends to a great extent on adopting a logical method of approach. Usually, this can be taken in conventional stages, as follows:

(*a*) To define, as a first step, the real problem requiring solution; this should determine whether any principle is involved. Given a complex problem, it may be helpful to break it down into component parts.

(*b*) To look at the problem, when defined, in its full appropriate environment; it is wise not to attempt a solution in isolation purely on its theoretical content. There is considerable practical value in assembling all the available facts relevant to a problem and setting them down on paper. In this way the various aspects of a situation can be brought together, classified and weighted, and a logical pattern gradually evolved. It may be found, too, that a diagram will clarify the essential relationships and reveal gaps or irregularities requiring further investigation. Unfortunately, executives are often unable or are reluctant to do this exercise; could it be delegated perhaps?

(*c*) To arrive at the best possible solution, taking into account all reasonable alternatives. This involves weighing the pros and cons of each alternative before deciding on what appears to be the right solution in the given circumstances. It may mean going a step further, by way of compromise or concession, to achieve a workable solution, preferably one acceptable to all concerned. In the process, practical consideration should be given to the channels through which any decision reached would need to be implemented.

There are, of course, many other factors involved in the process of decision-making. For example, both the long- and short-term aspects have to be considered; any risk involved must be assessed quantitatively. Should the present be sacrificed for future gain or vice versa? What is the worst that can happen, given the wrong decision?

Finally, as usual, there should be feedback of some kind to check on the results of decisions as seen to work out in practice. In important cases the decision-maker might consider it worthwhile to carry out a check by personal visit or by delegating the task to a responsible assistant. It is not enough just to make decisions; they must always be followed through to the point of action.

Completed Staff Work

Taking a problem to a superior for decision is a technique in itself, and there are at least two very different ways in which this can be done:

(a) The subordinate can simply say, or state in writing, that there appears to be a problem here and could he be told what to do about it.

(b) He can set out the basic facts in logical order, evaluate the alternatives, make an intelligent and practical recommendation, and suggest the course of action needed to be taken.

It is not necessary to state which of these is the better (and more rewarding!) course for an up-and-coming subordinate to adopt, but it is surprising how often the easier way is taken both by the superior and by the subordinate. The superior may feel that his ego has been flattered, when in fact he should refer the matter back as "half-baked" and insist on the staff work being properly completed to enable him to make an informed judgment from the facts. The subordinate, on the other hand, may be lazy, unambitious, lacking judgment himself, or perhaps even working in a hostile atmosphere where his opinion is neither required nor valued.

Basically, the subordinate recommends and the superior decides. But the submission of decisions can be delegated right down the line provided that they are effectively programmed within the policy framework emanating from the top.

DECISIONS UNDER
CONDITIONS OF UNCERTAINTY

In the previous section consideration was given to making the right decisions, but more often than not decisions have to be based on imperfect knowledge. Although analytical skills can be developed, and the chances of success strengthened, it is seldom possible to obtain *all* the information one would like to have. There are many types of decisions, but at least those having a long time-span and therefore looking well into the future have to be made under conditions of uncertainty.

Quite apart, however, from the dynamic environment and the problems of forecasting, outlined in Chapter Two, it is difficult to know, for example, what competitors are planning to do in the same basic situation. Despite industrial espionage and the poaching of informed executives, it can still be possible for several boards of directors to be meeting at virtually the same time, each arriving at similar policy decisions likely to make a significant impact on the others. This kind of situation can, to some extent, be offset by intercompany consultation and conference, either by occasional meetings of top management representatives or, more formally, through a relevant trade association. Even so, there are still likely to be key policy decisions which remain closely guarded for as long as possible, if only in the interests of corporate survival.

Probability Techniques

In management education today considerable prominence is given to the "quantitative aspects" of business. This relates basically to using such measurement tools as mathematics, statistics, and so on, inevitably linked to the computer, specifically electronic data processing, or E.D.P. for short. The use of these tools is of particular importance to the consideration of strategic decisions, especially those which have to be made well ahead in an atmosphere of uncertainty and risk.

It may be felt that these require subjective or value judgments of the old-fashioned kind, the entrepreneurial hunch or intuition, rather than objective or quantitative appraisal. However, it is at least possible to assess probabilities and thereby reduce the odds by scientific methodology. Most areas of investigation contain certain fixed elements as well as variables; given that the fixed elements can be identified and evaluated, then the variables can each be taken in turn, or in relevant combinations, to quantify the strength of alternative possibilities. If these possibilities can be turned into probabilities, the margin of error, and risk, may be considerably minimized before any substantial value judgments need be invoked.

There is generally held to be a hierarchy of decisions, from the routine day-to-day operating decisions to strategic decisions, mentioned above, which have long-range planning significance. It is with the latter that we are mainly concerned in this chapter and it is here, too, that industry has begun to make more effective use of scientific methods.

Operations Research

With growth, a firm tends to become more capital intensive—in other words it has relatively more equipment than personnel—and even a small mistake in decision-making can result in substantial loss. To reduce the margin of error, by providing as much relevant and factual information as possible, it is wise to employ scientific methods, with special reference to operations research. All levels of management require basic information for decision-making, but the higher the position held in the hierarchy, the more significant and critical becomes the need for that information to be quantified and reliable.

In the main, operations research (O.R.) uses mathematical techniques. It is important, therefore, that managers of all kinds should be able to appreciate their value and interpretation in the analysis and solution of business problems. This does not necessarily require a knowledge of higher mathematics or advanced statistics, other than a few basic principles and formulas, but rather an ability to understand the proper use of tables, graphs, and the like and their validity and relevance to any decision necessarily based on them.

Among the specific mathematical techniques that have been developed or adapted to help solve complex management problems are the following:

(a) *Statistical analysis*, which relates to the variables in an analysis, the determination of their values, and the part played by them in the process of arriving at a decision.

(b) *Queueing theory*, which deals with goods or people arriving at and flowing through certain service points, the ways in which delays and bottlenecks can be avoided, and the ways in which waiting time can be reduced to an absolute minimum.

(c) *Linear programming*, which attempts to tackle problems involving a number of interacting variables by an organized trial-and-error procedure of selecting better and better solutions from a given mixture until the best solution is found. This may be to achieve the highest profit, the lowest cost, or whatever the particular problem in hand requires by way of solution.

(d) *Simulation*, which consists of producing and operating a realistic model of a given system or of any of its components so that its operations can be studied and quantified, in varying combinations, usually over a considerable period of time.

(e) *Stock-control systems*, which connote a special application of scientific method for ensuring adequate service based on minimum stocks.

These are just some of the O.R. techniques currently being used to provide a hard core of relevant data on which intelligent judgments can be based in a variety of decision-making situations.

Mathematical Models and the Computer

Reference was made in Chapter Two to a statistical model of the economy; and it is convenient here to consider briefly similar mathematical models constructed for industries and firms. In the process such O.R. techniques as linear programming and simulation are invoked and, in view of the complex nature of model-building, it is virtually essential to make extensive use of a computer.

In simple terms, a model consists of a wide range of mathematical equations to a particular business organization; these equations contain unknown factors, or variables, as well as all the fixed information that can be obtained. By putting values to these variables, in a variety of combinations, it is possible to judge the consequences of all the possible decisions which could be reached. Trying it out on the computer first may save heavy losses later. This has particular value for planning decisions.

It should be recognized, however, that model-building has a long way yet to go before it can be said to be universally accepted and employed. This is partly because of the complexity and cost, partly because the computer may have more urgent needs to satisfy first, and partly perhaps because of a shortage of specialized expertise.

Problems exist also with regard to the essential information that should be fed in; there is often, for example, a lack of accurate marketing data. The increasing popularity of computer time-sharing facilities, with one or more terminals, may encourage more interest in simulation at a controlled cost.

Other Approaches to Decision-making

There are many other management techniques now in vogue that can be used to help with decision-making. Of these the following examples justify brief mention:

(a) *Decision theory* attempts to sort out top-management decisions from those which can be made just as well, or better, at lower levels of management. Having delegated as much decision-making as possible down the line, there still remains a limited number of significant or controlling factors that require the special attention of top management in any given set of circumstances. These need to be identified, isolated, and analyzed.

(b) *Algorithms or decision trees* deal with a whole network of decisions branching out from the trunk, according to the answers given, or decisions made, at each stage. In an algorithmic diagram this may start with "yes" or "no" alternatives leading, according to the choice made, to "yes" or "no" questions, until the branch route taken arrives at its required destination. Other types of decision trees introduce (percentage) probabilities and costs related to the consequences of alternative decisions, which need to be considered and selected from at each intermediate stage. Indication may be given, too, of maximum, middle, and minimum effects that could result and the respective repercussions of each of these taken separately and carried forward to the next step.

(c) *Game theory* attempts mathematically to produce optimized answers to problems arising from business systems in competition with each other. Postulating a "malevolent force" such as competition or nature, this approach involves the maximization of gains and the minimizing of losses. It is largely theoretical and to that extent related to business games, used for educational purposes, described more appropriately in Chapter Fourteen.

Judgment Still Essential

In order to keep this chapter in perspective, it is necessary to emphasize that advanced decision-making techniques are still in the developing stage. With the greater and more sophisticated use of computers, however, their value in this context must become increasingly, if slowly, recognized. Nevertheless, even with long-range strategic decisions, where such techniques have particular application, there will still be ample room, and need, for the basic ingredient of judgment. With short-term operating decisions it could be argued further that judgment may long continue to play the major role. But all judgment decisions must be supported by as much factual information as the situation demands, and such information needs scientific analysis and effective presentation.

TOTAL MANAGEMENT INFORMATION

In order to facilitate decision-making, at the top level, it has always been necessary for management to have the right kind of information at the right time. In the main, this has been collected by, and processed through, various functional departments such as those dealing with marketing, production, finance, and personnel. With increasing size and complexity, however, any management information system today needs to become much more total and sophisticated.

Three trends are relevant. In the first place there is less emphasis now on functional organization; second, new coordinating units have sprung up, such as those for corporate planning and management services; third, electronics has added a new dimension to data processing.

The Impact of E.D.P.

Apart from production, most computers to date have concentrated their power on the many routine operational tasks associated with running the business side. They have largely taken the place of the functional departments in dealing with such matters as payroll, accounting records, stock control, and invoicing. The structural effect on organization has already been mentioned, in Chapter Four, including brief reference to the making of many routine decisions formerly the job of middle management. This highlights a grouping of functions, at routine level, as a first approach to a coordinated concept of total management information.

The computer has been seen to be particularly well suited to dealing with complicated mathematical research problems, including the construction of models for forecasting and planning. The further step is to build in all relevant additional information regarded as essential for providing the right kind of output, coupled with routine information, to assist the higher grades of management with their decision-making. The planning of the input data in this context is a major problem in itself. Nevertheless, the more effective that planning becomes, the more informed will be those areas of decision-making requiring judgment.

Management Information Systems

Basically, any business undertaking is made up of two parts: the management information side, which collects the data and does the thinking, and the operational side, which acts on that thinking. For purposes of control it is essential to regard all data as interrelated and to think in terms of total management information, whatever the system, or systems, installed.

Information sources and characteristics can be divided into categories. For the present purpose it is sufficient to note internal as against external information, and regular as against *ad hoc* information. Special mention can also be made of "feedback" information used for testing the effectiveness of planning and policy decisions in action. This operates in what is generally known as a "loop," sometimes a "cybernetic loop," the usual route (shown in Fig. 8) being as follows:

(a) Plan produced based on the management information system.

(b) Action taken by the relevant part of the operating system.

(c) Action performance measured against the plan.

(d) Results fed back into the management information system.

(e) Action taken by operating system, if corrective action indicated, OR

(f) New or modified plan again based on the management information system.

(g) Route continues as before, back to (b) above.

An associated simulation based on the way information is converted into decisions and action, with appropriate feedback, is that of "industrial dynamics." This concept demonstrates, for example, how reaction to market information, starting with the customers and passing backwards through retailers, wholesalers, and so on to the factory, can cause serious planning disequilibrium. This is the result of delays occurring, and/or magnified reaction, in response to that information.

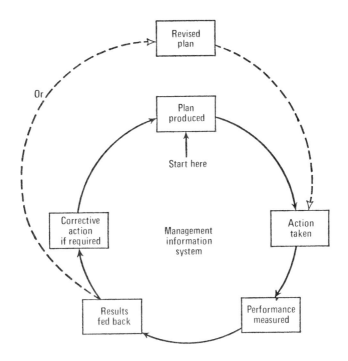

FIGURE 8. Management information loop

Management by Exception

There is always a danger of top management allowing an indiscriminate collection of facts and figures to be placed before it from which decisions have to be made and control exercised. With corporate growth and complexity, however, top management's time tends to become increasingly critical (see Chapter Four), and ways and means have therefore to be found to economize on the use of that time. Hence the popularity of "management by exception," which means that only those facts and figures which differ from the norm, and therefore relate to exceptional circumstances, need be referred to the top. While everything continues to proceed according to plan, there is obviously no point in top management becoming involved. To a lesser extent this is true at the lower levels of management. In all other cases, decisions have to be made, and action taken, in accordance with the objectives and policies as circulated through procedure manuals and office instructions.

In an introductory book of this kind, it is not possible to do much more than indicate scientific management techniques and outline the most important aspects of their uses. Attention is therefore directed to the bibliography below, which indicates sources of more detailed information. Events are continually on the move, however, and the serious student must keep in touch with those events by reading as widely as possible, with special reference to the many excellent management journals available (usually monthly), or the business and scientific sections of the more responsible newspapers.

Summary

1. *Definitions*
    a. Business policy is an all-embracing term covering management practice.
    b. A policy is a guideline laid down to help achieve objectives.
2. *Major Policy Decisions*
    a. These emanate from the boardroom, but may originate lower down.

b. Broad treatment is required.
c. Decisions should be based on facts available plus sound judgment.
d. Effective policy decisions cannot always be achieved.
e. Major policies cover marketing, production, finance, and personnel.

3. *Decision-making*
a. The problem is first defined in an appropriate setting.
b. An acceptable solution is then chosen from alternatives available.
c. Subordinates must complete staff-work before seeking any decision from a superior.

4. *Under Conditions of Uncertainty*
a. Most decisions are based on imperfect knowledge.
b. Quantitative techniques assess probabilities.
c. Operations research is used for this purpose.
d. Uncertainty is minimized, but judgment is still essential.

5. *Management Information Systems*
a. These provide the right kind of information for decision-making.
b. Information systems cover internal and external data.
c. Computers help, given appropriate inputs.
d. Feedback through a cybernetic loop helps in testing effectiveness.

6. *Management by Exception*
a. Too many facts and figures tend to confuse.
b. Select only those data differing from the norm.

Suggested Future Reading

AITCHISON, J. *Choice Against Chance: An Introduction to Statistical Decision Theory.* Reading, Mass.: Addison-Wesley, 1970.

ALEXIS, M., AND C.Z. WILSON. *Organizational Decision Making.* Englewood Cliffs, N.J.: Prentice-Hall, 1967.

ARGENTI, J. *Systematic Corporate Planning.* New York: Wiley, 1974.

BIERMAN, H., JR., ET AL. *Quantitative Analysis for Business Decisions.* 4th ed. Homewood, Ill.: Irwin, 1973.

EDEN, C., AND J. HARRIS. *Management Decision and Decision Analysis.* New York: Halsted Press, 1975.

HARRISON, E.F. *The Managerial Decision-Making Process.* Boston: Houghton Mifflin, 1975.

MILLER, D.W., AND M.K. STARR. *Executive Decisions and Operations Research.* 2d ed. Englewood Cliffs, N.J.: Prentice-Hall, 1969.

NEWMAN, J.W. *Management Applications of Decision Theory.* New York: Harper & Row, 1971.

RAIA, A.P. *Managing by Objectives.* Glenview, Ill.: Scott Foresman, 1974.

RICHARDS, M.D., AND P.S. GREENLAW. *Management: Decisions and Behavior.* Rev. ed. Homewood, Ill.: Irwin, 1972.

RIGGS, J.L., AND M.S. INOUE. *Operations Research and Management Science.* New York: McGraw-Hill, 1975.

SHULL, F.A., JR., ET AL. *Organizational Decision Making.* New York: McGraw-Hill, 1970.

SMITH, L.M. *Managers Digest: A Handbook for Decision-making.* New York: Exposition Press, 1975.

THOMAS, H. *Decision Theory and the Manager.* New York: Beekman, 1972.

NINE

Marketing and Sales Policies

Having discussed corporate objectives and policies generally in the previous chapter, it is appropriate to focus on the policy implications for the essential functions in industry—marketing, production, finance, and personnel. Although many enterprises are not concerned with manufacturing, this is a convenient way in which to cover the management scene effectively. Even the providers of services (as opposed to goods), such as government departments or bankers, may derive valuable background information for the framing of policy from knowing something of the problems of industry in *all* aspects.

THE EMPHASIS ON MARKETING

Traditionally, American industry has made the goods and *then* tried to sell them; many firms still do this. But the modern concept is the other way around, to start with marketing and the needs of the consumer. In management terms, a firm should be "marketing oriented" rather than "production oriented," a philosophy or attitude of mind based on the sound logic that it is no good making anything that cannot be sold and that it is better to start with customer needs and try to satisfy those needs. Some needs can be created, the customer being attracted to something he did not know he wanted; but even there it is better to think about or test the market first rather than produce in bulk with a selling policy based on blind hope.

Most companies today, with good records of growth, have a top management with a keen appreciation of the importance of this attitude toward marketing; less effective concerns should follow their example. Putting the customer before production is by far the most logical and profitable way of conducting a business.

Marketing Defined

"Marketing" embraces selling and covers the full gamut of analysis, promotion, and coordination. This involves studying the environment, assessing the outlook, analyzing actual and potential markets, finding out what goods and services customers want, where they want them, how best to advise them of what is available, assessing the strength of competition, anticipating changes in demand, and other policy considerations.

In practical terms the following are the main constituent parts of what is usually called the "marketing mix": marketing and consumer research; product planning, brands, and pricing; public relations, advertising, other forms of promotion and display; personal selling and incentives; distribution channels, warehouses and transportation; packaging and servicing. All these must be coordinated by top management, who should at the same time aim to optimize the use of productive resources by effective liaison and feedback.

Basic Policy Decisions

In setting marketing objectives in an existing organization, one of the first questions asked is usually "What business are we *really* in?"; in a new enterprise, or an old one in process of change, it is "What business are we going to be in?" Too narrow a concept here could mean eventual failure to survive, classical examples being "entertainment," not just films, and "transportation," not just railways. This leads to policy decisions on what products or services to sell and over what range. To arrive at tenable conclusions, it is essential to take an objective view, actual or potential, of the strengths and weaknesses of resources available, with stress on market opportunities likely to lead to profit and growth. This suggests a hard look at the long- and short-term trends of the adopted industry, using all available information and research facilities, coupled with quantitative estimates of the likely rise or fall in the demand for the goods or services in question. Marketing, of course, occupies an important place in the life of the community, affecting as it does the well-being of so many people. All the effort (and resources) devoted to achieving the right marketing objectives and successful policies is, therefore, worthwhile.

Opportunity Cost

In deciding what to sell (and make) or what services to provide, there enters into the calculation the factor of alternative uses to which given resources, human and material, can be put. Basically, in choosing to sell (and manufacture) A instead of B, or A and B instead of C and D, the gain of one or more means the loss of the other or others. Similarly with regard to markets, the areas and customers being supplied are chosen at the expense of others not being supplied. The "loss," i.e., the opportunity foregone in order to take up a better (it is hoped) alternative use of resources, is usually referred to as the "opportunity cost." This concept has to be taken into account and reviewed continually when setting or rethinking corporate objectives.

Once the opportunity (alternative) appears to be foregone at too heavy a cost, then possibly it is time to decide whether the resources are currently being used to maximum advantage or whether the company is now in fact operating in the wrong business or at the wrong place.

Organization for Marketing

Before attempting to be successful in marketing, with large-scale profitable expansion in mind, a company must be efficiently organized with the right kind of expertise on hand to tackle the progress envisaged. Good motivation and high company morale should be salient features.

In a large organization the key man would probably be a marketing director, but in every firm there should be a top-level executive with special responsibilities for marketing and direct access to the chief executive officer.

With a centralized organization, the marketing director might have some, or all, of the following managers under his command, to coordinate and control: public relations officer (P.R.O.), market research manager (possibly with specialists in sales statistics and forecasting), advertising (and sales promotion) manager, new-product planning manager, and sales manager (with a sales force and responsibility for distribution). In addition there could be an export manager.

An alternative arrangement might be based on organization by product or brand, in which case there would be a manager for each (product manager) under the marketing director; each of these managers would have his own separate advertising, sales promotion, and sales team concentrating on that product or brand. Marketing services, that is to say market research, sales statistics, forecasting, and the like, would be available, as usual, in support of *all* products or brands. In a very large organization the whole structure could be broken down into product divisions, each with its own divisional head and supporting hierarchy. Regional managers centrally, with territorial responsibilities, could each be in charge of a given area of the country, divided up among divisional managers on the spot and their sales teams.

KNOWING THE CUSTOMER
AND HIS NEEDS

On the chicken-and-egg principle, it is not easy to decide whether a pioneer business starts its thinking with the product or service it intends to offer or with the market. An entrepreneur might first look at people, or firms (which are people in groups), and try to identify a need for a product or service yet to be thought up; or he might first find a product (perhaps an invention) or service (perhaps a new technique) and then look for customers likely to be interested. To some extent, the entrepreneur would keep both sides of the equation in mind, probably with a bias one way or the other.

Market Research

It is essential to produce what the customer needs, when and where he wants it, bearing in mind that it may be possible to create an awareness of fresh needs by offering new products or variations on old products. This is a continuing process based on a dynamic, in the sense of a changing, environment which must be kept constantly under review.

"Market research" may be defined as a method employed to find out about people and their needs, thereby ensuring better sales figures, with the intention of improving profitability. It may be carried out by outside specialists, such as market research firms and advertising agents, or by in-company technicians. Essentially, it is an investigation into the buying habits of customers, potential customers, or even into the peculiarities of those who refuse to become customers. Using statistical methods based on sampling, the investigation attempts to discover the needs of customers by looking into what they buy and how often, where they buy, why they buy, frequency of use, how they use what they have bought, and their comments for and against the product itself. By finding out why people *don't* buy or use certain products or services, objections may be overcome or taken into account when devising appropriate marketing strategies.

Field market research techniques range from questionnaires filled up *ad hoc* by students stopping passersby in the street, to organized test panels conducted along scientific lines by specialists. In addition, a great deal of desk research can be done by analyzing government and other statistics relevant to the particular type of product, service, or market. The cost of market research has to be considered, but in the right hands it can more than earn its keep.

As a management tool, market research has great value, but its natural limitations must also be appreciated and understood. There are negative aspects in that a survey of current habits, or even of declared intention, does not necessarily point the way ahead. Apart from statistical review, however accurately carried out, there are important sociological and psychological overtones to be given their full value. Fashions are notoriously fickle, and habits tend to change unpredictably. Then, again, a market survey carried out in selected areas, on a sample basis, does not necessarily indicate with any accuracy a likely pattern for *national* characteristics. In planning, say, five years ahead, market research alone is insufficient; but it is a good starting point for sales forecasting, coupled with managerial flair and judgment.

Identifying the Customer

For some firms the customer is the final consumer, whether an industrial, commercial, or household user; for other firms he is a "middleman" such as a dealer in the distribution network. Having identified the *type* of customer, whether a firm, group, or individual purchaser, it is vital to recognize who, by their power of making buying decisions, are the influential people likely to tip the scales of success or failure, either collectively or individually. Full satisfaction can be given only if the key customer is known, fully understood, and evaluated. If this key customer is in fact the dealer, including the shopkeeper, then market research should also cover this area of market characteristics as well.

With industrial marketing, which relates to selling capital goods used in manufacturing consumer goods, the situation is even more complex, but the need for identification and understanding remains.

The Market and Market Segments

Related to knowing the customer is the need to identify and understand the total market to be served. This involves deciding whether to concentrate on specilialization or whether to diversify, meaning whether to aim at a class or classes of consumer and concentrate on their needs, or to try to cover the widest possible range within the resources available to the enterprise concerned. It is possible, for example, either to focus attention on a particular kind of product, perhaps a high-quality exclusive product geared to what has been called the "top end" of the market, or to aim at a much wider market by producing relatively cheap or popular goods.

It may be decided to aim at more than one market segment at the same time; for instance, aiming at the "top end" with a quality product projected under an expensive brand name, coupled with the firm's reputation, and aiming at the "bottom end" with a second-rate anonymous product.

This market segmentation, or stratification, requires intensive research into the size and breakdown of each market by areas, customer, and the like and its opportunity potentials. By systematically and continuously studying the strengths and weaknesses of each segment, or finding segments not yet covered (or at least not yet saturated) by competitors, it should be possible to keep attention objectively focused on the way ahead.

Of course, both geographic segmentation and the use of demographics (segmentation by such variables as age, sex, social class, education level, income, and color) have been in vogue with marketing specialists for decades. Among the more recent approaches to targeting in on special groups of consumers that are being tested here and there are "benefit" and "volume" segmentation and the even more modern "psychographics." Potential customers are classified according to the kinds of benefits they are seeking in a particular product or service (such as the desire for a "clean breath" in the selection of a dentifrice) or according to their frequency of use of the item (heavy, medium, or light users), or even in light of their lifestyles or personalities.

It is not enough, however, to find a profitable segment, or even segments, and then settle down complacently expecting a successful sales program to continue indefinitely. For, given evidence of success, other enterprises tend to move in, either competitively to share that success or aggressively to stave off a threatened loss of total market share. With or without competition there is always the danger of a segment becoming unprofitable through eventual saturation. Given an attack, for example, by market leaders on their competitors' market segments, there is always the inherent risk of diminishing returns through that saturation. So the progressive firm must always keep in mind the continuous need to look for new segments to replace or augment the old: this can mean having to search for other products and markets, including exports. In the automobile industry, for example, gaps in the price range have to be strategically filled from time to time; as an example we may note the successful introduction of compact cars underneath an existing price range. Whatever plans are made, however, market strategy must always take into account the likely time-scale, and impact, of potential competition and the need to keep at least one jump ahead.

A progressive company would maintain a continuous research program into markets and products throughout the whole field of its business activities. It would have regular breakdown analyses, pin-pointing its competitive position in each market and segment; in the process it would find out how it is progressing relative to the efforts of competitors, and it would investigate such domestic facets as customer reaction to its products, complaints, the views of salesmen, and the attitudes of dealers and agents. It would also research into every opportunity, at home and abroad, looking for vacant market segments, however narrow, with a view to profitable exploitation, bearing in mind that other firms could be going through the same exercise and coming to similar conclusions. In this context it should be appreciated that there is a "lead time," often several years, between conception and physical innovation.

SELECTING THE PRODUCT OR SERVICE

Any realistic marketing plan should contain full provision for implementing continuous product/service selection and review in order to keep the business alive and prosperous. This starts with considering whether to sell a narrow range of goods or services (specialization), or to concentrate instead on a fuller range (diversification). Product policy takes account of market needs, with future profits in mind, and product planning sets the pattern for research and development (dealt with in Chapter Ten).

In dealing with products, it is appropriate to draw a distinction between consumer goods for domestic use and industrial goods such as capital equipment. Whereas with the domestic market there may be preference for a given make or brand, the purchasing officer of an industrial concern may show a natural reluctance to be too dependent on, and possibly held to ransom by, a single manufacturer. Other than that, it is convenient to treat consumer and industrial products alike in the comments that follow.

Specialization or Diversification

Any decision of this kind must relate to the present or potential resources of the firm: resources in marketing, production, finance, and personnel, with special reference to skills and managerial ability available or able to be acquired. It may, for example, pay a firm to make use of consultants or hire specialized knowledge, which means a deliberate policy to engage proved experts from other companies to augment its own management, rather than just survive with existing resources. One of the problems of a small firm growing rapidly is that it tends to grow beyond its quota of skills and abilities. At the end of the exercise, however carried out, there must be adequate profits for continued survival and growth.

Success depends on being especially good at something, particularly where a firm has a patent, technological, or marketing advantage over its competitors for the time being. A policy choice has therefore to be made between being a leader on a small front, with special expertise to offer, or an ordinary contributor to a wider area with other firms in competition offering much the same commodity or service. Often the most successful firms are those which specialize, but a firm in a field with limited potential would be wise to diversify into an area offering more opportunity for growth. But diversification must not be allowed to go beyond the resources and skills available.

Among the advantages of diversification are the offering of a range of products or services, or a complete system, so that a dealer can specialize in a brand name if he so desires, supported by effective promotion. Too wide a choice tends to confuse the customer choosing, for example, from a large number of wallpaper pattern books. For this reason it might be advisable to limit the range, compensating the bringing in of new lines by taking out old, and possibly dated, lines on their way to becoming losers.

Salesmen are always happy to have extra lines, particularly when up against competition or when aiming to maximize the value of calls made, but in practice they tend to concentrate on a few lines only. This can often mean that new exciting products are exploited to the detriment of less attractive lines, or concentration on lines easiest to sell (with commission in mind) instead of those most profitable to the firm. This, however, may be offset by special incentives for the sales force to channel effort in the right direction.

Diversification implies the spreading of risk by having many irons in the fire at any given time. But it is wise to consider the concept of compatibility, which means keeping within the parameters of existing "know-how" and managerial ability to control. This concept is dealt with more fully in Chapter Sixteen, when dealing with takeovers, in particular the acquiring of new businesses one after the other. For here a choice has to be made between conglomerate structure, essentially a haphazard diversification, and compatibility, defined as strategically planned specialization within existing managerial ability, experience, and qualities.

Variety Reduction

Although it is necessary to study what motivates customers when choosing between alternatives and to satisfy their needs by offering variety through a range of goods, there must be limits related to profitability and cost. Take into account, for example, the varieties of appearance, size, and style, linked with fashion or seasonal changes; or price ranges, linked with varying quality, accuracy, or durability; and it soon becomes possible to think up a very wide range of alternatives, as, for instance, in an ordinary shoe store.

Given a catalog, for example, with thousands of items in it, there is a real opportunity for using the technique of "variety reduction." Each item can be taken and studied separately to see what contribution the price makes to the fixed costs (overhead expenses) of the company, having already covered the variable costs (mainly materials and labor) relating to the product itself as manufactured or otherwise supplied. Those making insufficient contribution—the potential losers—can then be eliminated, leaving the best contributors as a reduced but more profitable range. This contribution theory will be developed in more detail in Chapter Ten, under Production, with special reference to a statistical approach called "Pareto analysis."

It is not always easy to drop even a recognized loser because of tradition, face-saving, effect on staff morale, or company enthusiasm for the product itself; but where resources can be more profitably used elsewhere, a low-contribution product should be pruned from the product line or mix. It is wrong to spend further time and money on advertising, etc., in the hope of resurrecting a former winner now in the doldrums; instead of dissipating management energies and time or throwing good money after bad, such valuable resources could be better used on a new product or service.

Product Innovation

The managerial ability to mount successful product innovations (in other words, to launch new products) means the maintenance of momentum and the keeping up to date of the firm's range of goods. This is not the only factor in growth, however, which usually takes one or more of the following forms:

(a) Existing products in existing markets.

(b) Existing products in new markets.

(c) New products in existing markets.

(d) New products in new markets.

Having invented or devised a new product, usually from the company's own research staff, or ideas from salesmen or other members of the staff generally, it does not necessarily follow that such a product can be successfully launched. There can be, for example, initial resistance or scepticism in the boardroom or at executive level. For old products sometimes die hard, and new ideas, like new brooms, tend to be looked at with suspicion. What is still imperfectly understood is the "product life-cycle," dealt with below, which connotes that as soon as a new product is succesfully launched it has already started to become obsolete. Complacency must therefore be overcome, old products regularly reviewed and, subject to reasonable safeguards, innovation planned and welcomed.

Unfortunately, many new products fall by the wayside, usually well within a year from being launched, and it is essential to prevent this if possible by test marketing or by learning from experience, possibly the painful experience of others in comparable circumstances. There is, in fact, a school of thought that sees merit in always being second, deliberately deciding to let others innovate and make mistakes, then move in with an improved "me too" product, more sophisticated "know-how," and perhaps better equipment for production.

However, initiative in being first often produces exceptional market growth and pricing advantages until competitors eventually enter the field (bearing in mind lead-time problems) and limit the opportunities. But by then, there could be further innovation and/or new markets entered.

Essentials—but without guarantee—for successful innovation seem to be:

(a) Effective market research into acceptable price levels, size of market, etc.

(b) Adequate test marketing.

(c) Optimum marketing effort, including a well-planned sales drive and proper distribution arrangements.

(d) Making sure that the product is fully tested and developed, thereby being well able to stand up to the claims made on its behalf without latent defect.

(e) Good timing.

(f) Hitting on the right strategic price backed by realistic costing.

(g) Realizing in advance that competitors could affect potential by imitation; making allowance for such an effect in estimates.

(h) Continuing to seek further innovations.

Before going ahead, full investigation should be made into the implications and costs for inventory maintenance, distribution, and delivery; appropriate policy decisions can then be made on firmer ground.

The "Life-cycle" Concept

Products which survive innovation go on to flourish, mature, and die, sometimes (as with fashion goods) in a matter of months. The classic pattern, as shown in Figure 9, consists of four main stages:

(a) Innovation. This is the critical period, when early development takes place, during which considerable resources have to be devoted to the venture, but without much hope of immediate return.

(b) Growth. Here, assuming a successful launch, the product becomes established and enters the most profitable period of its life,

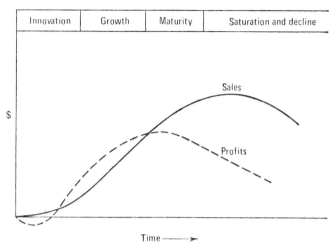

FIGURE 9. Product life-cycle

during which it is able to make optimum impact through having a temporary monopoly.

(c) Maturity.   At this point it is likely that competitors will have entered the field, and although sales may still be rising, they are doing so against a background of increased costs, such as for extra advertising, and possibly reduced price in the process of trying to hold the market.

(d) Saturation and Decline.   Eventually the market becomes oversupplied by the concerted efforts of imitators, sales decline, and profits fade away. But by this time the firm should be well organized with other inventions. Clearly, as the life-cycle gets shorter the need for a new product becomes more urgent. Bearing in mind the problems of lead time, fresh innovations should be sought as early as possible.

As with most concepts, this is an oversimplification, but a useful one to keep in mind when devising market strategy. When forecasting, it should be possible to judge the likely limits of market growth, involving saturation, given reasonable market research, but it is not so easy to predict the timing pace of eventual decline. A good parallel here is financial knowledge of the Stock Exchange—it is easy enough to state from theory when to buy or sell securities, but a very different matter in practice.

The concept has merit, too, for those wishing to be second and thereby provide the competition. Obviously the time to enter the market is during the early stages of the growth period while the profit opportunities can still be seen and exploited.

There is some wisdom in having several products each with its life-cycle at a different stage of growth, so that they tend to compensate for each other and even out growth and profitability. The tragedy is to hold onto any given product too long. Occasionally, a product can have a new lease on life, that is to say, go back a stage or remain longer at a current stage, by the discovery of new uses or improvements. Apart from these aspects, however, it is usually better to divert the firm's resources to other products where the return is likely to be more rewarding.

Some manufacturers consider that household and other "durable" goods have too long a life! Such firms are anxious not only to increase sales by adding new customers but to persuade existing owners of similar products to buy again. Hence, they hope that innovations (by new appearance or technical improvement) will tempt existing owners to discard the old and replace with new, if only to keep up with the people next door. To help with this choice, and in order to limit durability, it is not unusual to adopt the policy of "built-in obsolescence."

This life-cycle theory can be adapted to market trends as well as product trends; the strategy of making hay while the sun shines applies equally to both.

Seasonal Patterns

Firms selling goods that have seasonal peaks and troughs may find it worthwhile to have other products with an inverted seasonal pattern; the peaks and troughs of *all* products may then offset each other. Fashion firms with seasonal goods have the problem of thinking ahead, planning in the summer for winter fashions and in the winter for summer fashions, thus attempting to anticipate or perhaps create fashion trends at least six months in advance.

THE SIGNIFICANCE OF PRICE

The theoretical fixing of a price for goods or services starts with the interplay of supply and demand.

Marginal Theory

In economic terms, supply and demand can be studied "at the margin." Without wishing to confuse the practical aspects of marketing with such terms as "marginal utility," the "marginal propensity to consume" as against the "marginal propensity to save," "marginal revenue," and "marginal cost," it is still essential to know something of marginal theory to be able to appreciate the economic background to pricing policy.

Stripped of complications (the book list at the end of the chapter will point the way to more advanced economic study), the following basic but relevant statements may seem obvious; they are nevertheless essential.

(a) The marginal purchaser—there may in fact be many of these —is the consumer who thinks it just worthwhile to pay a given price rather than not buy the commodity, or service, at all. It is that price which governs the volume (in money terms, "revenue") of goods that can be sold. If the price is raised, former marginal purchasers stop buying because they now find themselves below the margin. If the price is lowered, a new layer of would-be purchasers becomes marginal as they are just prepared, or just able, to pay the reduced price.

(b) From the firm's point of view, *marginal revenue* is the extra revenue arising from the sale of an extra unit of commodity, or service, taking into account the possible effect of that marginal sale on market price. Where there are many other firms in the market, the sale of that extra (marginal) unit would tend to have little or no effect. Using jargon again, the "marginal revenue" would equate with "average revenue," or price. But given only a few firms in the market, then any price reduction aimed at selling those extra units in the face of

competition would require similar price reductions of all *existing* units sold. In economic terms, "marginal revenue" would not be the same as "average revenue."

(c) There is a similar theory related to *marginal costs* and *average costs*. It is sufficient here to state that the right theoretical concept of profitable market strategy is for a firm to continue expanding its sales to the point where its marginal costs are just lower than marginal revenue. Beyond that point the profit on further units ceases.

The equilibrium of supply and demand in terms of marginal theory is illustrated in Figure 10. In Chapter Thirteen this theme is developed to include "total revenue" and "total costs" in the determination of a break-even point as between profit and loss.

Pricing in Practice

Although there is no infallible guide to effective pricing policy, there are many examples of workable formulas—such as the "cost-

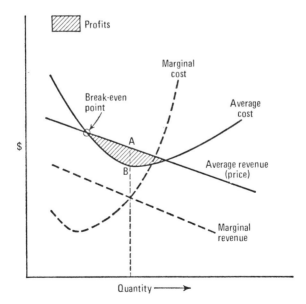

FIGURE 10. Traditional marginal theory

plus" method practiced particularly by those firms providing industrial (capital) goods. Certainly the price should be high enough to keep the business going, that is to say, to cover costs of production, distribution, overhead and a margin of profit. But with a marketing approach, it should be what the (marginal) customer will pay, sometimes referred to as "what the traffic will bear," with a healthy respect for other prices, especially those of competitors selling a similar product. If the feasible price for the quantity envisaged is too low, having in mind the costs of production, then the emphasis should be on reducing those costs.

Cost-plus is simple and popular where it can be made to work, and has a long history with regard to government contracts in war and peace. It presupposes a "normal" profit, neither so high that it attracts an influx of competition nor so low that overhead expenses, reserves, and the dividend interests of stockholders are inadequately covered.

While on the subject of competition, it is worth noting that a large manufacturer, being a recognized market leader, can usually initiate price changes up or down. Even so, it would be wise to communicate intent, or indicate reasons, to other leading firms in the industry, if only to prevent misunderstanding and the danger of misinformed retaliation.

Research into what the customer expects to pay is a vital part of pricing policy, for the average consumer usually has a preconception of what the price level should be, based on conventional buying habits covering a wide range of products. This again suggests a marketing approach, tailoring product development to a selected price or range of prices.

By and large, consumers tend to judge quality by the price charged; given a low price they may well wonder what is wrong with the product that it can be sold so cheaply. Housewives, for example, will often pay the higher of two prices for comparable goods, usually packaged differently, thinking that they are thereby getting better value and quality.

Similar considerations apply to isolated price changes against the competitive stream. A rise in price may well suggest that the demand for this particular product must be rising and that it must therefore be especially good. A price cut, on the other hand, may suggest difficulties in selling or perhaps the imminent launch of an improved product.

These are necessarily generalizations; nevertheless many

specific examples can be found in daily transactions. In this respect, as well as others, marketing has strong psychological characteristics which need to be fully understood.

Once customers get used to a stated price and sales remain satisfactory, it may be risky policy to alter that price. Given the necessity for an increase in price, it becomes common practice instead to adjust consumer value by reducing the contents of a package slightly or making the commodity itself fractionally smaller.

Faced with price cuts, other suppliers may feel compelled to follow suit or even start a price war. But it should not be forgotten that it may well be better to face such competition by marketing an improved product, such as a new model, or by more effective salesmanship. This reinforces the need to keep product development, innovation, or improvement constantly on the boil.

Summarizing the practical aspects of pricing policy, it can be stated in simple terms that price setting becomes an amalgam of being:

(a) Sufficiently above unit cost to ensure that the business will continue.

(b) In line with the prices charged by competitors, other marketing aspects being taken into account.

(c) What the traffic (customer) will bear.

Protecting the Consumer

Setting prices does not necessarily reflect value or quality. There may be monopoly aspects, tax burdens, inefficient manufacturing processes, costly overhead that should be reduced, and so on; but provided a sufficient number of consumers are willing and able to pay the price, "exploitation" becomes feasible.

Traditionally, there has long been that well-known caveat "let the buyer beware," but in a complex economy, it is no longer sufficient to leave the innocent to his own devices. Hence the compulsory, as well as the voluntary, aids which exist today for consumer protection.

Monopoly prices and profits are a detailed study on their own, illustrated by deliberate price-fixing and other agreements to isolate prices from competitive influences, all likely to operate to the detriment of the consumer. With mergers and acquisitions becoming increasingly popular, such practices could have resulted in sections of the populace being held to ransom. However, it lies within the very essence of a capitalistic society to encourage competition. The general posture of the federal government *vis-à-vis* large combines and trusts that might tend to restrict free competition dates back to the latter part of the nineteenth century and the Sherman Antitrust Act. Large-scale activity is not necessarily wrong; given the right product and market, mass production could just as easily mean a reduction of costs, lower prices, and customer satisfaction.

Monopoly relates more to restrictive practices. Whereas the Sherman Antitrust Act was aimed at preventing monopolies and other combinations and "conspiracies" in restraint of trade, the Clayton Act of 1914 broadened the base of public policy in this area by banning price discrimination, tying arrangements, and interlocking directorates, where these tended to substantially lessen competition. In that same year, the Federal Trade Commission (FTC) was established to, among other things, monitor unfair methods of competition. Subsequent legislation in the same vein included the Robinson-Patman Act (1936), which prohibited unfair discounts and other discriminatory pricing practices; the Wheeler-Lea Act (1938), which extended the powers of the FTC to protect the consumer from unfair business practices—including the fraudulent advertising of foods, cosmetics, and other items; and the Celler-Kefauver Act (1950), designed to block mergers that might lead to the restraint of trade.

Under resale-price maintenance, retail prices were fixed by manufacturers to prevent undercutting. The aim is to safeguard distributors' margins, wholesale and retail, usually based on stated percentage "markups." The approach dates back to the Depression years, when individual states, in attempts to maintain resale prices, began to pass the "fair-trade" laws. Because of the obvious potential of conflict by such statutes with the intent of federal antitrust legislation, the government passed the Miller-Tydings Act in 1937, exempting fair trade from possible prosecution under antitrust law. Since the early 1950s, however, the fair trade concept has come increasingly under attack, especially in the area of "nonsigner" clauses that bind retailers who have not been party to a contract to the contract price. Despite the passage of the McGuire Act in 1952, which attempted to reinforce fair trade, fewer than half of the individual states today still have such statutes on their books.

Legal protection for the consumer also exists in other areas, afforded by a series of legislative acts that date back over the decades, beginning with the Pure Food and Drug Act (1906) and the Meat Inspection Act (1906). These early laws not only banned the manufacture, sale, and interstate transfer of foodstuffs and drugs that had been adulterated or wrongly labeled, but also sought to enforce sanitary conditions and plant inspection. It was strengthened—and the Food and Drug Administration (FDA) given "teeth"—by the enactment of the Food, Drug, and Cosmetic Act (1938). In addition to these, a number of "labeling" laws have been passed over the years, covering a variety of items such as wool, fur, and textile fiber products; alcohol; cigarettes; and hazardous substances. Safety standards for the automobile industry were assured with the enactment of the Highway Safety Act (1966); protection against flammable clothing was given by the Flammable Fabrics Act (1953) and against dangerous toys by the Child Protection and Safety Act (1969); and "truth-in-lending" was made a household catchword by the Consumer Credit Protection Act (1968).

Then there are various organizations available to advise the consumer with respect to defective goods and services, misrepresentation, or other problems such as the departments of consumer affairs in many of our nation's cities, Better Business Bureaus, and any number of consumer groups. In many instances, state and/or local laws will cover the situation in question.

Today there is a second caveat, "let the seller beware," for clearly there are likely to be many more claims—given legal aid and small-claims court procedures—against those who (perhaps irresponsibly) supply goods and services.

But protection does not absolve the purchaser himself from taking reasonable precautions. He should carefully read the information now required to be printed on leaflets, advertisements, packages, and the like; make sure he is comparing like with like (for example, a large package may contain less than a smaller package); use common sense; and shop around.

ADVERTISING, PROMOTION, AND SALESMANSHIP

Having accepted the practical logic of marketing orientation, dealing in turn with the customer, the product, and pricing, it is now essential to consider how best to *sell* the goods to be manufactured or the services to be offered. To this end, we shall consider public relations, advertising, and the selling side of the business, with special reference to motivating the personal sales force to maximum effort with full backing from the home office.

The Corporate "Image"

The attraction of having a high-class image, prestige, standing, or call it what you will is obvious yet often overlooked. To start with, a company's name can be a significant factor, hence the change to a new name sometimes adopted. This is a moot point, however, in that if large sums have been spent in the past on advertising coupled with the old name, the advantages of that advertising may temporarily be lost. Second, some firms with awkward names have turned a weakness into strength by clever advertising capitalizing on the name and its peculiarities, thus building up an acceptable, perhaps humorous, reputation for itself in the process.

It is often considered advantageous to adopt some sort of clever symbol, coat of arms, apt slogan, or typeface as an image-building "logo," which will convey the desired personality of the company on its stationery and everything else it issues to the world at large. It can be displayed, too, on factory premises, office buildings, delivery vans, containers, and even shopping bags. Advertising also plays a major part in creating the right impression, given goods or services that justify public confidence, which aspect will be developed later.

In the meantime, it is clear that corporate prestige of the right kind enhances marketing success, particularly in new markets; the standing of products; the ability to raise finance, attract the right kind of staff, and generally achieve its long-term objectives. Research on behalf of a firm to test its real standing in the eyes of the public can be carried out by scientific inquiry over a wide market population, but it tends to be expensive.

Public Relations

Because of the importance of creating or preserving the right corporate image, it is usual to give special attention to the function of public relations (P.R. for short). This attention should begin at the top and extend throughout the whole organization. Examples can be found in every government department, as well as in most areas of industry and commerce. Almost any large enterprise today will have its P.R. department or someone responsible for P.R. or will make use of a firm of P.R. consultants. Whatever the form, P.R. includes supplying information about the firm's activities to the general public, its own customers, stockholders and staff, using the newspapers, television, radio, and other types of news service whenever they can be persuaded to give the right kind of free coverage.

It follows that the enterprise, its management, products or service should be basically sound, for however good the P.R. organization may be, it is doubtful whether it can hope to succeed for long with indifferent wares to market. Truth, it is said, has a way of coming out.

Reporters and other members of the press are always keen to talk with top managers, to ask them questions and to learn their frank and honest views, whether for publication or as "off the record" background information. With judicious handling, a mutual respect can be built up in this way. Help can often be given,' for example, to journals seeking advice in writing articles on what may be, to them, less familiar topics. By being friendly, available, and useful to the press, senior managers may well ensure generous press comment on their firm's successes and, what is no less important, sympathetic coverage in times of difficulties. The P.R.O., whether on the staff or a consultant, should not be a bottleneck; he should act as a middleman, bringing the two sides together, diplomatically interpreting one to the other, thereby building up important and direct channels of communication. In order to be able to advise management, without fear or favor, when occasion demands, he should be given adequate status and the right of access to the top. The good P.R. man is not just another apostle of advertising, but a mixture of campaigner and watchdog in his own right.

In supplying information to the press, it is essential to look at the news release from the editor's point of view. To check this, the following questions should be asked.

(a) Is there real news value, a good story, or an unusual slant likely to interest the public reading the paper or papers concerned?

(b) Is the news release written in the form that would make it easy to accept for publication, that is to say, not too long and in the form it would most likely appear after editing?

(c) Has the ground been prepared in advance, where possible, by personal contact? This presupposes that the P.R.O. has, by background or cultivation, the right kind of entrée to the press or other media concerned.

Building up prestige may not be just a matter of wooing the customer. A great deal of P.R. may indeed be directed towards influencing those business leaders of the community to whom consumers, in any given context, naturally turn for advice and recommendations.

Editors should not, of course, be deluged with news releases, lest they grow weary with the enterprise concerned and indifferent to its virtues.

Invitations to the press and other news agencies to attend opening ceremonies, exhibitions, annual general meetings, press conferences and similar occasions at which journalists can ask questions, preferably over cocktails or lunch, are all within the province of P.R. enterprise.

Clearly, then, a P.R.O. plays an important part in helping management select and develop policies and courses of action which will be compatible with good public relations. His job is to highlight corporate strengths and play down any weaknesses; management's job is to develop those strengths and overcome the weaknesses.

In dealing with in-person, mail, or telephone inquiries, complaints and correspondence, at any level in an organization, each staff member concerned becomes effectively a P.R.O. As far as the general public is concerned, this may be their only contact; they will judge the firm accordingly.

Advertising Budgets

To achieve quantified sales results, as detailed through corporate planning, it may be necessary to spend considerable sums on all kinds of advertising relevant to the type of business concerned. It might be thought easy to decide how much to allocate for this purpose, usually annually, within the limits of overall finance, but in practice this is often far from being the case. Research into how companies do in fact fix their overall advertising budget usually reveals little more method than setting appropriate objectives with an arbitrary formula, trial and error, previous figures adjusted, or pure guesswork as to the amount that should be spent over any given period. One of the problems of advertising is that almost any administrator—company president or other top executive—tends to consider himself an expert on the subject. Another problem is that a great deal of advertising must necessarily be wasted. Although, for example, an advertisement may be placed in the kind of newspaper likely to attract the class of readership relevant to the product or service, only a proportion of those readers, at any point of time, will actually be interested. And many of those will miss seeing the advertisement altogether.

In assessing the cost of advertisements as between different newspapers, allowance must be made for audited circulation figures. Actual readership is normally higher than the number of papers sold.

Efforts made to seek a scientific formula, to quantify advertising expenditure with optimum impact in mind, have seldom been more than partly successful. By relating annual appropriation amounts to a percentage of actual sales, profits, or other criterion, either historically or as planned for in the year ahead, such a percentage inevitably becomes an arbitrary choice in the light of what can be afforded. Even after years of adjusting such a percentage, by trial and error in the light of hard-won experience, it may still be too much or too little for the future results planned. There are usually variables and unknowns to be sorted out and uncovered. For example, advertising by competitors can go up and down, thus affecting the situation one way or the other.

In place of an arbitrary formula, management decision tends to revert to the exercise of judgment, perhaps using selected formulas as a first approximation. These can be related in turn to the probability of achieving certain annual sales amounts at given points over a range of selected appropriations, coupled with estimated probability for each alternative.

Using an Agency

Advertising tends to be an emotive subject, but one requiring objectivity as well. To help in this, it is usual to employ the services of a reputable advertising agency. By such a liaison, it is possible to hire a wide creative experience of advertising in all its forms, a technical knowledge of artwork, copywriting, printing, media selection, and of buying time and space. The company's own marketing organization will, it is hoped, supply clearly defined objectives, including the kind of corporate image to be projected, the sales it plans to achieve, the market aimed at, and the positive qualities of its product or service.

Regular meetings are usually held between the principal and agency to discuss and translate policy into practical effect. Whether one side or the other has the greater influence on the final result is a moot point, but certainly both sides have an effective and complementary contribution to make.

An agency may well have reserach and other specialized marketing departments and will certainly be able to give practical advice on how to allocate an advertising appropriation between alternative media, how to run advertising and sales campaigns, set up trade shows and carry out pilot test schemes. It can suggest logotypes and advise on point-of-sale display material, including brochures, catalogs, and marketing literature generally.

Employing an advertising agency need not necessarily be expensive; part of its agency income is received from newspapers, etc. as commission on the amount of advertising space sold on their behalf. The client, of course, will have a bill to meet, if only for artwork, typesetting, layout, and so on. This bill may be on the basis of a fixed annual sum, as a retainer, with other payments for special and technical services rendered; or payments for those services may be charged *ad hoc*, presumably at a higher rate. Some organizations employ the same advertising agency for years, relying on the turnover in creative artists and copywriters to produce fresh ideas; other firms prefer to change their agency from time to time, perhaps to offset possible staleness or even complacency. For obvious reasons, an agency usually will not deal with two or more organizations in active competition with each other in the same line of business.

Forms of Advertising Media

The choice of media is governed by advertising objectives, relevance to the product or service, and the type of customer to be courted. Briefly, the main alternatives are:

(a) Newspapers and Magazines. More than $25 billion are spent each year for advertising in the United States. Our daily and weekly newspapers account for close to one third of this staggering total. The booking of space is usually effected through the advertising agency, which also recommends detailed schedules based on selected newspapers; submits ideas for artwork, copy, layout, and so on; deals with the technical aspects; and handles the media placements. In addition, there are trade journals in which an appeal can be made to dealers and all kinds of magazines, both specialized and general. Incidentally, these additional publications bring the country's total print media bill up to well over $10 billion annually.

(b) Television. Whereas many press appeals are partly intended as part of a long-term or short-term buildup of impressions, television advertising aims at quick results. It is hoped by the firms concerned that brand images built up during the afternoons and evenings will lead to point-of-sale purchases during the days that follow. Hence, much TV advertising relates to household and other ordinary consumer goods available locally. Here again, the coverage can be national or regional, through the appropriate networks. Cost naturally varies with the day of the week, peak or other viewing time, length of the show or commercial, and the number of estimated viewers in the area being covered. Television ranks second to the print media in volume, with some 20 per cent of all advertising expenditures assigned to this medium. By contrast, less than 7 per cent is involved in radio advertising, though the total annual figure of over $1.5 billion is by no means insignificant.

For these media, which together account for the bulk of total expenditures on advertising, it is possible to obtain considerable information about readers and viewers, broken down statistically by income groups, sex, households, buying habits, and the like. As usual, such information suffers from the faults of being history or, at the best, today's situation, not probabilities for effective forecasting. Insofar as such information is made available, however, it tends to minimize waste in selecting where and when to place advertisements.

The whole subject is highly complicated, taking at random such knotty problems as which is the best day to advertise a given product in the newspapers? How big should an advertisement be to attract optimum attention? What is the best position in the paper itself? When is the best TV day and time for a particular good? Should newspaper exposure or TV coverage be spread out evenly over the whole period, or should it be concentrated to attract special attention and then spread thinly until the next concentrated barrage? To what extent should there be indirect, long-term, institutional or image-building advertising as opposed to direct advertising aimed at an immediate sales response? Should there be humor in advertisements or not? And so on *ad nauseam*.

(c) Miscellaneous Media.   Brief mention may be made here of billboards and other bill-posting sites, railroad, subway, and bus advertising, all offering opportunities for a wide range of merchandise with special appeal to the "captive" traveler or passerby.

Then, there are various "on the spot" forms of advertising, such as neon and other exterior signs, window displays, dealers' aids, and catalogs, often provided and subsidized by manufacturers. Manufacturers may also back up their goods with appropriate advertising —newspaper, TV, etc.—aiming to "pull the goods" through retail outlets. "Pull" strategy simply means concentrating the advertising on the consumer and his needs. This creates demand because the customer exerts increased pressure on retailers to supply the advertised goods to satisfy those needs. The opposite is "push" strategy, which means concentrating the advertising and other sales efforts on the retailer. By this means he is urged to stock and display the goods prominently and try to create increased demand by pushing the sales of these goods. Then there are the many uses of "direct mail," including samples, circulars, and handbills sent by mail or distributed from door to door.

Other methods of getting new ideas or products off to a good start, nationally or locally, include shows, conventions, authors signing copies of their latest books, film stars opening new stores, and cocktail parties held to celebrate new factories, offices, or branches.

(d) Sales Promotion. It is a current convention, in dealing with a manufacturer's total sales effort, that advertising and salesmen's salaries and commissions, on the one hand, should be distinguished from the cost of premium promotions and sales incentives, on the other. Obvious examples are a reduced-price offer printed on the package or other container, two for the price of one, giveaways, free samples, contests with prizes, gift vouchers, coupons, and trading stamps. The success of these ventures usually depends on their ingenuity, skill in presentation, and psychological appeal to the average purchaser. Somewhat similar are the "attractions" of cut-rate stores, credit terms and accounts, check cashing, acceptance of credit cards, and special customer facilities such as the availability of expert technical advice (advisory customer service) and reliable after-sales service.

There is no royal road to obtaining optimum value from given advertising expenditures, nor is it easy to measure results achieved. Various techniques are used such as coded coupons included in newspaper advertisements, prepaid inquiry cards with catalogs, and special addresses or telephone numbers to which potential customers are invited to make immediate personal requests for further information. But these are not scientific tools, only broad indicators. Advertising effect cannot be isolated from collective marketing efforts, including P.R. and the activities of the personal sales force. What can be assessed is the achievement, or otherwise, of the short- and long-term targets set for sales; in the light of such results, appropriate adjustments can follow.

Organizing the Sales Force

The personal-approach or "direct" salesmen, who make calls to stimulate sales and collect orders, are the front-line troops; their motivation, equated with self-interest, and field organization are well worth careful study. Assuming that the company has the right kind of reputation, and that the product or service is satisfactory, there still remains the sales-promotion problem of hiring, training, and launching a sales force with the right collective personality and ability.

It is too easy to generalize that it takes an extrovert to be a successful salesman; a salesman should, however, be well liked by local retailers, have the right temperament and enthusiasm, perhaps unaffected by failure and disappointment, and be well versed in the art and techniques of effective salesmanship. In point of fact, a good listener feeling his way sensitively through his sales interviews, with the ability to bring out the vital sales points convincingly at the end, is at least as likely to succeed as the fictional traveling salesman with his forced good humor and fund of "blue" jokes.

Salesmen vary from what are known as "missionary salesmen" who spread the gospel of a particular brand or commodity and are salesmen exclusively to engineering specialists who add technical knowledge and skill to salesmanship when dealing with industrial products. In the latter instance, a policy choice has to be made between using a first-class salesman who has a smattering of technical know-how or a first-class engineering expert who can turn his hand to selling. In practice, this may call for a joint effort: the salesman-cum-technician softening up the customers by "hard sell," and the engineer-cum-salesman cementing the transaction with his top-level specialized ability and knowledge.

The art of salesmanship, covering consumer or industrial goods, cannot be dealt with in a few sentences, for it is a vast amalgam of basic psychology, hard-won practical experience, trial and error, and good marketing enterprise. A few comments can be made, however, on the organizing of a sales force, with special reference to the best way of directing and using the services of those responsible for face-to-face personal selling.

Before making calls, for instance, it is essential for salesmen to find out, and build up card records of, all relevant information about the factories, offices, or shops, considered to be worth calling upon, to find out (a) who is actually empowered to make decisions with regard to placing orders, (b) when such executives are likely to be available, and (c) how best to interest them. Calls can then be planned in groups to cover the territory systematically and economically, so that every firm can be visited regularly and effectively. Orders accepted must be dealt with promptly; they should also be recorded, with any other helpful sales intelligence, for future reference just before making repeat calls.

The sales manager is normally responsible for selecting and organizing the sales force to achieve maximum performance. Special training, including refresher courses, should be arranged to cover all the marketing aspects, including the strengths and weaknesses (if any) of the product or service that has to be sold. On the principle of "know your enemy," information would be made available concerning the strengths and weaknesses of rival products and services with a "run-down" on the known tactics of competitors. Regular reports by salesmen would maintain up-to-date feedback to management.

Sales conferences held centrally or locally have great value in that they provide a regular opportunity for *(a)* management to restate objectives and fill in the details of new policies, plans, and strategies and *(b)* salesmen to report on, and discuss, market conditions, opportunities, trends, problems, and the like for the information of management and each other. Given effective chairmanship, probably by the marketing director himself, or the sales manager or regional manager as appropriate, sales coordination can be achieved, new ideas sparked off, grievances aired and dealt with, and enthusiasm generally brought back to concert pitch.

Enthusiasm is largely tied up with motivation, which has been shown to be the harnessing of self-interest to company interest. In the case of salesmen, motivation takes into account financial incentive —usually sales commission paid on top of basic salary. In any given set of circumstances, the proportion of basic salary, representing security, to expected commission, constituting incentive, needs careful consideration and decision. Too much security may mean blunted effort; too much incentive may result in over-aggressive tactics. Motivation also relates to maintaining the interest and enthusiasm of salesmen over difficult periods or when dealing with difficult areas, and here the sales manager has a very human task to perform. On occasion, too, he may arrange for new men to be attached to experienced salesmen, so that they can see success in action and thereby increase their own confidence.

PROBLEMS OF DISTRIBUTION

As the costs of distribution, from production line to customers, can range from 10 to 30 per cent of sales, any saving here, usually identified with storage and transportation, tends to be appreciable.

Total Distribution Cost

Because they are so closely related, the costs of storage and transportation should be taken and studied together. This concept of "total distribution cost" is analogous to "total commuter cost" as related to deciding where to live: proportionate to the distance from a large city center, housing gets progressively cheaper but fares become progressively dearer. The two elements must therefore be looked at together and dealt with as a whole.

Reckoning the total distribution cost calls for accurate and complete accounting. For example, the cost of occupying the premises owned by a company should take account of the quantified effects of inflation. Due allowance, too, should be made for inventory financing, with a proper rate of interest being charged on the value of inventory held, the "proper" rate being a matter for board decision in the light of events.

The marketing concept takes account of *total* distribution costs so that it might pay to increase storage costs by $x if transport costs could thereby be reduced by at least $x, preferably $x + y. This means in practice taking a hard look at the map and strategically juggling the locations of factories and warehouses with transportation facilities to achieve optimum economies.

Logistics and Transportation

There are many alternative features to be taken into account when trying to achieve a strategic, and economic, deployment of factories and warehouses. This relates to total distribution cost with special reference to transportation, warehousing, stock inventory, and packaging. Facilities location has to take into account raw-material sources; the weight and bulk of raw materials as against that of the finished product; the type of product, especially whether perishable or not; the kind of service required, particularly the importance or otherwise of being near the markets to be served; relative costs of production, labor, warehousing inventory and delivery; and the availability of suitable labor and housing for any workers to be imported from other areas.

To obtain the best "mix" is no easy task, but the alternatives can be shuffled up and dealt with as a mathematical problem, falling within the scope of operations research. Among the objectives sought should be maximum managerial control and minimum service costs. Taking all the particular circumstances into account, operations research would determine whether factories and/or warehouses should be centralized or decentralized.

Facility location from a transportation point of view must keep in mind not only present facilities but all future trends such as new airfields, changing port facilities, sea-land routes, new highways and so on.

The main purpose of having warehouses lies in the saving that comes from "trunking," that is to say sending the goods long distance in bulk and having them broken down at the warehouses on arrival.

Warehouse managers should act as local executives, be responsible and accountable, and encouraged to use their own initiative. They should be given, and agree to, clear-cut objectives and have their delivery performances budgeted and checked, with the emphasis on keeping their costs to a minimum.

Ideally, production, transportation, and storage location should be linked together by computer to achieve optimum results in action. "Action" is the operative word, for wherever the products are at rest, that is to say as stock, they are costing money; it is essential therefore to keep them continually on the move.

As with advertising, most directors and other top transportation executives consider themselves to be experts in transportation policy, particularly with regard to truck specialization and rail. Transportation management, however, is a specialization in its own right. Among the policies to be settled are whether to use public carriers or to own, or lease, a company fleet of vehicles, or perhaps a mixture of both, depending to some extent on the operations research solution to the main problem above. This would justify a full-scale traffic analysis, with special reference to the true cost of each alternative linked with performance. The transportation industry has many facilities to offer, and these should be fully investigated in the light of the particular type of service required.

Having decided in favor of company transportation, it is important to ensure efficient routing and maximum use of vehicles and vehicle space: trucks in the garage or empty, wholly or partly, for instance on a return journey, can become a costly proposition. In a large firm such policy matters would be resolved in practice through a transportation manager, who would probably be responsible also for vehicle maintenance and repairs.

Distribution Channels

So far, we have studied the firm's distribution route—factory, depot, customer—noting the distribution costs involved in warehousing, transportation, advertising, salesmen, and final delivery either direct or through dealers. Costs of selling increase with the distance from customers, hence the choice between extensive coverage of the whole market area or intensive concentration on selected locations. Decentralized factories, and warehouses supporting local groups of dealers, ensure more effective regional coverage by localizing transportation and customer service generally.

The channels of distribution normally extend from the manufacturer who sells to wholesalers, either direct or through agents, and thence to retailers, each category specializing in a particular market service. The wholesalers can be bypassed, as a matter of policy, by the manufacturer selling direct to retailers; so can the retailers by selling direct to consumers. These policy decisions depend on the kind of business, the product, and the marketing strategy considered to be the most likely to ensure success. At each point in the chain there are extra costs to be balanced against the return expected, these costs making their impact on the final price. There is usually a percentage "markup," i.e., trade discount, which must not be confused with the credit discount offered for the quick settlement of bills. There may also be a quantity discount for bulk purchases. To ensure continuing sources of raw materials, and perhaps to control costs, it is not unusual for producers to acquire those sources by initiating a takeover, thereby integrating backwards. Similarly, on the wholesale and retail side, it may be good policy, strategy, or expediency to acquire such outlets, thereby integrating forwards. In any given set of circumstances, the pros and cons must be carefully weighed up before arriving at a definite decision.

Apart from acquisition, a manufacturer has the alternative of starting his own retail shops instead of, or in addition to, other outlets.

In this book, it is only possible to make brief mention of retail outlets, each of which justifies a chapter on its own. The field of department stores, chain stores, independents, supermarkets, cooperatives, and mail-order houses is, however, comprehensively covered in several of the texts listed at the conclusion of this chapter. Finally, the whole market structure must aim to provide maximum service to consumers at minimum cost. Modern organizational techniques should ensure taking the best distribution route to customers; shortcuts through the channels of distribution will be taken whenever they appear to be worthwhile. Customers are not necessarily consumers, but can be intermediaries in the chain to the final user, whether domestic or industrial. On a cost basis, it may be better to have a few large customers, unless there is a chance of being held for ransom by them, than many small customers, bearing in mind the expense of keeping records and accounts and of salesmen and drivers making many insignificant calls instead of a worthwhile few.

It goes without saying that there is a continuous need to keep up with competitors and to find out what and how they are doing in the channels of distribution. A simple example in the supermarket field suggests that a producer must make sure that his competitors are not taking over the most valuable shelf space in the shop, enjoying the advantage of having the right position for a quick turnover and thereby edging out his own goods. If he discovers that his own goods are being demoted to less prominent shelf space, he must find out why this has happened and take action accordingly. Other characteristics in the same field are

(a) The voluntary collective marketing system organized to gain the advantages of bulk purchases and bulk distribution;

(b) The wholesale cash-and-carry warehouses used by independent retailers;

(c) The "private label" goods brought in by the supermarkets and tending to take the place of established competitive brand leaders and even diluting brand "loyalty" in the process.

PLANNING FOR EXPORTS

For years now, the United States has been struggling to achieve a more favorable balance-of-payments situation in international trade.

Hence, it is essential to make reference here to exporting, the overseas approach to marketing, with its inherent problems and risks.

Overseas Information Facilities

There is no lack of general information on exporting, as evidenced by the various publications and sundry services currently available through the facilities of the U.S. Department of Commerce (most notably the Bureau of International Commerce and the Office of Field Services). Among other facts, it is possible to obtain:

(a) A general handbook on the field of exporting.

(b) Details of likely markets.

(c) Information on setting up business overseas in many different countries.

(d) Information on foreign tariffs, import regulations, and preparation of shipments.

(e) Help in finding agents and in making other trade contacts.

(f) Credit information on foreign countries.

(g) Statistics as to the kinds of goods purchased by foreign markets.

(h) Assistance in foreign trade fairs.

(i) Current developments in international trade.

Leading banks also provide customers with advice covering specific market information, finance, foreign currency and exchange control, credit inquiry reports on overseas firms, recommendations as to finding agents, and help with other export problems of all kinds.

Export Strategy and Structure

Success in overseas markets requires identifying and taking full advantage of opportunities available. This means continually finding new markets or market segments to exploit, a deep analysis of the situation in all its aspects, a competent home office organization for export, with first-class marketing services, including after-sales service, to back up a well-trained and motivated local sales force. This should result, or must be made to result, in competitive prices, reliable quality and effective delivery dates.

A company should be strongly motivated to export and have clearly defined objectives, with policies geared to devoting sufficient resources, long-term, to ensure the right kind of impact. Experience suggests that the best guarantee of high-level profits comes from understanding and concentrating on one market, or a few markets at the most, and building up a more extensive policy from there. This enables the exporter to increase his sales progressively, at the same time gaining maximum profits. He must, however, exhibit superior skills in marketing. In a period following devaluation he should make every effort to capitalize on opportunity while exchange rates are in his country's favor.

With regard to training in exporting, it is essential to include a full understanding of each country covered by the firm concerned, with the usual breakdown into political, institutional, economic, technological, and social aspects. It is essential, too, to acquire a detailed knowledge of foreign habits and customs, which means looking at the product from the consumer's point of view and wooing the overseas customer in his own language. One of the greatest obstacles to success in exporting is often bad overseas communication. This can be so, even when there is a "common" language, as between the United States and Great Britain, where the best advice, both ways, is to regard each other's country as being inherently foreign and not just an extension of one's own.

The use of export agents is common practice, but success depends on the right selection and control of agents. As indicated above, there are many ways of obtaining advice on how to find the right agent, which should be narrowed down to a short list, to be cemented by personal interview on the spot. The agent will work on commission, will probably take little responsibility for the product or for customers' credit, but he will nevertheless be in a key position to build up a market profitably. The exporter should control the agent with a loose rein, occasionally making a visit to meet his larger customers and reassess the relationship. Good communication, both ways, is an essential ingredient coupled with mutual trust.

Joint ventures are another way of exporting. To be successful these need to be on a flexible basis, geared to different overseas territories and partners, making sure that both partners have clear objectives, are well motivated, and jointly have a reasonable stake in the future of the business.

In these and other ventures into exporting there are clearly risks, but with all the export services, public and private, available to industry it should be possible to minimize these risks. In support are the services of the Export-Import Bank of the United States (Eximbank), which offers various financing plans for exporters, and the Foreign Credit Insurance Association at the World Trade Center in New York City.

Summary

1. Emphasis on Marketing
  a. It is important that the firm should be "marketing oriented."
  b. Marketing embraces selling.
  c. Constituent parts are known as the "marketing mix."
  d. The type of business should be expressed in broad terms.
  e. The right marketing objectives and/or policies then follow.
  f. "Opportunity cost" relates to alternative uses of scarce resources.
  g. Organization may be by function, product, brand, or territory.

2. Starting with the Customer
  a. The customer and his needs are identified by market research.
  b. Statistical methods used include sampling techniques.
  c. The customer may not be the final consumer.
  d. The total market needs to be investigated, and the appropriate market segment(s) determined.
  e. The market research program should be continuous.

3. Selecting the Product or Service
  a. A decision has to be made between specialization and diversification.

    b. If there are too many items, the variety-reduction technique can be used.

    c. Product innovation maintains momentum.

    d. It does not always pay to be first in the field.

    e. An optimum marketing effort determines success.

4. *Life-cycle Concept*

    a. All products have life-cycles of varying lengths.

    b. The classic pattern is innovation, growth, maturity, saturation, and decline.

    c. It is desirable to have several products, each at a different stage in its life-cycle.

    d. Built-in obsolescence makes way for innovation.

5. *Significance of Price*

    a. The interplay of supply and demand should be studied at the margin.

    b. Traditional marginal theory provides a first approach to pricing policy.

    c. Pricing ranges in practice from "cost-plus" to "what the traffic will bear."

    d. Psychological aspects need to be taken fully into account.

    e. Price policy changes by competitors should be monitored.

    f. The consumer must be protected.

6. *Advertising and Promotion*

    a. Corporate image may be reflected in the company logo.

    b. Public relations include liaison with the press.

    c. Advertising budgets are often based on arbitrary formulas, but judgment must be exercised as well.

    d. Advertising agencies should be employed to handle the media selected.

    e. The choice of media tends to be complicated.

    f. Sales promotion helps advertising.

    g. There is no easy way to judge the effectiveness of any given advertising expenditure.

7. *Sales Force and Salesmanship*

    a. Direct (personal approach) salesmen are the front-line troops.

    b. These vary from missionary salesmen to technical experts.

    c. A good salesman can be either extrovert or introvert.

    d. The sales force must have effective organization and records.

e. Conferences, reports, etc., motivate and produce feedback.

8. Problems of Distribution

a. Total distribution cost takes account of transportation, warehousing, stock inventory, and packaging.

b. A logistics approach is essential.

c. Distribution channels extend from manufacturer to final consumer.

9. Planning for Exports

a. Overseas information facilities help identify opportunities and determine strategy.

b. The selection and control of export agents is very important.

c. Use should be made of export services to minimize risks.

Suggested Further Reading

BOWERSOX, D.J. *Logistical Management.* New York: Macmillan, 1974.

DAVIDSON, W.R.,ET AL.*Retailing Management.* 4th ed. New York: Ronald Press, 1975.

DRUCKER, P.F. *Managing for Results.* New York: Harper & Row, 1964.

DUNCAN, D.J., ET AL. *Modern Retailing Management: Basic Concepts and Practices.* 8th ed. Homewood, Ill.: Irwin, 1972.

HILL, S.R. *The Distributive System.* New York: Pergamon, 1966.

HOWARD, J.A. *Marketing Management: Operating, Strategic, and Administrative.* 3d ed. Homewood, Ill.: Irwin, 1973.

KOTLER, P. *Marketing for Nonprofit Organizations.* Englewood Cliffs, N.J.: Prentice-Hall, 1975.

KOTLER, P. *Marketing Management: Analysis, Planning, and Control.* 2d ed. Englewood Cliffs, N.J.: Prentice-Hall, 1972.

McCARTHY, E.J. *Basic Marketing: A Managerial Approach.* 5th ed. Homewood, Ill.: Irwin, 1975.

McIVER, C. *Marketing for Managers: The Practical Man's Guide to a Complex Subject.* New York: Longman, 1973.

REDINBAUGH, L.D. *Retailing Management: A Planning Approach.* New York: McGraw-Hill, 1976.

SMYKAY, E.W. *Physical Distribution Management.* 3d ed. New York: Macmillan, 1973.

WALTERS, C.G. *Marketing Channels.* New York: Ronald Press, 1974.

WEBSTER, F.E., JR. *Marketing for Managers.* New York: Harper & Row, 1974.

TEN

Production Policies

In the previous chapter, emphasis was given to marketing, which must still be seen as part of overall corporate planning, which embodies all main functions, including production, now to be examined in its turn.

While accepting the concept of being "marketing oriented" rather than "production oriented," it would be fatal not to have full regard for the factory side. It is no good organizing sales that cannot be met. Marketing should be kept in step with low-cost, long-machine-run production, hence the tendency towards reasonable specialization rather than widespread diversification. In the last analysis, it is a question of achieving a proper balance between too much marketing, on the one hand, and too much production, on the other.

PROCESSES AND TECHNOLOGICAL CHOICE

The type of manufacturing process to be employed depends initially on the kind of product; feasibility may leave little or no choice. Once there is a choice, however, then policy decisions have to be made. The second relevant factor is the quantity required of that kind of product. This type of choice does not relate solely to manufacturing firms but applies equally to other kinds of organizations where alternatives exist as to how best to produce a particular service or services.

Manufacturing Alternatives

Basically, the main factory choice is between job, batch, and flow—terms which describe themselves adequately.

Job production is carried out specifically at the request of a customer, possibly in subcontract work, and the finished order is usually delivered direct to him, without the necessity of building up inventory. This job-lot process needs *(a)* setting up for that purpose only, *(b)* special labor skills, and *(c)* uneconomic machine runs. It needs flexibility to cope with frequent change.

It is often possible to overcome the manufacturing problems of small job lots, allied to batch production, by grouping them with other lots which, although apparently different, basically need similar productive resources. Known as "group technology," this system replaces the normal functional plant layout with group layout, in which event the parts to be produced are divided into families of comparable type, each family being produced on its own group of machines. Fundamentally, this means product specialization instead of process specialization. The advantages are significant, including increased capacity and output, lower costs, and reduced capital investment in machinery and stock. Such production can, therefore, compete on more or less equal terms with mass production.

Batch production is for longer runs, usually of standard products, either to meet orders received from customers or to build up stocks in anticipation of orders. Usually, much larger quantities are involved than under jobbing, but it does not necessarily follow that there can be indefinite runs. A batch, for instance, can still be a special order, but of a more economic size. In general terms, this process is a halfway stage to flow production.

Flow-line or mass production is continuous production, flowing from one operation to the next, where labor and plant can be used to optimum capacity. Machinery is designed and introduced to save manpower but, once installed, it must be kept in continuous production; otherwise, expensive capital equipment becomes a drain on financial resources. Furthermore, it will tend to become obsolete before it has had its useful life. That is why, apart from technical needs such as keeping furnaces or boilers going, there are such cost-spreading advantages in shiftwork, using machinery and other capital equipment virtually nonstop. This can be true also of office machinery, particularly with regard to the expensive computer equipment used in electronic data processing.

Originally, industry was entirely "labor intensive" with workmen in abundance using hand tools, but today the trend is increasingly towards being "capital intensive" with more and more machines tending to replace labor. Automation may well be the final answer, cutting labor to an absolute minimum, but so far the revolutionary high hopes for complete automation have been slow in coming to fruition. Theoretically, it is a standard exercise to combine amounts of capital and labor in varying proportions and to relate them to the total output for each combination. It is then possible to demonstrate, with varying prices of capital per unit and of labor per unit, the optimum combination and total output giving minimum average cost.

Apart from costing aspects, shortages or potential shortages of manpower in themselves imply that an industry or firm is becoming more capital intensive. This is so, too, in commercial institutions, where more mechanization, including electronic data processing, may well prove to be the only workable key to a future faced with full employment.

Automation

Factories in science fiction are visualized as operating without any labor at all, but present logic and conservatism suggest that, for the time being at least, this is not too realistic. Automation, for example, requires large-scale manufacturing centers, yet there is a strong tendency today towards product centers instead. In practice, automation has been hard to introduce and even harder to justify commercially. Nevertheless, properly conceived automation can increase productivity considerably. Most systems of automation so far have confined themselves to parts of factories only; rarely are there complete robot processes covering the whole of production.

Apart from a lack of sufficiently long production runs, which would perhaps be secured by large-scale mergers involving comparable products, there are managerial problems of decision. In order to install full automation, given an obvious case where this technique could be vital, management would need to face up to a major organizational upheaval that, perhaps not being technically minded, it would rather defer. Another reason is the traditional fear of unemployment or greater leisure for workers, which they may or may not want. Automation to deal with a situation of potential manpower shortage is logical and necessary, but there may be visions of an ultimate situation where machines replace too much labor. Whatever the arguments, it is an undisputable fact that automation has succeeded much better in the United States, the land of mass production, than elsewhere in the world.

Control of industrial processes by computer is such a complex issue that there is a tendency to leave everything, basically selection and installation, to engineers and data-processing experts. This can be fatal, for top management, with its wider experience of process and product, must be involved in policy decisions right from the start. The specialists would then back them as a team, keeping their expertise in proper perspective.

Automation in practice is usually based on the computer control of some mechanical operation such as boring, drilling, milling, or turning, and then directing the product on to the next operation —and so on, in sequence, throughout the whole process. This is generally done by means of digitally controlled (fully computerized) machine tools. Instructions are fed into the machine tools as a code of digits on paper or magnetic tape. Apart from large, expensive digital control systems, the various adaptations of automation include comparatively simple cheap attachments to existing machines, using hydraulic, pneumatic, or electrical power.

Whether to automate or not requires a major policy decision based on properly quantified long- and short-term objectives; a feasibility study of production requirements; selection of the right system; and a thorough appreciation of the structural, personnel, and other constraints that have to be taken fully into account.

Pros and Cons of Automation

Among the arguments put up for automation are that *(a)* savings will accrue from having continuous production runs with high efficiency in the use of machine tools, based on two or three shifts; *(b)* no separate jigs or tools would be needed; *(c)* setting up would be quicker; *(d)* consistent quality would minimize waste; *(e)* the need for inspection would be less; and *(f)* manpower would, of course, be reduced. Some of the arguments against automation have been mentioned already; in addition, there are *(a)* the heavy capital cost of the equipment itself; *(b)* the training of key personnel in programming, planning, and preparing the tapes or other techniques; and *(c)* possible labor problems, including resistance to change and to having even more de-skilling of work. Incidentally, there are experiments at hand to "improve the quality of working life" by replacing the monotonous assembly line with responsible group-assembly teams.

It goes without saying that a wrong decision on an issue of this kind, including electronic data processing in commercial use, could prove extremely costly. A right decision, on the other hand, could materially add to profits. Most automation systems take account of variables—in raw materials, processes, and products—substituting accurate measurement and control for less scientific methods. This must, inevitably, lead to better quality and reliability.

Automation or not, management should always be conversant with the latest improvements in plant and machinery, from the simplest operating aid to highly sophisticated mechanization. There are many ways in which this can be achieved, such as exhibitions, presentations, demonstrations, newspaper and magazine supplements, trade journals, catalogs, and visits from industrial salesmen. It is another matter, however, as to how frequently existing plant and machinery should be changed. The financial implications are discussed in Chapter Eleven, but there are, in addition, upheavals likely to stop or slow down production, problems of training, knowing when to change and whether the next technological breakthrough is a long way off or just around the corner.

In practice, therefore, it may pay to continue with machinery not quite up to date (to some extent all equipment tends to be obsolete even when first installed, as new ideas may already be on the drawing board), provided that it is good enough within the constraints of quantity output, cost, and reliability. Wear and tear may result in inaccuracy beyond acceptable tolerances, but this indicates a replacement of parts rather than the installation of an entirely new system. As usual, there are vital policy matters to be considered by management.

Nevertheless, it is essential to exploit all opportunities such as a move to another factory site, a new factory to match growth, or extensions to an existing plant. Additional machinery should be reasonably compatible with existing machinery unless the two systems can be worked in parallel without creating problems or adding to the cost of production. It is often argued that obsolete equipment superseded by new equipment should be scrapped, but the old plant may still serve a useful purpose in certain circumstances by being available to meet peak production requirements. Again, this is a matter of judgment, balancing the advantage of availability at such times against the waste of underemployment in normal times.

Throughout managerial policy making there must be constant and consistent attempts to capitalize on the virtues of simplification and standardization. For it is an unfortunate fact of life in almost every sphere that everything man touches tends to become more and more complicated. Efficiency, however, demands that complexity and overelaboration should be cut through and reduced systematically to essentials. A pertinent example is the confusion caused by having too many different automation systems and a variety of computer languages, developed by different manufacturers to bedevil industry.

All too often there is a vested interest in maintaining complexity, if only on the theory that most people tend to respect "learned" treatises or systems that they find hard to understand. They are, perhaps, "blinded by science." In practice, systems may start in a simple way, but haphazard additions are made to deal with each new feature or stage of growth until the eventual result is a costly confusion. The remedy, not always easy to achieve, is to throw everything into the melting-pot and straighten out the situation from first principles. It is here that industrial consultants can make a valuable contribution justifying their fees. This reorganization is developed when we come to consider work study and its various forms later in this chapter.

Size and Location of Plants

As indicated previously, manufacturing units are not necessarily planned to be as large as possible. Within the concept of mass production, this was a commonly held point of view, but today other considerations tend to be taken into account as well. There may be good reasons, for instance, for breaking down production into a number of separate operating units corresponding to the number of separate products.

If, in fact, large-scale mass production is essential, with or without automation, then the factory will be centralized up to the size where optimum manufacturing results are being achieved. Otherwise, there will tend to be decentralization of production to a given number of factories regionally situated. To some extent, the decision reached will be linked with the distribution network. Exact locations will take into account shipping costs and the distribution of the market, current or potential, as well as the availability of suitable manpower.

Each case must be decided on its merits. The key factor technologically is to have each of the manufacturing units working at its optimum size. If separate location is of academic interest only, then there could be a number of factories all on the same site but each at or near its individual optimum.

The same considerations apply to the production of a service, as in the case of a commercial or financial institution. To start with, there are the size and location of its home office; this may or may not be thought of as necessarily having to be in or near New York, or another large city, for prestige reasons, proximity to the money market, and large-scale availability of staff. Given full centralization, with or without computer facilities, the home office could be a large expensive building. The alternative, with a somewhat smaller home office, would have to be regional or area offices on a basis of decentralization. Each regional office would have a computer or terminal, if appropriate to the organization, and other management services insofar as they could reasonably be devolved from the home office without taking away the allocation of resources and final control.

From the marketing or service angle, a strategic network of branches would be built up with varying mandatory and other powers to match local requirements. These branches would be directly accountable to the home office, under a centralized plan, but attached to regional or area offices under decentralization.

This introduces the basic managerial policy problem of determining how far decentralization of production of goods or services should be carried in practice. The usual choice, as above, is between almost complete autonomy with all services under local control, and partial autonomy with access to central management services as and when required. There is no right answer, as both alternatives can be made to work, but the policy implications must still be faced one way or the other.

Furthermore, circumstances change as, for example, in financial institutions with regard to customers' bank accounts. Originally, all such accounts would have been kept centrally as a matter of convenience and control. Then, with growth and the bulk pressures of work on the central organization, these accounts may have been decentralized to the branches. There would have been the added advantage of being able to give better branch service by having customers' accounts under local control. The next, and current, stage could have been to withdraw local accounting facilities and recentralize them to take advantage of bulk computer production facilities. The problem of a reduced local service could then be considered as a problem of communication, of how to get speedy feedback to branches from the central computer.

Relocating the company out of a major metropolitan area, for example, would make it difficult (if not impossible) for most of the existing personnel to travel the distances required, even if the new building was only just outside the city. The final choice must, therefore, mean the voluntary transfer of key and other personnel, given acceptable incentives such as company housing and/or monetary help with relocation expenses. The remaining personnel required would be recruited in the new location. This, in turn, produces problems of training.

Organization for Production

The key figure on the production side, under the president or general manager, would normally be the production director or production manager. Depending on the size of his empire, he would have an organization including all or some of the following broad functions:

(a) Research and development.
(b) Production planning.

(c) Purchasing.

(d) Stock.

(e) Manufacturing.

(f) Maintenance.

(g) Inspection.

The detailed organization would be determined by policy considerations, type of product, and type of production. Managerial responsibility for maintaining productive efficiency can be emphasized by considering the following analysis of typical everyday problems in industry. The phrases in parentheses indicate possible techniques for control as described in this and other chapters.

(a) Too many different kinds of products *(product line management)*.

(b) Too wide a range of component parts, etc. *(simplification and standardization)*.

(c) Shortages in materials through mistakes in ordering, poor stock records, or wrong anticipation of requirements *(purchasing and stock control; production planning and control)*.

(d) Out-of-date and/or badly serviced plant, machinery, and supporting equipment; mechanical breakdowns *(automation, etc.; planned maintenance)*.

(e) Production bottlenecks *(balancing the flow lines)*.

(f) Waste of material and rejects of finished products *(quality control; waste control)*.

(g) Inefficient factory layout, routing, and work methods *(work study)*.

(h) Cost of production too high *(cost reduction methods and control)*.

Good organization for production is the first step towards maintaining effective control, which must be fully integrated by top management with all other functions in a properly balanced administration. In this administration, production must be given its fair share of importance and attention.

RESEARCH AND DEVELOPMENT

For convenience, research and development, or R. & D. as it is usually called, is included here with production; it could be argued, however, that a stronger link exists with marketing. Despite being technologically oriented, there must clearly be practical regard for commercial potential, profits being the end product. Research for its own sake is not enough.

It is characteristic for scientists to research and invent, yet some commercially minded countries have gone further, developing and marketing the results and, in the process, enjoying the profits. Foremost among them, perhaps, is the United States with concepts on the domestic front such as the "industrial campus" where university and commerce combine to succeed and, more generally, a quick ability to exploit other countries' innovations successfully.

The above does not imply that pure research is necessarily wasteful, simply that it must be properly applied. Whether or not pure research, sometimes called "basic" research, should be left to the universities entirely or dealt with by an in-company R. & D. unit as well is largely a matter of corporate policy and organization. The real need is for a harnessing of all such knowledge to coordinated productive ends.

Industry and the Scientist

Unstructured research provides considerable scope for individual initiative. The right climate of work may well be one where self-discipline is allowed rather than imposed discipline, for the successful scientist is often a nonconformist who must be given reasonable responsibility and latitude to enable his best work to emerge. Yet, research is costly, and the true researcher, given complete freedom from control, may never produce a viable proposition but only new areas of knowledge of purely academic value.

Hence, there must be a rigorous watch on progress, a regular weeding-out of projects, and continuous emphasis on the need for profitability. Organization, in terms of financial control, must not be allowed to become too loose. This, basically, is the job of top management, whereby all parts of the business must be effectively integrated to achieve the corporate objectives.

In particular, R. & D. should be geared to profit forecasts, which means not only applied research but potential commercial development as well. This is a difficult area, however, for forecasting, as spectacular "breakthroughs" can emerge unexpectedly, sometimes as "spin-offs" from main research, whereas many hard-worked projects may consistently fail to mature. A foolproof project evaluator to help with those forecasts would be of great assistance, if such could be found.

What has to be understood, too, is that (lead time permitting) any major breakthrough could change the nature of a business almost overnight. This, of course, has long been so, for that is the very nature of invention; the lesson still to be learned is how to recognize, and expedite, such changes without undue delay.

With the research itself, however, time is a problem equated with cost; the trick is to know (a) when to continue a project, and for how long, with a reasonable hope of achievement and (b) when to stop a project and avoid throwing good money after bad. In point of fact, much work is being done in this field, with some success in sorting out reasonable probabilities and eliminating obvious failures.

Looking at the financial implications, there may be occasions when a higher expenditure on R. & D. would yield more than proportionate returns in product and process breakthrough. However, it is not necessarily the total sum that matters but how it is allocated among various projects in hand. To control the scientist is very different from trying to stifle him; he must at all times be given room to breathe and encouraged to grow in stature. Part of the process may be to keep him aware of objectives and be willing to share with management the responsibility of increasing profits. Consistent with this thought is the system sometimes adopted of allowing a proportion of the individual's time to be unaccountable, when a research worker can try out "hobby horse" ideas of his own without reporting back to higher authority.

Given good management, usually translated through an R. & D. manager, the department's activities will start by being an outflow of cash, but eventually it should break even or pay for itself and then show increasing profits in line with expectations.

From the country's point of view, all university and industrial research should be coordinated and encouraged, with full support from government departments and appropriate trade associations. Current experience, however, suggests that a concept of this kind, while theoretically sound, is still some way from being achieved. Apart from vested interests, rivalries, industrial espionage, and possible leaks overseas, there has yet to be a practical official appreciation of the way in which this job could be organized. Properly integrated and directed research, with a pooling of resources, subject to reasonable safeguards, could produce impressive results.

In the meantime, only large organizations can afford full R. & D. with basic as well as applied research. For firms operating in science-based industries, substantial expenditure on R. & D. is clearly vital to continued success. Other firms may appear to have less need for it but, wherever innovation is included on the marketing plan, so R. & D. should be. Finally, various forms of research can be purchased from outside the firm as required for particular purposes.

Incidentally, it is worth noting that research has a valuable part to play in the context of management decision-making, insofar as it can replace subjective judgment with objective measured fact.

ORGANIZING THE CAPACITY

Among the many features that have to be integrated when deciding on required manufacturing capacity, sales forecasting probably comes first. This, however, needs further thought before a viable answer can be translated into actual productive processes. The vital issue is to make optimum use of the manufacturing plant, keeping abreast of change and balancing capacity with sales.

Production Planning and Control

By using the (management information) control loop outlined in Chapter Eight, it is possible to start with the sales forecast figures, then prepare a master production plan to be translated into detailed work orders, route sheets, or schedules. These set out the target loading figures for the guidance of the various production departments and sections. A production planning and control department is normally responsible for carrying out these duties.

The route sheets or schedules, often in the form of charts, highlight actual figures to date as against target figures and so give continuous visual indication of progress or shortfall. In the light of these results, production departments will speed up if necessary and possible, continue on target, or replan in liaison with the sales side, thereby going around the loop again.

The procedure adopted for scheduling must be practical and realistic, after consultation with all concerned. In line with this, it is essential to keep the purchasing, stock, and dispatch departments so fully informed that they can fit into the control pattern effectively. Their records would, in fact, be integrated with other planning and control records, making up the management information system for total control.

Mention was made previously of the use of charts. One of the best known of these is called a Gantt chart, which deals with scheduling as related to time. It should be noted in passing that most scheduling does relate to time, rather than quantity, as this is easier for everyone concerned. For all workers understand what is meant by production being x days behind target, but they may not be anywhere near so clear if told that production is y units of quantity behind. A Gantt chart shows the planned amount, the actual amount achieved week by week, and the actual cumulative amount over successive weeks. From this bar chart, consisting of one or more horizontal progress lines according to the detail of the productive process, it is possible for any worker to see at a glance how the plans are working out in practice.

Although the Gantt chart has rendered valuable service to production facilities for decades, newer approaches to planning and control, especially for more complex projects, are available, including those labeled "network analysis" methods. Methods such as CPA (critical path analysis) or CPM (critical path method) and PERT (program evaluation and review technique) are based on the breaking down of a project into its many components, then representing these components or segments in some fashion along a network of lines. Activities, time, and costs are indicated. These methods are treated more in depth in Chapter Thirteen.

Keeping Production Steady

In most industries, the four main environmental factors—political, economic, social, and technological—conspire together to unsettle production. Common examples are government encouragement or restriction at any given time, cyclical fluctuations, seasonal trends, R. & D. breakthroughs, or changes in fashion or customer habits. Their effect is that production, if simply left to meet requirements as and when they arise, tends to go forward in peaks and troughs—with resultant problems for management.

Should management, for example, plan its production at the level of peak performance? This could mean either continuing to produce at peak load during slack times, hoping to sell the surplus volume produced, or having part of the production capacity lying idle and not earning its keep.

If management decides instead to plan production at a level below peak performance, how then does it meet peak requirements? One answer is to stockpile during slack periods and build up supplies ready for peak needs. Another is to put on extra overtime to meet rush demand; but, of course, the plant may already be running on a shift basis 24 hours a day to maximize the use of machinery. A further solution is to purchase production on a subcontract basis, but it may not be wise to rely on such supplies being available at what could be the same peak for all similar manufacturers.

Charging customers extra at peak times, or offering an incentive price during slack times, may help to even out demand. Whatever is done, it is essential to balance production on the one hand with customer service on the other.

Corporate planning must always take growth into account; assuming the marketing side to be capable of expansion, then the production side must be able to keep pace with it. This means leaving room to expand when buying a factory site, allowing for increased capacity when building a factory, and generally thinking ahead how to add extra facilities economically and efficiently when they are likely to be required. Management must quantify the value of having potential facilities available with the cost of surplus capacity temporarily lying idle. Other important factors to keep in balance are the financial and personnel sides; these will be covered in succeeding chapters.

With standard products it is relatively easy to consider operating at full capacity, but this can be complicated by the introduction of special models. Insofar as the latter may produce extra profit, their inclusion in the product "mix" may be worthwhile; but this must be balanced against the cost of disrupting the manufacturing processes of standard products. In practice, it would pay to keep such disruption below the point where it could adversely affect the overall profit margin.

Balancing the Flow Lines

Emphasis has been given to the importance of factory production operating at optimum capacity, even to the extent of having separate factories on the same site each operating at its own optimum. Taking this a stage lower, it is just as important for each *part* of a productive process also to be at its optimum.

Given a process requiring three types of machines, *A*, *B*, and *C*, this means that the product passing through each of them in turn would tend to cause problems, unless each machine had the same optimum as the others. Assuming different optima at a ratio of 3:2:1 in quantity, this would require, in machine terms, working to a capacity of 6 in order to achieve balanced production. There should, therefore, be two type *A* machines working in parallel, followed by three machines of type *B*, and, finally, six machines of type *C*. Figure 11 illustrates this relationship.

Assuming further that there were only two machines of type *B*, then *B* would clearly constitute a bottleneck holding up the flow of production at this point.

This example is an oversimplification but illustrates the principle involved. In practice, the aim is to plan for as near a balance as possible consistent with overall productive requirements. Maintaining a flow-line balance needs constant attention to take change into account, removing bottlenecks and dealing with any stage going through a phase of under-capacity use.

The same considerations apply to the use of workers in an office. Common to machines and personnel is the theoretical problem of "indivisibility."

Given a situation where the work load had increased to the point where it was just too much for a particular machine or office worker, consideration would then be given to taking on an additional machine

(a) Balanced production

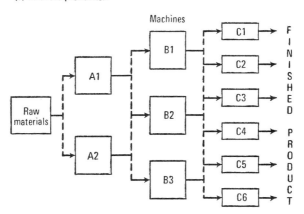

(b) Bottleneck

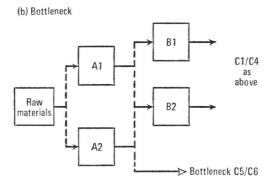

FIGURE 11. Balancing the flow lines

or clerk in order to increase capacity. But what is really wanted, for the time being at any rate, is one-fifth of a machine or clerk. Insofar as other necessary work can be found for the new machine or clerk, such addition to capacity may be economic. Where no additional work is available, there will be wasted capacity likely to prove costly. With personnel, this situation can shake down to the point where everyone is doing that much less work, so that Parkinson's famous law operates and efficiency tends to suffer.

There may be a case for methods study (described later in this chapter) in order to match the work to the original number of clerks; the essential feature is to achieve balance. The snowball effect of allowing staff to be taken on as needed, without inquiry, can be serious. A progressive bank with 1,000 branches, for example, could theoretically require, at a point of time, an extra, say, one-fifth of an accounts clerk for each of the branches. But people are indivisible so that, given lax administration, 1,000 accounts clerks could be taken onto the staff, whereas, in total, the extra work clearly justified no more than 200. It is this kind of argument that advocates of centralization or regionalization advance in support of their claims. In this banking context, the value of a central or regional computer becomes apparent.

Reference to bottlenecks would not be complete without some consideration of the problems involved in dealing with waiting lines or "queues": that is to say, queues of goods and equipment as well as queues of people. This is in fact the same basic problem of achieving a proper balance. For if service facilities are inadequate, waiting time proves expensive in terms of goods and people; if, on the other hand, such facilities are more than adequate, the operating costs may prove to be too high.

A "queuing theory" has been evolved during recent years, using the techniques of operations research, whereby the problem can be analyzed into its constituent parts, often to take account of random application, and a practical solution found. In general, statistical techniques are used, but highly complex problems go beyond the normal confines of queueing theory and are best solved by simulating the actual situation on a computer.

Preventive Maintenance

This is a most important function, usually carried out by a skilled maintenance department under a plant engineer, with the positive policy of preventing deterioration and breakdown well before they arise. This means continuous regular inspection and maintenance, usually when the factory is shut down, for example, overnight (subject to shift work); major jobs are carried out when the factory is closed for a longer period such as on Sundays and during recognized holiday breaks. When kilns, boilers, furnaces, and such are involved it may be an expensive business to let them cool down, so the only feasible approach might be a complete annual overhaul during the main holiday shutdown when all factory workers are required to take their summer vacation.

In carrying out regular maintenance, it may be good policy to replace all working parts before they reach the end of their effective life, meaning before they fail to keep within stated tolerances for the quality of production required.

Records of failures and breakdowns enable information to be built up that can help to prevent similar occurrences in the future. Action taken to deal with such trouble, which may, of course, be the result of operator negligence or accident, means loss of production through machinery being temporarily out of action. Therefore, as indicated above, preventative action, despite the cost of regular maintenance inspection and replacement of parts not completely worn out, must pay handsome dividends. Negligence and accidents come within the province of a safety officer, whose preventative and propaganda duties are outlined in Chapter Twelve.

Finally, it should be noted that here again it may be possible to invoke operations research techniques for working out optimum requirements for complete replacement of machines and renewal of parts, quantitatively based on all the relevant factors indicated above.

PURCHASING AND STOCK CONTROL

The normal purchasing and stock side of a business is sometimes a Cinderella, but it is in fact an important facet of production in its own right. Insofar as it concerns the buying of expensive capital equipment, it is likely also to involve a number of top people with company-wide experience.

Making or Buying

The first policy consideration is to determine how much of the finished product should be made in the factory and how much should be procured from outside. Taking extremes, this can range from making everything, down to the last nut and bolt, to buying everything, thereby confining production to final assembly only. The policy decisions made here will greatly affect the purchasing agent's task and that of the inventory supervisor.

In arriving at policy decisions, it may well be that the right approach would be to purchase components and the like whenever possible. There are several good reasons for this:

(a) It keeps the business less complex and enables top management to concentrate on more vital issues such as making more economic use of capital resources.

(b) It is often cheaper to do so when the supplier is operating at a higher optimum capacity than the firm itself could; also, the supplier could specialize in this component and supply many firms in the same line at reduced cost.

(c) It takes advantage of competitive conditions, as for example soliciting bids, thus keeping down the cost of purchasing from the outside.

(d) It provides flexibility, which means that the firm can buy more or buy less as conditions demand, or stop buying altogether, without the complications which would result from having its own production line for this kind of operation.

Given the following situations there may, however, be equally good reasons for making the components internally:

(a) If it was not possible to procure at the right price or quality.

(b) If the firm could economically produce such components itself at the right optimum capacity.

(c) If there was only one effective supplier which could, whenever it chose, hold the firm for ransom.

(d) If there were special advantages in achieving complete independence.

In comparing costs, as between buying a product from outside or making it inside, a useful concept is to adopt a marginal approach.

The arguments for and against are just as relevant to purchasing or providing services, which follow much the same policy-decision approach as in the case of components. A choice can be made, for instance, between having a computer or using time-sharing terminal facilities; having a printing department for sales literature, office forms, and the like or buying the services instead from a commercial printer; having a lawyer on the staff or using the services of an outside firm of lawyers. with or without the payment of an annual retainer.

As an illustration of special services, an internal printing department can obviously give immediate facilities for printing, say, urgently required advertising literature, whereas an outside printer would require notice of such an order in view of other commitments from equally important customers. Possibly an extra payment could be made, or would be charged, for emergency services. Insofar as an internal printing department may prove to be more expensive than purchasing the same requirements, this extra cost can be considered by the firm as being worthwhile for the advantage of having instant availability. It could, in any case, fill in any spare time by printing office forms and dealing with routine printing requirements. Whatever the situation, it is always good practice to check internal costs, taking the precaution of including *all* relevant aspects in the calculation, with comparable estimates from outside.

A further relevant issue when purchasing outside services is that the suppliers of such services may prove to be more objective in outlook than an internal department and have much wider experience on which to draw when tendering advice or giving some other service.

When an internal services department is becoming an administrative headache, there may be a good reason for spinning it off as a separate company to take its chance in the competitive world outside. In such circumstances, it might be wrong to grant it concessional favors once it has started in business on its own.

Systematic Purchasing

Because materials usually constitute a high proportion of the cost of a product, it is essential to have an efficient purchasing department, generally a centralized function, to keep that cost to a minimum. This implies systematic purchase planning and analysis, with accurate budgeting, and control through being answerable to a cost or budgets department.

In all firms there must be a buying function of some kind, whether full-scale purchases of raw materials, finished parts, machine tools, and so on or just ordinary office stationery. Usually, an acceptable list of regular suppliers is built up over the years, but it is still essential to watch prices, quality, freedom from defects, and delivery dates. The availability of quantity and other discounts, special credit terms, guarantees, and so on, must be taken into account when looking at a price. Complacency, or inertia, can prove expensive; to offset this there should be a systematic search for new suppliers and new products and a periodic review of arrangements made with existing suppliers.

Industrial purchasing may need systematic planning, too, possibly with a team of experts to look into new sources and opportunities. This is particularly so with regard to the purchase of expensive capital equipment, such as a computer, requiring demonstrations by sales engineers, feasibility studies, and expert comparison with alternatives. Ideally, all leading makes in the particular field should be considered if only to ensure that no reasonable opportunity has been overlooked.

Nor is it sufficient just to examine existing equipment already on the market, for a leading manufacturer may be on the verge of a major breakthrough still on the drawing-board. In this event, it may pay to wait—"may" being the operative word, as teething troubles can be frustrating and expensive. This, as always, requires a policy decision to be taken in the light of all known circumstances.

Often an element of reciprocation enters into the placing of buying orders. Purchasing policy may determine that the power to place such business should be used strategically to get orders for the firm's goods in return. Normally this only applies to industrial goods in which another firm would or could be specifically interested.

Overdependence on any one supplier, for example, of raw materials, may prove to be a dangerous policy. Assuming a lack of competition in this field, a good case could be argued for attempting backward integration to secure and control that source of future operations.

The choice of a particular supplier can be made on the grounds of whether he offers reliable delivery, repair and maintenance services, technical advice, and so on. There are, indeed, many factors that can influence choice of supplier, even old ties or the personality of its salesman, all of which should be weighed objectively.

Stocks and Warehousing

It has been demonstrated that sales and production must be kept in step; by inference this coordination also extends to purchasing.

Working backward from planned sales, it can be seen that ideally these are matched by productive capacity exactly kept going by the volume of materials and components purchased. But obviously this is much too simple, hence the buffer states inserted in Figure 12, shown to consist of stocks of materials and the like and stocks of finished

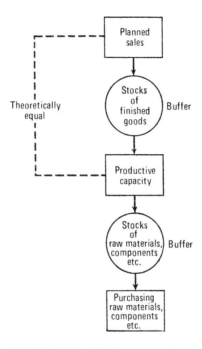

FIGURE 12. Flexibility through stock control

goods. These buffers provide essential flexibility and absorb the effects of change.

It was demonstrated in Chapter Nine that every time goods stop *en route* from production to consumer they cost money; similar arguments apply to dormant materials on the way to production. Put in another way, this means that stocks of all kinds tend to be expensive, hence the need for stock control.

Judging how much raw material, purchased components, parts, and so on to keep in stock needs careful policy decision with special reference to timing. Buying bulk supplies, possibly with instalment deliveries, now rather than later, to take account of inflationary trends, price opportunities, market glut, or seasonal advantages, are some of the reasons for building up stocks while the going happens to be good. Against this policy has to be weighed the cost (reflected in rent, interest charges, etc.) of holding above-average stocks for any length of time. Any stocks no longer relevant to production, possibly because of a change in the product itself, should be disposed of without delay. This means instituting an efficient materials-control system, including effective stock records, graphs, and other visual aids, so that the exact situation at any given time, compared with requirements, can be kept constantly under review. Apart from instantly revealing any stocks running down to minimum safety levels, it also indicates where potential savings can be made by reductions in any stocks trending towards too high a level.

Looking into future needs as a part of inventory-taking and stock control generally, it is usual to apply what is called "exponential smoothing." This high-sounding phrase simply means that unimportant short-term graphical fluctuations are ironed out to leave the significant long-term basic trend clearly discernible. In arriving at this situation, more statistical weighting is given to recent data than to older data, the argument being that the more up-to-date information is likely to have a greater effect on future activities.

Although some goods are made to order, as seen earlier, most products are sold from stock, whether direct from factory stock, from wholesalers' stock, or from retail outlets carrying stock. As would be expected, retailers' stock levels tend to result from established practice based on experience gained. Usually only standard products are carried, any variation required by a particular customer being obtained from the factory direct. Because of the desire to give efficient customer service, there is a natural tendency to keep too much stock, even when levels are watched with a keen eye on the financial control of the cost of investment in inventory. By careful planning, using operations research techniques on a computer, around one-fifth of retail stocks held can usually be proved to have been unnecessary. Indeed, the figure can be much higher than that.

Automated inventory control in department stores and supermarkets, showing the current position in detail at a glance, has much to commend it (to date it is, however, the exception rather than the rule). Such a system highlights, by warning signals, inventories of popular goods running down, slowly moving lines, and lines that are "dead wood." To keep all the stock on the move is clearly the best way to ensure profits even out of narrow margins, if only through the practice of giving away all dormant goods in order to release valuable shopping space for faster-selling lines.

While the sales mix is proceeding in accordance with marketing plans, the building up and control of stocks becomes a matter of routine. But sudden changes in demand for that mix, to meet such aspects as the vagaries of fashion, could result in a sudden build-up of surplus stocks now unwanted. It could also mean a surplus of specialized raw materials or component parts. Management, however, should be aware of such possibilities and, as a matter of policy, be ready at all times to adapt to change. What is pertinent here is to make sure that the purchasing and stock departments are alerted in sufficient time to make effective adjustment.

The location of a warehouse, or depot, was discussed in Chapter Nine. It was shown that an efficient warehouse, in the right position and with proper stock control, could be a vital cost saver in the distribution network. It could be on the same site as, for example, the main factory, for central-control purposes, or decentralized to be near important market areas. Whatever the logistics, the warehouse itself must be properly designed, built, and controlled. In deciding on the number of depots, it should be borne in mind that extra costs will be involved in the stock itself, for there must be duplication for service reasons, so that more stock would be required for *all* depots than would be the case for a single central warehouse.

Having chosen a site, the next stage is to plan the building; experience here generally suggests a rectangular shape and single-storey construction. This keeps building cost down to a minimum, maximizes natural lighting, and obviates problems of weight loading. It also eases delivery, flow, and dispatch of stock and facilitates supervision and administration generally. In addition, fire precautions and safety regulations are easier and cheaper to put into effect. A multi-storey warehouse, on the other hand, needs wasteful staircases or elevators, an external fire escape, and other expensive compulsory features.

Layout planning depends on the type of goods stored, but the important features to be taken into account are the best and most economical use of space, quick identification and speedy access to stocks, easy logical flow, and instant facility for stock control.

Mechanical handling devices should be carefully selected, introduced, properly used, and employed to capacity. For the outstanding task here is to solve the handling problems at all stages, for materials coming in, through their initial storage, to intermediate storage at the point where they are partly made up as work in progress, to final storage as finished products ready for delivery. Much of this problem area comes within the framework of logistics discussed elsewhere, which means that everything must be in its proper place for the purpose required.

Handling equipment includes such items as wall and movable racks, fork lifts, overhead rails, and continuous conveyor belts; there may also be a case for automation. The policy decision, however, would depend on the capital cost of installation, and loss of interest on that capital, as against the labor-saving that might be achieved. In most cases the answer would stop at partial automation—if indeed it got as far as that in today's situation.

CONTROLLING AND REDUCING COSTS

Centralized production may gain from economies of scale and/or make the best use of specialized machinery; we also know that a central warehouse minimizes stock levels. But there are other considerations to be taken into account as well, such as saving transportation costs through trunking and giving on-the-spot service to local markets. Running through this, and similar policy considerations, is the awareness of cost and the need to keep it firmly under control at all times. This means cutting across functional boundaries and looking at the problems from the top on an overall company basis, possibly through the establishment of a cost-reduction action committee with regular meetings, perhaps monthly or quarterly. There is also value in making comparison, where possible, with the labor, material, and machine costs of other firms in the same or similar industry. It is essential, however, to make sure of comparing like with like, using, where feasible, a common basis of physical or monetary measure.

Value Analysis

Cost reduction can start with the products by having a "brainstorming" session using a technique known as "value analysis."

Representatives of departments such as R. & D., purchasing, production, sales, and cost get together at regular meetings to compare the cost of a product with the value being obtained from it and in the event decide, as against possible alternatives. whether the expenditure involved in making it is really justified. This analysis should periodically be applied to innovations as well as having a hard new look at all existing products. When the technique aims at preventing, instead of identifying, unnecessary cost, it is more usual to refer to "value engineering." But the team approach is the same, with a full-scale attack on design and development right through to final production.

This means asking simple basic questions such as What exactly does the product or component part do? and, in the latter case, Is it indeed really needed at all? How much does the product or part cost? Could some alternative do the job equally well and be produced more cheaply? With objective thought, the team may be able to recommend substantial cost-saving changes in design, material, or process. A typical cost breakdown shows that more than 40 per cent of that cost could be made up of raw materials and purchased components and about 10 per cent in direct labor; hence there remains considerable scope for economy.

Among the reasons for unnecessary cost are conservative attitudes ("we have always done it this way and with these materials"), lack of ideas and information concerning alternatives, and too high a quality or accuracy in the light of practical requirements. Like all attempts at change it is necessary to overcome initial resistance from managers, staff, and workers. Thus it is essential that the right attitude to cost saving should percolate from the top downwards.

Quality and Reliability

These two terms (Q. & R. for short) relate to the manufacture of products, but each has its own individual significance.

Quality control is a management system for making sure that all products have the right quality for full customer satisfaction, and at minimum cost (maximum profitability) for that quality. This not only applies to completed products but operates as interim checks as well during the course of production, and even further back as specification at the design stage. "Right quality," often referred to as the optimum level of quality, connotes that the product will be just good enough for the purpose required. If it is too good for that purpose it will tend to be uneconomic, in terms of production cost, when a cheaper job would serve the customer equally well, or tend to have a life beyond that required from it in practice. This ties in with a policy of helping future sales through "built-in obsolescence" referred to in the previous chapter. If the quality is not good enough, the answer would soon make itself felt by customer complaint and falling turnover. In the case of an important order to be placed with a manufacturer, a large (e.g., industrial) consumer will often carry out a "vendor survey," by a team of observers put in to investigate quality policies, practice, and personnel, to make sure that the required quality will be forthcoming.

Basically, quality is tested statistically, usually by sample, sometimes taking quite small samples where the results are likely to be sufficiently sound mathematically in representing the whole. Obviously, this is a much cheaper process than a 100 per cent inspection. Other applications of quality control include "capability studies" where process or machine accuracy is tested and "process control" where present performance is measured as a guide to future performance. This is a large subject, but the aim throughout is to minimize waste through scrap and the remaking of rejects. Sufficient has been indicated, however, to show how variations in the manufacturing through wear and tear, in materials used, human error, and so on can be actively prevented from the start, not just found out after production has taken place, evidenced perhaps as complaints from customers.

Human error arises from such negative characteristics as indifference to the job, boredom, fatigue, and lack of vigilance. It can, of course, be obviated by automation, or it can be overcome by the creation of a far more positive atmosphere as evidenced by a "zero-defects" program with financial and nonfinancial rewards for workers achieving "right quality" perfection or near-perfection in output. The cost of such rewards may well be a minute percentage of overall savings in product cost.

As always, the prevention of waste must be encouraged from the top. Unless management has the right attitude, and this applies to office materials as well as to factory products, it can hardly be expected that staff and workers will take the initiative. Passive acceptance of traditional levels of waste, in whatever form, must be turned into positive action to reduce that waste by clear direction from above.

Reliability is in much the same vein as quality control. It means checking against technical specifications for accuracy, as in instruments, ability to stand up to given weather conditions and so on, where customers have to depend on the efficiency or effectiveness of the products which they purchase.

Work Study

This is an omnibus term covering a number of productivity techniques vital to the control of costs. In essence it consists of a detailed analytical look at work carried out, the object being to improve efficiency, and thereby obtain better performance, and, if possible, reduce expenditure. The main techniques are methods study and work measurement.

Methods study is a systematic approach, review, and reconstruction of existing methods, or new methods, in order to effect an improvement and cut costs. Having selected the actual job for detailed study, it is broken down into constituent parts for critical evaluation by one or more of many processes, such as using a movie camera with fast and slow speeds, flow diagrams, work-place-layout plans, etc. The object is to demonstrate as clearly as possible the sequence of hand and foot movements, use of tools, routes taken between machines or around a workshop, etc., as appropriate to any given job or proposed job.

The next stage is to examine the evidence as critically as possible, in proper sequence, and then work out the most economic and effective method possible. It may, for instance, be decided to use both hands at once, instead of one at a time, or cut out unnecessary walking about by a rearrangement of sequence; the opportunities are endless. However, having decided on the most suitable method and having sorted out any initial troubles, this method should then be put into operation as standard practice. Finally, it is always advisable to keep a running check on the new method to make sure that the standard practice is still being maintained.

Methods study engineers have a language of their own, as well as standardized charts, etc., and the whole technique is highly scientific in approach. As with all such specialized functions, the long-term savings in cost should be far more than the actual expense of the methods study service; in other words, methods, or any comparable, study must be made to pay for itself over a given period and show a profit. If this is not likely to be so, then management would be wise to reconsider the situation and engage a new team in place of the old, or drop the idea completely.

Common to all aspects of work study is the human element which, as usual, must be taken fully into consideration. Any attempt to change methods—the classic example is the man going around the factory with a stop watch—is viewed by the productive workers on the shop floor with fear and suspicion. It is essential, therefore, when installing and maintaining new methods to "sell" the idea to the staff or workers concerned. Experience dictates how best to overcome initial and/or persistent resistance to change, by preparing the ground in advance, showing in the process how much could be saved by more economical methods. If the total amount saved could be shared in some way with the workers, then quantified motivation can be substituted for opposition. This aspect is developed further in Chapter Twelve.

One other personnel requirement is the ease with which workers can be trained in the new methods, and this depends partly on the preparation of detailed specifications for each of the jobs concerned. In the preparation of such job specifications, as with the installing of the new method in the first place, it is good policy to secure the full cooperation of supervisors and workers by inviting their participation. It could also be argued, as a matter of policy, that gradual change would be more acceptable, and more likely to succeed, than sudden and dramatic change.

Work measurement is the use of various techniques to ascertain how long a batch, job, or part of a job should take, assuming that it is carried out to the right standard of quality. The obvious method —back to the man with the stopwatch—is "time study," an emotive term historically, but one now more or less taken for granted. Work measurement is carried out scientifically today by qualified engineers, taking into account all relevant factors. This results in the calculation of a "basic time" for a given job, after making sure that the operator (or operators) being observed is (are) working neither too fast nor too slow. Certain allowances will be added to basic time, such as time for rest and contingencies in order to estimate total standard time. Note also the concept here of a "standard minute."

So-called predetermined-motion time systems are a development of time study. Manuals can be obtained setting out detailed timings on a wide variety of hand, arm, and leg movements against which an engineer can check his own measurements.

Mention must also be made of "activity or work sampling," employing statistical techniques, which simply means taking a few random observations of machine operations and the like during the course of, say, a week instead of mounting a costly study covering the whole week. The extent of sampling, however, should be sufficient to guarantee the required mathematical accuracy of measurement for the purpose in hand. Finally, work measurement can be extended to nonrepetitive work and indirect activity by a process of "analytical estimating." In particular, it can be applied to storekeeping and maintenance and to office workers covering a wide range of employment. In this latter context, it is usual today to refer to "clerical-work measurement" where, despite less precise standards having necessarily to be applied, considerable progress has been made.

The value of work measurement enters into such fields as production planning and scheduling, balancing flow lines, estimating, costing, job analysis and the fixing of incentives. It is worthwhile, therefore, for top management to take a keen interest in methods study generally and its main applications.

One other cost-reduction medium that needs to be mentioned here is variety reduction. This was discussed in Chapter Nine in its marketing context. Reducing the number of different products to be sold must simplify production through standardization and specialization, and thereby make it a more economical proposition. In planning to gain the full benefits of variety reduction, it is usual to employ what is called "Pareto analysis" based on a "Pareto curve" as shown in Figure 13. This technique can be used for the evaluation of cost and profit, product by product, on the fundamental concept that when dealing with large numbers of people or items most of the effective influence comes from a significant few of them, about one-fifth of the whole. If, therefore, the significant few, in this case products, can be identified, isolated, and given special analytical attention, then major benefits will flow automatically. The remaining bulk can virtually be ignored.

Similar to work study is organization and methods (O. & M.), introduced in Chapter Four. O. & M. relates to administrative and office work, seeking to have the most effective management structure and reducing clerical tasks to essentials. When all unnecessary jobs have been systematically eliminated, and paperwork reduced to a minimum, there follows a maximized use of manpower. In much the same way, too, as under work study, office machinery can be planned for optimum use. As with systems analysis, the same techniques have already been seen to extend into the computer field.

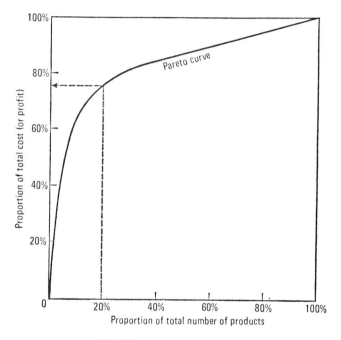

FIGURE 13. Pareto analysis

Cost Centers

The importance of controlling costs starts as a management philosophy; it can be reinforced by making managers and workers down the line responsible and accountable for the costs incurred within their particular province. This accountability ensures that the managers and supervisors concerned will take positive action to keep materials waste, defective work, and general inefficiency to an absolute minimum.

Having decided on appropriate cost centers, which can be either personal, i.e., related to a person or group of people, or impersonal, i.e., attached to a given function or machine, the next stage is to allocate all relevant costs. Direct materials, direct labor, and the like present no practical difficulty, but with the apportionment of indirect costs such as factory overhead expenses, there can be many problems. In order to fix responsibility, the cost center concerned must be properly charged with costs; for any arbitrary allocation can evoke opposition or at least damp down enthusiasm.

The allocation of variable overhead expenses, therefore, should be kept as fair and logical as possible. There are many alternative methods for achieving this, such as allocation by space occupied by the center, by number of machine hours, by percentage of direct labor or direct materials cost, but whichever methods are adopted they must be reasonably easy to understand and generally acceptable to all concerned. It then remains for management to exercise continuous control by routine and comparative study of cost-center totals. The financial implications are elaborated in Chapter Eleven.

Summary

1. Processes and Technological Choice
   a. The type of manufacturing process depends on product and the quantity required.
   b. The choice lies mainly between job, batch, and flow-line production.
   c. Industry is becoming more capital intensive: machines are replacing labor, but automation has limitations in practice.
   d. When to bring in new plants and machinery is a matter of judgment.
   e. The virtues of simplification and standardization should be borne in mind.
   f. Production needs effective organization.

2. Size and Location of Plants
   a. Mass production suggests a large centralized factory, but manufacturing can be decentralized.

  b. The key factor is for each unit to be at optimum size.
  c. Similar considerations apply to the production of a service.
  d. Choice here lies between centralized home office and branches with local autonomy.

3. Research and Development
  a. R. & D. has strong links with marketing as well as production.
  b. Unstructured research gives scientists full scope; but it must be geared to profitability, and costs must be watched.
  c. Coordination of American research has not yet been achieved.

4. Organizing the Capacity
  a. Optimum use must be made of manufacturing plant.
  b. This implies production planning and control.
  c. In practice, programs or schedules need to be translated into Gantt charts.
  d. Production must be kept steady and bottlenecks avoided.
  e. To achieve this, the flow lines have to be balanced.
  f. Planned maintenance avoids breakdowns.

5. Purchasing and Stock Control
  a. A decision must be made as to how much of the finished product should be purchased rather than manufactured.
  b. The cost of providing special services should be weighed against the cost of purchasing them.
  c. An efficient purchasing department minimizes costs.
  d. Systematic purchasing makes best use of suppliers.
  e. Effective stock control keeps down costs of holding materials and finished goods.
  f. Location, building, and layout of warehouses calls for careful planning.

6. Controlling and Reducing Costs
  a. Cost awareness should be encouraged from the top.
  b. Action should be initiated through a cost-reduction committee.
  c. Action starts with value analysis, looking critically at every product and component used.
  d. Quality (and reliability) control ensures the right quality at minimum cost.
  e. It may include vendor surveys with respect to goods bought in.
  f. Human error can be minimized by a "zero defects" program.
  g. Pareto analysis pinpoints significant areas for cost saving.

7. Work Study
   a. This includes productivity techniques for improved performance.
   b. It is made up of methods study and work measurement.
   c. Jobs should be analyzed, reviewed, and reconstructed where necessary.
   d. Work measurement takes the time factor into account.
   e. Psychological aspects must not be overlooked.

8. Cost Centers
   a. Direct costs are allocated to appropriate centers.
   b. Managers and workers concerned are held responsible and accountable for the direct costs.
   c. Overhead expenses are allocated on a basis that is accepted as fair and logical.

Suggested Further Reading

BUFFA, E.S. *Modern Production Management.* 2d ed. New York: Wiley, 1975.

ENRICK, N.L. *Quality Control and Reliability.* 6th ed. New York: Industrial Press, 1972.

ERICSSON, D. *Materials Administration.* New York: McGraw-Hill, 1974.

GAGE, W.L. *Value Analysis.* New York: McGraw-Hill, 1968.

GRANT, E.L., AND R.S. LEAVENWORTH. *Statistical Quality Control.* 4th ed. New York: McGraw-Hill, 1972.

HULL, J. *Control of Manufacturing.* New York: Beekman, 1973.

JOHNSON, R.A., ET AL. *Production and Operations Management: A Systems Concept.* Boston: Houghton Mifflin, 1974.

JURAN, J.M., AND F.M. GRYNA, JR. *Quality Planning and Analysis: From Product Development Through Usage.* New York: McGraw-Hill, 1970.

LUKE, H.D. *Automation for Productivity.* New York: Beeker and Hayes, 1972.

MAYER, R.E. *Production and Operations Management*. New York: McGraw-Hill, 1975.

McLEOD, T.S. *Management of Research, Development, and Design in Industry*. New York: Beekman, 1970.

RIDGE, W.J. *Value Analysis for Better Management*. New York: American Management Association, 1969.

VOLLMAN, T.E. *Operations Management: A Systems Model-Building Approach*. Reading, Mass.: Addison-Wesley, 1973.

ELEVEN

Financial Policies

Although the previous two chapters have dealt respectively with marketing and production, it is obvious that nothing could have taken
place without the necessary finance. Yet the order is not illogical. A
would-be entrepreneur usually starts with a good idea for a product
or service that he thinks would sell; he then works out how it could
be made; and, finally, he seeks to convince one or more financial
backers that the product is viable and worth the risk. Naturally, the
greater the risk the higher the cost of raising funds.

Chapter Fifteen deals with the special problems of a small firm
in acquiring all the capital it needs, demonstrating the transition from
sole proprietorship or partnership to private corporation, with the
money still more or less in the family, and finally to becoming a public
corporation, with control divorced from capital ownership. It is with
this last situation, assuming a well-established corporation having a
wide range of stockholders, that we are mainly concerned with at
present.

Cash or Funds Flow

The modern approach to capital is through the concept of cash flow, which reflects changes in the sources and uses of funds employed in the business. It starts by asking what those funds are required for and where they can be obtained; the next stage is to draw up a cash-flow statement that quantifies the changes in those sources and uses over a given financial period as reflected in balance-sheet figures at the beginning and end. This recording of the flow of money in the firm is the well-established province of the accountants. At any point or time, *sources* of funds, i.e., funds raised, are shown as liabilities, and *uses* of funds as assets. The composition of assets and liabilities is illustrated by the simplified vertical balance sheet included later in this chapter. Incidentally, share capital is considered a "liability" because that money may have to be repaid to the stockholders by the company should the company go into liquidation.

While the terms "cash" and "funds" are often used synonymously, as they are here, in strict balance-sheet terminology there is a difference: "cash" refers to actual cash on hand or in the bank, whereas "funds" covers both sides of the balance sheet, including cash. However, in the present context, cash flow can be considered as being identical with funds flow, particularly when dealing later with the refinements called "discounted cash flow" (abbreviated to D.C.F.) which recognizes that present dollars are worth more than future dollars and makes adjustment accordingly.

Management policy is continually directed towards making the best use of funds, bearing in mind corporate responsibilities to stockholders and others who have invested those funds, and matching the needs of growth by finding additional resources as and when they may be required.

USES OF CAPITAL

Although it is convenient to discuss the uses of capital (funds) before looking into the sources, in practice these two opposing aspects interlock. Clearly each use of funds must be financed from one or more sources, so that total uses and total sources must always be equal.

Basic Capital Needs

Any new business must have cash to buy raw materials, obtain the use of premises, plant, and equipment, pay salaries and wages, meet selling and administrative expenses and so on, well before it can expect funds to flow back after the first goods or services have been sold. Even then, there may be further delay before the invoices for those sales or services are actually paid in cash. Capital is therefore needed to cover this time-lag between the initial outflow of funds and the much slower flow of funds back in again.

A further basic distinction is between capital needed for acquiring more-or-less permanent assets, called "fixed" assets, and capital required for everyday use as working capital or circulating capital.

Long-term Funds

Investment in fixed assets, such as land, buildings, plant and machinery, transportation, fixtures and furnishings, is clearly a matter for top-management decision, starting with an objective and detailed "capital-investment appraisal." This means taking a hard look at each long-term outlay of funds to make sure of achieving a maximum return on capital invested (R.O.I. for short) over its projected lifespan. What that return should be depends on an amalgam of factors such as the long-term interest rate, the degree of risk involved, and the return being obtained by main competitors.

Management should therefore continually ask itself whether the fixed assets in the business are earning a satisfactory rate of return based on a reasonable target rate for the industry as a whole. If not, then perhaps the firm is in the wrong business. This connotes that a "minimum" rate of return, say 10–15 per cent per annum, on the capital sum (after providing for depreciation and taxes) must be obtained, not only on existing fixed assets but with respect to every new proposal to invest funds in additional fixed assets. Management policy, however, must include a clear definition as to how that minimum rate is to be calculated and make sure that it is not set too low. In arriving at the decision it is reasonable to suggest that the higher the forecast risk and uncertainty, the higher the minimum rate would need to be to compensate.

Capital Investment Policy

In view of the permanence and heavy cost of fixed assets, it is vital not to make any errors of judgment when deciding upon special capital expenditures. Often this is a selection from alternatives, using scarce resources, made centrally through a regulated system of capital budgeting. This implies taking a relatively long-term view of all proposed capital expenditures, usually in the form of a moving three-year or five-year schedule having next year's proposals set out in detail and the other years in broad outline. This schedule is usually submitted to the board of directors, possibly first through a finance committee, as part of the annual budgeting procedure (to be discussed later).

A moving schedule is simply one that is made out to cover x years ahead. As each financial year passes, and the items for that year are dealt with in one way or another, a further year's proposals are added to the end of the schedule, so that at each annual review the board or committee is still looking x years ahead. The inclusion of an item on the schedule is a first step towards acceptance of the expenditure involved. It follows that at each annual review, perhaps more frequently, the whole position must be looked at afresh in the light of change. By the time an item has survived to appear in detail in the next year's proposals, it has a good chance of going through. Nevertheless, it should still be dealt with specifically before the expenditure is actually made.

It follows from this that unless an item appears on the moving schedule, there must be a sound, perhaps opportunity cost, reason why it should receive consideration at all. Too many such items make long-term budgeting unreal; yet, as always, managerial policy must be tempered with flexibility.

An example may help. In a commercial firm with a network of branches and an expansion policy of so many new branches per annum, the process would start with the selection of a list of towns strategically chosen in order of marketing priorities for the opening of new branches. For each of x years ahead, on a moving basis, the total cost of premises would be estimated as part of the overall capital budget. By the time the name of a particular town appeared on the next year's list, it is likely that a specific proposition would be in course of being negotiated. At the eventual point when a decision had to be made, a full-scale proposal would be submitted, perhaps to a premises committee, quoting chapter and verse, including a profitable rate of return on the capital to be invested. But when seeking premises in a range of towns, it could happen that a once-for-all opportunity presented itself, in which case the appropriate body would exercise reasoned flexibility and, other things remaining equal, take advantage of the opportunity. This might mean that some other proposition would have to be set back in priority, in order that the capital budget totals would not be invalidated. Similar provision would need to be made with regard to extensions, improvements, repairs, and redecoration relating to existing premises, when the annual capital expenditure should be on the same moving basis as before, as part of an overall premises budget.

The next problem is how to decide between alternative propositions. As a first approach, any request for capital expenditure not consistent with management policies should automatically be rejected. Then, having detailed the advantages and disadvantages as related to the estimated cost, the R.O.I. calculation could be made, by the formula adopted, excluding any proposition not matching up to the minimum rate as laid down.

On occasion, however, there may be strategic reasons for accepting a substandard economic proposition. In the example given above, it may pay to buy certain premises, on a particularly valuable site, despite the fact that the return on capital would be low. One reason could be the prestige value of that location, *vis-à-vis* competitors, the advertising value of the premises, and the potential business likely to be attracted from a large passing trade. Yet even here the R.O.I. situation should be kept in mind. Consideration should be given, for example, to the feasibility of taking on adjoining premises, with a view to letting, on the most favorable terms, any of the accommodations not actually required by the firm for its own use.

Apart from special opportunities, which must be balanced out with other propositions providing a higher than minimum rate of return on capital, there still remains the problem of selection from among given alternatives. This could be effected by taking all the proposals offering the highest rates of return right down to the point where the budgeted capital expenditures had been completely used up. Here again, in individual cases, there must be full allowance for other relevant factors, mathematical calculations on their own simply being a first claim for serious consideration. But *overall* there must be an adequate rate of return on capital if the firm is to continue to flourish. For the return expected on each different type of capital expenditure must be brought into line with the profit objectives of the business as a whole.

Having decided on the most effective way to achieve the objectives and policies laid down for capital projects, it is essential to make sure that the process selected includes keeping the costs to a minimum. This cost aspect is developed later. Furthermore, it is a wise precaution to check up on past capital projects, from time to time, to learn how previous decisions have worked out in practice. This type of follow-through action usually provides valuable experience as a guide to future investment planning.

Discounted Cash Flow

With fixed assets of any kind the capital investment decision is crucial, but far from easy to make. Apart from the difficulties of choosing between alternatives, there are risk problems of obsolescence, such as the hazard of buying the latest computer when a future-generation computer is already nearing the point of dramatic breakthrough.

However, having narrowed down the alternatives with a clear idea of cost, and what each will achieve, it is possible to apply the R.O.I. calculation. This starts with the initial cash-flow outlay, i.e., the purchase price, followed by estimated cash inflows for each year of useful life. At a point of time the original price will be covered by these inflows and thereafter the asset, having paid for itself, continues to make a profit. By averaging out the profit over the useful life, it is possible to get an average annual profit, which, related to the capital investment outlay, gives the rate of return.

The following simplified example (see Table A), taking two alternative machines X and Y, will illustrate this type of calculation. Machine X will apparently pay for itself by the end of the fourth year, and machine Y will do so by the end of the third year; but on a rate-of-return basis, assuming a life of five years, it seems that machine X would be the better buy, other things remaining equal.

But, as suggested earlier, present dollars are worth more than

TABLE A. Comparing Alternatives for R.O.I.

	Machine X	*Machine Y*
Outflow (purchase price)	$4,000	$4,000
Annual cash inflows		
1st year	600	1,400
2nd year	800	1,400
3rd year	1,200	1,200
4th year	1,400	400
5th year	2,000	400
	6,000	4,800
Total profit	2,000	800
Average profit per annum	400	160
Return on capital	10%	4%

future dollars and this must be so, quite apart from inflation, because a dollar today can be invested to earn interest. The appropriate figures can be obtained by looking up discount tables under "Present Value of $1" for each successive year hence, there being a column for any given rate of interest. Bearing in mind the need to have a minimum return on capital this could conveniently be fixed, for our present purpose, at 10%. Under the 10% column the discounted $1 for one year hence is 0.909, for two years hence 0.826 and so on to the fifth year, in our example, which is 0.621. It is now possible to recalculate our comparison figures on this more realistic basis, by using the net present value. The figures then become as shown in Table B.

It is usual, for purposes of easy comparison, particularly when there are different purchase prices, to reduce the figures to what is called a "profitability index." This is calculated by dividing the purchase price (present value) into total annual cash inflows as adjusted to present value, giving 1.076 for machine X as against 0.963 for machine Y. The choice again falls on machine X, other things remaining the same, as the figure here matches up to the 10% minimum return on capital, the index figure being more than unity. In fact, taking a second look at the cash inflows for machine Y, there would appear to be doubts about its useful life beyond the third year despite having already paid for itself.

TABLE B. Comparison in Terms of Discounted Dollars

	Machine X	Machine Y
Present value of annual cash inflows (at 10%):		
1st year	$ 545.4	$1,272.6
2nd year	660.8	1,156.4
3rd year	901.2	901.2
4th year	956.2	273.2
5th year	1,242.0	248.4
	4,305.6	3,851.8
Outflow (purchase price)	4,000.0	4,000.0
Profitability index	1.076	0.963

It has been seen that, in capital budgeting, the cash outflow and the cash inflow can be estimated for any given project, but that the rate of return remains an unknown quantity. It is possible, however, to determine a rate of interest by experimenting with different rates until one is found which will balance out the transaction over its given life. On this basis, the rate for the project is the one which just makes the present value of total inflows equal to the original purchase price. Taking the example given above, based on a useful life of five years, the alternatives work out to a discounted interest rate of approximately 12% for machine X and 8% for machine Y. It must be mentioned, however, that different answers will be produced given different estimates of useful life.

In the last analysis, the capital investment decision between stated alternatives will inevitably rest on managerial judgment and common sense, but quantification must be given its full weight, when considered with the nonmonetary factors.

In practice the "net present value" method is refined in various ways, such as allowing for taxation, with special reference to actual times of payment as reflected in the cash flow. Because tax is often paid long after assessment, the return on capital is likely to be effectively more attractive than under the pre-tax method. But the principle behind discounted-cash-flow (D.C.F.) techniques remains the same, a valuable management tool for estimating future financial benefits as between alternative fixed assets. Incidentally, a simple electronic calculator is now available to ease the burden of D.C.F.

The above deals with the purchase of a new machine, looked at in isolation, but often the requirement is for a new machine to replace an old one. In this case consideration must also be given to the remaining useful life (if any) of the old machine, the rate of obsolescence, the increasing cost of maintenance and repairs, tax relief on depreciation, and the likely secondhand (or scrap) value it could attract. Any car owner is aware of such financial considerations, excluding tax relief, when deciding to trade in an old car for a new one.

In private life, the economics of changing a car are likely to result in a rough and ready calculation, with bargaining in mind, but top management must determine a firm's transportation replacement policy more scientifically. In general, such policy relates to delivery trucks, salesmen's vans or cars, and executive cars, and each of these categories requires separate consideration. Basically, a policy decision has to be made between time and mileage, and then quantified. It may be policy, for example, to change executive cars every three years, or 40,000 miles, whichever comes first, but to change salesmen's vans or cars annually, possibly under a fleet agreement with a dealer or manufacturer, whatever the mileage. Each category must be decided on its merits, and the policy decisions incorporated in the total capital budgeting.

In all matters related to fixed assets, there is the added problem of inflation, but this is considered in a wider context later in the chapter.

Purchasing or Leasing

So far, consideration has been confined to the purchase of fixed assets, namely land, buildings, plant and machinery, transportation, fixtures and furnishings; but there is also available the alternative of leasing. Even a chief executive's private office, from executive desk to hat-stand, can be leased from one of the firms specializing in this kind of transaction.

Leasing, particularly on a long-term basis, is a worthwhile method when there are more capital opportunities than capital or when it is desired to conserve capital. In other words, leasing enables a company to acquire expensive capital equipment without tying up its working capital, which can then be put to better use elsewhere. Leasing could be used, for example, for modernization or re-equipment, thus enabling a company otherwise unable to find the finance to keep its capital equipment in good shape. Among the financial benefits usually listed are a no-deposit scheme, easy rental calculation for budgeting purposes, and the fact that rentals are allowable for tax purposes. By agreeing on fixed payments in advance there is a protection against inflation; furthermore these payments will be made out of the profits produced by the new plant and equipment.

To purchase or to lease is a matter for managerial policy decision. Some firms may wish to use leasing as a regular feature, others for particular, usually large-scale transactions such as a home-office building, heavy machinery, or a fleet of delivery trucks. Whatever the policy, it must be translated into practice with due care, still using comparative techniques, even though the subject matter of the lease obviously does not appear on the balance sheet among the company's own assets. A long-term leasing arrangement must not be entered into which could embarrass the company financially at some later stage.

In the case of premises—home office, factories, branches—the conditions may include certain breaks in the lease, for example, at seven, 14, or 21 years, when the rental is to be increased automatically by stated annual amounts to keep pace with rising market prices; there may also be onerous clauses as to repairs and redecoration, such as in a "full-repairing" lease. As leases of this kind are long-term commitments, it is essential to make sure that all the financial implications are fully understood right from the outset. For once the lease is signed, it may be too late to have second thoughts. There could be problems, too, about renewal at the end of a lease: one approach is to have an option to purchase the premises, or other asset, on agreed terms, on the expiration of that lease.

An arrangement often adopted is that of "sale and lease back," which means disposing of an asset already owned, by selling it to a financial concern and taking a long lease in exchange. This releases capital for use in other directions or helps to get over temporary financial difficulties. A company could, for instance, have a block of premises built to its own design and for its own occupation and after the completion date dispose of it to an insurance company or large pension fund (each normally seeking investment outlets for considerable surplus income) on a sale-and-lease-back basis.

In all these matters management should be mainly concerned

with the broad principles of overall financial policy; the finer points of detail must be left to the accountants, and the legal intricacies to the lawyers.

A real need exists today in industry to increase the average level of long-term fixed investment in new buildings and machinery. The overall problem here is to find ways and means of stimulating such investment. While this is partially a matter for government concern and official policy, one of the priorities of the 1970s is that individual companies should still make the best use of opportunities to become more capital intensive, within existing constraints.

Working or Circulating Funds

Apart from capital expenditures on fixed assets, it is necessary to have working capital, consisting of cash or assets intended eventually to be converted into cash, for everyday business transactions. Particularly important examples are:

(a) Cash on hand and in the bank.
(b) Marketable (short-term) securities.
(c) Accounts receivable.
(d) Inventory.

The financial problems of inventory maintenance have already been indicated in the context of marketing and production. There must clearly be a sufficient stock of finished goods to ensure good customer delivery, and a steady flow of raw materials is necessary for production purposes; but stock at rest, even as work in progress, tends to be costly. Working capital tied up in stock inventory must not be wasted, therefore, by keeping levels unnecessarily high, nor by having too wide a range of variety, nor by allowing stock to perish or become obsolete or unwanted. In the latter circumstances, early action can and should be taken to clear the deck. Hence the previous emphasis on stock *control*.

Cash on hand and in the bank can also be expensive, bearing in mind the overall minimum return required on capital invested. Cash in the till earns no interest at all, nor does a business checking account at the bank (in fact it could be subject to bank charges). Yet there must be sufficient cash available to pay bills and take advantage of opportunities requiring ready money. However, as always, experience generally suggests a happy medium between keeping too much cash and too little. Beyond a reasonable level for everyday operations, checking account balances are usually transferred to a deposit account earning interest at the appropriate rate.

When bank balances in total become too large, the excess is normally invested in short-term *marketable securities* in order to produce a higher return. The ability to turn assets quickly into cash is known as *liquidity*. It is, of course, essential that assets should be realizable, without loss, at a time of need. This might not apply to long-term *investments* in high-risk securities which, at a given point of time, could only be sold, if at all, at considerable loss. Less risky long-term investments include government bonds or other first-class securities, preferably within a few years of redemption date in order to ensure easier realizability when required. There is a risk, of course, with regard to all securities, but this can be minimized by careful selection on a basis of wise investment not wild speculation. Management must be continually aware of money-market trends and take action accordingly, keeping in mind the liquidity requirements of financing everyday transactions, including any seasonal peaks.

Apart from interest or dividends on the investment, there is the factor of capital gains, hence the expression "redemption yield," which includes an element of capital appreciation. Any yield will be "gross" or "net" according to whether the amount is quoted before or after deduction of tax.

A company can, of course, use excess liquid capital to pay off any outstanding debts, assuming satisfactory arrangements can be made for doing so, and will need funds for the payment of taxes and dividends to shareholders as described later.

Accounts receivable consist of money owed to the business by customers. Because outstanding debts can be an expensive loss of working funds, every effort should be made to collect them as promptly as possible. But from the customers' point of view, particularly at a time of credit stringency and high interest rates, there is a financial advantage in delaying the payment of outstanding bills until the very last minute. Even the most credit-worthy concerns tend to seize the chance, on any pretext, of keeping their money two months or more longer in order to earn a high return on that money before paying it over for goods previously supplied. In addition, there is always a core of bad and doubtful debts, even after taking all reasonable safeguards such as obtaining effective credit references for new customers. All accounts *should* pay their creditors promptly, but there may be good reasons why they cannot do so, the outstanding one being that *their* accounts receivable may be suffering from delayed settlement, too, thus preventing funds from being available as optimistically budgeted. Thus it pays top management to organize proper credit control with a specialist credit manager in charge, both to reduce the credit risk as far as possible and deal with any defaulters not meeting their obligations, despite the taking of normal precautions. Action to be initiated will naturally vary from gentle reminder, and helpful arrangements in genuine cases of difficulty, to legal action for recovery as a last resort. Management must, of course, weigh collection costs against net results expected, and any repercussions on customer goodwill likely to affect future business transactions and therefore profits.

There are, however, a number of firms called *factors* that will take over the job of collecting debts, not when they have become bad or doubtful but right from the actual date of invoice, paying over the bulk of the invoiced amount to the client immediately. At a time of credit squeeze such accommodation is naturally harder to provide. Usually the payment for it is a given rate of interest plus a service charge. Factors can also provide other services, such as acting as the client's accounts department, thus saving staff costs or, in many cases, giving a guarantee against bad debts. Often, as a safeguard against incurring large bad debts, a client will consult the factor before undertaking different types of transactions and/or accepting new customers.

SOURCES OF FINANCE

Having analyzed in broad outline what capital is used for—fixed assets and working funds—it is logical to review the various sources from which capital can be obtained and at what relative cost. Generally the problem is one of trying to get enough finance to match growth rather than being embarrassed by excessive capital.

Up to a point, a small firm can grow on its own resources by ploughing back profits, the owner taking out only a modest sum for his personal needs. Much depends on the nature of the business, for some firms require a much larger investment in fixed assets than others. Beyond that point, however, depending on the plans for growth, resort will have to be made to external finance. Briefly, the principal sources available for funds are permanent capital, medium-term capital, and current capital.

Permanent or Long-term Capital

The two main forms in which share capital is issued are:

(a) Preferred stock, with a prior claim to dividends.

(b) Common stock (equity capital), with voting rights and the expectation of a fair rate of return.

Holders of common stock take the risks and share the rewards, both of which will vary with the type of enterprise concerned. These shareholders are in fact the owners of the business and exercise control through a board of directors appointed from among their number as described in Chapter Three.

After ascertaining the total annual profit earned, the holders of preferred stock if any, are paid their fixed dividend (which may perhaps—according to the terms of issue—be cumulative, being carried forward to another year if there are insufficient profits to pay it this year). What remains of that total becomes the property of the ordinary shareholders: part of it is distributed to them as dividends and the rest ploughed back into the business to help further growth and the making of future profits. This continuous ploughing-back process is usually referred to as *retained profits*, which form an important part of the financial structure analyzed later in this chapter.

The administrative and legal intricacies of dealing with registration, new capital issues, using an investment firm, offers for sale and private placings by brokers, tenders, and so on are mainly the concern of the company secretary and fall outside the scope of this book. The advantages of "going public" and the status of having a Stock Exchange listing are practical management considerations dealt with in Chapter Fifteen.

Management is, however, concerned with broad principles and one of these is the relationship between common stock capital and total capital. The ratio of total capital to common stock capital is known as "gearing" (a more detailed formula is given later). If holders of common stock constitute only a small proportion of total capital, the gearing is high and this represents a speculative investment for those stockholders. The reason is obvious, for in a bad year preferred stock (and other long-term capital) will absorb the profits through their fixed interest claim, but, in a really good year, the balance available to be shared among a relatively small number of holders of common stock could be considerable.

Preferred stock may be "callable," i.e., bought back by the company, or "convertible" to shares of common.

Bonds or Loan Capital constitute another form of raising funds. Bond holders are long-term creditors with a prior charge against the company's profits for fixed annual interest, which must be paid in good years or bad, before meeting any claims by stockholders. In deciding between taking preferred stock capital or loan capital, the greater flexibility of the former has to be considered against the lower cost of servicing the latter.

Usually the bonds are secured on specific fixed assets or on the assets in general by means of a floating charge. When the trend of interest rates is downwards, any bond fixed-interest charge becomes an increasing burden. This point, of course, applies to any annual commitment involving fixed interest rates. The problem is deciding on the amount of fixed interest that the firm can stand, that is to say the maximum amount of debt it could sustain during a serious recession. This is often called the "debt-equity decision," equity being the alternative of raising further capital in common shares where the dividend varies with profits. The reverse is also true, whereby issuers of fixed-interest preferred stock obtain an advantage in years when the general trend of interest rates is upwards.

Insurance companies are usually interested in taking bonds with a floating charge, such finance generally being used by industry for the purchase of fixed assets. This provides more flexible security for the insurance company than the alternative of a mortgage (see later) specifically secured on those assets.

Medium-term Capital

Generally this means capital tied up for more than a year. *Bank loans* are an obvious source, usually related to the purchase of fixed assets, and can extend for as long as ten years. Overdrafts of any kind, however, even up to previously agreed limits, take the chance of being called in at short notice and are therefore regarded as current liabilities.

A *mortgage* from a bank, insurance company, etc. can normally be raised on bricks-and-mortar assets, but it must not be forgotten that the fixed annual interest (even without any capital repayment) can be a burden in difficult years. There may also be *lease with option to buy* facilities for buying fixed assets, *sale-and-lease-back* opportunities, as mentioned earlier, and *equipment leasing*, all of which need careful investigation before making any financial commitment affecting the years ahead.

Short-term Capital

Being for less than a year, short-term capital is used for such bridging purposes as building up inventory in anticipation of seasonal demands. It may also be used for building up resources to invest in fixed assets at a later date. By its very nature, therefore, it is temporary finance and a useful buffer for leveling out fluctuations in the required amount of working capital. Commercial banks are the first line of call, through *bank overdraft* facilities with day-to-day interest (subject to a percentage base rate) on the outstanding balance. *Loans* for a definite period can also be arranged but with interest, at a higher rate, over the full term. The amount that can be borrowed basically depends upon the firm's profit record, the collateral security offered, and the cash-flow ability to repay the loan, with interest, on the date agreed upon. The bank will also be concerned with the purpose for which a loan is required. For the small business, assistance in securing bank loans can be obtained through the offices of the Small Business Administration, as described in Chapter Fifteen.

With regard to exports and imports, *bills of exchange* are another source of finance. Usually self-liquidating over three months, these bills are, in effect, short-term borrowings from merchant banks or similar sources.

Trade credit is another accepted method for obtaining short-term funds, with the added advantage that no interest or dividend has to be paid. Every opportunity should be taken, therefore, to obtain maximum credit from suppliers; this has to be weighed, of course, in interest terms, against any cash discounts offered for prompt payment. Suppliers of raw materials and services customarily offer credit facilities, payment to be made, for example, one month after delivery. Delays in making payment (to creditors) can extend such facilities as seen earlier when dealing with accounts receivable, for buying on credit is but the other side of the coin from selling on credit. The counterbalancing advantages and disadvantages depend on financial policy, relative size of the firms involved, the importance of reciprocation, established reputation, and any similar factors that consciously or subconsciously need to be taken into account.

Depreciation

Although it is not obvious at first sight, depreciation today is an important source of finance.

All fixed assets (except land) tend to depreciate in real value as they wear out and/or become obsolescent, so provision has to be made for such depreciation annually out of current profits. This is another way of stating the main objective of charging depreciation, which is that, in arriving at the annual profits, full account must be taken of the cost of using those assets. There are many different accounting approaches to quantifying this problem, including the controversy as to whether the calculation should be made on original cost (recommended) or replacement cost, the annual allowance for depreciation being itself based on an arbitrary judgment. Thus the written-down balance-sheet "value" (cost less depreciation) of fixed assets also tends to be arbitrary. As consistently reduced over the years, this book value may become significantly different from *current* value (ignoring inflation), theoretically representing the price that could be realized in the open market at any given time. Formerly, it was considered to be a policy virtue and a sign of strength (hidden assets) to write off fixed assets, including premises, even to the point of their not appearing on the balance sheet at all. Modern statutory requirements, however, demand a more accurate and realistic picture of a firm's affairs.

However, depreciation is only a book entry, not a payment of cash. When ascertaining cash flows from published figures, it is therefore usual to add back the amount charged for depreciation, as shown in the accounts, to the annual profit after taxation. In fact, it is not unknown for a firm to show a loss and yet (through the above concept) enjoy an abundant cash flow arising from the same business.

The quantitative aspects are magnified considerably when inflationary trends are also brought into the picture. This is particularly true of land and buildings that have appreciated substantially in value during recent years, in money terms not real terms, despite the buildings becoming physically older year by year. Full weight, too, must be given to improved values due to external conditions, such as well-selected sites that become more valuable as larger communities develop around them.

Whatever the chosen rate of depreciation, therefore, it is clear that if a mortgage was to be arranged (or a sale and lease back) to raise funds, the basis of the transaction would be the current market value, not the book value. Ignoring depreciation entirely, there could be a considerable "cashing in on inflation." For example, a freehold building bought for $50,000 could be depreciated on a "straight-line" basis at $2,500 per annum over ten years, reducing the book value to $25,000 at the end of that period. The current market value could by then be inflated to $70,000 thus (in money terms) giving an extra margin of $20,000 on which to raise finance. This ignores the quantitative aspects of real terms as against money terms, a problem that is dealt with later in a different context.

Apart from the above, there is also the practical factor of building up a fund from profits to replace such assets when they become obsolete or physically worn out. This, however, is a separate financial decision affecting the appropriation of profits, not the determination of profits. It is worth noting that, because of technological advances and perhaps entirely new processes, replacement assets may sometimes be cheaper than the old ones.

Management Flexibility

There is nothing static about finance: It varies with the company's progress and requirements at any given time, with the relative availability of funds, and with the cost of borrowing from alternative sources. The continual problem facing top management is how to make sure that sufficient capital is forthcoming, that the cost of it is reasonable, and that the future of the company is not endangered by accepting undue risk. For example, if considerable surplus funds were unwisely invested in Stock Exchange securities, there might be a heavy loss if they had to be realized for urgent liquidity purposes in time of need. Any investment portfolio must be flexibly managed, balancing revenue return with capital gain, and long- and medium-term opportunities with short-term liquidity needs. Similarly, in view of the effects of corporation taxes, it is cheaper to raise finance through loan capital (whose interest is a charge against profits) than preferred share capital (whose dividends are an appropriation of profits). But, of course, loan interest *must* be paid out even in bad times.

The changing money-market environment must therefore be kept continually under review, as a background to budgeted cash flow for the years ahead. Too much reliance should not be placed on short-term sources, such as banks, because they tend to call in loans and seek to reduce overdrafts just when business in general is faced with recession. At a time of credit squeeze, therefore, companies may well resort to other fields for raising capital instead of continuing to tap the traditional source of short-term funds.

It is for these and allied reasons that top management should be vitally concerned at all times to frame viable and flexible financial policies tailored to fit the changing scene.

Management is also responsible for protecting the company's capital and must arrange effective coverage for all insurable risks over a wide range of hazards. The list of these is highly complicated and includes such diverse examples as fire, flood, burglary, theft, plate-glass, third-party liability, vehicle insurance, cash or goods in transit, workmen's compensation, and fidelity bonds. It is, of course, important to have the right amount of coverage, to appreciate exactly what the conditions are with regard to each policy, and above all to choose a reputable insurance company or companies. Streamlined arrangements made with such companies, designed to reduce paperwork, ease premium renewals, speed up claims and so on, may well be worthwhile when dealing with many transactions of the same kind. For with insurance, as with other functions, management must keep its judgments flexible and maximize every opportunity to reduce costs and improve profitability.

ANALYZING THE FINANCIAL STRUCTURE

Having just looked at the main uses and sources of funds, what interests us now is the relationship between them. In traditional accounting format it would have been sufficient to list the assets and liabilities respectively. Given below, however, is a simplified version of a *balance sheet* in vertical form, which sets out the various items in a more modern combination.

A balance sheet is often likened to a photograph of a company's affairs at a specific point of time, featured in terms of money. As illustrated under the section on depreciation, this is not necessarily a completely accurate picture. For example, the asset figure for inventory, or work in progress, is usually valued at whichever is the lower of either cost or net realizable value. Both cost and value, however, are arbitrary judgments. It has been said that in fact only the cash on hand and in the bank can be accurately stated. Theoretically, "window-dressing" tactics (for the stockholders' benefit) can be made to show different figures on the balance sheet date from those appearing in the accounts for the day after—when temporary financial arrangements have returned to normal. Fortunately, no auditors will give a favorable report today for such tactics.

Sufficient has been stated already to show the difficulties of reading a balance sheet in the context of the current situation. Apart from a variety of nonmonetary factors, such as the quality of management, industrial relations, organization and effectiveness of machinery, even the monetary figures themselves are bedevilled by inflation when attempting to compare one point of time with another. Nevertheless, despite these limitations, each succeeding balance sheet should suggest a number of "discerning questions" to be asked in the boardroom; the true value could then be derived from the answers.

Stockholders' Equity

The balancing figure in a company balance sheet is the accumulated amount of retained profits; it is, in fact, the excess of total assets

TABLE C. Simplified Vertical Balance Sheet

Assets

Current Assets:		
Cash (on hand and in bank)		$ 34,500
Accounts receivable	$ 25,500	
Less allowance for uncollectibles	1,275	
		24,225
Merchandise inventory		44,700
Supply inventory		2,600
TOTAL CURRENT ASSETS		*106,025*
Fixed Assets:		
Land		20,000
Plant & equipment	125,000	
Less allowance for depreciation	15,000	
		110,000
TOTAL FIXED ASSETS		*130,000*
Intangibles:		
Patents		6,000
Goodwill		1,000
TOTAL INTANGIBLES		*7,000*
		$243,025

Liabilities & Net Worth

Current Liabilities:		
Accounts payable		$ 16,000
Notes payable		1,500
Accrued taxes		5,525
TOTAL CURRENT LIABILITIES		*$ 23,025*
Long-term Liabilities:		
Mortgage		40,000
Note due, 1984		20,000
TOTAL LONG-TERM LIABILITIES		*60,000*
Net Worth:		
Capital		
Preferred stock	$ 15,000	
Common stock	120,000	
		135,000
Retained earnings		25,000
TOTAL LIABILITIES & NET WORTH		**$243,025**

over total liabilities. Should the liabilities exceed the assets, some very searching questions would need to be asked!

As proprietors of the business, those that hold the common stock own not only the common share capital but the balancing amount as well. Taken together, this total can be referred to as the "stockholders' equity," "total equity capital," or "net worth of the company." In the balance sheet itself, the balancing figure usually appears as "retained earnings," "surplus," or "reserves," kept on hand to meet any future losses. Total reserves consist of capital and revenue reserves.

For reserves can be added to by *capital* gains as, for example, from the sale of premises or marketable securities or by the process of revaluing the fixed assets in general to take into account inflationary effects, as already mentioned. Profits from normal business transactions are, of course, *revenue* gains. Premiums paid on bonds, or on shares of preferred stock, are capital reserves belonging to the common shareholders. They are a payment to the shareholders for the privilege of joining (preferred shares) or lending money to (bonds) the prosperous firm the common shareholders have created.

It is the duty of the directors to build up the total equity funds, that is to say to maximize revenue and capital earnings in the best interests of the common shareholders. In the process due regard has to be paid to gearing, as seen earlier, which can now be more accurately redefined as the ratio between the total of (equity + preferred share capital + long-term liabilities, including bonds) and equity. Without these other forms of capital the gearing ratio is obviously 1. Top management, when thinking of increasing gearing by raising further fixed-interest funds, must weigh the significance to common shareholders of potentially greater profits, with a higher net return than the net cost of borrowing, but increased risk.

Common share capital ("equities") appears on the balance sheet at *book* value, but each share has a *market* value as well, which rises or falls daily according to Stock Exchange dealings in those shares and the business outlook generally. All of which is a favorite topic in school mathematics with the working out of dividend yields and other associated calculations.

The book value of the shareholders' *total equity* capital is theoretically the value in event of liquidation, with revaluation of assets and the like to produce a more realistic basis for sale. The market value of that equity, on the other hand, is its value in the context of a growing concern: in this case the total consists of the quoted price multiplied by the number of common shares issued.

The *earnings per share of common stock* consist of the total annual profits, less fixed loan interest, preferred share dividend and taxation, divided by the number of common shares issued. Generally speaking, the trend should be rising, as it is the duty of management to maximize the earnings per share of common stock upon which the market price of that share will depend. These earnings are, however, usually looked at in conjunction with the "price/earnings ratio" described below.

Dividend Policy

Having settled for the time being on the "right" proportion of fixed debt to equity capital in the financial structure, a further problem remains in deciding how much of the profits after tax to distribute to stockholders as dividends. The total earnings per share are simple to understand in theory—they can be defined as the residue of profits after the company has deducted all the costs and paid all the tax—but, of course, part of those earnings should be retained by the company to create reserves or should be ploughed back into new plant and equipment to facilitate the making of future profits.

In practice, the average shareholder buys and sells his way into and out of companies and is only interested in reserves academically. His main concern is with the so-called *price/earnings ratio* which, simply stated, consists of the market price, as quoted on the Stock Exchange, divided by the latest published earnings per share, both usually converted into convenient units for ease of calculation. A price/earnings ratio of 15 or slightly more would be reasonable (at the time of writing), depending on the industry concerned and the overall environment. A useful way of understanding the significance of this particular ratio is to imagine buying shares of common stock on the basis of so many years' purchase of profits (e.g., 15) or earnings per share in the same way that property is bought for investment at so many times the annual rent. Any ratio less than average would tend to indicate a poor, perhaps erratic, record to date or doubts about the level of profitability likely to be achieved in the current year. Another way of looking at the price/earnings ratio is to regard it as the reciprocal of the earnings yield.

Management, trying to keep the stockholders happy and the business prospering at the same time, is faced with the old adage "not too much, not too little, but just right." If it distributes too much of the profits as dividends, the company has that much less to plough back into the business and has to cover this deficiency from other, more expensive, sources. If it is replaced by further equity issues, then the earnings per share of common are diluted and become less attractive. Much depends, of course, on whether the stockholders' mood in general is for income now or capital gains later, or even for something in between.

If too little is distributed, then the stockholders may be fair game for a takeover offer, leaving top management in a difficult situation tactically. So the dividend distribution must be just right, to match the current scene, keeping a close watch on industrial trends generally. But "just right" varies from firm to firm: an established thriving business may well be keen to give its stockholders the maximum possible dividend, but a relatively new firm, particularly one with strong R. & D. implications, would be wiser to conserve resources, offering growth prospects rather than immediate income.

Dividends can be kept steady from year to year by relating the proportion of profits distributed on a long-term average, and this may be preferred by the stockholders to a dividend that fluctuates with the annual profits. This means keeping back profits in good years, in an equalization account, to help out the bad years.

Profit Planning

Consideration has been given to the distribution of profits arising out of business transactions over a financial year, assuming such profits to have been made. Traditionally, the amount of that profit, or loss, was hardly known until the books were balanced, usually annually only, but occasionally as an interim measure instituted by more advanced managements. Today, the emphasis is on profit planning and keeping a close watch on the financial situation all the time, an aspect which will be developed further in Chapter Thirteen when dealing with the integrated aspects of managerial control.

In the meantime, the following simplified profit and loss statement, which generally complements a simplified balance sheet such as the one in Table C, completes the main outline on a firm's final accounts.

TABLE D   Simplified Profit & Loss Statement (Retail Store)

Gross sales for year		$227,000
Less returns and allowances		2,300
NET SALES		$224,700
Cost of goods sold:		
Inventory, Jan. 1	$ 40,000	
Purchases	136,500	
Freight-in	1,100	
Cost of goods available	177,600	
Inventory, Dec. 31	43,200	
COST OF GOODS SOLD		134,400
GROSS MARGIN		$ 90,300
Operating expenses:		
Rent	$ 21,000	
Salaries and wages	23,300	
Telephone	1,700	
Utilities	2,400	
Insurance	2,800	
Depreciation	6,500	
Advertising expense	4,000	
Other selling expenses	5,500	
Bad debt expense	1,200	
Other administrative expenses	6,200	
TOTAL OPERATING EXPENSES		74,600
OPERATING INCOME		$ 15,700
Other income—dividends		1,100
TOTAL INCOME BEFORE TAXES		16,800
Income tax expense		7,500
NET INCOME		$ 9,300

Business Ratios

To help with forecasting, planning, and control, various financial and operating ratios can be derived from the balance sheet and other accounting records. The price/earnings ratio has been met already, but there are many others that are worth consideration. For example, ratios should enable a check on the level of investment in fixed assets, on the adequacy of working capital, the rapid turnover of stock, and the keeping of liabilities within proper safety limits.

A word of warning is necessary before proceeding further: Ratios taken for comparison, however accurate statistically, should be regarded as indicators only. Even for the same firm, the building of a time series can be invalidated unless the changing environment is given full weight when evaluating the apparent trends. When comparing ratios with those of other firms in the same industry, or in different industries, it is essential, so far as possible, to make sure that like is being compared to like.

The following simplified business ratios, often referred to as management ratios, are included by way of example. There are a large number of others in common use, and most industries have special key ratios of their own relevant only to themselves in their particular line of business.

1. PROFITABILITY RATIOS

(a) Return on Investment. The R.O.I. consists of profit for the year, expressed as a percentage of capital employed. In this context, capital employed consists of share capital (common and preferred) and reserves, plus any borrowed money including bonds, loans, and bank overdrafts. The R.O.I. will vary considerably, depending on industrial trends and the state of the economy.

(b) Return on Equity. This ratio consists of the net income for the year, *after* preferred stock dividends, interest charges, and taxes, expressed as a percentage of common share capital and reserves at the start of the year. Ordinary dividends and retained profits can also conveniently be expressed as a percentage of total equity capital.

2. LIQUIDITY RATIOS

(a) Current Ratio. This measures the short-term ability of a company to convert its current assets (inventory, receivables, marketable securities, and cash) into cash in order to meet its current liabilities (creditors, bank overdraft, taxation provisions, and dividends due) as appropriate. The ratio is determined by

dividing the current assets by current liabilities. An acceptable value is usually 2:1. Apart from the actual ratio at any particular time, some importance should be given to the trend; for should this be downwards, it probably means that sales are growing faster than (and overloading) working capital. This situation suggests a need for more long-term finance to support continued development.

(b) Quick Ratio. Often known as the *Acid-test Ratio*, this streamlines the Current Ratio down to basic elements by excluding inventory from the calculation. It attempts to measure the financial ability of a company to meet its obligations day by day. In this revised form, a ratio of 1:1 is normally considered to be acceptable; but here again trends are important and every situation must be judged overall, not merely on mathematical results.

(c) Solvency Ratio. Expressed as a percentage of total equity capital to total assets, this ratio speaks for itself. The practical realizability of these assets, without significant loss in the event of liquidation, is a material point to be kept in mind.

3. OTHER FINANCIAL RATIOS

By relating profit to sales, it is possible to assess the efficiency of management in keeping down costs of all kinds, thereby achieving a satisfactory overall margin. Similarly, by appropriate ratios, it is also possible to demonstrate the proportion of sales income taken by various costs. Sales, in turn, can be related to capital invested to show how many times the capital is converted into sales; for example, an answer of 3 means that every $1 invested produces $3 in sales.

Then it is important to ascertain, by dividing stocks by sales (preferably the cost of those sales), how many months' stocks are actually in hand. A rising trend in this ratio will suggest that stocks are increasing and/or sales falling off, thus indicating a possible liquidity problem for the future.

As a final example, it is worthwhile to keep ratios for receivables and payables as a check on the average length of trade credit given and received, the effects of which have been mentioned earlier in the chapter. Here the total for accounts receivable is divided by annual sales in one case, and for accounts payable by annual purchases in the other. The trend, as usual, is the main guide for management action and indicates the likely effects on liquidity and profits.

It is the province of management to look at all sides of any problem; business ratios, provided that they are carefully selected and used with understanding and discretion, can serve as a valuable tool in the process of decision-making.

Liquidity versus Profitability

These two terms are basically in opposition and require managerial judgment if a realistic balance is to be achieved between them. It can be readily appreciated, for example, that holding a great deal of cash as working capital, over and above all normal requirements, can be reassuring as liquidity. But, at the same time, it can be highly expensive as against being used in the business as fixed assets or invested profitably outside the business. Liquidity ratios must be high enough to keep everyday activities satisfactorily on the move, with a reasonable buffer for any sudden emergency, but not excessive to the detriment of planned profits. Here again, therefore, is a case of "not too much, not too little, but just right"; what is "just right" can vary from one period to another, demanding continual vigilance and flexibility.

Interfirm Comparison

A company that is content to compare its current business ratios, or results in some other form, with past performance, even its best performance to date, may be burying its head in the sand or be guilty of complacency. Simply to be satisfied with doing better this month than last month, or the same month last year, ignores the vital environmental fact that the overriding situation may be completely different, thereby vitiating true comparison. Even trend figures, including moving annual totals, tend to suffer from inbred isolation.

A more significant test is to compare one's own progress, or recession, with the performance and financial results of other firms in the same industry operating over the same period and under similar conditions.

It may be argued that such competitors will tend to keep their key results secret, other than those which they have by law to publish in final-account form. But even these final-account results can be analyzed, and comparative deductions made, coupled with such statements as are made to stockholders in annual and interim reports. The basis is necessarily historical, but is an objective step in the right direction.

Trade associations for separate industries often provide comparisons among firms, their operations and financial comparisons being geared to include the inherent peculiarities of the particular industry. Each participating firm may be asked to supply its results monthly, or quarterly, on the promise of a quick return of analyzed results, suitably camouflaged for security reasons, for managerial action as appropriate.

In order to obtain valid figures and strict uniformity, the trade association concerned must be careful to define the exact accounting, costing, and other information required. On the secrecy issues there must also be safeguards against intelligent guesswork by a competitor. For example, taking an extreme case, if one particular size bracket contained two firms only, either firm could deduce the figures of the other simply by eliminating its own results from the combined totals. This assumes the usual situation that averages and so on are broken down into separate data for large, medium, and small companies as well as for all companies taken as a whole.

Here again there is an historical basis, and that history is sufficiently recent for the information to be significantly studied and lessons drawn period by period. Trends can be built up and projected as a first approximation in practical planning.

Within an industry, and to a lesser extent between industries, opportunities arise for managements of different firms to get together for policy discussions and to pool experience in general. Trade associations, apart from supplying figures as indicated above, may also be active in making recommendations to firms within their province. In formulating such recommendations the participating firms, represented by directors or executives on councils and committees, must inevitably talk a great deal of "shop" together and share such information as they are prepared to divulge in the common interest.

Such discussions would probably include the interpretation of collective results and explanations for causes of difference as between one period and the next. They might be concerned with the average performance and range of performance as between all competing firms in the industry. Certainly, they should keep a close watch on the business ratios, to make sure of their continued relevance as a measure of interfirm comparison on all major issues; or perhaps of inter-industry comparison in general matters, such as return on investment. The objective behind all such trade association activity must be to help improve results for the future, and, as a neutral body, be ready at all times to give advice to member firms.

It may be felt that the efficient firms in an industry are helping less effective rivals to become more competitive, simply by contributing to the common pool of knowledge. But experience shows that efficient firms usually gain the most from comparative tables, and other published information, being geared for positive action, and that in practice they have little to fear. The real test is the relative quality of the respective managements.

Most of the business ratios already indicated are "critical" ratios essential to top management for control purposes. Usually, such key ratios are kept to a working minimum to focus attention on the vital issues. Other ratios, less critical, also need careful selection, but these can be studied, and departmental action be taken, at lower levels of management.

At any time a need could arise for further information to help planning, requiring additional facts about the industry. In this context, the alternatives include instituting special research, internally or externally, or stimulating the trade association to fill in the gap by approaches to its member firms making the results obtained available to them all. The association could also, in appropriate cases, seek government help by making, for example, a case for additional official statistics to be produced in the interests of the industry or the community at large.

To have proper managerial control there must be meaningful standards of performance. The comparison of actual results against previous results leaves much to be desired, as has been seen, and the better, more scientific, method is therefore to compare actual with budgeted figures based on forecasts. Budgeting techniques will be developed in some detail in Chapter Thirteen, but in the meantime it should be clear why emphasis has been placed on the part to be played by interfirm comparison.

The Effect of Inflation

Even when differences in environment, accounting definitions, and so on have been rationalized for purposes of accurate comparison, there are still problems caused by changes in the value of money that can weaken validity to the point of absurdity. Comparing, say, the growth of assets over the past 20 years, a given result could suggest highly satisfactory progress. But, adjusting for the effects of inflation, the true "progress" could in fact be negative.

Government statements on changes in the value of money suggest that it needed more than $3 by 1973 to equal the purchasing power of a dollar in 1940. The full effects of this are not always sufficiently appreciated, bearing in mind that the value of money will seemingly continue to fall and must be allowed for even when comparing figures with those of only a year or so previously. This means adjusting balance sheets and statements of all kinds to obtain a true record free from misleading information likely to affect decision-making and bedevil policy. A practical example of this kind of problem has already been encountered in connection with the depreciation of fixed assets.

The changing situation implies a need for rethinking orthodox historical accounting and the substitution of what has been called "purchasing-power accounting." Obvious though the need for realism may be, it is regrettable, but understandable, that many managements (where old habits tend to die hard) have been slow to adopt its logic.

The most important effect of continued inflation is that, by allowing fixed assets to remain on the books at cost less depreciation, the key ratio of return on investment (R.O.I.) shows profits, at face value, as being proportionately better than they really are. This may appeal to conservative managements, content for balance-sheet figures to be understated in the tradition of "secret reserves" (or "hidden assets," to put it another way), but it can open the door for possible takeover bids from more sophisticated competitors. In any case, it may lead to complacency and the misuse of capital resources to the detriment of future development.

Quite apart from inflation, it may be said in parenthesis that many companies still tend to clear what are called "intangible assets" from their balance sheet, even though they still have a value that should be shown among the other assets. Examples are goodwill, usually created from the acquisition of subsidiary companies and patents, copyrights, trade-marks, and brand names that still have a cash market value to be recorded.

The second effect is with respect to the capital itself. Being subject to the same monetary erosion of purchasing power, the capital will therefore need the injection of fresh funds over the years to maintain its *status quo* quite apart from any growth that has been planned. The stockholders, too, will tend to argue that any dividend policy should take full account of currency debasement as a matter of common justice.

In using inflation accounting, a general price index, built up over the years and extended realistically into the future, would seem to be an essential tool of management. Although emphasis has been placed on inflation, management at any given time may need to give attention to deflation instead, or to cyclical trends involving a mixture of both.

Some progressive companies take a modern viewpoint of inflationary changes in monetary values and periodically revalue their fixed assets, showing the current value on their balance sheet, thereby adding to total assets and increasing general reserves correspondingly. Ideally, such revaluation should be carried out annually, if only for business-ratio and other control purposes outside the published statements themselves.

In the same context, there is often some misunderstanding about the concept of "replacement cost" mentioned earlier. This might seem to presuppose a regular (perhaps annual) need for an expensive professional revaluation of fixed or other assets if purchasing-power accounting is adopted. But, insofar as the technique is confined to offsetting the effects of inflation, all that is needed is a simple recalculation of asset figures by the application of the appropriate price indices reflecting inflation. It is then an easy matter to adjust each asset figure, in money terms, from the date of purchase until the current year or other year required for true comparison.

Inflation also affects contracts, particularly those requiring payment in the distant future when the value of money could be quite different from that obtaining at the date of contract. A long-term loan to purchase premises, for example, with deferred-repayment facilities could result in the property itself becoming a "hedge against inflation" and the eventual repayments being made in depreciated currency. Given both advantages over a long enough period, interest charges could be offset by capital appreciation or eliminated entirely. Responsible managements, on both sides of any long-term contract, should therefore be on guard for any detrimental effects and make provision accordingly.

PROFIT AND COST CENTERS

The decentralization of authority has been described in Chapter Four, including the concept of divisionalization. This latter was seen to be the breaking down of a complex business into a number of operating divisions, each with its own largely autonomous management. To help maximize profits or minimize costs, according to the particular point of view, it is a convenient technique to pinpoint responsibility for either, or both, as effectively as possible, by means of "profit centers" or "cost centers," each controlling its own marketing, production, and financial operations.

Although divisions, based on product line or territory, have been mentioned in this context, *any* separate unit, such as a department or branch, which can be given autonomy, qualifies automatically as a potential profit or cost center. It is generally agreed, however, that conglomerates, i.e., large concerns having fingers in many pies, with their essentially self-contained divisions or subsidiaries, appear to offer the best scope for evaluating unit contributions to a group's progress as a whole.

The Profit Center Concept

The key to managerial success is the setting of feasible targets and the measuring against them of results achieved. Divisional managers, each working to financial targets laid down by the parent board of directors, can be given wide responsibility and powers of control based on a self-contained profit center. This means that they have freedom to operate as they consider best, subject to achieving the profits laid down for the division, preferably after mutual discussion and agreement with the overall targets set.

Emphasis must be laid on the need for consultation, as targets can be too low, leading to complacency, or too high, resulting in frustration and feelings of unfairness. The most effective level should still be somewhat higher than that normally attainable, as any executive should be stretched to his utmost, given the right degree of motivation, if only for his own development. In addition, there is usually some benefit to be derived from the activities of the group as a whole, for example, the building up of a good public relations image for a national enterprise, which helps to produce better collective results than could be achieved by the units working locally in isolation. This extra group benefit is often called "synergy," where the sum of the parts through cooperation can be greater than the whole.

Incidentally, the running of such a center can prove to be an excellent training ground for future top managers. They become indoctrinated at an early stage with the search for profits and the importance of achieving the right return on capital employed. Certain criteria other than R.O.I. are also essential for success. In particular, the unit objectives must be identical with those of the group, and the assessment of a unit's performance must be independent of the assessment of other units' performances. In equity a unit should only be judged by the effectiveness of decisions made by its own management, not by those imposed on such management from outside. Failure to comply with such criteria can lead, and often does lead, to difficulties and dispute.

Top management must, of course, continue to exercise overall control, concern itself with planning and the allocation of resources, and make essential policy decisions. But in maximizing group profits generally, it should not place any division at a disadvantage without accepting at least some of the responsibility for any relative falling off in its growth rate of profits.

Problems to be Overcome

Breaking down a large concern into a number of watertight compartments, each becoming a virtually independent business, is no easy task. To make the exercise worth while there must be an overall advantage to be gained, with special reference to profits. Any self-contained unit not capable of making a profit, or sufficient profit, would be better closed down unless there were special policy reasons, such as prestige, advertising value, or customers' service for continuing its existence. Even so, such substandard profit results must be satisfactorily offset by other units geared to above-average returns.

Most of the problems arising from profit centers are accounting problems, with particular reference to *(a)* the comparative use of assets, *(b)* the allocation of overhead expenses, and *(c)* the fixing of internal transfer prices when one unit sells to another. These three issues are the cause of much dispute and divisional or other unit dissatisfaction, especially when there are no firm bases for assessment.

Taking the use of assets first, it can be readily appreciated that two profit centers, each occupying business premises, can have very different accounting figures when one center has a building bought many years ago on a long lease and the other center a building just erected on a newly acquired site. Attempts to equalize profit opportunity, for example, by fixing a speculative rent (interest) on updated valuation (capital), are necessarily arbitrary and tend to get away from reality.

Central overhead expenses, such as the cost of home office administration, can be allocated to divisions; but to avoid arbitrary bases for certain expenses, such expenses may preferably be absorbed at the home office itself. Where specific services are called upon, such as O. & M. facilities, it could be argued that these should be paid for according to the amount used. There might be a case for assessing what such services would cost if imported from outside the group. The main factor is to ensure that any basis for allocation is reasonable and seen to be fair to all concerned. Arbitrary allocations of overhead expenses, such as group advertising or research and development, made according to unit turnover, profits, and the like, seldom come within this area of acceptability.

The profit center must not be considered merely as a means of allocating home office costs. In fact, many of the accounting pitfalls can be avoided simply by excluding *all* central overhead expenses from profit center accounts. On this basis the self-contained unit is judged on its contribution to the group's profit, related, of course, to capital employed, without having the frustrations of being debited with costs over which it had no control. There may also be a saving in accounting work centrally and divisionally. Another approach used in practice is to pass on to a unit only those overhead expenses which would cease if the unit itself went out of business. If, however, it is decided to allocate *all* costs, then the bases chosen must be seen, and accepted, as equitable and fair to all concerned.

The third issue, internal pricing, is another thorny problem: how to determine, for example, the basis for transfering goods or services from one division to another. The two obvious alternatives are the open-market price, as charged to customers, and the actual cost, however that may be defined. But the former may include an element of central overhead expenses; and the latter could be a higher cost than it should be, simply as a result of inefficiency.

As responsibility must be laid fairly and squarely on a profit center, it is essential that there should be no loopholes for managerial excuse. In the above case, there are certain accounting adjustments that could be made, but room for argument could still remain. One answer might be a buying price and a selling price, central accounts absorbing the difference.

Similarly, long-term interests should not be allowed to be sacrificed for short-term advantage. An ambitious profit center manager, who could be a divisional president, might be tempted to make an impressive impact. With this aim he could strategically keep his costs down, and thereby increase the R.O.I., by not spending resources on such items as advertising, staff training, research, or property maintenance, relying on past impetus to keep the center going for the time being. Should he succeed in his strategy, to gain promotion, there would be headaches for *his* successor.

Divisional, or other profit center, accountants having submitted their annual figures, the comptroller or central accountant will prepare consolidated final accounts, including the balance sheet and profit and loss statement, making such adjustments, including contra items, as become necessary between one division and another. During the year his department will prepare regular interim consolidated statements—daily, weekly, monthly, or quarterly—coupled with the business ratios and so on; these are submitted to top management for purposes of control, profit center managements being kept informed as appropriate.

A Further Look at Cost Centers

An introduction to cost centers was given in Chapter Ten. It has been assumed so far that divisionalization, or other self-contained organization, has been possible, either through divisions or subsidiary companies. There is, however, a "half-way house" type of organization where it is not feasible to have complete autonomy, but where responsibility can be fixed for incurring costs and other expenses. Here the concept of cost centers is well worth consideration.

Briefly, the organization is divided up into departments, branches and so on, each with authority to incur expenditure within a given mandate. Cost control can be invoked at all vertical points in an organization—marketing, production, finance, personnel—and at all levels. Even in the office there are many expenses that should be controlled. Granted that rates and rents are fixed, there can be considerable saving in lighting, heating, stationery, telephones and postage, quite apart from the more dramatic savings in personnel cost through increased productivity as dealt with in Chapter Twelve.

Responsibility for costs can only be fixed if complete local control is given over the costs and expenses under review. Ideally, an atmosphere of cost consciousness should be stimulated from the top, including the issue of comparative schedules from time to time, so that cumulative results can be checked against budget figures and action taken as indicated.

The idea of cost consciousness as a missionary policy connotes the concept of *cost clinics,* where all interested parties can be brought together in committee to discuss ways and means of reducing costs effectively. A similar type of committee can be created with regard to the broader opportunities of *profit clinics*. In the latter, in particular, agents, dealers, and other members of the marketing organization can be made to play a vital part in liaison with the accountants. Free-for-all "brainstorming" sessions often produce valuable ideas, some of which have practical possibilities, but such meetings also help to emphasize managerial policy at first hand.

Cost Accounting and Standard Costs

Before leaving the topic of costs, brief mention should be made of the build-up and analysis of cost information. The main components of costing are *(a)* direct materials and direct labor, being those costs which can be identified and charged to a particular product or service supplied, and *(b)* overhead expenses.

Overhead expenses are usually broken down into three main

categories: those attributable to factory, to sales, and to administration. They include, for example, the cost of power, supervisors, and clerical labor in the case of the factory; the salaries of executives and staff in the case of administration; advertising, sales commission and transportation costs with regard to the marketing side. The usual object is to determine the total cost (average unit cost) of a product, service, department, project, or other unit as appropriate to a given organization.

The problem of equitably allocating central (home office) overhead expenses to divisions, or excluding them entirely, has already been introduced with regard to the motivational effects on divisional profit centers. Similar difficulties must be overcome when allocating factory, administrative and sales overhead expenses within any firm, whether divisionalized or not, if cost-accounting information is to be put to effective use.

Given the attainment of acceptable figures, after imposing suitable checks on the accuracy of data collected, they must still be used with understanding and discretion. As historical costs they have obvious limits, particularly when attempting to use them for planning purposes without due regard for environmental change. However, they are a useful first approximation of the cost implications of any proposed business strategy.

A more sophisticated approach is the concept of *standard costs*, which is an estimate of what the costs of a given product or operation are likely to be in a future environment, the figures being based on certain realistic assumptions. Actual costs achieved can then be checked against standard costs (determined in advance) and appropriate managerial action taken in the light of variances. But this is an aspect of control which receives more detailed treatment in Chapter Thirteen.

SITES, PREMISES, LAYOUT, AND EQUIPMENT

Arising from accounting considerations of capital investment in fixed assets, with special reference to land and buildings, it is appropriate here to have a look at sites, premises, layout and equipment from a financial point of view. There are other approaches equally tenable—marketing, production, personnel—but these can be conveniently covered at the same time.

Nevertheless, there must be emphasis on economic viability, in order to achieve at least the agreed minimum return on the investment to be made. Any departure from this rule would need a strong case to back it up. It is also essential that there should be a proper balance between capital cost, maintenance, and productivity. Consideration has already been given to the financial alternative of owning or leasing plant, warehouses, or office accomodations.

Site Location and Investigation

It is the function of top management to provide effective and adequate accommodations consistent with the corporate objectives, in the right place or places. Originally, the choice would have been that of the entrepreneur, but in a dynamic environment there must be continuous reassessment of existing locations, and the buildings erected on them, even for a business which has long been established.

The vital issues for consideration with respect to plant location include:

(a) The proximity of raw materials.

(b) The availability of local (preferably lower-cost) labor.

(c) Economic transport facilities by air, sea, river, canal, railroad and highway, as appropriate.

(d) The right climatic conditions, where necessary for production.

(e) Adequate power and other public utility services.

(f) Convenience to markets at home and abroad.

In the process, feasibility surveys would be made and costed with a systematic narrowing down of alternatives available. First, the particular areas of the country would be selected, then the actual localities, and finally, the individual sites that happen to be available at the time.

The negotiation of sites is normally the province of specialist industrial or business real estate agents; engineers and architects may be brought in at a later stage to advise on the technical issues of site development. Management must, however, be clear as to what is required from an administrative point of view, based on a preliminary scheme and the working out of budget costs, and must brief the specialists accordingly. The importance of a thorough briefing, setting out all the essentials envisaged, cannot be overemphasized.

Where an element of secrecy is required, there may be a good case for using a leading agent to act for a "client" unspecified. This may be a large firm wishing to conceal from its competitors the extent of its plans or aiming to help negotiations by not revealing initially that it is a well-known firm with ample resources. This may be particularly relevant to competitive trading ventures, such as department stores, operating in centers of population for limited markets. Here we have a combination of strategy to consider as well as economic viability.

Building Construction

Once a site is finally settled upon, and feasibility studies have been carried out, the full-scale effects of planning and building must go forward. A valuable technique here, known as "critical path analysis" or "network planning," is described in some detail in Chapter Thirteen.

The company would normally engage a building contractor to carry out the construction work. It is usual here to go to tender, with a detailed bill of quantities upon which costs can be reasonably quoted, the lowest estimate being accepted. Tenders should be sought only from firms that would be acceptable as builders; otherwise a successful tender might result in a cheap contract being placed but a bad job in the ultimate. There is an opportunity for price fixing, in tendering, which needs watching. The other practical danger lies in the invoking of "penalty clauses" for not finishing by the contracted completion date. The builder in difficulty can defensively "create" a file of correspondence and site-meeting notes, seeking to prove that his failure to complete in time was really due to the client changing his mind on the original plans and/or causing delays by being slow in giving opinions.

The builder thereby seeks to prove, with the possibility of legal action against him in mind, that any losses incurred were in fact the fault of the client himself. Penalty clauses are void at common law unless they represent a genuine attempt to agree upon liquidated damages. Also any attempt to frighten would be void under so-called *in terrorem* rules. Management must be continually aware of problems such as these and keep a watchful eye on progress.

·An alternative method is not to go to tender at all but to arrange a "package deal" with a reputable contractor who will take over the full practical burden. The company would still need to agree on the architectural and engineering design, a firm price, and a guaranteed completion date.

Apart from new construction on a site, there is the alternative of adapting an existing building already situated in the right location. Architectural plans would be drawn up for alterations of additions and costs estimated in much the same way as for a new building. Another variation is to take over an old building and demolish it for the advantages of obtaining the site. Comparative costs, *vis-à-vis* potential profits from alternatives, must constantly be borne in mind.

In looking at the costs of construction, managerial decisions are required on total floor-space capacity, materials, height of building, whether it is to have permanent internal walls or be erected as an empty shell with movable departmental divisions for flexibility. It should be noted that multistorey construction can prove to be expensive because of elevators, fire escapes, and other necessary additional items. Provision must also be made for physical expansion, as and when required, to match planned business growth. This should not mean, however, leaving valuable space empty and producing no revenue at all.

Planning a Factory or Warehouse

There is no need to emphasize that plant layout requires careful planning and starts with the collection and analysis of the necessary data. Then, having taken care of all legal and other constraints, it should be possible to develop a logical layout with economy of space, strategic and balanced flow of materials, work, and finished products, coupled with flexibility for growth and change. Quantitative techniques such as "linear programming," which is a mathematical system of allocating resources in such a way as to achieve optimum effectiveness, and "queueing theory," dealt with earlier, may play an important part. The various specialists will take care of floor loadings, heating, lighting and power, waste disposal, and other industrial building requirements.

Scale plans and made-up models, for example, of machine tools, drawn to the same scale, enable factory layout planning to be worked out accurately in miniature. This may be part of a feasibility study or a choice between alternative systems allied to a given floor space.

But planning based on work studies of technical processes is not enough; there must also be provision for achieving the best possible environment for those who will occupy the premises as workers. Well-designed architecturally and properly planned, such buildings can improve productivity, help profits, assist labor recruitment and aid publicity and good public relations. There are, of course, certain minimum standards for the working environment, but these should be regarded by any progressive organization solely as the starting-point.

Office Planning

Wherever offices are built, or taken over, there still remains the *managerial* problem of planning. Broadly, the choice exists between the old-fashioned divided type of layout, consisting of many separate departments and private offices, all with more-or-less permanent walls, and open planning where there are hardly any walls at all.

Open-plan offices—the concept also applies to open-plan factories—do away with most of the internal walls and substitute low screens and horticultural plants instead. Because of the indoor vegetation, an alternative term used is "landscaped" offices.

An analysis of the advantages and disadvantages of walls soon demonstrates a physical balance in favor of open planning. But consideration must also be given to the welfare and efficiency of the personnel working in one or another environment, either singly or as part of a group. While some claim that open planning is distracting and others, theoretically losing private-office status, tend to stand on their dignity, the majority soon find that the new conditions are pleasant, effective, and acceptable. But before knocking down any walls, management would be wise to sound out reaction to change and prepare its plans accordingly.

Clearly, open planning is economic in space requirements, makes supervision easier, speeds up communication and the flow of work, and is thereby a great time-saver for clerical staff. It has considerable flexibility and provides for changing individual and group identities, on functional lines, by the strategic placing of mobile equipment. Private offices are few and far between, being mainly reserved for top managers needing privacy for interviews with customers and staff.

Yet, despite the apparent attractions, open-plan offices in industry as a whole are still an exception to the general rule. Opponents, arguing that they are expensive to start with, have in mind the cost of carpeting and acoustic ceilings needed to combat increased noise, together with the mobile screens, plants, and low furniture. But they tend to forget that, in the long run, all these costs can be taken care of by the more economic use of space and increased productivity. For this is no gimmick, but a serious attempt at designing a realistic and methodical office layout.

Moving a Factory or Office

A managerial decision to move from an existing site to a new one some considerable distance away, for example as part of a policy to decentralize production, requires careful investigation before any action is taken. Although the choice of a new location may be in line with previous discussion, there is a factor of comparative costs to be taken into account here, problems of removal, and special responsibility with regard to personnel.

The availability of suitable labor in the new area, skilled or unskilled, is a starting-point, coupled with the level of pay and associated conditions of employment. But there are managers and other personnel already in the existing factory or office, some of whom may be vital as key employees, either in a supervisory capacity or as instructors to take over training in the new locality. This raises two main problems: first, which members of staff should be transferred to the new location and how can they and their families be motivated to move, and second, what should be done about the remainder, many of whom may be long and faithful servants of the company?

Acceptance by the new community is another vital issue and may mean instituting some form of regular liaison with the local powers and personalities to demonstrate good faith and gain access to informed local opinion and goodwill.

Key personnel to be transferred will be vitally concerned with the availability of suitable local housing and with comparative levels of house prices, rates, and rents. They will be concerned also about schools and other essential services and amenities. They may need help with legal and real estate agent costs of changing houses and with relocation costs. All these and similar matters require advance managerial planning of a most practical character. The frequency or availability of local transportation between the new site and residential areas is a matter not to be overlooked. It is with facilities of this kind that development areas have a built-in advantage. As to personnel no longer required or not willing to move, suitable compensation (or at least, severance pay) would require policy consideration. Trade union attitudes would, of course, have to be kept well in mind.

TAX CONSIDERATIONS

No chapter on the financial aspects of business operation would be complete without at least some minimal reference to the complex tax environment for the American firm, although a comprehensive treatment would be outside the purview of a basic management work. In view of the intricacies of tax legislation at federal and state levels, numerous and frequent changes in provisions and regulations, and the amassing of a large body of tax rulings, it is just about mandatory these days for even the smallest business to seek assistance in this general area of taxation from an accounting firm or tax specialist, both of which can manage to keep current with the rapidly changing situation. The function of such specialists, of course, would be to seek to minimize the overall tax liability of the company.

Among the major taxes affecting business are:

(a) Income taxes.

(b) Social security taxes.

(c) Sales taxes.

(d) Property taxes.

(e) Excise taxes.

Management must play two roles within this tax environment; not only must it pay taxes of various types, but it is also required to act as an agent for the government in collecting tax monies. In performing these two functions, a not inconsiderable amount of record-keeping and paperwork is involved, reflecting in increased costs both in time and in dollars for the company. Taxes are imposed upon business at all three levels: federal, state, and local.

Federal Taxes

More than sixty years ago, a constitutional amendment gave Congress the right to collect taxes on incomes. The major tax facing business firms today, on the federal level, is the income tax. Businesses as well as employed persons are required to pay this tax on earnings. Under present law, however, neither the sole proprietorship nor the partnership, as a legal form of business, is considered a taxable entity in and of itself; consequently, income earned from the operating of such enterprises is taxable to the individual owners or partners. Such income is to be added to other personal income these individuals may earn during the taxable year and reported annually on the ordinary individual income tax form (Form 1040). However, partnerships are required to file special informational returns each year with the federal government (Form 1065).

On the other hand, as corporations are treated legally as separate entities, such companies are taxed directly on their annual earnings, currently at the rate of 22 per cent of the first $25,000 of taxable earnings and 48 per cent on income in excess of $25,000. The federal government provides a corporation tax form (Form 1120) for purposes of accounting. It should be noted that small business corporations may elect to be treated much as partnerships; in this latter case, an information return is filed with the government, and earnings from the corporation are then added to the individual tax returns of the stockholders, for tax liability.

A "Declaration of Estimated Tax" must be filed with the government by incorporated businesses as well as by individuals, on a quarterly basis. When submitted, these forms are generally accompanied by the prepayment of a portion of their expected income tax for the current year. With regard to this steady accounting to the government, firms must also report on information returns payments made to employees, consultants, and the like as salaries or wages, commissions, fees, and so on.

The firm is required to act as tax agent in withholding tax from the wages and salaries paid to its employees. This is done according to established percentages of earned income, at the end of each regular payroll period. Such monies must be deposited frequently in a special account as well as reported, on a quarterly basis, to the federal government.

In similar vein, the employing firm must collect social security tax, under the provisions of the Social Security Act of 1935 and subsequent amendments; these sums are destined to provide for unemployment insurance to workers (through a cooperative federal-state arrangement), for old age benefits, and for disability coverage. Further, the firm must make a matching contribution on its own.

Federal excise taxes are placed on a variety of products including gasoline, automobiles, liquor, telephone calls, tobacco, and theatre admissions. Retailers as well as manufacturers are responsible for collecting these amounts and must, in turn, deposit same regularly, in addition to filing quarterly returns.

State and Local Taxes

In addition to the federal income tax on earnings, most states and some large cities also levy tax on incomes. As a general rule, the filing of such returns is expedited by tying in the forms to entries on the federal income tax form. Of course, rates as well as regulations differ substantially from state to state.

Similarly, states, cities, and some county governments set sales taxes in varying percentages on most merchandise purchased by consumers. These are paid directly by the consumer, collected by the firm, and deposited with the appropriate agency. Certain products are exempted from such taxes as well as certain types of purchasers (as, for example, churches or other nonprofit institutions).

Most of the revenue that goes toward the support of local governments come from taxes levied on real and personal property. Usually, such property taxes are based on a fixed dollar rate per each $100 of the property's "assessed valuation," as determined by the local taxing agency. Of course, as the costs of operating local government continue to climb, the property tax rate is adjusted upward from time to time, as has been happening frequently in these inflationary times. Businesses, as they own larger buildings and more land and put in more improvements, pay a proportionately greater share of this revenue than do homeowners.

Another source of revenue to local governments, of course, is the licensing of a variety of business types, including beauty parlors, liquor stores, pharmacies, hotels, restaurants, and others. Licenses or permits are also intended to enforce zoning ordinances and otherwise regulate business.

Although not a tax problem *per se* (though a necessary expense), brief mention ought to be made at this point of the necessity for business firms to carry, in compliance with state law, workmen's compensation insurance. This type of mandatory coverage provides protection for employees against expenses incurred because of personal injuries suffered on the job and for work-related illness. It also provides protection for the firm itself, in the event that lawsuits are filed against the company by employees. This insurance covers medical bills incurred and also pays the employee weekly benefits, usually after a short waiting period. In general, premiums for workmen's compensation policies are based upon the particular industry, the nature of the work including the hazards involved, and the number of prior claims submitted by the company insured.

Summary

1. *Modern Approach to Capital*
   a. The important concept is that of cash or funds flow.
   b. It is quantified by changes in assets and/or liabilities.
   c. The aim is to make the best use of funds.

2. *Investment in Fixed Assets*
   a. Capital investment appraisal must be objective.
   b. It should be based on a moving 3-5 year schedule.
   c. A given return must be achieved on capital employed.
   d. Selection on R.O.I. basis takes account of discounted cash flow.
   e. Comparison is facilitated by the profitability index.
   f. Leasing instead of buying conserves capital.
   g. Existing assets can be subject to "sale and lease back."

3. Working or Circulating Funds
   a. Adequate working capital is essential.
   b. Liquidity measures the ability to turn assets into cash.
   c. Working capital must not be tied up unprofitably.
   d. Accounts receivable can be collected by factors.

4. Sources of Finance
   a. Permanent or long-term share capital comprises two main forms: preferred and common stocks.
   b. Bonds or loan capital are also long-term.
   c. Other sources of finance (medium- and short-term) are trade credit and borrowing from commercial banks.
   d. Financial policy needs to be kept flexible.
   e. Capital (assets) should normally be protected by insurance.

5. The Financial Structure and Stockholders
   a. A balance sheet shows the financial position at a point of time.
   b. Stockholders' equity includes the reserves.
   c. Gearing reflects equity relationship with fixed-interest funds.
   d. Management has a duty to maximize earnings per share of common stock.
   e. The amount of dividend distribution is a matter of policy.
   f. The average shareholder is concerned with the price/earnings ratio.
   g. Emphasis should be placed on profit planning.

6. Business Ratios
   a. Financial indicators help with forecasting.
   b. They should be studied in the context of changing environment.
   c. They may relate to profitability, liquidity, or other assessments of management efficiency.
   d. Interfirm comparison constitutes a valuable independent check.
   e. Comparison of one period with another is affected by inflation.

7. Profit and Cost Centers
   a. These must be properly identified and understood.
   b. The concept of a self-contained profit center should be based on achievement of feasible targets.
   c. Profit centers are an excellent training ground for future top managers.
   d. Problems arise from comparative use of assets, allocation of home office costs and internal transfer pricing.

e. It may be better to confine control to the narrower concept of a cost center.

f. This introduces cost accounting and standard costs.

8. Sites, Premises, Layout, and Equipment

a. Plant location involves complex decisions, but negotiation is best left to specialists.

b. Building construction is a matter for experts; penalty clauses are of limited value.

c. Plant layout and equipment should be planned for optimum effectiveness.

d. Open-plan offices are still the exception.

e. The decision to move a factory or office must take into account the reactions of key personnel and acceptance by the new community.

9. Tax Considerations

a. The complexity of tax legislation and frequent changes in regulations require detailed record-keeping and specialized accounting assistance.

b. Among the major federal taxes for business firms are the corporate income tax, social security taxes, and general sales taxes.

c. Business is taxed at the state and local levels as well.

Suggested Further Reading

ALFRED, A.M., AND J.B. EVANS. *Discounted Cash Flow: Principles of Some Short Cut Techniques.* 3d ed. New York: Halsted Press, 1971.

ANTHONY, R.N., AND J.S. REECE. *Management Accounting Principles.* 3d ed. Homewood, Ill.: Irwin, 1975.

BATTY, J. *Accountancy for Managers.* New York: International Publications, 1971.

BRIGHAM, E.F., AND J.L. PAPPAS. *Managerial Economics.* Hinsdale, Ill.: Dryden, 1972.

CLARKSON, G.P., AND B.J. ELLIOT. *Managing Money and Finance.* 2d ed. New York: Beekman, 1973.

DeCoster, D.T., et al. *Accounting for Managerial Decision-Making.* Los Angeles: Melville, 1974.

DePaula, F.C. *Management Accounting in Practice.* 4th ed. New York: Beekman, 1972.

Gray, J.C., and K.S. Johnston. *Accounting and Management Action.* New York: McGraw-Hill, 1973.

Holzman, R.S. *Tax Basis for Managerial Decisions.* New York: Holt, Rinehart and Winston, 1965.

Lewellen, W.G. *The Cost of Capital.* Belmont, Calif.: Wadsworth, 1969.

Schattke, R.W., et al. *Managerial Accounting: Concepts and Uses.* Boston: Allyn and Bacon, 1975.

Smith, D.T. *Tax Factors in Business Decisions.* Englewood Cliffs, N.J.: Prentice-Hall, 1968.

Wett, J.E., and C.L. Prather. *Financing Business Firms.* 5th ed. Homewood, Ill.: Irwin, 1975.

TWELVE

Personnel Policies

Management today places greater stress on the human factor than at any time in the past. Even so, the personnel side of numerous business organizations still remains something of a backwater. How many firms, for example, have a personnel *director,* comparable with other functional executives who are directors of the board, instead of just a manager at some lower level? In the boardroom, it is natural that most directors should consider themselves to be experts on personnel matters, yet this is a specialized function, quite as important as marketing, production, and finance, with its own independent expertise.

In the framing of personnel policies, it is a useful corrective, from time to time, to study the changing attitudes of workers and staff. In fact, this very demarcation between workers and staff is itself a danger point, at least emotionally, with time-honored overtones of class distinction. It is, however, a convenient way of dealing with factory work and production as against office work and administration, for the strategic purposes of textbook analysis. But, in human terms, such arbitrary distinction should diplomatically end there.

Although personnel policies are conveniently dealt with in a separate chapter, for purposes of exposition, it must be emphasized that the personnel function cannot be isolated in practice. This has already been demonstrated, as for example in Chapter Six, where "line" authority is clearly identified with immediate responsibility for personnel *management*. Nevertheless, personnel *policies* laid down centrally have a coordinating influence.

THE HUMAN FACTOR IN MANAGEMENT

Top managers are becoming increasingly aware of the many new techniques of management and the need to anticipate the changing environment in all its aspects through corporate strategy, the mainspring of long-range planning. They are beginning to appreciate the advantages of the computer as an aid to decision-making. They are clearly concerned with physical assets and costs. But there still remains a tendency, for example in mathematical model-building, to leave the human aspects to take care of themselves. Yet human resources, unpredictable though they may be in practice, are of the utmost importance to corporate success whether on the shop floor, in the office, or as the energizing force in management itself.

Changing Worker Attitudes

The younger worker today, in the factory or office, is no longer much concerned with security and pensions but wants early involvement, interesting jobs, quick promotion, and the rewards for work now rather than later. Traditional apprenticeships and clerical probation-periods are now mainly a matter of history, with a new emphasis on receiving the full rate of pay at the earliest possible date. Even the trainee typist, with or without shorthand, seeks immediate secretarial status, wherever it can be found, and a salary to match, whether justified by potential or not.

Such impatience has its merits, for it demonstrates a growing self-confidence, energy and enthusiasm, that must be sought out and developed, whenever possible, by increased opportunities for active participation. There is unfortunately the inherent danger of youthful initiative becoming blunted by bureaucratic red tape and too much routine. But even in such a restrictive atmosphere as that, it may still be feasible for the more progressive managers to encourage their juniors to take greater responsibility, either individually, or through personal involvement in group activity.

On the management ladder, opportunities for promotion, with increasing freedom of self-expression, often depend on the rate of corporate growth; but it is in the large-scale organizations that there tends to be that excessive regulation and undue constraint on individual flair just mentioned. Even the entrepreneurial extrovert stands in danger of regimentation.

As for the young graduates now entering business, it is probably true that they have no immediate expectations of grandeur, knowing full well (whatever they may say) that they have first to win their spurs. At the same time, however, evidence suggests that they can quickly become baffled by ultraconservative and unimaginative attitudes, feeling compelled to question the logic of established practice. Unfortunately, in expressing their controversial points of view, or even in making positive but critical comment, however tactfully, they are soon likely to run into difficulties and frustrating opposition. For the old guard ever tend to close their ranks, if only to defend themselves against youthful invaders.

Yet it is this very freshness of approach that should be welcomed by all those long in authority but tending to be over-conditioned by the past. This managerial "generation gap" must be bridged, however, for each side has much to offer to the other. Young graduates understandably have a realistic attitude to financial incentives, but what they want most of all is a chance to develop a satisfying and worthwhile career. They are beginning to appreciate that life has much more to offer than just the money and, so far as possible, this plus quality must be built into the job itself.

In the determination of personnel policies, such changing attitudes throughout the firm must be given their full weight. Managing "personnel," a term which conveniently covers workers of all kinds, whether symbolically clad in blue overalls, white jackets or black office suits, clearly demands a sympathetic personal approach and thereby the establishment of sound human relations. This leads inevitably to the more efficient running of a business through greater interest in the firm, better cooperation, and increased productivity. As shown in

Chapter Six, this interest in people starts at the top, as a positive management philosophy, and permeates right through the hierarchy down to the lowest levels and the latest recruit.

The concept of involvement is illustrated by the use of "attitude surveys" aimed at finding out what personnel really feel about the company they work for and to obtain their ideas for improvement. Basically, an attitude survey is a carefully worded questionnaire seeking employees' opinions on management policies. It is a kind of corporate self-analysis in which all personnel can take part, either through an outside agency or anonymously inside. This camouflaged method of approach may be considered essential if full and frank answers are to be obtained, although experience shows that positive helpful contributions are usually received at least as frequently as merely negative comment. As a result, some surprisingly unexpected attitudes are likely to emerge, with valuable repercussions on future policy deliberation.

Among the objectives of an attitude-survey program are the improvement of morale and standard of work; greater interest in the firm and a more positive sense of cooperation; the receipt of information, ideas and suggestions; the identification and analysis of problems at certain levels; better communication and understanding; and, of course, the expression of attitudes toward a variety of corporate issues ranging from product price levels and advertising to the quality of food in the factory lunchroom.

Attitude surveys can be carried out by experienced interviewers, meeting individuals or groups, as well as by (or instead of) a formal questionnaire. But whatever the method adopted, the end result should be a large collection of information and opinion needing to be sifted and classified for managerial attention and action, as appropriate. For once the rank and file feel that full consideration is being given to their collective points of view, management/worker relationships tend to take on a better meaning. Conversely, if a sense of merely "going through the motions" is allowed to arise, irretrievable damage to such relations may well result.

The Behavioral Scientist

The managerial contribution of the behavioral scientists, direct or indirect, is well known, covering as it does such a wide area of human aspects. Just to take one example from the sphere of organization structures, a clear distinction is drawn between the "mechanistic" and the "organic," the former denoting a cold rigid material approach to organization and the latter the much more fluid concept of a living and human creation. Nevertheless, without being too emotive, it must be admitted that either of these alternatives may be appropriate in given conditions. There is no one right system to cover all sets of circumstances, and it is imperative that any structure should be evolved from the needs of the situation. If a more human organization happens to be applicable, so much the better.

In fact, the behavioral approach covers a multitude of management concepts, and scientific experiments, with special reference to people and personalities, individually and in groups. Examples include theories of management style, interviewing techniques, personality testing, skills analysis, communication networks, and the assessment of motivational needs. All these and many others are associated with the valuable contributions to knowledge made by well-known behavioral scientists. It is a moot point, however, whether any of these authorities actually thought of themselves by that title or whether they considered themselves instead as social researchers into human characteristics.

In recent years, two high-sounding titles have emerged in this field: "ergonomics," the study of the interaction of physical and human systems, and "cybernetics," which is the study of information, communication, and control systems.

Ergonomics aims to produce the right kind of relationship between a man and his environment, whether at a factory bench, office desk, sales counter, or other place of work. It means helping to increase his efficiency and output by ensuring satisfactory working conditions so that physically and mentally he is freed from distracting influences and unnecessary stress and strain. In practice, this implies proper seating, logical layout of machine controls and of the workplace itself; the right levels of heating, lighting, and noise; better design of instruments; protective clothing; all according to the individual and collective needs of employed personnel seeking to do their jobs more effectively.

Cybernetics, on the other hand, relates to the connected fields of information, communication, and control. In Chapter Eight reference was made to the management information loop, illustrated in Figure 8, showing the nature of planning and replanning, based on action, measurement of results, feedback and control. Insofar as this loop demonstrates the nature and use of information and the solving of communication problems, particularly in complex systems, it is clearly a "cybernetic loop." This type of approach helps with the understanding of communication and its problems in the community as a whole, or in any organization (such as a firm) within that community.

Personnel Management Defined

The many responsibilities of a personnel department may be summarized as follows:

(a) Employment. Recruitment, including liaison with the local state employment agency and any other appropriate sources of labor supply; formulating terms and conditions of service; interviewing, selecting, appointing, organizing transfers, filling out termination papers, and discharging personnel; induction and follow-up of newcomers; keeping personnel records and statistics; complying with employment legislation.

(b) Wages and Salary Administration. Maintaining the company's accepted wage structure, salary grading schemes, and the like; authorizing rate changes, deductions, and special payments; assessing and controlling differentials; liaison with time-study engineers and other specialists in work measurement.

(c) Education and Training. Organizing in-company and external training courses at induction, specialist, supervisor, and management levels; liaison with local institutions of higher education; encouraging further education of all kinds; dealing with information services, library facilities, house organs, and so on as appropriate.

(d) Health and Safety. Making arrangements for employees' medical examinations on appointment and thereafter; making sick visits and arranging for convalescence; keeping health records; accident prevention and investigation; dealing with accident claims; compliance with the requirements of workmen's compensation, unemployment insurance, and other relevant legislation.

(e) Welfare. Providing social club and sports facilities, as appro-

priate; supervising employee lunchrooms and cafeterias; arranging for savings plans; dealing with superannuation, pension funds, and severance pay; making loans in hardship cases; giving advice on personal problems and arranging for legal aid when necessary; providing assistance with relocation expenses to staff transferred to another area; and looking after fringe benefits.

(f) Industrial Relations. Serving as negotiating officers with trade unions and other outside bodies; keeping a watchful eye on joint consultative procedures; helping to make known the spirit of company policy; becoming conversant with arbitration and conciliation; suggestion-box systems and providing opportunities for dealing with workers' complaints.

MANPOWER PLANNING

There is nothing to stop any organization from taking on personnel as and when required, which has usually been the case in the past. But manpower, like any other expensive resource, must be carefully planned and quantified, not just left to arbitrary, perhaps isolated, decision.

Watching the Cost

The personnel side of a business cannot disregard the constraints of cost. Although comparative statistics of total numbers of workers and staff, taken in isolation, have a limited value, rising wages/salaries costs, unless kept under control, may well have serious financial implications.

It is commendable that those responsible for personnel administration should be concerned with paying the rate for the job, and should negotiate higher wages, salaries, and benefits as necessary. But they must be aware, at the same time, that by increasing costs they may be reducing profits.

Looked at on its own, therefore, personnel management could appear to be a negative and expensive function, bearing in mind the cost of recruitment, cost of training, salaries and wages, social security and pension contributions, various fringe payments, welfare, and so on. But whenever benefits accrue to the firm in excess of those costs, the human resources employed are seen to be, as they are, the firm's most important asset. This means that all personnel costs must be made to give adequate value in return, with special emphasis on productivity. Apart from purely humanitarian reasons, a well-motivated labor force can become a good corporate investment for future success. In keeping with this policy, nothing must be done to endanger that motivation, a point taken further when dealing with industrial relations later in the chapter.

Having decided that human assets can prove expensive and that policies adopted must be made to produce value for money, it is appropriate to have a look at manpower planning and its special implications for top management. The process starts by an objective analysis of the present use of human resources, followed by realistic forecasting and the drawing up of a detailed manpower plan properly integrated with all other plans. Participation in the drawing up of such plans, by all managers and others concerned with the use of human resources, is implicit.

Forecasting Future Needs

In theory the manpower requirements of any organization over, say, the next five years, need to be estimated as realistically as possible so that recruitment, training, promotion, transfer, and retirement can be geared to the overall plan of corporate development. In many concerns, manpower planning can usefully be considered even as far ahead as twenty years or more, as an integral part of long-range planning. This would take into account all expectations in marketing, production, finance, and technological change.

From a practical point of view, however, most firms seem to rely on "hunch" or play it "off the cuff" as events unfold, or even in anticipation of events. Nor is this amateur approach surprising in view of the many difficulties of scientific manpower planning in the context of the changing industrial scene. To that extent, at any rate, such planning is perhaps more of an art than a science. However, most organizations have some sort of manpower planning, even if only based on a rough-and-ready kind of guesswork; but whether this looks far enough ahead is generally doubtful. There are even firms today, mainly large ones, who do not know at any given point of time just how many personnel they do have on their books.

Nevertheless, despite the difficulties, long- and short-term forecasting must be attempted with such flexible adjustments to match external pressures as may become inevitable. This is not just an overall forecast of total numbers, but a serious attempt to have the right *kinds* of personnel at each level and function, properly trained and available by the time they are needed. Without having the right people ready at the right time, the whole future of an enterprise may be jeopardized.

There are, or course, arbitrary monetary measures of total manpower requirements. For example, one might relate the annual salaries/wages cost to total capital or total annual sales, but this cannot be more than a first approximation. A useful index is the trend of total annual sales per employee, with appropriate price-level adjustments to offset inflation, with respect to the commodities or services being sold.

Then again it may be possible to project forward all existing information on recruitment, labor turnover, absenteeism, retirements, and so on, broken down into organizational groups and departments, as significant. This in turn requires an understanding of how such groupings will themselves develop, for some departments may be due for rapid growth, and others for pruning or phasing out altogether. Nor can the level of efficiency be ignored, for it may be possible perhaps through the efforts of an outside management consultant, to produce economies in numbers through the introduction of more effective techniques. In this context increased mechanization can be an important factor, an aspect already mentioned elsewhere from the extreme points of view that some organizations are basically labor intensive and others basically capital intensive.

The creation on paper of a simple flexible manpower model year by year is a worthwhile exercise, leading eventually to a sophisticated model with all the variables and possibilities built into a computer program.

A further source of information can be an interfirm comparison of manpower, preferably from within the same industry, on much the same lines as comparing financial information and business ratios, as outlined in Chapter Eleven.

Planning Considerations

Whether the procedure adopted is scientific approach or hunch, the end result must indicate either a shortfall in staff or a surplus (for example following a merger or reorganization). A shortfall would be made up by recruitment augmented with training; a surplus might be transferred elsewhere, or discharged, or allowed to dissipate through natural attrition by stopping or reducing further intake for the time being.

Policy aspects are involved here, as well as in the special case of industrial manpower geared to trade cycles alternating prosperity with recession. Personnel requirements in times of boom may be augmented by temporary labor, total manpower having been deliberately maintained below peak level; and in times of slump by keeping and using the skilled labor, bearing in mind the current shortage of adequately qualified technicians, to build up stocks of finished goods ready for the return of better times. By contrast, the policy could simply be to hire and fire, as dictated by events, taking a pure gamble on future manpower supply and demand.

A practical necessity is to prepare a moving five-year chart of manpower needs, quantified and costed, and broken down into such groups as will give a clear indication of the tasks ahead, subject to the overriding safety valve of budgetary flexibility. A full appreciation must be made of existing abilities and potential, and this must be molded to future requirements, as foreseen, gearing training at all levels to ensure optimum quality throughout. Without a chart or other forecast of future needs, it is hard to see how any personnel department can carry out its duties effectively.

In dealing with forecasting, a prime objective must be the matching of jobs with people, or people with jobs, depending on the emphasis preferred. Greater efficiency, and thereby increased productivity, will result from people being given satisfying jobs that suit their abilities and fully stretch their capacities. This involves seeking greater participation, and thereby a breaking down of the management/worker distinction; granting more responsibility to those that can take it; and giving positive recognition to the results achieved. Coupled with this kind of approach, reiterated here to show that there is more to manpower planning than merely counting heads and assessing cost, is the proper provision of modern equipment, methods and conditions of work. The trade union attitude is important here, but more conveniently dealt with under the heading of "Industrial Relations" later in this chapter.

MAKING THE RIGHT SELECTION

Having stressed the importance of quality, as well as quantity, in the planning of manpower, it can be seen that the initial appointment of people, their progress through the organization, even their discharge, all depend on the right personnel policies and selection techniques.

Recruitment Policies

Taking on new employees is an expensive business, involving as it does advertising the jobs, interviewing applicants, accepting a temporarily lower standard until sufficiently trained, providing that training, conducting relevant correspondence, keeping records, and submitting periodic reports.

Furthermore, apart from meeting the manpower needs of expansion, recruiting must also deal with labor turnover, which at times can be considerable. In this context, every organization should study its turnover figures, and trend, and try to ascertain the *real* reasons why employees have decided to leave. The resultant information should then prove to be a valuable guide for the framing of future policies. The word "real" is emphasized here, because people when leaving are not always prepared to state the true situation but may give instead some other, perhaps less embarrassing, reason. In any event, the total cost of replacement can be high; therefore everything possible must be done to keep the turnover percentage, usually related to a financial year, to an absolute minimum.

The number of new recruits required, in addition to turnover replacement needs, period by period, can be obtained from the manpower chart. Plans can then be laid accordingly. This means taking into account the level of skills and experience required for the various jobs to be filled, in each geographical location, and then creating the appropriate machinery for selection and appointment. Recruitment is usually a centralized function in the smaller firms, but with large-scale organizations much of the recruiting and selection procedure may be carried out locally, subject to overriding central control.

Companies considered to be worth working for, with prestige names and good employment records, naturally find it easier to obtain the right kinds of applicants for recruitment. Terms of service and conditions of employment must, of course, be acceptable, but these may well be secondary, at least initially, to the attractions of a firm's public image and established reputation.

Sources of recruits, depending on the types of jobs to be filled, include:

(a) Employment agencies.

(b) Advertisements in newspapers and trade journals, ranging from routine help-wanted columns to prestige announcements seeking managers.

(c) Notices of vacancies, posted up in or near places of work.

(d) "Office-temporaries" agencies.

(e) Schools, universities, technical colleges, and business schools.

(f) Professional institutes, with regard to their own members registering for appointments before or after qualifying by examination.

(g) Personnel consultants or management consultants, with the emphasis on higher managerial appointments and the initial preserving of anonymity.

In seeking recruits it is essential to issue realistic job descriptions; otherwise wrong applications and even wrong appointments are likely to follow, or good applicants exclude themselves. Successful candidates may well feel resentful afterwards if the job turns out to be somewhat different from what was advertised. To avoid such dangers, progressive steps must be taken through job study, job analysis, job specification and then job description.

As a matter of normal policy, in a firm of any size, selection will be made whenever possible from within the organization itself, by transfer or promotion; selection from the outside, by recruitment, is particularly relevant to the lowest level of vacancies to be filled. The advantages of promoting from inside, given suitable applicants, are:

(a) The persons appointed should already be well versed in company policies, procedures, and personalities.
(b) Their work records are already known from first-hand experience.
(c) Assuming fair appointments, the general effect on personnel morale and motivation is likely to be appreciable.

It may be argued, however, that because the object is to make the best possible appointment, *all* vacancies involving transfer or promotion should be advertised externally as well as internally. The advantage of this kind of approach is that existing personnel cease to rely on mere seniority of service and know that they must be at least as good as the best candidates likely to come forward from outside. Given equality of ability and experience, it may be decided in the end to promote "the devil you know" from inside, but the alternative of bringing in "fresh blood" is a tenable policy not to be ignored without careful thought.

With rapid growth and innovation, suitable candidates may not be available inside, in which case appointments from outside become the obvious course. There is still a danger, however, in that rather than go outside, a selection may be made from inside, perhaps for morale reasons, even though this is known to be a second-best solution. In such a situation, some promoted personnel surprisingly rise to the occasion, but by and large such potential as exists should already have been detected, recorded, and developed.

In recruiting external applicants, every opportunity should be taken to strengthen the manpower quality, particularly where it is known to be below the average of the organization as a whole. The qualifications required may be general or specific, the former being geared to the type of personnel sought as a whole, the latter relating to the particular job. Top-level recruits are sometimes sought by prestige advertisement or professional "head-hunting" from *any* source, even though this may prove to be right outside the industry itself. On occasion, such bringing in of *completely* fresh blood has been deliberate development policy.

Company policies may exclude the taking on of relatives, thus preventing any suspicion of nepotism, and may or may not actively seek to attract experienced personnel from rival organizations. "Head-hunting" at the top end, referred to above, is a development of the latter, often conducted confidentially through a specialist intermediary.

Selection Procedures

Among the techniques adopted for selection purposes are various tests covering aptitude, general interest, intelligence and even personality, as considered appropriate to a given job. Aptitude tests, being designed to evaluate physical dexterity, etc. at lower levels of labor, may be noncontroversial, and for some time now intelligence tests have been well established and widely used. But any test intended to measure personality tends to be viewed with suspicion.

Nevertheless, top managers are beginning to turn to the psychologists for help with their senior appointments. Even at a lower level it may be valuable to know just how literate or numerate job applicants are, to assess their potentialities for the work offered and for future promotion. Intelligence and personality tests can probe deeply into human characteristics, whether such tests are conducted by properly qualified people within the firm itself or through outside consultant specialists.

Intelligence tests, on paper, are now largely routine and consist of such items as *(a)* completing diagrammatic patterns and *(b)* solving problems to demonstrate fluency with words and ability to juggle figures. These tests are normally carried out against a stop watch. Personality tests are rather different and of various kinds, but usually they appear as a lengthy questionnaire aiming to discover a candidate's inner feelings, points of view, preferences, tastes, and attitudes, as relevant. The answers given must then be scientifically analyzed according to carefully devised rules, subject to built-in checks to offset any attempt to demonstrate a "right" image rather than the true one.

Projective tests give a candidate full scope to use his imagination and then attempt to draw inferences from the results achieved. The most quoted variety relies on ink blots, where a candidate is required to state what they look like or suggest to him. There are many varieties of such tests, but few of them can claim scientific "validation" and should therefore be used with caution.

All tests, of course, are designed to provide a more scientific basis for selection, as compared with the subjective nature of decision by interview. They should not, however, be regarded as the sole basis of selection, but merely as a part of the selection procedure.

Interviewing is a basic but thorny selection technique. To start with, an interviewer is likely to be conditioned by first impressions, which can often prove to be wrong in the light of better acquaintance. A candidate who has created a favorable first impression may then be credited with better answers to questions than he actually gives: conversely, an adverse first impression may lead to good answers being treated with reserve and any bad ones magnified. For an interviewer, experienced or not, is still subject to the frailties of being human. The extent of such frailty will naturally vary with the individual, his make-up and personnel experience generally.

There are a variety of influencing factors here, too, that can affect personal judgment. Some interviewers consider physical characteristics as vital issues: for example, a long nose may signify natural leadership; the wearing of glasses may denote intelligence; short stature may suggest a tendency towards aggression, and so on *ad nauseam*. Whether or not one subscribes to such beliefs, however, the general appearance and bearing of a candidate, his smartness, voice, and so on, should certainly be taken into account where these are factors deemed essential to the vacancy being filled. But a foreman taking on a laborer might only be concerned with physical strength; and an R. & D. manager could be completely happy to acquire the services of a highly qualified back-room scientist despite his having an unorthodox idea of how to dress. Many similar examples can be quoted, but basically this is simply an extension of making sure that a person selected matches up effectively to the job to be filled.

Good selection procedures ensure that bias is eliminated so far as possible, that interviewers have as much information before them as is considered appropriate, and that there are independent checks such as the tests described earlier.

Most interviews are concerned with physical characteristics; family background; educational and other attainments; previous experience, including any military service; special aptitudes, intelligence, and personality; particular interests, hobbies, and sports; and attitude to life generally. Much of this information should be documented on the application form, but attitudes and points of view can be revealed only by the right kind of question after the candidate has been put at his ease and helped over any initial nervousness. Often a general visual assessment is made as well, the interviewer trying to imagine the applicant actually doing the job and deciding whether he would in fact seem to be suitable.

From this short review it should be appreciated that an interview must be properly structured, with scientific rating assessments, point by point, not just left to haphazard conversation. It should also be apparent that as much care must be taken in selecting interviewers as those being interviewed.

Selection procedures vary according to the level of job being offered, from taking on school dropouts, experienced workers, supervisors, middle managers, and so on, right up to the appointment of a new chief executive. At the lower levels, single-person interviews may be considered appropriate, but in making higher-level appointments, interviews will normally be conducted by a selection committee, subject to group decisions being distilled from individual judgments, through the chairman, and the independent validation of results.

Practical Aspects of Promotion

In the course of promoting personnel by selection from within the organization, whether in competition with outside candidates or not, careful consideration has to be given to the best route to be taken upwards. This can be:

(a) Vertically up the ladder, in which case an employee is promoted in rank, keeping within his present function, department, or branch.

(b) Horizontally, where he has a sideways transfer to another part of the organization.

(c) By zigzagging, where the employee has the opportunity of progressing upwards through a planned series of promotions combining routes (a and b).

Vertical promotion is a popular method and has the advantage that each job at the next highest rank can be understudied in advance of promotion. This rests on a theory that a responsible employee should not only do his own job effectively, but train the person doing the job just below and learn everything possible about the job just above. This method, however, has disadvantages in that the employee concerned tends to become more and more of a specialist and acquires restricted practical experience of the organization as a whole. His chances of promotion, being confined to a single ladder, are thereby limited in scope.

The alternative, of horizontal promotion, deals with these disadvantages effectively. In practice, this takes two main forms: promotion in rank to another comparable department or promotion to a larger unit, remaining for the time being at the same rank but enjoying the advantage of enlarged opportunities, including prospects of further promotion. This horizontal method of approach naturally depends on the type of organization concerned, but the main objectives of increasing expertise and broadening experience have wide application. On the debit side is the time required to learn the new job, which may involve acquiring new technical detail or a special knowledge of personalities, including customers.

Where promotion involves a sideways transfer to a smaller unit, offering leadership responsibility instead of being at the most a second in charge as before, the development value is inestimable. This is just as true whether it relates to becoming a supervisor, foreman, or manager. The other factor to be taken into account is the psychological advantage of arriving at a new unit with the status of leader, there being a subtle difference here from being promoted to that rank within the same unit. A compromise is to promote the selected person sideways to develop his leadership qualities elsewhere and then return him to the original unit, as manager, by a reverse sideways transfer.

In the zigzag method, maximum use is made of gaining experience in a number of different parts of the organization, in relevant cases abroad as well as at home. Promotion may be vertical or horizontal, as appropriate at any given time, but each move should be a planned step upwards. By such broadening of experience, coupled with the right type of training, specialists can become less specialized and be able to graduate more effectively into general management. But many specialists are tied to their specialty, perhaps by policy considerations, hidebound limitations, or personal choice, and consequently promotion must be constantly within the same field. In this event, to maintain motivation, there should be a clearly observed ladder of promotion right to the top of the area of specialization, within the overriding pyramid covering the organization as a whole.

To ease the personal expenses involved in sideways promotions to other geographical areas, policy decisions have to be made as to whether any financial assistance should be given to key employees concerned, and, if so, how much. Such assistance could be an arbitrarily fixed amount for *any* transfer, or a variable sum geared to individual circumstances. In order to facilitate mobility, the provision of company houses may be worth consideration. Married employees clearly have special problems, such as children settled at school, the wife at work, joint local interests and so on, which may suggest the need for some incentive by way of increased remuneration. In most cases the transfer of bachelors would create lesser problems, but in equity this should not influence promotion prospects in general.

As to opportunities for promotion, these are generally more apparent in a large organization than in a small firm where progress may well depend on filling dead men's shoes. Decentralization, too, provides more effectively for creative leadership, thus making promotion to the local units concerned more responsible and demanding.

In some establishments, it is customary to have regular interviewing boards to assess the potential of *all* personnel at or above certain levels, or simply those submitting applications for interview, depending on company policy. With this arrangement, or some other selection machinery, it is possible to "pencil in" the names of suitable people for promotion generally, or tentatively to fill future vacancies, well ahead of events. However, because people can change (they may, for example, be late developers), any advance-selection policy or action program should be kept reasonably fluid for the time being.

Whether employees initially earmarked for promotion should be told of this fact or not is a moot point, bearing in mind the above caveat. But there is always a danger that personnel who leave for better jobs elsewhere are usually the best personnel, the lesser lights remaining *in situ*. Thus it could be argued that potential promotees should be told where they stand so as to retain their interest and services. To be consistent, those unlikely to be promoted should also be told, but this more negative aspect needs to be treated with caution.

There is a popular contention that all personnel who are progressively promoted, eventually reach what has been called their particular "level of incompetence." This is a controversial thesis, bearing in mind the kinds of management development programs that can be set up, but further consideration is deferred until Chapter Fourteen.

Maintaining Personnel Records

Apart from the usual routine personnel records dealing with remuneration, withholding tax, absenteeism, and other general matters, most firms maintain an individual record of each person employed. This can range from a simple index card, for operators and general workers, stating the bare details only, to a complete dossier, for more senior employees, containing the fullest possible information regularly updated and documented for future reference.

Where a complete dossier is relevant to the type of job in question, the individual file usually starts with the initial application form summarizing personal information as at that date, including family background, education, qualifications, special interests, and previous employment experience. Any references that have been taken up, and this is a problematical subject in itself, would also be in the file, along with any medical report required as a matter of company policy. Subsequent updating covers periodic assessment forms completed by superiors, details of in-company training received, including reports from training officers, private study undertaken and examination results achieved, external courses attended, promotions, interview notes, and anything else that would help to create a complete picture of an individual. In a small firm, of course, everyone is known to everyone else, but with a large-scale enterprise there must be considerable dependence on comprehensive records in support of special interviews. Each file may include a photograph, but this would obviously need renewal from time to time. Sometimes group photographs of training courses can be adapted to this purpose.

Periodic evaluation reports must be used with care, whether consisting of completed proformas or unstructured reports. Whatever the format, these reports may be made at half-yearly or yearly intervals, at the end of a probationary period, or when personnel are leaving one job to take up another within the same organization. Even having designed the right kind of form to be completed, there is still a danger of bias being imparted by the raters. This does not necessarily mean bias with respect to individuals, favoring some and disliking others on purely personal grounds, but overall bias. For experience shows that some departmental managers will try to keep all their reports favorable, others will be jaundiced throughout, and many will take the easy middle course. Hence there must be an assessment of raters, or more than one rater related to each individual monitored, coupled with various techniques to assist in achieving objective critical judgment. As an arbitrary example, a middle-of-the-road type of manager would be forced to think more deeply if he had to divide his departmental personnel into, say, one third promotables, one third ordinary, and one third dischargeable.

There are many subtle aspects to bias. For instance, a key employee working away from the central office may feel that he is at a disadvantage compared with his opposite numbers who are in closer daily contact with top management, thereby having greater opportunities to demonstrate their capabilities. In practice, this could just as easily operate the other way round, for the distant key employee could enjoy the benefit of an untarnished reputation, built up from results achieved and carefully worded reports, whereas the key personality daily working next to authority could easily be taken for granted, and find himself unable to camouflage for long any peculiarities or weaknesses. Thus it sometimes happens that a "young lion" brought into the home office from the hinterlands will fail to live up to inflated expectations.

Another subtle example of bias is where a meticulously fair-minded manager, knowing that he instinctively likes or dislikes certain members of his team, quite apart from their work abilities, tries to compensate for his natural personal feelings when making out evaluation reports. In the process there may be a danger that he will underplay the value of "favorites" and be overgenerous to those he dislikes. The obvious more cynical version of this, demonstrating the natural tendency towards bias, needs no comment. It is to prevent this kind of situation from arising that objectively maintained personnel records can be of special value, coupled with check reports whenever practicable.

Layoffs and Dismissal

However careful an organization may be with regard to its personnel policy and long-term manpower planning, there is always the likelihood of excess personnel and dismissal needing special decisions. Dismissal starts with induction and probation periods, if any, those failing to match up to requirements being given another chance (a debatable practice) or discharged. In either case, this labor turnover is *prima facie* evidence of imperfect selection, although much depends on circumstances. At a time of overall manpower shortage, for example, it might seem pointless to have any probation periods at all.

As a general policy, some concerns would rather transfer unsatisfactory staff, after some lengthy period of service, to another part of the organization than just discharge them outright. This takes account of the fact that personalities sometimes clash and that square pegs may be unhappy in round holes. Other firms prefer to part company with any employee failing to match up to minimum standards.

Among the usual reasons for dismissal are the obvious ones of inefficiency, dishonesty, failure to respond to authority, and disability, as well as the cessation of work, seasonally, during a recession or permanently, leading to layoffs, which may have little relationship to an individual's abilities and performance. Whatever the situation, the discharge itself must be handled diplomatically and objectively, not in a sudden burst of temper that may subsequently damage continuing relationships with other subordinates. As always, justice must not only be done but be seen to be done.

Termination plans arising from the dynamic environment, or from necessary changes in company policy, including the aftermath of mergers, require special understanding and care when dealing with the actual dismissals. Usually, a *fait accompli* approach is made to the appropriate trade unions so that acceptable and equitable arrangements can be worked out, in liaison with shop stewards, so far as possible. Official opinion, however, suggests that the unions should be consulted at an earlier stage, before any final management decision has been made concerning layoffs.

To start with, every effort should be exerted to keep key personnel, including skilled production workers, and to minimize the remaining excess personnel problem by relying on natural attrition. This would include a temporary ban on recruitment, coupled with normal retirements, or induced voluntary retirements at an earlier age, with adequate financial incentives. Nonproductive workers and office staff should be pruned as appropriate.

In selecting for staff reduction, a logic based on profits suggests dispensing with the least efficient workers and perhaps the oldest workers, but a strong trade union influence might argue that those last joining the firm should be the first to go. Where this is a fact of . life, any concern would be wise to tighten up its selection procedures to ensure the elimination of its least efficient workers at an earlier stage, or, by an efficient training program, to convert them into better workers.

It should not be forgotten that wholesale layoffs, such as that caused by withdrawing a large undertaking from a particular area, could have hardship effects on the local community. This may be softened by a phased program, in liaison with the unions and local authorities concerned. With respect to hardship, it is feasible that special consideration would be given to marital status, as against single status, but this is only one factor out of many to be taken into policy account.

At managerial level the terms of service are usually subject to written agreement, but in any event such cases are nearly always decided individually on their merits. Whenever possible, effective managers are employed elsewhere in the organization; others may be compensated with a "golden handshake," where applicable, or granted a full pension (or a proportionate but augmented pension) at an earlier age than is normal for retirement. Much depends, however, on corporate policy, expediency, and the circumstances at the time.

TRAINING THE WORKER

Our national policy commitment to the support of vocational preparation for our citizens extends back over the decades to the Smith-Hughes Act (1917), which encouraged such training at the secondary school level, and the National Apprenticeship Act (1937), through which the Bureau of Apprenticeship and Training was initiated. The coordinating and facilitating activities of this federal bureau has, over the years, helped to prepare literally hundreds of thousands of new certificated journeymen in several hundred different trades. Outside of these areas, however, with the additional burgeonning of veterans' training activities in the post-World War II period, little else existed in the way of job-learning opportunities for the average worker. Of course, there was the opportunity for learning by watching, whether or not the person already doing the job had any ability at instructing, or even whether the job was being done as well as possible in the first place.

Fortunately, this situation has been somewhat ameliorated since the passage of the Area Redevelopment Act (1961) and the subsequent Manpower Development and Training Act (1962). With these two pieces of legislation, the federal government began to provide training (as well as subsistence payments) to unemployed and underemployed individuals, in occupational skills that were locally needed in depressed areas. Such training is provided through the U.S. Employment Service in conjunction with state employment offices. In 1964, The Economic Opportunity Act further strengthened the intent behind the ARA and MDTA. Such programs and organizations as the Neighborhood Youth Corps, the Job Corps, Vista, and Head Start have since originated in the activities of the Office of Economic Opportunity set up under the EOA.

Training within Industry

Special mention should be made here of the "Training Within Industry" program originally conceived of and initiated back in 1940 through a combined government/industry effort. Its main objective was to train and develop supervisory personnel for the defense plants of America. Well over one million supervisors were trained through the war years, and after the war ended these efforts were continued by the Training Within Industry Foundation, a nonprofit organization. Their special training approaches, refined over the years, continue to be of help to domestic firms and have since been exported to other countries.

Company Training and Types of Training

As a first step, policy decisions are needed to determine the management objectives of training, the types of training and the place(s) of training. Having made the best possible recruitment selection, it is common sense to capitalize on the basic qualities of new personnel and develop potential. In this way there will be higher morale, quicker production results, more effective use of machines, less defects, less material wastage, less tool damage and less need for close supervision in the case of factory workers; greater efficiency, on similar lines, with regard to office staff; and better chances of success on the part of salesmen. Training should start with induction and continue systematically throughout all subsequent service. Progressively, this should include apprenticeship, if any, instruction in semi-skilled work, specialized training for technical or clerical work, training for supervisors, and, finally, training for management.

First impressions tend to be lasting, and apart from the importance of having the right kind of policy for easing a newcomer into the work environment (a subject in itself), it is important to institute organized induction training as a corollary.

The primary object of an induction course is to introduce a new employee to the background of the firm, its objectives, organization, general policy, leading personalities, and amenities, and to describe the highlights of its achievements in providing goods or services, and consequent importance to the community. It is an attempt to make the recruit feel that he is now a part of a firm worth working for, to help him understand how his job fits into the general framework, and enable him to find his way about and understand the rules and regulations that will affect his future. There are various ways of doing this in practice, including films, talks and conducted tours, coupled with frank answers to spontaneous questions raised in the process. A large enough firm could set up regular courses covering all the intake during a given period, where this is feasible in view of travelling and other constraints, but a smaller concern may have to content itself with something less ambitious.

Policy decision is involved here, insofar as judgment needs to be exercised as to when recruits should report for indoctrination. If this is to be at the very beginning of their employment, it may be felt that they are not yet settled down sufficiently to absorb the induction message properly. On the other hand, if left until much later they may by then have acquired wrong impressions from anti-establishment fellow workers with a "chip on their shoulders."

Induction may be followed by basic instruction in the work itself either through apprenticeship or other on-the-job training by properly qualified instructors. With semi-skilled work, it is best that training should be carried out away from the job itself, ideally at a training center organized for this purpose. The value of a properly structured systematic program of training at this level cannot be overemphasized, particularly as semi-skilled work applies to considerably more employees than does skilled work. In fact, where skilled workers are hard to find, the policy may be one of de-skilling operations to broaden the intake of labor generally. De-skilling,however, may result in the loss of job satisfaction and the substitution of continuous worker boredom, but this is a separate problem to be dealt with on its own.

To some extent training requirements are linked with recruitment policy. Some firms prefer to recruit at a relatively young age and maximize training opportunities as an incentive for school dropouts to join the firm and learn a trade. Other firms prefer to take on workers trained elsewhere, and thereby minimize their own training requirements at those levels. The choice here may reflect the state of the labor market.

Given, for example, office recruitment difficulties in attracting secretary-typists, it may be decided to take on young girls straight from school and have them professionally trained so many days a week. For the remainder of the time they may be used as internal mail room girls and later on as copy-typists. There is a risk, of course, that once they are sufficiently trained they will be tempted away by the many advertised opportunities, and the lure of agencies, into more remunerative employment. This may mean imposing certain initial safeguards, such as signing an agreement to stay for a given period after training, but in practice this is not easy to enforce. However, as a calculated risk it may be decided that the cost/benefit of retaining, say, half of them permanently would be well worth the trouble and expense involved. Alternatively, it may be decided, again as a matter of policy, to change the whole system of secretarial work into a central pool of audio-typists, thereby cutting out the need for shorthand and economizing in the numbers of personnel required.

In the training of various skills at a separate center, there are many techniques that can be employed, ranging from straightforward instruction by lectures and discussion to the use of practical simulation.

Simulation, in this context, has many applications. It can be used for reproducing workshop situations of all kinds, it can be a mock shop counter or a model branch of a bank; in fact, anything that can give a sense of realism without actually being reality itself. Here mistakes can be made without upsetting production or customers, and the job learned effectively in true-to-life conditions. The wartime R.A.F. Link trainer was an early example, whereby the cockpit of an aircraft was accurately simulated; although not airborne, pilots could, under expert instruction and with plotted performance, "fly" a course and deal with situations and emergencies as if actually in the sky. More recently, the Apollo astronauts were able to practice the whole of their journey to the moon, while remaining firmly on the ground in Texas. Today, therefore, simulation techniques are no longer an idea but taken for granted. But they are still not used as widely, in a business context, as their value would seem to justify.

Part of the problem may be one of cost, or of not being able to provide full-scale training facilities at the right level and/or in the right place. A firm may in fact wish to contract out much of the educational work and leave it instead to the professionals. This is a question of policy, but in any case it is essential to have a responsible training officer to coordinate all the training activities whether in-company or external.

External cooperation should start with basic instruction. Apprentices or other workers can have the benefit of either day release, which means attendance one day a week at a local technical school or commercial institute, or block release, which means attendance over several weeks at a time. In both cases there is a marriage between "know-how" picked up on the job and the theory/practice learned elsewhere.

In-company training can provide progressive courses of instruction by formal programs at regular intervals, including refresher courses and retraining where appropriate. A large organization would use a special lecture room or suite, within the main building or a purpose-built training school at some geographically convenient center; a smaller concern would necessarily have to be less ambitious.

Having planned the most appropriate types of training courses, using visual aids, instruction manuals, specialized equipment and the like, the selection of instructors becomes a matter of prime importance. This again is a question of policy, and the answer may be to select operators, supervisors, and so on from the firm's own personnel and have them properly trained as instructors. Appointments may be on a basis of temporary assignment for a given period, rather than permanently, so as to keep the instructors' feet firmly on the ground as practitioners. Resort would also be made to the use of outside specialists on a weekly part-time basis, or as and when needed. Policy considerations would be likely to suggest making the best possible use of local training facilities at technical or commercial level. These practical points will be elaborated further in Chapter Fourteen when dealing with in-company management development schemes.

PROBLEMS OF REMUNERATION

In addition to recruiting and training personnel, including motivating them by effective induction, policy consideration must be given to paying the right level of salaries, wages, commission, or whatever other remuneration is relevant. It has been seen that financial incentive is not the sole incentive; nevertheless, the average amount of take-home pay must necessarily be of vital concern to the bulk of employees and their families.

Prices and Income

Most workers today appreciate the difference between money wages and real wages, being concerned with how far the money will go in practice. The effects of inflation have long been a hard fact of life, particularly with regard to people living on fixed incomes, hence the waves of industrial unrest that continue to make themselves felt whenever prices in general seem to be rising faster than income.

The Consumer Price Index prepared by the Bureau of Labor Statistics, reflecting changes in retail prices, demonstrates substantial and continuing increases year by year. Taking a wider view than retail prices, however, and basing the comparison on domestic weekly budgets, including the rising cost of housing, fares, fuel, electricity, income tax, and other deductions from pay, the increased *cost* of living then appears to be getting out of hand. Hence the use of "escalator" clauses in union contracts covering more than five million workers, whereby rounds of salary/wage increases could be kept in step with the cost of living. This concept of indexation, i.e., relating pay to a relevant index, is seen as an attempt to maintain real purchasing power, and as such it may well be developed further in the light of experience. Speaking comparatively, however, the basic take-home pay of the ordinary householder is still scarcely any higher, in real terms, than it was, say, some thirty years ago.

Yet, many wage-earners today seem to be better off than before, for their *standard* of living has clearly risen. This may be partly due to the householder's basic wage being augmented by overtime, made possible (or necessary) through shorter working hours or even by having a part-time job as well. The main reason, however, is probably to be found in the increased proportion of working wives today who, with other members of the family, contribute appreciably to the *household* income.

The effects of such family affluence on the economy, through rising consumption demand, despite being damped down by taxes of various kinds, cannot be developed here; nor can the effects of the rising wage-cost burden on industry. This is a fascinating subject on its own. But mention must be made of the well-known inflationary spiral arising from increased wages (and other income) pushing up prices, increased prices then pushing up wages, and so on *ad infinitum*. Whether the spiral starts with wages going up or with prices going up, the end result is still inflationary.

Fixing Wages and Salaries

Consideration has already been given to total v ages and salaries costs and the need for keeping them under control. It was also indicated that the proper rate must be paid for the job a d that such rate had necessarily to take inflation into account. The final level at any given time must be fair to both the employer and the employed, taking productivity fully into account.

Basically, "wages" refer to manual workers of all kinds, and "salaries" to office staff and administration generally; but the borderline between the two categories often tends to become blurred. Here again there is the same emotive danger of implied class distinction that exists in the labels "worker" and "staff." It might in fact be better to have a common term covering both types of remuneration. In addition, there are still other kinds of pay, such as directors' "fees" and salesmen's "commissions."

Usually, too, wages relate to the actual work done, or number of hours worked, on a weekly basis, whereas salaries imply uniform payments from one pay period to the next that are not explicitly related to the number of hours worked. For this reason, basic wage rates are usually quoted as being so much an hour, with a weekly total, while salaries are quoted as being so much per week, per month, or per annum.

Because of this distinction, it can happen that a first-rate factory worker promoted to supervisor, thereby becoming a salaried member of the staff, could initially earn less than he did when enjoying a guaranteed minimum wage augmented by incentive payments related to results. Being on the staff, however, implies a greater degree of permanence in employment, with allied status benefits, and could well lead to further promotion.

Throughout the fixing of levels of remuneration there must be proper coordination between the rewards given to personnel doing the same, or similar, kinds of work. This should take account of differences in degrees of difficulty, the relative importance of jobs, the need for special abilities, judgment, and experience. Ideally, the assessment should take account of national and industrial levels, the latter often reflecting the bargaining strength of individual trade unions.

In practice, leading firms in an industry may be prepared to make their wage rates and salary scales available, perhaps by exchanging them for those of their competitors. If corporate identities are to be concealed, then the appropriate trade association can, as usual, act as an intermediary.

The comparative level eventually sought may be a matter of deliberate board policy. Some concerns, for instance, may decide to pay above the norm in order to attract the best personnel, and minimize their rate of turnover; others may prefer to pay standard remuneration offset by certain corporate prestige advantages or other benefits. These latter comments, of course, refer mainly to salaried staff; in any case nonmonetary "attractions" tend to wear thin over the course of time. In general, there is the well-known observation that employers offering peanuts can only expect to get monkeys. Where individual firms in the same industry try to keep ahead of their rivals, when periodically fixing levels of pay over the whole range, there tends to be a degree of leap-frogging. This naturally depends on the degree of trade union activity.

Getting the comparative wage/salary structure right is only the first step, for it still remains necessary to ensure justice internally, an important aspect psychologically. This ties up with the problem concerning whether individual wages and/or salaries should be published for all to know, thus taking the place of intelligent guess or grapevine communication. Wage and salary rates, as negotiated with trade unions, or adopted as salary grading plans, are often common knowledge, but there may still be room for flexibility when fixing the exact remuneration of certain individuals within the range of a published grade.

Higher-salaried employees may be outside any grading consideration, depending on policy and practice; but at board level, in a publicly held company at any rate, remuneration must now be legally disclosed in annual reports. Government appointments, at that kind of level, have long been subject to the same control. In general terms, to publish as much information concerning wages and salaries as seems reasonable is probably better than trying to maintain an air of secrecy.

In achieving a correlation between the level of remuneration, the job done, and the ability or capacity of the individual concerned, it is only equitable to treat men and women alike. Traditionally, of course, there has always been a considerable wage/salary differential, with a few notable exceptions, but current thought has been conditioned towards the widespread adoption of equal pay ever since the passage of the Equal Pay Act in 1963. Similarly, the providing of equal opportunity has been ensured through the enactment of the Civil Rights Act (1964). From the managerial standpoint, equal pay means extra cost, but this is a problem to be solved with extra productivity in mind.

In fixing levels of remuneration, much research work has been done on what has been called the "time-span of discretion." Briefly, this research classifies current and potential earnings according to an individual's conceptual capacity. For some people can only deal with the concrete, being confined mentally to what they can actually see and touch, while others have the imagination to range effectively over a wide area of abstract thought without any physical contact at all. This latter class can visualize circumstances and events and plan effectively a long way ahead. The wage or salary levels can then be related to this academic transition from the immediate concrete to the remote conceptual. The bench worker, for instance, being only concerned with the problems of the moment, is paid infinitely less than the corporation president who is able and required to think ten years or more ahead, making recommendations or decisions likely to have long-term effects on the company's profits. This research has been scientifically graphed, illustrating observed relationships between age, time-span, and levels of pay. It is a valuable concept, although some doubts have been expressed as to its detailed practical application.

Staff Salary-grading Plans

The fixing of individual levels of pay suggests a systematic approach through job evaluation, ignoring the titles given to jobs but assessing the value and nature of the work itself. This may mean a general reclassification of jobs. Where a staff salary-grading plan results, it is usual to fix a minimum and a maximum for each job-classified ladder (probably covering a range of comparable jobs) related to age or other criterion which can be easily understood and accepted by all concerned. It should be noted that the United States Civil Service Commission employs just such a classification system.

Once an employee is allocated to a grade, he could normally expect to enjoy automatic progression up the ladder, subject to satisfactory routine personnel reports, marking time eventually on reaching the top. Such an arrangement may mean staying for the rest of his service with the firm at the maximum salary for that grade, which raises an incentive problem with regard to the long-service employee, continually doing his best but having limited ability. This suggests a special case to be decided individually on its merits. A more talented employee could expect to receive promotion, at some stage or another, as a result of which he would be able to climb on to the rungs of a higher ladder (grade) well before reaching the top of the present shorter ladder. Eventually he could be promoted right outside the plan and become classified as "ungraded staff."

Age has been mentioned in connection with salary scales, but a strong case can be made out for pay at any level being related to the job in hand, irrespective of age. In practice, particularly where grading schemes are in force, it often happens that a younger man replacing an older and more experienced colleague will start in the same job but at a lower salary than that currently being paid. Grading plan apart, however, it could be felt that a top-quality young management recruit would merit at least comparable pay with that being received by the more experienced colleague, now possibly past his best and thinking of retirement. Against that argument it may be considered inadvisable to give the newcomer too much too soon; by starting at a lower level than that enjoyed by his predecessor, there is room to move to enable more substantial increments to be granted later. But it is dangerous to generalize and in any case the final answer may depend on such external factors as labor supply and demand, at any given time, and whether there is any bias towards "full" employment or recession.

Grading schemes must be brought into line with inflationary trends, the scales being brought realistically up to date, at appropriate intervals. Adjustments to changes in the cost of living may result from automatic voluntary management review (periodically or according to an agreed rise in the cost of living), or from collective bargaining. Whether the outcome is a flat rate percentage increase throughout the organization, or a more sophisticated graduated adjustment to take account of income taxes and the like at various levels of pay, is primarily a matter for individual boards of directors to resolve.

Boards should also give automatic consideration to scheduled progression within a salary grade, perhaps annually, subject to satisfactory work, and to promotions from one grade to another as and when they arise.

In a large corporate body, a wages and salary policy would be laid down as a matter of course, but the routine responsibility and authority would be delegated to the personnel department for carrying grading implications into practical effect. The board would consider top-level salaries for ungraded staff, and deal with any exceptional circumstances, but the remainder would largely be a matter of "rubber-stamping" bulk decisions made in accordance with policy.

Cost-of-living increases, however, are not the only adjustments that must be made, for in a large organization operating over a wide area it is still necessary to relate salary scales to geographical differences in that cost of living. Using a broad brush, overall differentials may be painted in to cover extra costs of traveling downtown and differences in the levels of housing and subsistence costs. The actual pattern to emerge will depend as usual on corporate policy, as periodically reviewed. There may, of course, be no attempt at *any* form of grading, all salaries being left to arbitrary judgments—as is often the case in smaller organizations.

Whatever the agreed pattern of remuneration, there must be room for flexibility. Although the sum total of all the figures concerned must be integrated with the financial plan and kept within agreed limits, it must not be forgotten that basically this is an exercise involving the well-being of personnel.

Incentives and Profit-sharing

While there is a different conceptual approach to remuneration as between wages and salaries, both alternatives recognize the importance of monetary incentive.

Wages calculated according to actual time clocked in, on a weekly or hourly basis of pay, take no account of relative ability. Consequently, a slacker, going through the motions of work when in sight of the foreman, receives as much as the keener employee producing a greater output. In other words, there is no incentive here for productivity. Payment by results, on the other hand, offers opportunity for increased wages where merited by performance. Under this approach, skimping of work just to earn more take-home pay can usually be prevented by quality inspection.

Such a plan requires comparison with agreed standards set, and here there is considerable room for labor dissatisfaction. In fixing the standard, it would clearly be wrong to take the best or fastest worker, or conversely (from management's point of view) to take the worst or slowest; an acceptable logic is to take an average worker, subject to work- or time-study supervision to ensure optimum efficiency. Where the fixing of standard times is specifically geared to work study, the incentive plan is generally known as "measured day work."

In the interests of the workers, and for any type of incentive plan, it is usually considered advisable to negotiate for a guaranteed minimum wage so as to provide for reasonable personal security. Incentive amounts, in addition to basic pay, would then depend on individual effort. Similar considerations can be applied, for instance, to salesmen by agreeing a basic salary plus specified commission on sales made.

It is generally agreed that any incentive plan must therefore satisfy the following minimum requirements:

(a) The results achieved must be due to the actual efforts of the worker himself. There are difficulties here with regard to team incentive plans, but workers can always find a way of dealing with any slackers.

(b) Any plan should be as simple as possible so that all workers can understand it without difficulty. Any attempt at a highly sophisticated plan, however equitable, would tend to be suspect right from the start.

(c) The receipt of the incentive should be timed to be as near to the completion of the work as possible. Any delay in making such incentive payment tends to cause confusion and misunderstanding.

(d) Any plan put forward should be acceptable to workers as being fair and not a device of management likely to operate against their best interests. Usually there would be full consultation between management and workers before and after any plan was introduced. Any disputes or changes would be dealt with through joint consultation in the usual way.

Attempts have been made from time to time to introduce incentive plans where the savings are shared equally between the employer and employed, the theory being that the former provides facilities for better output and the worker puts in extra effort. But to date such plans have not proved to be at all popular.

Incentives for direct individual effort are usually simple to appreciate, but problems arise with regard to indirect workers. An efficient operator can, for example, earn far more than the foreman, or other supervisor, in charge of his activities. The difficulty here cannot be resolved by relating money to individual effort, but rough justice can be achieved by the payment of bonuses reflecting overall *group* efficiency. A departmental manager, for example, could be given the incentive of a bonus, related by percentage to his salary, geared to *departmental* efficiency, thus reflecting the combined results of all the workers under his personal control. There may be a case, too, for incentive bonuses to be made available for clerical staff as a reward for special effort which cannot be directly quantified.

More-senior managers still could be given bonuses, in this case related to *company* achievements, which introduces the controversial incentive of profit-sharing. When top managers are high enough in the hierarchy to influence business results by their decisions, there is a fair analogy here with direct incentives to workers in that they are also entitled to be rewarded for significant personal effort. But at any lower level of management the profit-sharing concept is much less easy to defend, and for workers generally the plan has little value in logic, except, of course, as a welcome addition to ordinary pay. Furthermore, at a time of losses not profits, the effect on workers can be demoralizing, particularly if they have become accustomed to living on their salary or wages plus the former profit-sharing bonus. An alternative to bonus payments in cash is the issue of company shares on a "co-partnership" basis, but this again is still considered as an exceptional and controversial arrangement.

INDUSTRIAL RELATIONS

Fundamentally, the term "industrial relations" defines the relationship that exists between managements and the workers they employ. The rights of management to hire and fire and the rights of workers to receive a fair day's pay for a fair day's work are inherent in any scheme of employment, but in practice these are opposing viewpoints not easy to reconcile. Hence both sides have their allies: the bosses have employers' associations, and the workers have trade unions. Overall is the role to be played by the federal government. Unfortunately, industrial relations can so easily deteriorate into industrial strife.

Unions and Labor Legislation

Unionism in America extends back to the late eighteenth and early nineteenth centuries when small, localized groups of skilled craftsmen in such trades as carpentry, shoemaking, and printing joined forces. These artisans sought not only to maintain and strengthen their economic positions within their particular towns and villages but also to control, through the apprenticeship system, the labor supply in their trades. Nearly fifty years passed before some of these local craft unions joined others across the country to form national groups. Only a score or so of these national craft unions were in existence by the Civil War period.

A giant step forward in unionism was the organization, in 1886, of the American Federation of Labor (AFL), although in its early years, it faced not only growing pains but a fast-changing economic and political scene.

Impetus to industrial unionization was lent by the passage of the National Labor Relations Act (NLRA) in 1935. Also known as the Wagner Act, this landmark legislation, passed during the Depression years, gave workers the right to organize, to vote for union representation, and to engage in collective bargaining. It also restricted employers by listing and prohibiting some of the more commonly exercised "unfair practices," such as threatening employees' security for union activities, the use of "blacklists," and refusal to bargain in good faith. The Wagner Act also established the National Labor Relations Board to adjudicate employer unfair labor practices.

Soon after the passage of the Wagner Act, the Congress of Industrial Organizations (CIO) split off from the AFL and proceeded to make heavy inroads into the ranks of workers in the steel, automobile, aircraft, and other major industries. Throughout the World War II period, union membership in industry grew by leaps and bounds.

Minimum hourly wages for employees of most companies engaged in interstate commerce were provided for in the Fair Labor Standards Act of 1938. In more recent years, this legislation has been amended several times. Today, most states have minimum wage laws of their own—as well as child labor laws (also touched upon in the FLSA), "equal pay" legislation, and other "protective" laws sheltering workers.

As a counterbalancing force to the rapid growth and occasional mismanagement of union power, the federal government enacted, soon after World War II, the Taft-Hartley Act (Labor-Management Relations Act) in 1947. This law restricted unions even as the earlier Wagner Act had sought to restrict the power of employer firms. Under its provisions, the "closed shop" was outlawed, workers were given the right *not* to join unions, and the federal government assumed the right/power to enjoin union violators. The Taft-Hartley Act also established a Federal Mediation and Conciliation Service.

Some eight years later, in 1955, the AFL merged with the CIO.

Reports of malpractices continued to plague the economic scene, and in 1959, the Landrum-Griffin Act (Labor-Management Reporting and Disclosure Act) was passed to regulate the internal affairs of unions and to protect workers from the abuse of union power. Through this legislative act, the government was given oversight of the internal conduct of unions.

More recent labor legislation at the federal level includes both the Equal Pay Act of 1963 and the Civil Rights Act of 1964. Mention, too, should be made of the early Social Security Act (1935) and the Employment Security Amendments (1970), which have provided a considerable measure of economic security to most workers in the country, and of the many state laws that cover accidents, sicknesses, and unemployment.

Unions Today

Union membership today in America has been estimated at more than one fifth of the entire labor force. It should be noted also that some 75 per cent of all union members in the country are affiliated with the AFL-CIO, for the most part through their national (or international) unions. Such affiliation, of course, gives even the smallest union considerable leverage at the bargaining table, because it can count upon the full support of the huge AFL-CIO in the event of a strike.

The individual local lies at the heart of the typical union's organizational structure. Its officers are democratically elected by the union members. In most cases, the various locals send representatives to the national-level meeting, where major policies are decided upon. Day-to-day administration of the local's affairs usually lie in the hands of the local president and the business agent. Shop stewards, elected in firms by the workers and approved by the local, have the task of increasing membership and dealing with disputes on the spot, calling in higher union authority as necessary.

Government intervention in industrial relations can be on general grounds, such as equal pay for women or fixing a national minimum wage, leaving the unions to negotiate with specific industries or firms. Linked up with this is the justification of increasing pay by increasing productivity, a positive approach replacing the usual negative attitude of "higher pay regardless." Arguments are advanced, too, for realistic all-embracing binding contracts to become feasible policy as between managements and unions.

From management's point of view one of the biggest problems is having to deal with a variety of unions, and common sense suggests that there should be one bargaining agent only, covering all workers collectively within a given organization. Another problem is that of trying to negotiate with certain unions no longer enjoying the full confidence of their members.

Internally, there is much that can be done through joint consultation, whereby representatives of management and workers can meet periodically in committee. This provides machinery for clearing the ai⁻ of grievances, gives a regular opportunity to discuss negotiations on wages and salaries, working conditions, and other terms as appropriate at any given time, and generally to inculcate a spirit of understanding and cooperation. A positive approach is required from both sides, otherwise the atmosphere will tend to degenerate into mutual suspicion and produce only negative and harmful results.

There is always the possibility, too, in appropriate cases, that a management held to ransom by a militant trade union, or affected by continual labor unrest and disturbance, will eventually replace that labor by new and highly sophisticated capital equipment.

Productivity Bargaining

Evidence suggests that boards of directors are taking an increasing interest in manpower policy as part of their overall responsibility for managing *all* resources under their control as effectively as possible. Valuable, and expensive, human resources should figure high on their list.

Productivity bargaining is an advance on the natural bargaining for wages, hours, and working conditions that has always taken place between employer and employed, the balance of power sometimes being biased towards the former, during periods of substantial unemployment, and sometimes towards the latter, given full employment. Collective bargaining then took individual bargaining a step forward, with the trade unions exerting pressure on behalf of groups of workers to even up their chances of success against the powerful employers.

Productivity bargaining usually starts with the employer, traditionally on the defensive, who initiates negotiations aiming at *(a)* meeting the higher wages, etc. demanded by the workers, coupled with *(b)* agreed higher output per worker, and/or *(c)* lower costs through some change being accepted in organization, technique, etc. requiring worker cooperation. It is this aspect of the bargain that pinpoints the difference from traditional collective bargaining which simply increases labor costs without any corresponding benefits accruing to the employer. The most important form is a "comprehensive" arrangement covering all manual workers in a factory or in a self-contained part of a factory.

Obviously, productivity bargaining is a sound approach for raising the workers' standard of living and reducing costs of production, without adding to the national problem of rising inflation. This is a cost/benefit arrangement with much to commend it; additionally, it tends to produce good industrial relations. But the spirit of the agreement must be honored in the deed, not just the word. To be effective in practice, productivity bargaining requires long and patient preliminary negotiations and continuous cooperation and understanding from both sides. It goes without saying that management must itself be at peak efficiency before seeking to "improve" the workers' performance. With productivity in mind, management could perhaps start at the top.

There are two main industrial situations in which productivity bargaining is likely to be essential. The first is where there is already appreciable evidence of labor inefficiency and friction, such as demarcation problems. slowdown tactics, and excessive overtime. It is here that room exists for progress to be made in exchange for a higher-wage incentive. The second situation covers technological or other change, usually resulting in a more capital-intensive organization needing fewer workers proportionately, where special motivation may well be required to facilitate the acceptance of such change.

As always, there are weaknesses as well as strengths. In these cases the improved wages are geared to manual labor, thus tending to make office staff, for example, feel financially underprivileged. But this is simply another problem needing special solution. A more vital issue is the amount of work required initially, and perhaps continuously, to achieve extra productivity and the need to motivate those managers and supervisors on whom it devolves.

Given successful productivity bargaining, there should be a better understanding all around between management, workers, and the unions concerned. Such an ideal can only be achieved, however, through a new and sustained spirit of cooperation and substantial freedom from the restrictive practices of the past.

Before leaving the subject of industrial relations, brief reference must be made to arbitration. The use of voluntary arbitration as a means of settling differences between labor and management is widespread in America. Most labor contracts delineate grievance-arbitration procedures. On occasion, the federal government has required compulsory arbitration, generally to protect the public against the serious consequences of strikes in essential industries. Many states, too, will require compulsory arbitration in certain cases such as the strike threat on the part of such firms as telephone, gas, and electric companies. Both the American Arbitration Association and the Federal Mediation and Conciliation Service maintain lists of arbitrators.

HEALTH, SAFETY, AND SECURITY

Apart from purely financial implications, managements have a legal, as well as a moral, responsibility for the well-being of their employees. Legally, not only in view of the state workmens' compensation laws in existence for decades but more since the establishment, in 1970, of the Occupational Safety and Health Administration; morally, as part of the emerging social consciousness of American managements generally.

Working Terms and Conditions

In addition to seeking the right level of remuneration, workers are naturally concerned with hours of work, holidays, and working conditions generally. Flexible working hours, no Saturdays, paid holidays, and the current trend towards a demand for more public holidays are all developments of a long struggle towards more worker leisure and the opportunity to enjoy a private as well as a working life. At the management end, however, it is often difficult to determine where one life starts and the other finishes. For the so-called company man must be constantly available to meet external contacts, deal with extra work pressures, or sort out emergencies.

Policy decisions in these personnel areas are related more to containing the demands of workers for increased leisure, for example a 35-hour week, than seeking to relieve excessive pressure through onerous working constraints. The social problem then becomes one of education for leisure, which to some extent is now a forgotten art. But, of course, it is dangerous to generalize, as often it becomes essential to adjust working hours to the type of operations carried out. There may be, for example, a need for continuous production shifts to maximize the use of expensive plant and machinery, or Saturday-afternoon opening for retail shops in order to capture peak passing trade. Even so, it is usually possible to arrange for extra pay or extra time off to compensate those concerned for specially onerous or inconvenient duties.

It is usually necessary to stagger annual vacations throughout the year to ensure the availability of adequate personnel at all times in order to maintain continuous production or essential services. This then becomes a matter for policy decision, or mutual agreement, perhaps based on seniority, dovetailing all annual vacations to minimize disturbance. Alternatively, it may be decided to close a whole factory so that plant equipment such as boilers can cool off and give the maintenance staff a chance to clear, clean, and overhaul it as necessary.

Working conditions today, with the force of legislation behind them, are generally satisfactory. Proper heating, lighting, and ventilation, the provision of suitable toilet accommodations, rest rooms, staff lunchrooms, and lockers all tend to be taken for granted. But there is still room for wide aesthetic differences as, for instance, between the bare essentials to satisfy the law and the landscaping delights of open planning as previously described. The attitude of management may be to comply with minimum legal requirements only or to show a progressive attitude by providing as many welcome amenities as financial resources will reasonably allow.

The provision of amenities does not necessarily mean that all workers will be satisfied. Elaborate air-conditioning installations and double-glazing may be anathema to claustrophobic personnel anxious to open windows to the fresh air. Canned music, however cheerful, may easily offend as many as it would tend to please, and so on throughout the full gamut of human variety in taste and satisfaction.

Nevertheless, the important factor is the creation of the right atmosphere in which workers can genuinely feel that management has at least taken the trouble to provide for their comfort and well-being collectively. Often they can add the personal touches themselves, but not so as to spoil strategically planned interior decoration. Prior consultation, where it can take place, might prove to be worthwhile; but, as indicated above, it is seldom possible to satisfy more than a majority.

Retirement, Sickness, and Welfare

Although younger workers today have been shown to be less interested in security than formerly, proper provision for old age must become increasingly significant with advancing years. Most employees of course are covered by Social Security (over 90 per cent of the labor force), except perhaps for civil service and other public employees who participate in government pension plans. The main issue here is that provision is made for all workers to enjoy some basic level of security in their old age, with or without their own personal arrangements in support. Several years ago, well over one third of the labor force was covered by some form of group retirement plan; since then, the growth of Individual Retirement Accounts endorsed by the Internal Revenue Service has added substantially to the millions of employees who will be able to count on more than their basic social security payments after retirement.

A serious problem relates to the effects of inflation, there being a need to deal with this erosion both during the build-up of pension rights and while actually paying out the pension. Some firms, for example, voluntarily adjust their pensions periodically to prevent undue hardship to their retired employees; these augmented payments are made possible by skillfully investing the pension funds as a whole, outside the business.

Although accidental injuries on the job and occupation-related diseases are covered financially by workmen's compensation insurance, many large firms provide in addition on-the-spot facilities such as a company doctor or nurse. At least there should be a suitable room for the treatment of sickness or accident, with first-aid equipment and fully trained personnel quickly available. Finally, a good many companies today provide group health insurance coverage for their employees.

A great deal could be written about employee welfare, but this would follow much the same lines as the arguments used when dealing with working conditions. Essentially, there must be a genuine desire to make all reasonable facilities available to personnel with *their* interests firmly in mind; any suggestion of gimmickry or other insincerity is bound to be sensed and resented. This is no cut-and-dried subject, however, as there are many thorny problems to be faced and solved. One cardinal principle here is that personnel tends to become more interested in social clubs, sports, and so on if these are organized and run by the workers themselves. It could be argued, on the other hand, that it might be better not to have any such clubs, as it is in the best interests of personnel to mix with people in other walks of life, during their leisure hours, and to gain from the change of getting away from the corporate environment entirely.

So-called fringe benefits allied to welfare include subsidized group life insurance, help with home purchasing, sick pay, lunch vouchers, and other indirect advantages. Then there may be accounting assistance through payroll deductions for bonds or savings plans. Such advantages are currently more generous with respect to salaried staff than to wage-earners, this being particularly so at managerial levels where executive life insurance plans, company cars, overseas trips, conferences, expense accounts, and other status (but necessary) symbols enter into the higher executive way of life. As welfare and fringe benefits essentially form a material addition to the annual wages and salaries costs, they must be kept in mind when assessing total manpower cost.

Protection from Hazards

Local ordinances as well as city and state regulations lay down any number of safety provisions, such as fencing off all dangerous and moving parts of machinery, safeguards against being overcome by fumes in confined spaces, adequate fire precautions, and so on; these are all provisions that have been built up over the years, often in the light of bitter experience.

Safety matters of this kind usually come within the province of the personnel side, through a safety officer, and should have the full support of management at all levels. This item could, however, be included under production, because fire, accidents, and other disasters can play havoc with costs, even though well covered by insurance. As with other matters of cost control, there is a strong case for all staff to be kept constantly aware of the need to comply with safety regulations at all times. Often this is achieved by having a safety committee, made up of representatives from all main departments, usually with the safety officer as chairman.

All accidents should be thoroughly investigated and charts or other records kept analyzing the reasons for them. For example, were the workers themselves at fault, or had management failed to foresee, or properly safeguard against the hazard? A main object should be to prevent similar accidents from happening in the future, by publicity and/or installing new safety measures.

Finally, there is the growing problem of security related to losses from factory, office, store, trucks, and other areas, ranging in degree from armed robbery to petty pilfering. In many cases such losses can be minimized through the employment of security organizations, or store detectives, and by using such devices as television cameras at strategic points or silent alarms connected to the nearest police station. However, where the culprit is inside the firm, the case should be dealt with as a personnel function or through internal audit. Often a retired police officer is engaged as a security officer, which may well be a good investment. (The use of retired citizens, too old to defend themselves, as night-watchmen is another matter entirely.) Managerial policy would naturally include all types of insurance coverage, but danger to life and limb is by far the harder problem to overcome.

Summary

1. *Human Factor in Management*
   a. Human assets are of the utmost importance to corporate success, but they are not always sufficiently stressed.
   b. Worker attitudes are becoming more self-assured.
   c. The generation gap between management and graduate recruits must be bridged.

    d. Attitude surveys illustrate the concept of involvement.

    e. Behavioral scientists have much to offer.

    f. A personnel department should cover the full range of responsibilities for dealing with employees.

2. Manpower Planning

    a. Such planning cannot disregard constraints of cost.

    b. The first step is to make an objective analysis of existing human resources.

    c. Requirements should then be forecast well ahead, taking quality into account as well as quantity.

    d. Practice suggests a flexible five-year manpower chart, quantified and costed.

3. Selection for Recruitment and Promotion

    a. Taking on new employees is an expensive process.

    b. It normally covers expansion needs and labor turnover.

    c. The source of recruits depends on the type of job.

    d. Promotion is normally from within, but a firm may recruit externally to strengthen manpower quality.

    e. Whereas aptitude and intelligence tests are now standard, personality tests are viewed with suspicion.

    f. Interviewing is a basic but thorny selection technique.

    g. Planned promotion routes develop potential abilities.

    h. Selection/interviewing committees are used for higher appointments.

    i. Effective personnel records must be maintained.

    j. The negative side of selection deals with layoffs and dismissal.

4. Training the Worker

    a. Vocational preparation for its citizens has long been espoused by the federal government.

    b. Federally-supported training was accelerated after the passage of the Manpower Development and Training and the Economic Opportunity Acts.

    c. The company training program should include induction and training for semi-skilled work.

    d. Techniques range from lectures to simulation of work environment.

    e. In-company training should be supplemented externally.

5. Problems of Remuneration

    a. Inflationary trends are causing concern.

b. A wages or salaries structure is a matter of board policy taking comparative rates or scales into account.

c. Remuneration should reflect the job done as well as the ability and capacity of the individual.

d. The "time span of discretion" concept is worthy of attention, and so is the grading of staff salaries.

e. Incentive plans, including profit-sharing, must satisfy minimum requirements.

6. *Industrial Relations*

a. Industrial unrest is increasingly in evidence.

b. Although unions may still be in need of reform, they do have an important role to play.

c. Joint consultation requires a more positive approach.

d. Productivity bargaining is a valuable cost/benefit arrangement.

e. Most labor-management contracts contain provisions for voluntary grievance arbitration.

7. *Health, Safety, and Security*

a. Management must ensure satisfactory working terms and conditions.

b. Besides benefits provided by the Social Security system, company pension plans and welfare facilities are also important.

c. Safety provisions are essential to protect employees from hazards.

Suggested Further Reading

BASS, B.M., AND J.A. VAUGHAN. *Training in Industry: The Management of Learning.* Belmont, Calif.: Wadsworth Publishing, 1966.

BEACH, D.S. *Personnel: The Management of People at Work.* 2d ed. New York: Macmillan, 1970.

DUNN, J.D., AND E.C. STEPHENS. *Management of Personnel: Manpower Management and Organizational Behavior.* New York: McGraw-Hill, 1972.

FORMULARO, J.J., ed. *Handbook of Modern Personnel Administration.* New York: McGraw-Hill, 1972.

FRENCH, W. *The Personnel Management Process: Human Resource Administration.* 2d ed. Boston: Houghton Mifflin, 1970.

HAMBLIN, A.C. *Evaluation and Control of Training.* New York: McGraw-Hill, 1974.

HICKS, H.G., AND C.R. GULLETT. *The Management of Organizations.* 3d ed. New York: McGraw-Hill, 1976.

MAIER, N.R.F. *Psychology in Industrial Organizations.* 4th ed. Boston: Houghton Mifflin, 1973.

McGREGOR, D. *The Human Side of Enterprise.* New York: McGraw-Hill, 1960.

MINER, J.B., AND M.G. MINER. *Personnel and Industrial Relations: A Managerial Approach.* 2d ed. New York: Macmillan, 1973.

ODIORNE, G.S. *Personnel Administration by Objectives.* Homewood, Ill.: Irwin, 1971.

OTTO, C.P., AND R.O. GLASER. *The Management of Training: A Handbook for Training and Development of Personnel.* Reading, Mass.: Addison-Wesley, 1970.

PIGORS, P., AND C.A. MYERS. *Personnel Administration: A Point of View and a Method.* 7th ed. New York: McGraw-Hill, 1973.

SINGER, E.J., AND J. RAMSDEN. *Human Resources: Obtaining Results from People at Work.* New York: McGraw-Hill, 1972.

STRAUSS, G., AND L.R. SAYLES. *Personnel: The Human Problems of Management.* 3d ed. Englewood Cliffs, N.J.: Prentice-Hall, 1972.

WILLSMORE, A.W. *Managing Modern Man.* New York: Beekman, 1973.

THIRTEEN

Integration and Control

In the preceding four chapters, the major policy areas—marketing, production, finance, and personnel—have been studied in isolation. This is to say, in such isolation as is possible, because with both theory and practice there are inherent tendencies towards overlapping and integration, as well as towards departmental interests trying to pull their separate, sometimes independent, ways. Before looking at the business as a whole, it is convenient to review the main functions and responsibilities that must be properly integrated and controlled.

RELATIONSHIPS BETWEEN POLICY AREAS

The following four sections are not intended as a detailed summary of main policy areas, but rather as an illustration of the character and extent of natural interdependence.

Marketing Aspects

Being "marketing oriented" not "production oriented," a distinction considered in Chapter Nine, emphasizes the essential and quantitative need to balance marketing with production, the former acting as the pace-setter. This in turn requires a keen appreciation of the environment, a knowledge of the market in all its aspects, including customer attitudes, leading to forecasting based on taking a view of the future, and departmental planning. It is, of course, planning in this and other departments that must finally be integrated into the corporate plan.

Reference was made to centralization and decentralization in the marketing organization, bringing out the value and use of "staff" functions, including the cooperation of management services as and when required. This special use of computer facilities for automated stock control was given as a case in point. It was shown, too, that certain marketing appointments were necessary and that sales staff, internally and externally, had to be recruited, promoted and trained; in such a context the services of the personnel side are clearly vital.

"Variety reduction" in products or services was shown to link up with the theory of contribution towards fixed costs, thus bringing marketing together with production again, and finance. Any change in the products or services, whether specialized or diversified, must have interdepartmental repercussions through their claims on materials, personnel, and and other resources allocated centrally. For product policy must be reconciled with all other claimants on scarce resources, including finance, to ensure feasibility and profitability of performance. The marginal theory, too, is clearly linked with revenue on the marketing side and costs on the production side, finance being a kind of balancing medium. The significance of price obviously has departmental repercussions well outside pure marketing considerations. A wrong pricing policy can have far reaching consequences, for it is the aim of good policy to balance the reasonable demands of customers with the need to make sufficient profits to continue prosperously in business. Changes in pricing policy cannot therefore be made without considering their effects on production, material and personnel resources, and finance.

Publicity, promotion, and salesmanship in all its different forms must be reconciled with finance (everything has to be paid for), with production (to make sure that increased demand can be met), and with personnel (as to incentive and pay schemes for the selling side).

Finally, the problems of distribution, logistics, and transportation all have claims on other departments' activities and specialized areas.

Implications for Production

The interdependence of production with marketing, and other functions, is well illustrated by a consideration of processes and technological choice. Automation, for example, has financial implications in the selection and purchase of sophisticated plant and equipment, psychological problems such as the acceptance of change, new aspects of training and retraining, and similar matters all requiring the cooperation of other departmental specialists.

The size and location of plants have obvious marketing overtones from a customer-service angle. Even the management organization for production is governed by the type and range of product. Similarly the organization of R. and D. harnesses personal academic integrity and individual freedom with the corporate needs of marketing, production, and the financial constraints of cost.

With production planning and control, there is a natural element of integration in the many different features that have to be reconciled for successful operations. Policy decisions concerning the purchasing and/or making of raw materials, partly finished goods, and the like must affect the claims to be made on other managerial resources. The financial structure, for instance, has to take into account the working capital required to meet commitments and the level of stock to be carried at any given time.

There are personnel implications, too, in making a decision to produce for stock (and future sales) during a period of recession, in order to retain skilled labor, rather than declare such labor temporarily excess. Similarly with the consideration of incentives in the search for quality and reliability and of psychological aspects inherent in the use of work study.

Enough has been indicated, however, to show that production policies cannot exist in a vacuum, but need to be complemented by the other policy aspects of management in varying degrees of importance.

Financial Considerations

Watching the cash flow, meeting long- and short-term capital needs, the shape of the financial structure, effects of taxation, capital-investment policy, and a range of other allied topics are essentially multi-discipline activities. Although it could be argued, by an accountant, that financial policy governs everything, and that accounts record everything, clearly no single aspect of management can ignore its relationship with other management aspects. For finance is required for marketing purposes, to meet costs of production, including plant and machinery, to pay administrative costs, salaries, and wages, with the accountants coordinating and integrating all these various activities into comprehensive published accounts.

All assets used by any sector of the enterprise should be reconciled with the R.O.I. policy adopted; planning for profit involves total cooperation; profit centers and cost centers require active support from all fronts. Business ratios, too, point the way to improvements throughout the organization, linked with interfirm comparison covering a wide range of departmental activity.

The discussion on sites, premises, layout, and equipment was included *faux de mieux* among "Financial Policies" in Chapter Eleven, but the intersectional implications, being obvious in that context, need no further emphasis here.

Finally, budgetary control is clearly such an across-the-board company-wide technique that logic suggests its inclusion here under "Integration and Control," not, as is customary, in a chapter dealing solely with financial policy.

Personnel Policies

Manpower planning is based on the rate of progress anticipated over the years ahead. This in turn depends on the marketing outlook, the backing to be required from production, and the expectation of providing sufficient finance throughout. Technological change, the introduction of the latest generations in plant and equipment, and other production aspects, can make the demands on labor relatively less than they were formerly. They can in fact convert a labor-intensive enterprise into one that is capital-intensive. Note also the effects of the computer on managerial structure and office staff.

In providing for recruitment, selection, promotion, training, salaries, wages and retirement, personnel policies affect all aspects of an enterprise, and even more so when the training side includes general "management development." Dealing with trade unions, and other industrial relations, can also have wide repercussions on the production side, particularly in an industry or firm which is prone to the withdrawal of labor, i.e., strikes, official or unofficial.

However, enough has been included in these major policy sections to demonstrate, in practical terms, that functional interaction is not only necessary but, to a large extent, inevitable.

Achieving a Balance

The problem remaining is one of balancing these major policy areas, coordinating and streamlining the separate activities, and achieving integrated control. The main relationships involved are summarized in Figure 14 overleaf.

Figure 14 demonstrates the interplay between environment and corporate objectives, the forecasting which leads to corporate planning, and the identification of the objectives with the planning. This leads to major policies including the rate and nature of growth as set out by the objectives, with special reference to merger and/or acquisition, and their integration and balance.

The board of directors initiates and becomes conditioned by the corporate objectives; it is responsible for the major policy decisions and for overall, total control. In achieving that control, it is clearly essential to measure performance against the objectives and the planning.

The president is shown as the catalyst between the board on one hand and the staff on the other, between policy decision above and executive action below. But he must essentially view the organization from the top, whether, at any given time, he happens to be in the boardroom or at his office desk.

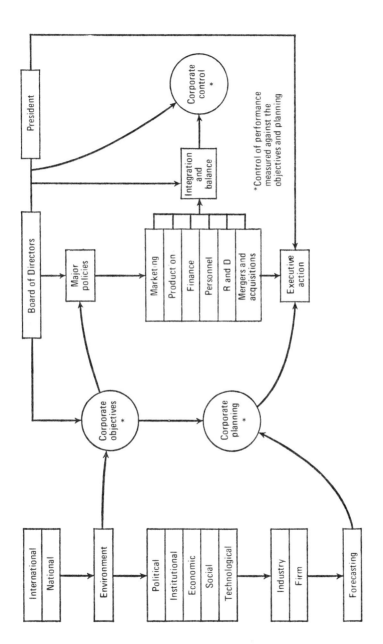

FIGURE 14. Schematic diagram of integrating relationships

VIEWING FROM THE TOP

"Business policy," an all-embracing term, is in essence concerned with that total enterprise, looking at the functions and responsibilities of general management, viewing the organization from the top. The board of directors, including the chief executive officer, are absorbed with problems which generate success, or failure, for the business as a whole. They have the duty of developing and implementing corporate objectives, major policies, plans, and strategies; and of making far-reaching decisions for the enterprise in a changing and uncertain world.

In the process they can, of course, influence the whole character of the business and make all the difference to results by the efficiency with which they keep the main policy areas in clear perspective, integrate them, and achieve overall control.

Integrated Problem Solving

In dealing with specific problems, top management is often required to look at departmental difficulties and biased points of view. At a staff conference, in management committee, seeking recommendations or initiating action, it often happens that the subject matter under discussion is highly specialized and must necessarily be analyzed and broken down into its constituent parts. The next step in the procedure is to determine which of these parts affect other departments, sections, etc., and to evaluate the strength and extent of each facet of global interaction. This may require some determination of relative importance, or priority, and the taking of appropriate action to ensure that other interests concerned are fully aware of these problems and their effects. They should be consulted whenever necessary. In this way the solution, usually the deciding of a principle or policy or the formulation of a plan, is far more likely to be effective when finally translated into practical terms.

In the interlocking of departmental problems, top management must essentially view the business as a whole and indoctrinate all other levels of management to share this fundamental total concept. One of the most important results of a study of "business policy," academically or practically, is that specialized managers and any others taking part soon acquire an understanding of how the president looks at their job and how he has to tie together all the related ends. This concept of the business as a whole is based on an integrated view of the firm's objectives. It means overall planning, leading to final control as the full responsibility of top management.

Coordinating Influences

Left to their own devices, marketing personnel are apt to concentrate on creative activities such as advertising, selling, and product development, with little or no concern for the financial implications involved in the outcome. For them the sky tends to be the limit, in an extrovert kind of atmosphere. Similarly, the financial people tend to be inhibited by their accounts and costs and fail to appreciate the life blood of marketing in the future of the firm. Both sides are, of course, wrapped up in their jobs and largely conditioned by them. In other words, they are commendable and committed specialists needing to be integrated.

It is here that the president, the arch-apostle of the general (i.e., total) approach, can bridge the gap and help each specialist to understand and appreciate the value of the other specialists. For he would be conscious of the remaining functions also in need of being conditioned and coordinated.

To some extent this would be achieved through regular interaction at board meetings, through top management committees, periodic conferences at various levels, and certain techniques such as budgetary control to be described later. By being brought together with other functions, marketing men become conscious of the need for profits, and accountants begin to look at marketing with a less jaundiced eye.

This approach to a total viewpoint is also helped by various forms of training—in-company, external course or seminar—possibly with the accent on appreciation rather than on the working tools of the other man's craft.

Coordination is one of the main problems of growth; in particular how to ensure that, having delegated all possible responsibility and authority, every part of the organization will keep firmly in step with all other parts. At each level up the scale, coordination is limited to the span of control, which may mean having more layers in the hierarchy. The breaking of administrative bulk, through greater decentralization, may ease control and provide for local autonomy, but overall total coordination must still remain the final responsibility of top management. Even a holding company has to produce a consolidated balance sheet covering all the subsidiaries.

Apart from purely formal attempts to achieve coordination, much value can be gained from social contacts and informal lines of communication. Interdepartmental understanding can, as indicated in Chapter Four, be fostered daily round the executive bar and at the luncheon table.

Ultimate success or failure in integration depends to a large extent on the kind of leadership emanating from the top on the philosophy of management that inevitably sets the tone for the whole organization.

PROGRAMS AND PROJECTS

Policies have been described as rules of action for the rank and file to show them how they are expected to attain the desired results, to enable the enterprise to reach the long-range target, or targets, set by the objectives. This implies motivating and directing all concerned, coordinating their activities, bringing in all other necessary resources, and checking the results achieved with the plans laid down. Objectives are, however, subject to time-scales and it is possible to have short-term programs and projects consistent with the long-term objectives.

Short-term Programs

Laying down a short-term program with a time span of anything between a few months and a few years, requires careful planning throughout, from initiation to final achievement. This means identifying the number and extent of operations involved and making a realistic assessment of the length of time required for the whole program. These operations may relate to a single department or extend right across the functional board.

Programs may be of a routine nature, illustrated by production planning and control, or refer to *ad hoc* activities such as unit- and job-improvement plans. The former may be the manufacture of so many units per month, and the latter the building of a new factory or the installation of a new technique. It is with this latter variety, i.e., short-term programming for a specific purpose, that we are mainly concerned in this section.

The various operations must then be arranged in order so that resources can be allocated, detailed time-scales drawn up for each stage of achievement, and responsibilities and authorities given as necessary. In particular, it must be made clear who is to be in overall charge of the whole program so that he may be made accountable for the operations, step by step, to the target date.

Top management, or other appropriate level of management, would require regular reports to be made by the program controller, by whatever name he might be called, so that they could be reassured from time to time that all was going according to plan. There could be a number of short-term programs to be dovetailed together, and each one completed, before proceeding to a more advanced stage involving other programs. As usual, all plans are subject to changes in the prevailing conditions; and even short-term programs must be kept flexible in operation. Any alteration, however, in target dates must be fully justified by chapter and verse, and realistic adjustments made accordingly. Any other programs affected by such a change would also need to be reviewed, as, for example, in the light of altered target dates, possibly extending right along the line. The alternative, depending on the degree of urgency, is to bring in additional resources with a view to maintaining at least the final target date. This latter decision will have to weigh the cost of those extra resources against the cost of not completing the program as originally planned.

Insofar as only one major policy area is concerned, the problem of allocating resources and appointing a controller may present no particular difficulty, except perhaps that of fitting in a special short-term program with everyday work of a more routine character. This may require additional personnel and/or training for existing personnel.

Where the resources required are right across the functional board, omnibus arrangements may be necessary. One such method is to appoint a project team, taking the best available people, possibly from different organizational levels, to bring into that team all such expertise as may be considered essential for the job in hand. These hand-picked specialists can then be kept together as a task force until the project has been successfully achieved. This makes good sense, but needs tactful handling from the point of view of line management, since the possibly prolonged reassignment of such experts may well prove to be a problem to their normal superiors. The alternative may be to appoint a permanent (costly) team, depending on the number and nature of projects, but it must be borne in mind that different projects often require a different selection of expertise.

Critical Path Analysis

In recent years a great deal has been heard about "critical path analysis" (C.P.A.), which is simply a systematic way of programming economically in sequence. Known also as "network analysis" and "program evaluation and review technique" (P.E.R.T.), and other names emphasizing slight differences in practice, its aim is to ensure the shortest possible time between inception and completion, to keep delay and cost to an absolute minimum. Thus a diagrammatic network of "events" is drawn up in logical order, with a time-scale for each part, the total time being determined by the shortest way home, through taking the critical path.

C.P.A. is basically an operations research technique, and in line with that it is essential to construct a progressive model of the real system. In this case it takes the form of an arrow diagram such as that shown in Figure 15. The example given is a simple one, but in practice, particularly with regard to construction projects, the network can be highly complicated, the critical path threading its way through a veritable maze of highways and by-ways to achieve a minimum sequence of significant events. It will be seen that each event is given a progressive reference number in a circle, called a "node," and that between adjacent events, conveniently placed in a square, there is a figure indicating estimated duration, usually expressed as so many units of working days. A refinement includes minimum and maximum times of expected duration.

The critical path in the example given is the horizontal line extending right across the center of Figure 15.

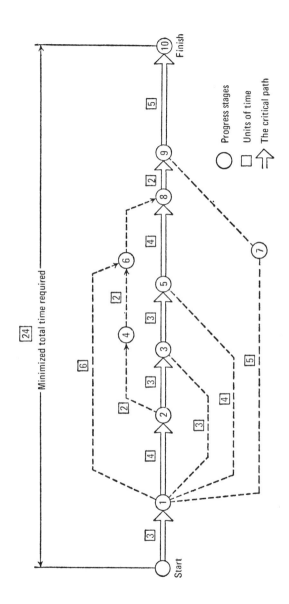

FIGURE 15. Critical Path Analysis

This shows that stage ① takes three units of time to complete from the start of the program; at this point certain side sequences are set in motion to slot into and help complete stages ③, ⑤, ⑧, and ⑨ along the critical path. By the time stage ⑧ is reached, for example, side programs ④ and ⑥ have been finished, thereby enabling stage ⑧ to be completed. By stage ⑩ the program as a whole has been finally achieved in the least possible total time.

Network analysis has many applications in practice. A typical example is the building of a new factory, with successive critical stages from leveling and marking out the site, and cutting out the footings, right through to the last coat of paint. Side programs can be the obtaining and delivery of concrete, bricks, timber, including prefabricated doors, window frames and partitions to the site, the digging and laying of drains, electrical wiring, putting up fences and roads, and so on. The critical path is then the arrangement of all these sequences, in logical order, to minimize the total time to be allowed for the project as a whole.

Similarly with a move to a new factory: each phase of the removal procedure would need to be planned, with military precision on a C.P.A. basis, to minimize disruption and keep down the cost of the operation in total. Such a network analysis could extend well beyond physical factors, in that new personnel, for instance, would have to be recruited locally, and properly trained by the time they would be required to help restart production. Key personnel would need to be transferred, and rehoused, by specific stages in the program, in order to supervise events on the spot, recruit and train the new workers, or simply to be there in time for resumed production. Operations at the old factory would have to be phased out, as part of the network analysis for the entire operation. It can easily be seen how such detailed programming can usefully be translated into a network diagram with all the necessary logical sequences and time-scales.

A further example is the planning of a new product, from initial design stage to full production. In this case, the C.P.A. network could indicate the parts to be played by R. and D., technical design, market research, materials planning, production engineering, and the like on the way to the achievement of profitable results in minimum lead time. In fact, this example could be extended to cover full marketing, including the launching of a product, equally amenable to C.P.A. treatment, adding in advertising, sales promotion, personal selling and distribution.

"Lead time," incidentally, is the total interval between thinking up a new idea and its translation into practical effect. Where it is essential to the meeting of competition, the shorter the time taken to establish a lead over competitors, the better the chances of improving the market share. Innovation and change must always respond quickly to events, whether to meet a new challenge or maximize an opportunity.

Although the above examples are related to construction or manufacturing, the same technique can be successfully used for planning office work or accounting systems—leading, for example, to budgetary control as discussed later in the chapter.

It may be argued from Figure 15 that the critical-path time allowed for progress from stage ① to stage ③ is ④ plus ③ units (perhaps working weeks) of time, that is to say ⑦, whereas the by-way from ① to ③ can be done in ③ weeks. This, however, is immaterial, the balance of four weeks being called "float time." It simply means that the by-way operation, being noncritical, can be carried out either with minimum labor over the full seven weeks, or with normal labor in any three weeks, as convenient during the full seven weeks available. This, allows flexibility of planning while keeping as rigidly as possible to the critical path. In this way it may be possible to achieve a more even work load over the full project.

A highly complex network usually requires the use of a computer to deal with the assessment, analysis, and scheduling of input data. There may also be a case in practice for breaking down a vast network into a system of self-contained networks, these to be carried out in parallel and integrated into a master network.

Whatever the type of network, the program or project must be effectively controlled throughout the sequence of scheduled activities to ensure satisfactory progress as planned.

Few management systems can be considered as perfect, hence the need always to assess the pros and cons before making a decision to adopt any one of them. In the case of detailed network analysis, the other side of the coin is that by using the technique, in the process of which highly complex diagrams have to be drawn up, more time may be wasted than is likely to be saved.

The alternative technique used by firms who hold this point of view, whether arising from experience or hearsay, is the older system of Gantt or bar charts introduced in Chapter Ten. Here each component activity is shown, one under another, as a horizontal line running through a given number of units of time, usually weeks. This means that those responsible for the separate activities can easily see when they are individually due to start and when they are expected to finish. Such a system, however, has certain limits in so far as it cannot deal with interrelated activities. Nevertheless, within those limits, it is simple to operate and easy to understand.

On balance, with the increased use of computers, including time-sharing terminals, the most sophisticated C.P.A. can be fully expected to hold its own. Although so far related to short-term programs, network analysis obviously has relevance to longer-range more complex projects as well.

Long-range Projects

In Chapter Seven, general consideration was given to long-range planning covering the full gamut of a firm's future development. Within this overall planning there can be short-term programming and specific long-range projects of all kinds. We have seen that long-range planning has targets set by the corporate objectives, with "control standards" at intermediate stages. Clearly, by anticipating the future in this way, all concerned can be conditioned from the start to know what is expected of them—if only to comply with a time schedule based on those stages.

It means, too, for any specific long-range project with control standards of its own that realistic time-scales must be allocated for the acquisition of essential resources and for each progressive stage of development. For certain physical resources may take many months or even years to produce. Then there may be complicated legal and commercial aspects to be negotiated such as patents, concessions, and licenses, as relevant to any given type of business. Finally, and at various stages, labor has to be taken on, trained, and organized in the same way as for shorter-term ventures. And all this has to be translated into monetary considerations such as capital, income, costs, and profits, ranging from survival in the interim to success in the ultimate.

In the meantime, current operations will have to be fitted into the long-range pattern and reconciled with any special projects intended to form a future part of that pattern. This may mean some modification of the existing business as, for example, to release finance, physical resources, or key personnel, to help a project on its way.

CONTROLLING THE OPERATIONS

It was seen in Chapter One that the principal functions of management were *(a)* planning the activities, *(b)* organizing the structure, both of these being mechanical aspects, and *(c)* controlling, which was listed under "dynamics." Overall there was the crucial factor of leadership.

Planning and Control Complementary

Controlling, the checking of performance against predetermined standards, has already been shown as being virtually inseparable from planning. Control standards, of course, arise from plans, which must be consistent with objectives, translated into convenient stages for measurement and resultant, perhaps corrective, action.

This is by no means an easy undertaking, for action has to be taken, either to make the plans work or to amend them, using *current* information to deal with a changing, sometimes rapidly changing, environment. All kinds of future probabilities have to be weighed and resolved in the best interests of corporate progress, providing in the process testing evidence of managerial efficiency, or otherwise, in the control of planning.

The Exercise of Control

In exercising that control, management can do so rigidly with cold ruthless adherence to regimentation, red tape, and bureaucracy, call it what you will, or by the proper use of imagination and motivation. Imagination here means having sufficient insight to appreciate the problems of subordinates, through whom a manager must work, finding ways and means to supervise their activities in a firm but flexible way. Motivation, in the same context, implies ability to make the best use of worker interests, hopes, and ambitions; sensitivity to understand their individual pecularities and innate differences in comprehension and/or pace of work; wisdom to consult and brief them whenever feasible; and humility to ensure that orders given are seen to be necessary, and relevant, not just evidence of authority for the sake of authority. For human qualities of this kind are inherent in good leadership at every level, including supervision in the office or on the shop floor.

Orders in some form or other are necessary, of course, as part of the process of communicating policy decisions when translated into action. Instructions have to be passed down, procedures put into effect and ground rules devised to ensure that everyone concerned with plans in action has a clear understanding of what needs to be done and why. But, having issued orders, made rules, and laid down procedures, whether verbally or in writing, it is no use sitting back and considering that all will be well simply because everything and everybody in sight has been neatly organized into the total pattern. For communications can be misunderstood, genuinely or deliberately, circumstances can change, delays occur, or inertia set in with creeping but disastrous effect.

Hence the importance of organized control, a pattern of systematic "follow through" to ensure that the plans, rules, and procedures are in fact being observed and carried out effectively. This does not necessarily mean overzealous control, which can destroy initiative, but rather a check on activity, with encouragement to the conscientious and stimulation or censure to the less effective. This can be done by interested inquiry, by systematic progress reports, which in turn may need to be verified, or by instituting a number of routine control procedures, some of which have already been mentioned. In other words, the aim of control in its many applications is to be both positive and practical.

Controlling the Marketing Side

Starting with marketing, it can be assumed that the planners have assessed their total market trends, have chosen their market segment or segments, and have a clear idea of the market share that they are setting out their stall to attract. There will be sales forecasts, budgets, and so on, clearly expressed in financial terms, possibly also in physical terms, which will constitute the raw materials for future control.

Control is fundamentally based on comparison, and in its

elementary form means comparing sales figures each month with those for the previous month and with those for the same month last year. Cumulative figures will be compared with cumulative figures for the year before, and trends observed by "moving annual totals." The use of "Z charts" is a long-established, but still effective, way of dealing with such simple statistics. Figure 16 shows how monthly results, current and cumulative, can be built up by progressive graphs.

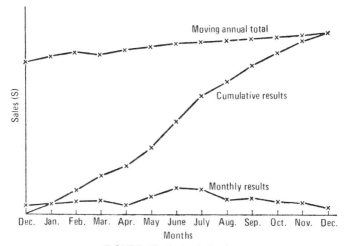

FIGURE 16. A chart of sales

The cumulative graph will naturally coincide at the end of the calendar year with the graph for moving annual totals, this being the total results, month by month, for a full year up to and including the current month.

Taking an example, the moving annual total at the end of March will be the figure for the year April to March inclusive. The value of this device is that it shows the sales trend free from purely seasonal effects, which in any case can easily be studied from the monthly figures. Such comparisons can be subdivided into products, sales territory areas, branches, or whatever other breakdown happens to be relevant and significant for the organization concerned.

This simple system shows at a glance whether the business as a whole, or in parts, is progressing or otherwise; but it makes no allowance for taking planning, that is to say standards of control, into account. In general, it is not sufficient to compare progress with historical results, but rather to compare achievement with realistic and planned estimates, made in anticipation of the changing scene. The next step is to compare results with the results of other firms operating in the same line of business, over the same period of time.

The first refinement is achieved through "budgetary control," a well-tried system which justifies a separate section to itself; the second refinement comes from "interfirm comparison," which is discussed in Chapter Eleven in the context of Finance. It is usually difficult to obtain the sales figures of competitors, and in any case these tend to be recent history at best by the time they are made available. It could be argued, therefore, that firms in the same line should get together at the planning stage and prepare their budget in liaison with each other. This would operate to the benefit of all concerned, but in today's environment, competition being what it is, such a comment is either before its time or naïve in its conception.

When dealing with the costs of marketing, selling, and distribution, arising from major policy decisions, there is a mixture of positive and negative control to be properly balanced. Positive, because with marketing and selling in general it often pays to *spend* money on market research, advertising, and other forms of promotion; control then consisting mainly of keeping to budget figures. This is well illustrated by matching up to advertising appropriations agreed by the board. Negative, because the emphasis should be on keeping distribution and allied costs to an absolute minimum, consistent always with acceptable efficiency and speed in dispatch.

But even with the positive aspect of control, it is still necessary to make sure that all money spent on market research, advertising, by salesmen in making their calls on customers, and with respect to other marketing features, has been well spent. In other words, control also connotes the evaluation of results achieved from given expenditures. But, as shown in Chapter Nine, there is no royal road to judging the effectiveness of advertising, only test checks and broad indications of success. The value of salesmen's calls can be more accurately assessed in the light of actual orders received, but even here there are cumulative and latent effects that have to be taken into account.

Reconciling Production Control

Production control, in physical as well as money terms, is also a matter of comparing actual results with budget figures. In this case the figures are based on production budgets, these in turn being reconciled with marketing budgets and manufacturing capacity available. It has been seen that there are many allied controls such as cost control, operating at various stages from design to final production, stock control, quality control, and network analysis. In addition, it is relevant to make special mention here of "standard costing," briefly introduced in Chapter Eleven.

In making forecasts of costs, reference is usually made to past costs, work-study data, and a range of estimated figures giving the likely trend of raw-material prices, wage rates, overhead expenses, expected output, general price levels and any other information that can usefully be brought to bear on the future situation. These forecast costs are known as "standard costs," being predetermined standards against which to judge actual costs. This being so, it is important to ensure that such standards represent realistic normal costs, not idealistic standards difficult if not impossible to achieve. With this kind of realism, standard costs constitute a useful basis for estimating, pricing and other managerial policy action, and are a valuable check on operating efficiency.

Financial Control Comprehensive

Financial controls are interwoven with all other functional controls, as every aspect of a business must eventually come to terms with accounting records and monetary profits. Mention may be made of the control of large capital expenditures, cost control, administrative expenditure control and, in particular, the annual balance sheet, as published in statutory form, whereby the shareholders or other proprietors can judge the final results for themselves. If not satisfied, they can exercise control through the annual general meeting.

Profit planning, inevitably tied to control, is a deliberate and strategic attempt to run the business in such a way as to attain certain stated profits over a given period. In practice, this involves a complex operation affecting all functions and requiring many significant features to be evaluated, interlinked and given their full effect. The main features may be listed as follows:

(a) Total sales in volume and prices.
(b) Total sales costs, including manufacturing and distribution costs; overhead expenses.

(c) Profit margins; contributions made by specific products or services.

(d) Effectiveness of employment of fixed assets; level of liquidity; capital-expenditure program; utilization of manufacturing capacity.

(e) Stock levels of raw materials, work in progress, and finished products.

All these, and allied aspects, are budgeted well ahead, and with the required aim of achieving a preconceived level of profits. In practice, however, difficulties arise with regard to a generally accepted definition of profits. In the first place, should maximization of profits be the main principle irrespective of social responsibility and the claims of the future? It may be possible, for example, to maximize profits in the short term by running down equipment, not making provision for depreciation, replacement of fixed assets and other costs, keeping salary and wage rates, welfare, and such to a minimum, and any other practice that can exploit tomorrow to today's advantage. There may also be disadvantages in maximizing profits for tax reasons, or even political reasons, such as not wanting to attract critical comment on exploitation, etc. likely to affect the corporate image and lead to more official control.

Second, what profits are we talking about? Basically, this is the return on capital employed translated into current values, not the book values of a company's assets as shown in the balance sheet after being adjusted for depreciation according to the particular policy adopted. In addition, the profit concept must always view the business as an "ongoing" concern, with long-range plans kept well in mind. This suggests working to an "optimum" profit, taking all relevant considerations into account, possibly with a minimum profit, below which it would be risky to go, as the critical limit.

Sensitivity Analysis and Break-even

Linked with profit planning is the sophisticated concept of "sensitivity analysis," which attempts, in graphical form, to indicate how sensitive the profits of any business are likely to be in response to changes in sales volume, prices, and costs. Most businesses, however, are more familiar with the well-known "break-even" chart, which deals with the same basic elements in their simplest forms. This chart is illustrated in Figure 17. Break-even can be seen as the point at which total revenue equals total costs and beyond which, with more sales (production), a profit can be made. From this chart a number of questions can be answered, such as what would happen to profits if total sales were to fall off, or what would happen to profits if prices were raised, with or without a reduction in costs, but less goods could

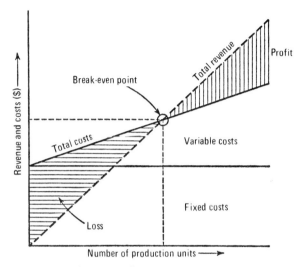

FIGURE 17. Sales break-even chart

be sold at these higher prices. The relevance of fixed and variable costs will already be appreciated from Chapter Nine, which introduced the contribution theory, the concept of a product or service covering its own variable costs and making some contribution towards the fixed costs.

There are certain assumptions that have to be made in the use of these charts, coupled with a narrow range of relevance (to accord with realism) on either side of the break-even point. Among these assumptions is the acceptance of a static environment, when a dynamic situation is more likely to be the case in practice. Being a static chart, therefore, it has greater validity when dealing with a relatively stable market than with a highly volatile market. Second, the chart can only be as effective as the extent and accuracy of the data which is built into it. Then there is an implied assumption that the revenue/cost relationship is linear, which produces its own limitations in application. Nor can the chart be used beyond the budget period of the firm. Finally, the total-revenue graph could be a curve instead of a straight line, and there could be more than one break-even point given a need for computations at different price levels.

But, despite these limitations, break-even charts have a basic practical value if only as a first approximation, coupled with value judgment and common sense, on the way to more sophisticated analysis.

Manpower Planning and Control

Personnel policies and problems complete the functional approach to control. Manpower planning is particularly important in the present context, because of the cost effects on nearly all other expenditures. More people being employed, in the factory or in the office, means extra working accommodations and equipment; a higher wages and salaries bill; greater unemployment insurance, workmen's compensation, pension, and other contributions including welfare expenditures; extra personnel records; problems of coordination, supervision, training and so on. Hence, in support of making better use of manpower, and aiming for greater productivity through work study and other aspects covered in Chapter Twelve, there are very real budgeting needs for planning and control to keep down the total cost of manpower.

A distinction may be drawn between direct and indirect labor, depending on the type of business and degree of automation, but this does not invalidate the general approach to control. Even in a commercial type of organization, there is still a budgeting need to determine an optimum staff establishment for each department. This implies provision for regular review, and resistance to any claims for additional staff unless a cast-iron case can be made out and substantiated financially.

Central Services and Control

Overall aspects of control can be internal or external. From a purely accounting point of view, for example, there must be legally appointed auditors responsible for ensuring that the bookkeeping entries are honest and accurate and that the final accounts (balance sheet, profit and loss statement, etc.) present a "true and fair view of the state of affairs" to the world at large. In support of this, in a large organization, there would probably be a team of internal auditors regularly checking the accounts and other records in departments and branches, with special regard to the accuracy of figures, accounting procedures, and the security of cash. Many a fraud or defalcation has been detected by an internal audit department of this kind. The external auditors would need to be assured of the effectiveness of such internal audit as a "branch" of their own responsibilities, in full support of their legal standing and statutory obligations.

Internally, too, various control procedures would be laid down to ensure that everything considered to be important, as expressed in company manuals and office instructions, was being properly observed and carried out. This might come within the province of a management services team working independently, but it could also be in the form of a "management audit," which would include higher authority and cover the full gamut of inspection. Such higher authority would be empowered to visit departments and branches, or whatever units of organization happened to be appropriate, and inspect every aspect of the work. The main aim would be to check efficiency, compliance with objectives, planning and policies, and any other aspect of company operations that came within the total concept of control. Usually there would be local consultation and discussion before any report was written, so that joint action mutually agreed as being necessary could be duly recorded, taken into account, and followed through at a later date. It must be kept in mind that any control and coordination of activities must be achieved, whenever possible, without alienating personnel and thereby destroying local morale.

Similarly, due regard must be paid to the cost of control, for in logic no control should cost more than it can hope to save in efficiency and monetary terms. An elaborate system could be built up, for instance, to keep a check on staff pilfering of stock, but theoretically (the ethical considerations may be different) if the cost of supervision became too great it might be more economic to let the staff continue their pilfering. Tied in with costs of control are the related merits of self-control, including participation in the setting of targets, which then become almost a point of honor to achieve. Where this attitude is channelled into profit centers and/or cost centers, such costs of control tend to become minimal. It can be argued that planning and controlling are opposite ends of the managerial scene, planning being positive and control negative, but as indicated before it all depends on the approach to people psychologically. It is here that management by objectives could be made to fit in.

Management is continually seeking information for control purposes, ranging from off-the-cuff reports made by salesmen to total management information systems based on a computer. Much of the basic reporting is done systematically—daily, weekly, monthly, quarterly, or annually, depending on its nature—by properly integrated documents such as divisional, departmental, or branch routine returns, with attention being drawn to any matters of exceptional merit. In addition to routine returns, special reports are usually initiated whenever they are required.

In processing information for central control purposes, this could be on the basis of management by exception, operating ratios, or other significant key results, aiming to pinpoint management attention to essentials and thereby save top people from wasting valuable time on matters of routine. By daily, weekly, or otherwise periodic reports submitted on this basis, top management would continually be made aware of trends and danger points requiring action. For figures and other data are not just to be looked at with passing interest: They are to be used as a basis for any managerial action considered appropriate. This may mean report and recommendation to the board for new policy decisions or executive action through the hierarchy to enforce policy already laid down, but not being sufficiently observed.

Central control is affected by organizational structure, with special reference to centralization versus decentralization. At one time the emphasis was always firmly on tight central control, but with growth, diversification, and new technologies, bulk has tended to be broken down, with local autonomy for ease of administration.

In such a context, central control must be largely based on reports from the circumference, but these would be reinforced by controls set up at various levels throughout the organization. The central problem would then be one of coordination of control.

With the introduction of computers, the tendency has been to continue centralized, or to re-centralize where this could effectively be carried out. Nevertheless, there are many organizational advantages of decentralization to offset the virtues of centralized accounting and information systems, so that the pendulum may well swing again in a decentralized direction.

BUDGETARY CONTROL

Budgetary control has a twofold value. In the first place many authorities believe that the preparation of the budgets themselves is almost *the* vital factor, in that the managers of all functions have to think ahead realistically and plan accordingly. Second, it has built-in comprehensive control elements based on a total company-wide system, each functional plan needing to be reconciled with the plans of every other function. In other words, budgetary control is probably the most effective device for integration yet produced.

This is no new system, however, but one that has stood the test of time and is still in common use. It is sometimes felt that the preparation of detailed budgets is time-consuming and therefore costly, but most users of the system would maintain that, properly carried out, it is time well spent.

The Basic Features

Budgeting is the concept of planning ahead to make ends meet, and if possible to have a surplus, in the same way that there are household budgets and national budgets. The broad issue is to ensure that income exceeds expenditure, which at times may require making more income, or cutting down expenditure, or both.

In management terms, budgets are normally on a year-to-year basis. Ideally, a budget is a forecast looking several years ahead, say, five years, broken up into moving annual budgets and then months, or other convenient periods, for purposes of control. Some far-seeing companies already follow this practice. All aspects of the business are covered by budgets, for example cash-flow budgets and sales budgets, with the long-range financial picture kept firmly in perspective. A master budget coordinates the departmental budgets and places the whole operation on a practical basis for sound future development.

As always, any attempt to look forward must be tempered with flexibility, in order to meet effectively any sudden emergency or unexpected change. Although all probabilities, even possibilities, must be given their full weighting in budgeting, it is always possible for events to prove materially different from the plans that have been laid down.

Preparing the Budgets

The focal point of the whole exercise could be the sales budget based on market expectations, with budgets for productive capacity, financial resources, and other areas over the short and long terms to be kept in step. Alternatively, it could be the achievement of certain profit figures, and/or growth of assets, for each of the years ahead, with budgets for sales, production, finance, and so on, juggled realistically to attain these objectives as quantified period by period. The approach then becomes a matter of policy decision and the laying down of basic budgeting requirements. Almost any departmental budget could be made the focal point, given limiting factors such as the availability of finance, labor, etc. likely to persist over the budgeting period in question. The final answer may well depend on the type of business and its location.

Whether by this name, or as part of other responsibilities, there should be a "budget controller" to initiate the preparation of budgets, make sure that the objectives and background are fully understood, to progress-chase the completion of the budgets, and finally weld them into a master budget for board approval.

Taking a planned income and expenditure approach, Figure 18 shows how overall budgeting covers every aspect of the business for an agreed period ahead. This budgeting is based on the objectives and main policies laid down by the board and communicated, through the chief executive, to all concerned.

The budget figures for income and expenditure will be given in detail month by month, for the first financial year, on a moving schedule basis, thereafter being roughed in with a broader brush. By and large, functional budgets are based on each departmental manager's assessment of the situation, as affecting his side of the business. He will have consulted and obtained in advance all possible background information to facilitate a realistic forward projection in accordance with declared policy. Continuous cooperation between all concerned is, of course, essential.

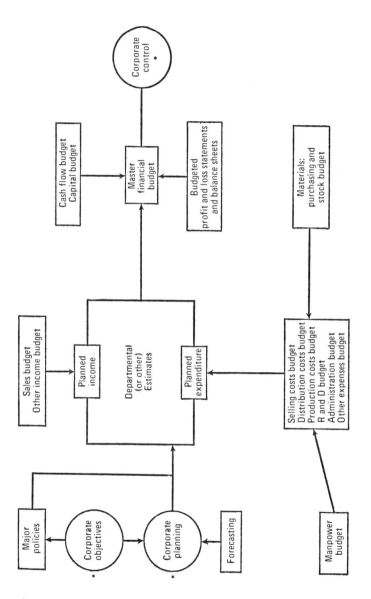

FIGURE 18. Simplified budgeting

Budgets in Use

Having been prepared in accordance with strategic require-ments, it becomes essential that budget figures should be im-plemented by actual performance. It is no use having a wealth of projected detail, unless that detail can in fact be used for purposes of control, for the budgets are the very essence of control. This means, in practice, the usual steps of comparing actual results with budget figures, noting any deviation, analyzing such variances, and making reports for managerial action at whatever level appears to be appro-priate.

In general, positive action would be the right course to adopt, but on occasion there may be an apparent need for a fresh look at the budgets themselves. In this context, it may be stated that budgets can imply constraint, keeping down to certain figures month by month, or targets, having to make special efforts to achieve above-average re-sults.

In order to ensure satisfactory budgetary control, it is essential that top management should take a keen interest in the technique, with special reference to regular boardroom review and policy deci-sion. The system itself should not be allowed to become overcompli-cated. There is a need here to keep essentials in focus, to have proper standards against which performance can be checked, and a firm appreciation of the value, and limitations, of the system by all who are required to use it. As a tool of top management, it should not become too mechanical, but leave sufficient room for informed managerial judgment.

The main checks are the monthly comparisons of actual with budget; but annually the budgeted profit and loss statements and balance sheets, for the years under review, would be reconciled with the statutory accounts.

When dealing with decentralized divisions, or other autonomous groups, the same system of budgets and monitoring performance against monthly standards is applicable. Managers of those divisions should be encouraged to make their own suggestions for divisional figures, in keeping with central policy and allocation of resources, and would have to explain discrepancies between actuals and budgets in the usual way. In extreme cases there could be a case for on-the-spot checks and consultation, as the budgets themselves may need to be amended in the light of hard practical experience. The important factor, as seen in an earlier context, is that divisional budgets, and any central costs unloaded on to divisions, should be accepted as a proper basis for a system of budgetary control operating from the central office. Usually, daily accounting figures would be submitted by each division, giving an opportunity centrally for a check to be kept on capital expenditure, cash flow, stock, accounts receivable, and other topics, as applicable to a given business. In addition, the monthly performance figures from each division would be checked against the divisional budgets.

It will have been noted that there is a close connection between budgetary control and management by objectives, the latter being in some respects an extension of budgetary control, not an entirely new technique. With this in mind, it may be worthwhile to refer back to Chapter Seven.

Adjustment to Change

Throughout budgetary control, the policy emphasis may well be on the profitability of the operations as a whole. This would in turn depend on achieving a growing share of the market, good R. and D., effective production, the right public image, positive leadership, and sound industrial relations. The advantage of budgetary control, as seen earlier, is the accent it places on the way ahead, leading naturally to a special interest in new products/services and markets, increased productivity, and improved techniques.

By such continuous concern for the future, coupled with the flexibility already emphasized, any company should be well set up for adjustment to change. Where an industry or firm is subjected to continuous change there is an increased need for flexibility; a good case exists for budgetary control in these circumstances being handled by a computer. Many of the background variables, given a management information system, could already be in its data bank.

Summary

1. Relationships between Policy Areas
    a. There is a natural interdependence between the areas of marketing, production, finance, and personnel.

b. These policy areas must be integrated, balanced, and coordinated.
c. Corporate control covers the whole, performance being measured against objectives and plans.
d. This implies viewing the organization from the top.
2. *Programs and Projects*
   a. Short-term programs suggest interfunctional project teams.
   b. Critical path analysis should be seen as a systematic way of programming economically in sequence.
   c. Long-range projects should be subject to intermediate control standards.
3. *Controlling the Operations*
   a. Organized control suggests systematic follow-through.
   b. Marketing control may start with a simple Z chart.
   c. Production control includes the use of standard costs.
   d. Financial control embraces sensitivity analysis and break-even.
   e. A functional approach is completed by manpower planning and control.
   f. Overall aspects of control can be internal or external.
4. *Budgetary Control*
   a. Budgets should be prepared departmentally to cover all aspects of business.
   b. All managers thereby have to think ahead realistically.
   c. Although budgets are normally on an annual basis, they should preferably cover the next five years.
   d. Monthly comparisons should be made between actual results and budget figures.
   e. Variances need to be analyzed, corrective action taken, or budgets adjusted in response to change.

Suggested Further Reading

BATTERSBY, A. *Network Analysis.* New York: Wiley, 1970.

BEER, S. *The Brain of the Firm: A Development in Management Cybernetics.* New York: McGraw-Hill, 1972.

DIXON, A.C. *Network Analysis.* Columbus: Merrill, 1973.

EDEY, H.C. *Business Budgets and Accounts.* 3d ed. Atlantic Highlands, N.J.: Humanities Press, 1966.

HECKERT, J.B., AND J.D. WILSON. *Business Budgeting and Control.* 3d ed. New York: Ronald Press, 1967.

LOCKYER, K.G. *Introduction to Critical Path Analysis.* New York: Beekman, 1969.

MALI, P. *Managing by Objectives: A Systems Approach.* New York: Wiley, 1972.

VAN VALKENBURG, M.E. *Network Analysis.* 3d ed. Englewood Cliffs, N.J.: Prentice-Hall, 1974.

WEBBER, R.A. *Time and Management.* New York: Van Nostrand Reinhold, 1972.

WILSON, R.M.S. *Cost Control Handbook.* New York: Wiley, 1975.

FOURTEEN

Management Development

It is easy to concentrate attention on the many advanced management techniques today, and the exciting sophisticated aids available in the shape of electronic and other forms of "hardware." But, in the last analysis, it is usually the quality of management itself that determines the knife-edge balance between corporate success and failure.

In Chapter Eleven it was demonstrated how the balance sheet of a company displays the assets and liabilities realistically at a point of time; yet the most important asset, executive strength, or the most insidious liability, managerial deficiency, remains outside such quantification. Nevertheless, it is absolutely vital that every organization should evaluate its executive strength and assess its potential.

EVALUATING EXECUTIVE STRENGTH

As a first step, in this type of situation, it is always useful to ask the right kind of questions; the more difficult problem is to find the right kind of answers.

Basic Questions to be Asked

These could be along the following practical lines:

(a) What form of organization do we envisage will be required in, say, five, ten, or even fifteen years time to deal with expected corporate growth, taking into account all probable environmental factors?

(b) What actual or potential executive strength do we have at the moment, which will be suitable in all relevant respects to match the needs of the organization by the time they are likely to be required?

(c) What are the deficiencies at each stage that become apparent when comparing *(b)* with *(a)*? What are our management weaknesses at the moment?

(d) What can be done to overcome these deficiencies and/or weaknesses by recruitment, training, additional experience, promotion, and the like?

(e) Can we keep existing strength (and potential strength) properly motivated, and maintained at top quality, until required for ultimate promotion to the level planned?

(f) In particular, have we provided for effective management succession at the top and middle levels?

Emphasizing the last point, there is always a basic duty to provide for succession, and for supporting expertise, with a realistic and flexible approach geared to the needs of the future. Whether candidates for succession are found internally, by normal recruitment, or through an outside specialist consultant is a matter of policy and judgment.

Taking Stock of Executive Ability

In a relatively small organization it is likely that the main strengths and weaknesses of all key executives will be well known to those in command. This may be largely an informal, intuitive process, based on personal contact, with little attempt, if any, to obtain a more detached viewpoint. Yet even in a small firm there ought to be at least a formal system of job-descriptions/personal-assessments, if only to maximize the proper matching of pegs and holes. This should certainly be the practice in a large company.

A convenient way of starting this operation is to take an ordinary organization chart (or prepare one) and make relevant notes in each rectangle containing the name of an office holder. The information to be noted can usefully include the date of appointment to the post now held, age, whether earmarked for further promotion, and normal date of retirement. Against each rectangle can then be listed the names and present positions of any candidates thought suitable for immediate or future promotion to that post. Certain likely people may be included on more than one short-list, but it must be remembered that they can only be promoted to one higher job at a time. Usually, there is a shortage of exceptional candidates. Other names can later be added to the lists (or original names deleted) in the light of recruitment, assessment reports, special achievements, ability demonstrated on training courses, etc.

Presumably, such an annotated chart would be regarded as confidential, bearing in mind the danger of raising expectations which might not eventually be realized. Nevertheless, as mentioned elsewhere, it is always a healthy sign to see a number of keen young hopefuls in active competition for promotion. Any obvious blanks in such a chart, with regard to certain key jobs, suggests immediate recruiting action, possibly at graduate level. This could be coupled with the granting of enhanced opportunities and training for existing personnel who, though having the right potential, still lack basic know-how and wider work experience.

Charting Future Executive Needs

Dealing with the present organization structure, however, is not enough on its own. For it still remains necessary to match future managerial requirements to new, perhaps completely different, structures envisaged as a natural consequence of long-range planning. This means, in practical terms, making a forecast of all types of managers, and the relative number of each, likely to be needed at each stage of future development.

This requirement suggests preparing separate, but progressive, organization charts for each of these strategic points in the future. Given steady expansion, there could be, for example, a case for new charts to be prepared at growth stages five years and ten years or even fifteen years ahead. Once again, appropriate names can be pencilled in on each of these futuristic charts where there are top jobs to be newly created, or senior vacancies arising in existing jobs, with alternatives to allow for natural attrition. Even so, many gaps can be expected to remain after all available executive ability, including that recognized as being potentially likely to emerge, has been carefully considered at each appropriate stage. Some present jobs, too, may be structured out of existence at one or other of the later stages of growth.

The next practical step is to prepare a comprehensive list of all the promotables to key posts, with a view to organizing individual management development schemes. At the same time, a further list should be made out of all new and existing jobs where no candidates have been seen to emerge from among present personnel, so as to enable comprehensive recruiting plans to be laid. It will already be appreciated that management development is but a logical extension of ordinary manpower planning, taken to a more exalted plane.

The concept of "individual management development programs" simply means making suitable arrangements to provide the optimum mixture of experience and training for each candidate earmarked for promotion, so that he will be ready to fit into the plans at the appropriate stage. In practice, there may be more than one suitable ladder for executive promotion, so that this alternative must be kept in mind as well. Furthermore, should the first scheduled promotion be some way ahead, a special problem arises of keeping the management trainee or other candidate properly satisfied with his progress in the meantime. Similarly, there may be interim difficulties with personal relationships when, for example, several ambitious candidates are known (or implied) to be on a short-list, for a particularly important top job, at some indefinite date in the future.

The alternative to earmarking for specific promotion is to have a pool of promotables, from which all suitable future management vacancies are normally to be filled. This has the disadvantage of excluding external competitors, and discouraging those internally who are not yet considered as being sufficiently competent to join the pool. In this context it is important that everyone should have equal initial opportunities for promotion, based on impartial selection procedures, and that due account is taken of the possibility that a later developer may well qualify for late promotion. Nor must it be forgotten that there are many executives in the middle reaches, or even well up the hierarchy, who do not *really* seek further promotion, with all the additional stresses and strains they would thereby have to face.

PLANNING FOR SUCCESSION

It is always the duty of top management to provide for its own continuity through effective planning for succession. Yet, all too often, little or no thought is given to the executive needs of the future, with consequent failure to provide a management development program as outlined later in this chapter. Such a lack of planning can result in frustration among senior executives, and, in the face of any unexpected vacancy arising at or near the summit, emergency recruitment from outside.

Achieving Objective Selection

Basically, it is the responsibility of the board of directors to ensure proper management succession at every level down the line. In particular, the board should be actively concerned with the continuing office of president, or other chief executive, as appropriate.

Apart from the top job itself, the remaining problems of maintaining effective succession could be delegated to the chief executive officer, with "rubber-stamping" approval by the board, as necessary. It is important, however, that his judgments should be known to be objective. A weak chief executive, for example, feeling himself likely to be embarrassed by an ambitious second line, may well be tempted to try and surround himself with lesser men, if only to preserve his own security. A strong chief executive would, of course, desire to build up the best possible team now and potentially. It is with this positive approach that management today should be vitally concerned.

Recruiting for Management

Chapter Twelve deals with the general approach to recruitment policies, selection procedures, and practical aspects of promotion. It is only necessary at this stage to make a few comments on particular aspects relating to potential manpower destined for top management jobs.

Fundamentally, the aim of management development is to make sure that the men set aside as future executives are properly trained, and ready for action, by the time they are due to take their appointed place in the overall plan. If the right initial selections are made, individual management development plans effectively organized, and the individuals themselves highly motivated, then strategic promotion through to the top would seem to be sufficient to provide for normal succession. But business life is seldom normal, and even highly motivated loyal executives can be enticed away by attractive offers, or become impatient, or see the value of a change of employment. In the process they gain a broadening of experience and speed up their route to the top, injecting fresh blood into the other organization at the same time.

Having made all possible provision for future managerial needs, it may still be necessary, from time to time, to "head-hunt," use a specialist consultant, or insert attractive advertisements in the responsible press or appropriate trade publication. Such a situation may rise from loss of key personnel as indicated above, needing replacement input, or simply because of technological change or rapid growth outstripping even optimistic plans. This suggests a special need to recruit ready-made managers and senior personnel able to tackle new products, processes, and techniques, or even the problems of growth to large-scale enterprise, not anticipated in the original plan or even in the amended plans. Computer evolution is a case in point. Hence it must be emphasized that even where there are proper management inventory and replacement charts, designed to make the best use of existing potential, these must be regularly reviewed and kept in line with reality.

In selecting for top management, at chief executive level, whether from inside or by external talent spotting, it may be considered advisable to use sophisticated tests designed to demonstrate managerial ability and general group effectiveness. As shown in Chapter Twelve, tests of any kind are by no means infallible; it can be re-emphasized that, despite all mechanical selection procedures, a first-class candidate may still prove highly successful in one firm's environment but quite ineffective in another. Nevertheless, a comprehensive battery of tests in expert (external) hands can be a help in the process of screening a short-list of apparently suitable candidates for the top job.

The group approach extends to such organized procedures as so-called psychological week-end or "country house" conditions, where candidates take part in public-speaking sessions, group discussions, debates, and exercises and are closely studied by specialists from all points of view. This includes an assessment of their social ability to mix well, to take part in intelligent conversation, and to conduct themselves correctly at table.

A simpler version is an invitation to dine with the chairman at his home or have lunch at his club. Probably by this stage there would be only one or two candidates left in the running. In the case of a visit to the chairman's home, or similar occasion, it may well be decided to include the candidate's wife, to test whether she would seem to be acceptable as a company president's wife.

All such selection experiences could be considered inhibiting, but it must be remembered that a potential chief executive should already have a full quota of poise and maturity.

MANAGEMENT DEVELOPMENT

Having decided on the promotables in any organization, including the recruitment of college graduates as management trainees, the next step is to organize management development training for them, either individually or collectively, with systematic appraisal from time to time. In a large enough undertaking, a trained management development executive could take charge of the whole operation; otherwise, this duty would fall into the province of the training officer already responsible for all other aspects of corporate training.

Any comprehensive policy for management development programs must start from the top, making sure that those in the seats of power are able to accept the full implications. They must not, for example, feel themselves likely to be at a disadvantage because of the enhanced knowledge of those at a lower level selected to take part. Anyone in this position should try to keep abreast of advanced techniques by attending the special conferences, seminars, and courses organized by such bodies as the American Management Association or by colleges of business administration and large universities. Given such top management cooperation and encouragement from the outset, young promotables returning from courses, full of new ideas and enthusiasm, will not be repressed as tends to be the case in certain companies at the present time. Instead, they feel motivated to press on with renewed energy.

Tuition Reimbursement

Many of the large companies today are prepared to reimburse their lower- and middle-management personnel for tuition fees and other attendant expenses at nearby universities for postgraduate studies or advanced management programs. Of course, it is to be hoped that even the regular employees at lower levels will receive encouragement and financial assistance to enable them to gain professional or technical qualifications likely to assist them in their jobs. Such qualifications may be obtained through part-time day release, by attendance at evening classes, by correspondence, or by private study at home. Furthermore, it should be a company's responsibility to make sure that all further education of this kind is properly recognized in any plans for individual executive development. For self-help demonstrates keenness and a desire to improve and should be taken into account when looking for promotables.

At this juncture, it should be noted that a number of the nation's giant corporations, such as IBM and General Motors, have established separate facilities, removed from their plants and home offices, for the advanced training of their executive personnel.

General Management Development

Progressive managements are aware of the fact that there is only a limited value in having, at top-management level, a team of specialists, each of whom is immersed in his own specialty and thereby tending to be biased in his thinking. They know that the ideal situation would be to have a number of highly qualified men, each with wide experience and a balanced viewpoint looking at the firm as a whole. At some stage, therefore, with regard to candidates for high office, there must be a transition from being a specialist to becoming competent as a generalist. It is here that a general program in Management Studies, such as that illustrated in Figure 19, has particular value.

Such comprehensive advanced management programs, designed to train professional managers for today's complex and competitive society, are the direct descendants of earlier executive development efforts organized decades ago by such august centers of learning as the Massachusetts Institute of Technology and the Har-

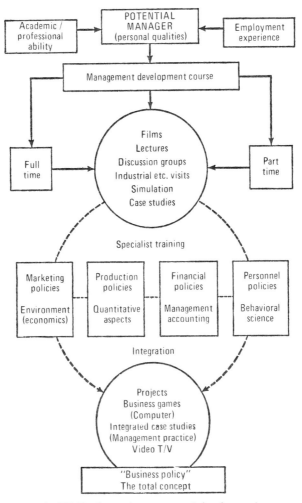

FIGURE 19. General management development

vard Business School. Generally, the students are men and women with good educational backgrounds and some years of practical business experience. They are first equipped with a broad-range overview of business fundamentals, among which are elements of management principles; management processes, tools, and techniques; economics and finance; industrial psychology and sociology; elementary statistics; human resource administration; and production and marketing managements.

Reference to Figure 19 shows how this stage of learning can be achieved by films, lectures, discussion groups, visits to plants, some simulation exercises, and functional case studies. These introductory sessions can be grouped as specialized training under four main headings—marketing, production, financial, and personnel policies—corresponding broadly to the subject matter of Chapters Nine to Twelve, respectively.

After the basics have been thoroughly grasped, this personal involvement and decision-making practice is assisted by integrated case studies, business games played by teams with or without the aid of a computer, and the carrying out of group and individual assignments or projects. This planned integration leads naturally to a study of "Business Policy" based on the total concept of the firm as a whole.

MANAGEMENT TRAINING TECHNIQUES

Whatever method of management training is adopted, externally, or in-company or a strategic combination of both, there are certain established management teaching techniques worth consideration. This is an evolving subject, however, and many new techniques are being tried out and developed; some of these will be indicated later. In the meantime, it is appropriate to trace the trend of management training philosophy. For gone are the teaching days of playing God, the average student today looking upon his mentor more as a personal friend.

The Importance of Student Participation

The lecture-and-listen technique still has its uses for imparting basic information, preferably in small doses, but the main ingredient adding zest to management education is active and enthusiastic student participation. The serried ranks of a captive audience have largely given away to the cut and thrust of group discussion where even the lecturer has to justify his performance with logic, knowledge, and experience. Nor can the students be passive for long, being required at any moment to join in discussion, making pertinent comment, answer a question, or play some other part requiring their active cooperation.

This is not intended, however, to decry the kind of stimulating talk given by guest speakers, with impressive managerial background. But even here, it is often found that the real benefit comes from question time; for keen students like to make the most of any opportunity to seek opinions from successful practitioners. With this in mind, a guest speaker will usually keep his talk to a minimum, leaving ample time available for interrogation at the end.

A professional management teacher knows that even when formal lectures are necessary, they should be properly punctuated with pauses for questions, comment, and discussion, making sure that every step in the argument is crystal clear. The disinterested reading of the same lectures year after year is fortunately a relic of the past, at least so far as management teaching is concerned. Instead, the accent today is on a pooling of practical experience, management students being well able to illustrate the theoretical points at issue from their specialized backgrounds often covering a wide range of public service, industry, finance, commerce, or other area of business activity. In fact, it is no exaggeration to state that, on occasion, the management teacher can learn almost as much from his students as he hopes they are learning from him. For management students are usually postgraduate, post-experience material of high caliber, thereby well qualified to contribute to collective thought.

This positive keynote presupposes the careful selection of good management material for internal or external courses. But, unfortunately, the selection process leaves a great deal to be desired; and not all managements are convinced of the value of such courses, particularly when they aim to take away the best staff from the daily routine. As a result, it may happen that the wrong people, perhaps those most easily spared, are sent on courses, and that, for the same reason, the courses themselves must be kept as short as possible. Furthermore, in order to cover an advertised syllabus, which may need to look impressive to attract participants, some trainers may attempt to do too much in the time available, particularly when faced with a mixed bag of willing and unwilling students. Consequently, there can be personal problems with respect to comprehension: the best course members being anxious for greater depth of knowledge, while the worst seem unable to follow most of what is being said and done.

Given a long management course, such problems can be largely overcome; but in a short course lasting only a week or two, solution is hardly possible, for participants need several days to adjust themselves to the strange environment, new personalities, and the unfamiliar subject matter of the course.

The efficient training officer, with management development in mind, will therefore be wise to make careful selection of employees possessing the right potential, ensure that they are sent on the right courses, and are properly briefed and motivated before they go. They may be asked, for instance, to do some guided reading in advance. They should also be required to report back afterwards as to whether the course was considered to be sufficiently worthwhile. In making such selection, a training officer must have proper authority, or at least be able to secure the cooperation of his colleagues, to ensure that those selected for courses are enabled to attend.

There is a place for short courses, particularly when getting to grips with specific management techniques, provided always that the members have been carefully selected with the course objectives well in mind. In such event, individual understanding of subject matter is assured and full participation can be seen to follow. Nevertheless, it still remains true that a comprehensive management course, for those destined for promotion to the top, should be long enough to cover the essential syllabus effectively. The danger of a "little learning" must, at all costs, be avoided.

Student participation is often achieved by the controversial use of task teams, small groups each having a common task to perform. Such groups may be organized by the tutor, with appointed chairmen, spokesmen, and secretaries, or left to evolve their own structures as applicable. In practice, teams can be highly effective, under good student chairmanship, but there can also be awkward personalities to contend with, clashes for power, and some crowding out of the remainder. In addition, there may be the usual "eager beavers," who delight in doing all the work, and lazier members more or less content to sit back and watch. However, even experience of this kind may help towards a more realistic appreciation of group behavior, such as will be encountered at some time or another with committees or boards of directors.

Another controversial topic, of more specialized interest, is the so-called T group, also referred to as "sensitivity training." The idea behind this unstructured psychological technique is to enable groups of people, say up to a dozen, to be with each other continuously over a period of time free to discuss almost any kind of topic. In the process they adjust to each other, are encouraged to be frank, can become emotional, and are helped to see themselves as others see them. The trained instructor in charge takes an indirect part in the proceedings, acting more or less as a catalyst, and makes sure that no psychological harm is being done. Those who have participated in such a T group find that the experience can be personally intense and revealing. It is hoped that this new understanding of one's self with other people will form a sound basis for future leadership success.

The Pros and Cons of Case Studies

Originating from the Harvard Business School, case studies today are an integral part of most courses concerned with management, whether related to disciplinary aspects or full-scale integration. Each case normally consists of comprehensive information about a given company with special reference to its history, background, progress, policies, and personalities, often supported by detailed appendices. In view of their importance to management training it is appropriate to list the pros and cons of case studies.

1. Main Advantages:

(a) They achieve participation, with opportunities for group discussion, including small group practice in chairmanship, speaking and the like.

(b) Representing real-life situations in the main, they provide management practice in problem-identification, problem-analysis and decision-making under conditions of imperfect knowledge.

(c) They encourage flexible thinking, demonstrating, for example, that more than one solution is tenable and that apparently easy problems may turn out to be more complex when given closer scrutiny.

2. *Main Disadvantages:*
   (a) They can be misused or overemployed, particularly as students may have difficulty in finding enough time to master the many pages of text and appendices.

   (b) It is often stressed that there can be no right answers and students accordingly tend to feel frustrated. The instructor can, however, recount what actually happened to the company (after the end of the case study) or suggest tenable solutions based on sound management practice.

The Use of Business Games

The popularity of business games, as a competitive feature, is attested to by their widespread use within government, the military services, universities, and industrial organizations such as American Telephone and Telegraph, International Business Machines, and Westinghouse.

Basically, of course, a management or business game is made up of small groups of students, each group representing a "company" operating competitively in a given business environment. The companies are well briefed in advance, and start their activities by outlining corporate objectives, devising a management structure, making strategic plans and formulating policies. Each game usually covers a number of simulated years, divided up into quarterly periods, each period requiring the submission of a range of operating decisions. The quantitative results of those decisions are fed back by the directing staff, who operate the market model, preferably with the aid of a computer, and generally keep up the pressure.

While the market model automatically provides for periods of prosperity and recession, the directing staff can introduce any complications they choose. These can include such items as base rate changes, budget statements, news flashes, industrial unrest, strikes, competition from overseas and so on as considered appropriate at any given time. Wrong company decisions, if not dealt with promptly, can easily lead to eventual liquidation. Mergers and acquisitions, initiated by successful companies, are by no means unknown.

The competitive success of individual companies is judged by balance sheet results, and as such materially assists in building up the essential atmosphere of involvement. But the main teaching objective of any game is to demonstrate the consequences of group decision-making, good and bad, in response to changing environmental situations. It is for this reason that sufficient time should be devoted to a comprehensive inquiry, in plenary session, with critical feedback from the directing staff.

In-company Projects

Group and individual projects are particularly suitable for training purposes as they provide management students with actual business problems to solve, often associated with their sponsoring firms. Such projects have a three-fold value: *(a)* to the students, by enabling them to gain practical industrial experience; *(b)* to the firms, by offering an impartial consultancy service; and *(c)* to the management teachers who, as project leaders, are thereby provided with valuable liaison opportunities when meeting practicing managers, at all levels, to discuss those projects. The setting up of project managers and project teams in the normal course of business, in itself a valuable training facility, is discussed in Chapter Thirteen when dealing with short-term programs.

Summary

1. *Evaluating Executive Strength*
   a. Both actual and potential executive strength should be assessed.
   b. It is desirable to chart the growth of an organization, forecasting future key positions.
   c. Potential strength can then be matched to future positions.
   d. Lists of promotables and plans for management development should be prepared in advance.
2. *Planning for Succession*
   a. The board has a duty to provide for management continuity.
   b. This involves objective selection in advance.
   c. It may mean planned recruiting for management.
   d. Special selection methods are used for top appointments.

3. *Management Development Programs*
  a. Policy for management development programs must start from the top.
  b. Professional and technical qualifications should be encouraged.
  c. The transition from specialist to generalist is helped by a program in Management Studies.
4. *Management Training Techniques*
  a. The modern approach encourages student participation.
  b. Employees to be sent to courses should be selected carefully.
  c. Participation includes small group efforts and the more controversial "T group."
  d. Case studies, business games, and in-company projects are regarded as integral parts of most management courses.

Suggested Further Reading

DINSMORE, F.W. *Developing Tomorrow's Managers Today.* New York: American Management Association, 1975.

FLORY, C.D., ed. *Managers for Tomorrow.* New York: New American Library, 1971.

HANSON, A.O. *Executive and Management Development for Business and Government: A Guide to Information Sources.* Detroit: Gale Research, 1976.

McLARNEY, W.J., AND W.M. BERLINER. *Management Training: Cases and Principles.* 5th ed. Homewood, Ill.: Irwin, 1970.

TORRINGTON, D.P., AND D.F. SUTTON. *Handbook of Management Development.* New York: Beekman, 1973.

TRACEY, W.R. *Managing Training and Development Systems.* New York: American Management Association, 1974.

VANCE, C.C. *Manager Today, Executive Tomorrow.* New York: McGraw-Hill, 1974.

FIFTEEN

Management
and the Small Firm

There is a tendency today, in any general discussion on management, to forget about the importance of small firms and their special needs. Fortunately, some excellent books have been devoted to this subject and suggestions are included in the reading list at the end of the chapter. Nevertheless, all that has been written throughout this book has relevance for the owner/manager of a small business, if only in minimal quantities, and may help him steer his firm through its struggles for survival to become a large organization in the course of time. In any small firm, it is expedient to start thinking about management, on conventional lines, at an early stage in its development. Yet the very word "conventional" is anathema to the entrepreneurial owner/manager enthusiastically charting a course with inspiration and a great deal of hard work.

In deciding how small is small, it is usual and convenient to make reference either to the company's annual sales or to the number of employees on the payroll. According to the Small Business Administration (SBA), the following firms are designated "small" and therefore may qualify for financial assistance:

(a) A *retail* concern with annual sales of less than $1 million.

(b) A *wholesale* enterprise with annual sales under $5 million (but up to $15 million, depending upon the industry).

(c) A *manufacturing* business with 250 employees or less (or as high as 500 to 1,000 employees, again depending upon the industry).

In short, size is relative and may well depend on the structure of the particular industry under discussion. With regard to American manufacturing firms, the Census of Manufacturers reports that, of the one third of a million such establishments in full-year operation in 1972, some 96 per cent had less than 250 employees—and less than 1 per cent were in the "over 1,000 employees" category. Indeed, more than 65 per cent employed less than 20 individuals.

In the retail trades, that same year, fewer than 5 per cent of the nation's 1.7 million stores enjoyed annual sales of more than $1 million. Much the same situation prevailed with regard to the wholesale trades. In summary, then, it would appear that the vast majority of American companies are indeed small—at least by SBA standards.

Need for Professional Management

Whereas a large company may have a policy of promoting its managers from being specialists to ultimate status as generalists, the owner/manager of a small firm normally starts at the top, keeping the overall viewpoint firmly in mind from the beginning. He may, of course, have acquired some specialized experience in previous capacities elsewhere. This overall viewpoint requires a comprehensive knowledge, or access to such knowledge, covering almost any business aspect likely to emerge in day-to-day practice. It implies that the owner/manager, seeking such a general background of management philosophy and techniques, will need to keep his management reading as wide as possible.

During the early years, all the functions of management may be vested in the entrepreneur, assisted initially perhaps only by his family. But although such an owner/manager may not need to apply *all* the techniques of management, for the time being, particularly in their more complex forms, it will certainly help him to know of their existence. He can at least benefit from the basic thinking, and better approach to problems, underlying those techniques. In the process he may well produce more effective results than he could achieve by the alternative gamble of expensive trial and error. For, as indicated in Chapter One, this is the era of the managerial revolution and the emergence of the professional manager. There are, of course, still amateurs hopefully setting up in business, but the casualty rate of the small firm is undoubtedly high.

THE PROBLEM OF SURVIVAL

Recent figures of bankruptcy and liquidation demonstrate a rising trend in the number of irrecoverable debts and business failures over a wide range of industries and for a variety of reasons. It may be noted in passing that bankruptcy relates to people and liquidation to corporations, but the end result is much the same.

It is essential to keep a sense of proportion, as some 300,000 new businesses are started up each year. Nearly 13 million firms of all kinds were in existence in 1972, some 75 per cent of them sole proprietorships, another 14 per cent corporations, and the balance (11 per cent) partnerships. Bankruptcies and liquidations, of course, were merely a fraction of the total. Nevertheless, they were still considerable in number, the failure rate being 38 per 1,000 firms in existence. It should be noted that although most new firms manage to get through their first year of operation, more than one half fail before their fifth year has ended.

Reasons for Business Failures

It is usually worthwhile to analyze the causes of failure, in any context, and learn the lessons that emerge. Naturally, it is far less painful to learn from other people's failures than one's own, which may thereby be avoided. The following main reasons, as to why companies and other firms fail, are worth studying.

Causes Stated for Bankruptcy/Liquidation:

(a) Insufficient capital to establish, maintain, and expand the business. This suggests that wrong calculations were made right from the start, the position being worsened by credit-squeeze restrictions on working capital.

(b) Too much reliance on the use of trade credit, coupled with insufficient capital. Whereas large companies can threaten to withdraw their business if debts are not settled to time, they tend to be regrettably slow in paying their own bills. Small firms dealing with large companies may suffer accordingly.

(c) Losses through irrecoverable debts. Where bad debts become proportionately high, they can bring financial disaster to a small firm not possessing the resources of larger firms to withstand such a set-back. Even good customers can be lax in making their payments, thus resulting in a build-up of past-due receivables.

(d) Inadequacy of management information, including defective accounting and costing systems, upon which decisions have been based, with unfortunate results.

But, of course, the main cause for failure is, often enough, mismanagement, although this is seldom admitted by those held responsible. Receivers, however, tend to be less sensitive about the truth.

Availability of Advice

There have always been sources of information for small firms but, on the basis of self-help, it is contended that owners/managers of many small companies could perhaps have helped themselves more than by just passively waiting, as some have done, for outside help to come and knock on their office door. They would argue, of course, that there was insufficient time left over from the day's work to be able to take advantage of such facilities. But it is often the busiest man who manages to find that critical but marginally extra time which may change a small firm's struggle for existence into steady growth. Possibly, too, part of the problem has not been knowing where to seek expert advice.

Yet, as far back as the mid-1950s, many offices of the Small Business Administration (SBA) were in operation around the country, providing information and assistance in exploiting opportunities or solving business problems. Institutes in small business operation were also established by major universities, offering services intended primarily to enable small and medium-sized firms to help themselves.

In similar vein is the help generally forthcoming from management teachers and advanced students anxious to carry out research projects in industry, preferably related to current problems exercising the minds of managers in small firms as well as in large firms.

Other advice facilities available to help the small firm sector include the Active Corps of Executives (ACE) and the Service Corps of Retired Executives (SCORE), both sponsored by the SBA, state departments of commerce, local Chambers of Commerce, and the appropriate trade associations for the industries concerned.

Part of the difficulty of small companies has been shown to be that they are usually started by entrepreneurs, often with technical ability, but lacking in overall management experience. Given the vast majority of firms, with limited resources and not more than, say, a dozen or so personnel, it is unlikely that such general management expertise could be found, or afforded, internally. Without offering any further examples, it seems clear that, although additional consultancy help is needed for the future, small firms have not been entirely neglected in the past. The main obstacle would appear to be prejudice toward such advisory services as evidenced by the owners/managers themselves.

The Small Business Administration

Recognizing the need to "aid, counsel, assist, and protect . . . the interests of small business concerns in order to preserve free competitive enterprise," the federal government in 1953 created the Small Business Administration (SBA) as a permanent government agency. Some years later, in a further attempt to stimulate the economy, the Small Business Investment Act (1958) was passed. This legislation authorized the licensing and regulation of Small Business Investment Companies (SBICs) to provide for the financial needs of small firms. Today, approximately 90 offices of the SBA service the nation. The SBA is an exceedingly active agency that makes available a wide-ranging variety of aids to small business including management, technical, procurement, and, of course, financial assistance. A number of these services are listed below:

1. Management Assistance:
    (a) The cosponsorship of business management courses at hundreds of public and private colleges and schools of business.

(b) Conferences, institutes, seminars, and workshops for both prospective and actual entrepreneurs on a variety of topic areas, including financial aspects, business organization, insurance requirements, and marketing.

(c) Clinics for small business owners in special problem areas, generally conducted by business or industry type.

(d) On-location management consulting, in coordination with such organizations as the Active Corps of Executives (ACE) and the Service Corps of Retired Executives (SCORE).

(e) Hundreds of printed aids, booklets, and so on available on every facet of business management.

(f) Information and counsel in the export field, in cooperation with the U.S. Department of Commerce.

2. *Technical and Procurement Assistance:*

(a) Specialized and technical help to small manufacturing plants with all types of production problems, including methods and techniques, product development, etc.

(b) Counsel on sources of and approaches to prime contracting and subcontracting for the federal government.

(c) Instruction in the preparation of contract bids—and the facilitation of same to various government agencies.

(d) Issuance of "Certificates of Competency," after due investigation, attesting to the small manufacturer's ability to fulfill satisfactorily government contracts.

3. *Financial Assistance:*

(a) Advice regarding short-term loans for business construction, purchasing machinery and equipment, expansion, and other purposes.

(b) Direct loans to small businesses, or, more often still, participation with banks in such loans by guaranteeing up to 90 per cent of the principal to the particular bank involved.

(c) Assistance in minority enterprise programs designed to enable members of minority groups to enter their own businesses, purchase franchises, or buy over established businesses.

(d) Provision for loans to small business investment companies (SBICs) as well as local or state development organizations to facilitate management and financial assistance to the disadvantaged.

(e) Loans to nonprofit organizations run for or by handicapped individuals, or directly to the handicapped persons themselves.

(f) Disaster loans to firms suffering physical damage (from earthquakes, floods, or other natural catastrophes) or serious economic losses.

(g) Special loans to firms wishing to undergo costly alterations in order to comply with the requisites of the Occupational Safety and Health Act (1970).

(h) Lease guarantees; arrangements for surety bonds; and other assistance.

Seeking Financial Assistance

Naturally, the commercial banks offer whatever advice is required in the control of financial matters, which is especially valuable where the staff of a small firm has no expertise of its own. The banks are undoubtedly the main source of external finance for small companies, often matching the entrepreneur's own funds with comparable bank funds, with or without security. The real bank security, of course, rests on its assessment of the expertise of the entrepreneur and the potential profits likely to be made by the business concerned. There is an inevitable risk but, in normal circumstances, the banks claim that they are prepared to respond to reasonable requests with flexible lending policies.

As stated in Chapter Eleven, bank finance is intended for current needs; with a small firm making satisfactory growth, however, these funds often become regarded more as permanent finance. Hence, at a time of credit squeeze, the small firm tends to find itself in a difficult financial situation. Even when funds are available, high interest rates, as at present, make it especially difficult for a small firm to commit itself to a loan with fixed terms extending some way ahead.

The assistance of factors, mentioned elsewhere as a means of finance and for dealing with customers' credit accounts, is usually denied to very small firms which, until they have reached a given sales volume, are considered to be uneconomic propositions.

For the young company that shows a great deal of promise, perhaps because of new products with substantial potential or because of brand new approaches, there is a growing number of "venture capitalists" willing to risk investment capital in exchange for an equity position in the enterprise. These range from individuals and small, informal groups to larger syndicates and venture-capital corporations, both private and publicly held. In the latter category are many of the Small Business Investment Companies (SBICs), as well as the more recent Minority Enterprise Small Business Investment Companies (MESBICs).

The traditional way for small firms to help themselves financially is by restricting money taken out of the firm, e.g., for personal use, and by ploughing back undistributed profits. Taxation is, of course, a major problem for small companies, especially a "closed corporation" (where the stock ownership is tightly controlled by directors, family, etc.). Experience suggests seeking expert tax advice, for some small firms may be paying more tax than they need.

Administrative Difficulties

It is easy for managers to become unduly concerned with daily problems in the factory, possibly forgetting to give at least equal attention to sources of supply and, as emphasized elsewhere, the market. They should be constantly concerned with acquiring sufficient capital, or credit, on the right terms to match planned development. This overall approach implies keeping abreast of the times, understanding the changing political and economic scene, and becoming aware of new management techniques.

They should, in particular, appreciate the importance of building up all-round efficiency in its widest sense. In the process they will at least learn the significance of business ratios and other self-help tests that can focus attention on weak spots in the firm's finances. For example, if current liabilities are found to be substantially greater than current assets, then something must be done about it, and quickly. However, the owner/manager, or director, of a small firm may already have translated the significance of previous chapters into his own particular situation. The basic principles remain the same; only the scale of relevance and application differs.

Probably, in a small private corporation, the main area of weakness lies in the boardroom itself where the leading shareholder/family directors, perhaps supported by a lawyer, banker, or accountant, meet at too infrequent intervals. In the meantime, the general management burden falls on the one or two executive directors coping as best they can with the daily problems. Whereas the president of a large firm merely has to use his intercom to obtain any specialist advice he requires, the small firm's chief executive has to depend, more or less, on himself. Furthermore, the onerous constraints of day-to-day work may well prevent him from making any positive attempt at short-term development, let alone long-range planning. It is here, however, that it may pay to seek some of the consultant advice that has been demonstrated as being available. Time must be made available by all possible means for planning at top level; for planning is essentially relevant to the small firm because it is so vulnerably exposed to the sudden effects of environmental change.

MAKING POSITIVE PROGRESS

A practical case exists for small firms to band together to help each other in every way possible and preserve a united front against constraints, political and otherwise, imposed from outside.

This introduces a more positive note, which suggests that there can be too much hiding behind excuses and difficulties. It has been stated, however, that the small businessman is quite prepared to face up to reality. He does not necessarily seek exemption from the burdens placed on industry generally, but he does require to receive a fair deal for his own kind of firm. He may also need help, if not time, to meet his obligations effectively.

Advantages of Being Small

Statistically, it must be easier to grow fast from a relatively low base-line than from one much higher up the scale. For whereas a very small firm can double its size almost overnight, a giant can only progress proportionately at a limited pace, however impressive that progress may be when expressed in absolute terms. This has particular relevance to such competitive aspects as market share, for a 1 per cent share could be doubled, but certainly not a 60 per cent share.

Research shows that small firms can often achieve remarkable success in narrow, often unexplored, market sectors and make considerable profits in the process while the going continues to be good. Once they begin to show too high a total market share, however, the main competitors will tend to sit up, take notice, and do something about it. But by then the successful small firms may have found other unexpected sectors to explore. It should be kept in mind that very few innovations actually succeed out of the many ideas submitted; the trick is to find and exploit the few.

The essence of the small firm's advantage lies in its flexibility; it is in line with this opportunity factor that so many valuable innovations have been produced covering such a wide range of activities. This is particularly well illustrated by the world of fashion, although it applies equally to any specialized product or service requiring flexibility, often resulting in substantial profits through well-timed anticipation of fleeting market demand. Part of the success lies in the speed of decision-making; but the owner/manager making such decisions must nearly always be right!

Linked up with this aspect is the importance of finding the right markets before actually making the goods, an essential precaution for a small firm likely to be ruined if too much working capital should become absorbed by unsaleable stock. From a practical standpoint, too, it is advisable to get as many orders in writing as possible, as verbal intentions may well prove to be misleading. Nor should there be more than temporary dependence on any single product; the alternative is to diversify.

On the export side, there are thousands of enterprising small firms engaged in overseas trade. Making the grade in exports is not easy, but there is assistance from the government, as explained in Chapter Nine, to help small exporters. This will encourage those firms wishing to set up overseas offices in particularly promising markets.

With regard to production control, there are the usual difficulties of short runs, but economies of scale can sometimes be achieved even with a restricted output, in terms of small-firm resources. The more difficult problem is with respect to "job lots" to deal with special orders. The essence, overall, lies in operating at peak efficiency, achieving effective stock control, including work in progress, and meeting delivery dates. This may be particularly important when, for example, a small manufacturing firm is specializing in subcontract work making parts for assembly by a large manufacturer located elsewhere.

This implies proper clerical support and the keeping of adequate records, or, ideally, the use of computer facilities. For if the small firm's accent is to be on its service to customers, then that service must be forthcoming. Problems may arise from sudden emergency orders, but, given proper planning, these should be minimized. In any event, there must be the usual balance between marketing and production, both needing to be flexible.

Financial aspects have been dealt with elsewhere, but some indications may be given here concerning small-firm attitudes toward personnel. A problem often arises in practice with regard to original employees of the firm who fail to match up to the demands of growth. For instance, a member of the staff, with limited ability but designated sales manager in the early days, may become, in the sophisticated light of progress, completely out of his depth. Should he realize this, he may expect some action to be taken, but, whether he does or not, in the best interests of the firm, he must be replaced. If other, less demanding, work can be found, presumably at a lower salary, this may serve as a reasonable solution.

The other universally accepted advantage of any small business is its marketing ability to provide the personal touch. This is illustrated by professional services, such as those sought from lawyers and accountants; by a small factory able to produce individual goods to order; or by the small corner shop still managing to compete with the large supermarket. For there is something satisfying to most people about being personally dealt with by the proprietor, director, or general manager, a personal touch also extending to suppliers and others having business relationships with the firm.

Finally, there can be a great deal of personal involvement by the staff in the fortunes of a small firm, with everyone taking an interest in successful development, in products that are selling well and in ideas that seem to be paying off. Small firms also tend to be valuable training grounds for young recruits, enabling them to see the woods as well as the trees. Such motivation is often made more effective by the short lines of communication, enabling everyone to know what is going on and to feel part of the team.

As already indicated, not all employees grow in stature with the firm's growth, but the owner/manager should be watching objectively for someone to succeed him at the right time. The main difficulty, usually, is with the man at the top, who, having built up a successful business, is unwilling to hand it over to the crown prince even when well past his prime.

The Process of Growth

Having survived the initial years, a firm eventually reaches a point where progress has become assured. At this stage there is a danger point in that, having found a viable product or service, there is a temptation to oversell. Even where production can keep up with marketing, insufficient regard is usually paid to the financial implications; for finance too must be balanced with marketing and production. It is a matter of record that many firms fail simply because they have become unbalanced.

The next stage is usually where the firm grows beyond the personal control of the entrepreneur and develops into a much more sophisticated structure. At this point of development many different kinds of plan may mature, including the provision of larger premises, new production facilities, new equipment and extra staff, together with added strength for management. Somewhere along this line of expansion there may arise a feeling that everything is at last going satisfactorily; this is yet another danger signal in that complacency is ever ready to take over from vigilant management.

Thereafter further progress needs to be interspersed with occasional periods of consolidation, until the firm eventually reaches maturity. If this is more than ten years from the outset, the time may well be ripe for the firm to "go public."

The Decision to "Go Public"

The timing in this context is a critical factor, to be decided in the light of the firm's record of past profits, the present trading situation, and its future prospects. The capital position is also significant as regards its structure, including the amount of working capital available. Before the securities can be listed on the New York Stock Exchange, for example, the corporation must meet a number of requirements, including earnings in excess of $2½ million for several years, a minimum number of stockholders, and public disclosure of annual results. The company will need to be thoroughly investigated before any issuing house will consent to take on the job of floating a public issue of its shares. Usually, it is necessary to start negotiations some two or three years before the firm actually requires access to the stock market. This will allow sufficient time for the right amount of confidence to be built up concerning the firm's affairs, and enable the ground to be prepared generally in anticipation of receiving public status.

Among the *advantages* of going public can be listed the following main points:

(a) The availability of additional finance to match planned growth, at the time and afterwards, by new issues. The valuation and marketability of having quoted shares.

(b) The status of being a public corporation, including the enhanced status of its directors, and the consequent advantages with regard to external relationships. It may, for example, be found easier to negotiate large contracts.

There are certain *disadvantages* that should also be taken into account before making any decision:

(a) There will be some loss of control, owing to the wider share base, with appropriate representation on the board.

(b) Future policy decisions will need to take the stockholders' interests into account, with special reference to planned profit growth and distributions.

(c) Vulnerability to unwelcome takeover.

This last point introduces the factor of mergers and acquisitions, for at any stage in the life of a small firm there may be the temptation to join forces with other small firms or to sell out to a larger company. But this is a subject relating to firms of *all* sizes and is conveniently left until the final chapter.

Summary

1. Importance of Small Firms
a. Size is relative, but "small" usually means less than 250 workers.
b. Roughly 96 per cent of all manufacturing firms are "small" in this sense.
c. Small firms demonstrate better capacity for profits growth than large firms.
d. Even a small firm needs professional management.

2. Problem of Survival
a. Reasons for the high casualty rate of small firms include insufficient capital, bad debts, and over-reliance on trade credit.
b. The main cause is usually mismanagement.

3. Special Help and Advice
a. There is still scope for subsidized consultancy services.
b. Tax constraints restrict the ploughing back of profits.

4. Administrative Difficulties
a. A manager runs the risk of becoming over-absorbed with daily problems.
b. Key employees may not grow with the firm.
c. Management must keep up to date with events and techniques.
d. Planning at top level continues to be essential.

5. Advantages of Being Small
a. Narrow market sectors can be explored with success, but too much success attracts competition.
b. Marketing flexibility suggests new opportunities.
c. The small firm is able to provide the personal touch.
d. Employees are more likely to be motivated by a sense of involvement.
e. But for the fact that managers are often unwilling to retire, the small firm provides valuable practical training for succession.

6. Process of Growth
a. At a certain stage of growth future progress is assured, but the firm may become unbalanced.
b. Such a firm is usually tempted into over-selling.

c. There is a danger of complacency when nearing maturity.
d. A critical point occurs when the firm is too large for personal control.
e. The decision to go public is a matter of careful timing.
f. The advantages and disadvantages of going public need to be considered in detail.
g. Possible merger or acquisition opportunities should not be overlooked.

Suggested Further Reading

BAUMBACK, C.M., ET AL. *How to Organize and Operate a Small Business.* 5th ed. Englewood Cliffs, N.J.: Prentice-Hall, 1973.

BAUMBACK, C.M., AND J.R. MANCUSO. *Entrepreneurship and Venture Management.* Englewood Cliffs, N.J.: Prentice-Hall, 1975.

BROOM, H.N., AND J.G. LONGENECKER. *Small Business Management.* 2d ed. Cincinnati, Ohio: South-Western, 1966.

CHAPMAN, E.N. *Getting into Business.* New York: Wiley, 1976.

HAZEL, A.C., AND A.S. REID. *Managing the Survival of Smaller Companies.* New York: Beekman, 1973.

KLATT, L.A. *Managing the Dynamic Small Firm: Readings.* Belmont, Calif.: Wadsworth, 1971.

KLATT, L.A. *Small Business Management: Essentials of Entrepreneurship.* Belmont, Calif.: Wadsworth, 1973.

SIXTEEN

Mergers and Acquisitions

In Chapter Seven, when dealing with objectives and long-range planning, brief reference was made to growth ambitions, including the
possibilities of mergers and acquisitions. It was noted that while the
taking of undue risks has dangers for a firm, so too has any half-
hearted development that is not positive enough in its approach. It is
certainly true that mergers and acquisitions need a bold attitude, regardless of whether the firm intends to be aggressive or cooperative
or is forced on to the defensive.

The terms "merger" and "acquisition" are often used synonymously, but the former implies a welding together of companies with
comparable bargaining strength, whereas the latter is basically the
taking over of a company by a stronger, usually much larger, organization.

Writers on this topic tend to elaborate on the clear analogy with
marriage; they describe the search for a partner, attractions and
counterattractions, courtship, the wedding ceremony, the honey-
moon, domestic bliss (or the complete reverse) thereafter. They refer
also to matchmaking, willing unions, marriages of convenience, shot-
gun weddings, and divorce. These are useful and relevant compari-

sons, which should be kept in mind, by way of illustration, to highlight the more conventional text that follows.

The Current Trend

Since the end of the nineteenth century, a number of broad merger movements have appeared on the American economic scene: one that brought a number of giant industrial trusts into the twentieth century, a second that preceded the Great Depression, and still a third (characterized by a major trend toward diversification) that extended from the mid-1950s throughout all of the following decade. In fact, mergers and acquisitions during the 1960s were at such a fever pitch that the decade has been described as the "Age of the Conglomerates." By the mid-1960s, for one example, Standard Oil had managed to acquire some 400 companies.

Thus far in the 1970s, there has been some leveling off of this activity. Some indication of this slowdown can be seen in the data below for 1972 and 1973:

Type of Company	Number of Companies Acquired 1972	1973
Manufacturing	997	877
Mining	39	52
Wholesale and Retail Trades	219	158
Services and miscellany	858	832
TOTALS:	2,113	1,919

Asset Size of Companies Acquired	1972	1973
Under $1 million	268	253
$1 to 9.9 million	254	249
$10 to 49.9 million	580	456
$50 to 99.9 million	272	208
$100 million and over	739	753
TOTALS:	2,113	1,919

The pattern of the last ten years, in numbers, is illustrated in Figure 20, which traces only the manufacturing and mining concerns acquired, as reported by Moody's Investors Service and Standard and Poor's. It should be noted that many small acquisitions are omitted by these sources.

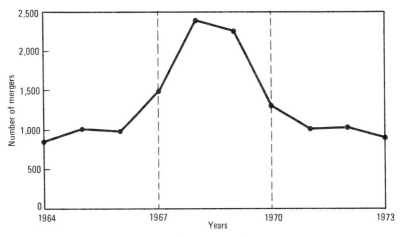

FIGURE 20. The pattern of mergers

DEVELOPING GROWTH OBJECTIVES

Normal business growth is a gradual process, faster at some times than at others. But growth by merger is an acceleration of that pace, often constituting a rapid jump ahead. Development is usually a more carefully planned and consolidated rate of progress, with every new activity being integrated into the organization, step by step, in accordance with policy.

A merger, on the other hand, can mean a complete realignment of physical and human assets, some of them being taken over without any real opportunity being afforded to find out how they will (or even if they will) fit effectively into the new pattern. This must be so with regard to the integration of two units brought together lock, stock, and barrel. In fact, some critics argue that, while there may be a quick leap forward, there may also be an early step backward caused by administrative indigestion and possibly by the discontinuing of certain parts not really required in the first place.

Planning for Mergers and Acquisitions

Having defined the company objectives as quantitatively as possible in relation to growth by merger, it is then necessary to reassess the corporate resources, in the light of the task in hand, and work out a plan of action. Given an objective to develop only by means of normal growth processes, there should at least be a policy to minimize vulnerability to the likely takeover ambitions of some other company. The more positive merger plan fits into the long-range plan as a way of progress and should be based on adding to company strengths and/or overcoming company weaknesses. Growth merely for the sake of growth is much harder to justify in the face of public interests. In planning for mergers, full consideration must be given to the reasons behind the policy, to ways and means of financing the operations involved, and to the likely after-effects if successful.

In general, the planning reason may well be to achieve quantified growth objectives as quickly as possible by bringing in additional resources, such as new products, services or markets, new manufacturing facilities, additional sources of finance, and/or new expertise in management. In this kind of situation it is important to appreciate the real reasons for whatever action is planned, for it is clearly wrong to proceed optimistically with a merger and then try to rationalize the situation afterwards.

Taking an example, it is likely that the integration of two large organizations, including human problems with regard to personnel, will be long and difficult; and these aspects must be taken fully into account at the planning stage. In particular, the financial implications must be clearly understood. For instance, will the operation be economical to mount or costly? What are the risks involved as against expanding in the normal way? Are these risks considered to be worthwhile in view of the benefits to be obtained? For this is another illustration of "synergy," where the value of the whole may prove to be greater than the sum of the two separate parts.

The Logic Behind the Planning

In addition to the general points already made, it may be helpful to summarize the usual advantages and disadvantages thought likely to arise from mergers looked at as a whole. These points may be regarded as key reasons, growth directions, or simply the case for and against. It must be emphasized, however, that circumstances alter cases and that, in addition to general policy, any given case should be flexibly assessed on its individual merits.

POTENTIAL ADVANTAGES
OF MERGERS AND ACQUISITIONS

(a) Marketing: increased turnover; more intensive use of existing markets, adding new markets, perhaps expanding from local or regional markets to national markets; access to new market-research information; adding new products or services to the product line to help existing customers and/or add new customers with associated needs; offsetting any seasonal or cyclical fluctuations related to the existing product line; acquiring brand names and any special market reputation.

(b) Production: new products and/or markets making greater use of existing plant and machinery, thus leading to increased economies of scale; acquiring patent rights, licenses, etc., and additional R. and D. facilities; augmenting or complementing productive capacity, additional factory buildings, plant and equipment; new manufacturing processes; vertical integration, acquiring sources of raw materials and/or customer outlets.

(c) Finance: better utilization of joint resources, employing idle capital or gaining additional funds (as, for example, a progressive company acquiring a dormant company having little ambition, but ample cash or marketable securities); taking advantage of a tax loss situation: spreading the business risk; minimizing stock-held balances; increasing the market value of shares; exploiting large-scale opportunities, enhanced profits and reserves.

(d) Management and Personnel: outlet for excess managerial capacity; acquiring additional management skills, key workers, trained staff, etc.; access to training facilities, management development plans, etc.

These are some of the reasons for mergers, but the list is by no means exhaustive. A key element in a given merger, for example, can be that a progressive chairman or president has visions of grandeur. In this event the main attraction will be the extra power and prestige emanating from an enlarged enterprise. Small companies, too, may be motivated to join together in order to become eligible to submit a formal application for a Stock Exchange quotation. Finally, to take a different kind of example, in a privately held corporation, the incentive for being taken over can be the problem of advancing age or indifferent health of the family shareholders, well aware of the constraints of estate taxes on their firm's finances.

Issues of Public Policy

Basically, any merger should result in some net benefit to the community; otherwise there would seem to be no intrinsic advantage in the exercise, other than personal advantage such as that indicated above. Usually, there is an increase in the scale of operations, with more monopoly power and possibly enhanced prices, coupled with economy in the use of scarce resources, and cost reduction. Often growth by large-scale merger is held to be the only way to achieve sufficient strength to compete successfully in international markets. But any mention of monopoly, or any other form of collective power, immediately raises national issues of policy. It is therefore convenient to look at the disadvantages of mergers in the context of the public interest.

Nevertheless, there are some very different sections of the public, some with conflicting points of view, and any policy issue of this kind can therefore become controversial. Authorities argue variously for the interests of stockholders, customers, suppliers, and personnel employed; or, with no special axe to grind, for the interests of the community at large. There are, of course, justifiable criticisms of merger operations, such as those which finish up as a structural anachronism, usually because of a basic lack of compatibility.

It is legally possible, for example, for two companies to merge with completely different objectives, policies, corporate character, personalities, and climate of work. But unless there are substantial advantages in other directions, the main result is likely to be resignations or discharge of key executives, bad morale, in-fighting for jobs temporarily duplicated, trade union difficulties, general dissatisfaction and loss of production. Couple this with unpopular rationalization, such as closing down duplicated factories, departments or branches or organizing new administrative structures, procedures, and jobs, and it may take years to overcome the initial shocks sustained. The natural resistance of workers to change of any kind has already been highlighted in Chapter Two.

Then there are charges of companies setting out their stall for improved bidding powers in the merger market, by juggling with short-term operations, effectively sacrificing future needs for current gain. To develop further the public-policy theme it is useful to examine briefly the implications of a takeover.

Takeover Implications

It might be thought that both parties to a possible union between companies of comparable size would be well able to look after themselves. But merger history has some interesting examples to offer of industrial giants caught complacently napping at particularly vulnerable times.

Most mergers, being by mutual agreement between the respective boards after painstaking investigation by both sides, are usually successful, subject to compatibility. It has been seen that larger units after voluntary merger can produce substantial net cost/benefits of increased managerial efficiency. While there may be some inherent danger of monopoly, this can be dealt with by the imposition of overriding constraints.

A more debatable approach by takeover is where vigorous attempts are made to obtain a majority holding in a company by making attractive bids direct to shareholders. These bids may well be made over the heads of the directors, who, in self-defense, will tend to retaliate by advising their stockholders to reject them. Much depends, however, on the general background, the company's record, the attractiveness of the bid, the tone of comment in the press and so on. Usually, whether directors recommend acceptance or rejection, their influence on the final outcome can be considerable.

It was suggested earlier that any company should ensure that its financial position is not vulnerable to attack by takeover. This assumes an efficient management (unfortunately not always a safe assumption to make) carefully watching the environmental situation, which, from time to time, provides opportunities for takeover. A long period of inflation, resulting in assets being allowed to become considerably undervalued on the balance sheet, is a good example. The wide variation between the true values and the book values of premises, investments, and other assets enables attractive, less costly, bids to be made.

In general, vulnerability is caused by an inefficient management not making maximum use of the company's assets and keeping dividends too low. For it is the duty of management to optimize the return on capital employed and to maximize the profit earnings ratio in the interests of the shareholders.

When a bid is made in such circumstances, the alleged intention is normally to improve managerial efficiency in respect of the combined unit, make full use of the underemployed assets, produce operating economies and pay more realistic dividends. The company making the bid, having assessed the situation, is quite prepared to take over existing resources, even though a loss is currently being made, visualizing what could be achieved with those resources given efficient management. For management is still the vital factor as between success and failure.

In making the offer the bidder will exploit the weaknesses of the company it wishes to take over, by arguing that more profits will be made and more profits will be distributed; and that the improved dividend situation will be maintained by more effective use of assets coupled with the divestment of unprofitable assets.

In seeking to persuade stockholders to reject a bid, the directors will probably support their recommendation with belated good intentions for improved growth activities and more generous distribution. These intentions, however, must be based on realistic profit forecasts which will tend to have a vital influence on the final decision by stockholders. Coupled with such forecasts may well be a statement setting out the true worth of assets as revalued professionally. Should the offer be rejected on this advice, then the bidding will probably be raised and the cost of the takeover may well become higher than it would if freely negotiated between two willing boards. There is always the chance, of course, that stockholders will be tempted into accepting a first or subsequent bid at too low a level, not appreciating the true value of their equity situation. Hence the importance of having a realistic profit forecast, etc., as indicated above, to enable a balanced judgment to be made.

There is a possibility, too, that a company making a bid may not be interested in the other company as a going concern, but simply as a means of acquiring the assets. These can then be sold to other firms likely to make better use of them, thereby netting a capital profit. This type of transaction, often referred to as "asset-stripping," is not, however, the most usual.

The intervention of other companies making counter-bids adds considerably to the problems of the directors of the company under attack; but it may be welcomed by stockholders for obvious reasons. Part of the directors' problem is that the company they would prefer to merge with may not be the one making the most attractive offer. It is essential, too, that all bids made should be capable of being implemented and that stockholders be given the fullest possible information and sufficient time in which to make up their minds whether to accept an offer or not. Inherent in any bid is the understanding that no section of the stockholders should be given more favorable terms than the remainder, and that minority rights should be safeguarded. For it is essential that the interests of *all* stockholders should be properly protected.

Usually, the initial intimation of a takeover is by a newspaper announcement, which may or may not set out the terms in detail. Where the takeover is an amicable arrangement, the announcement will include the board's recommendation; in more aggressive circumstances the directors may well get the first inkling of the proposed union from their morning newspapers.

It can happen, of course, that hints of talks and rumors of takeover will appear in the press, anticipating any formal announcement, thus tending to unsettle the share market by stimulating a rise in prices; it will also unsettle most of those in the company's employment. This being so, the board of the company likely to be taken over, whether willingly or not, will have some difficult decisions to make. It is a problem, in any case, to know exactly when to advise stockholders and employees of likely changes by merger. For there is a responsibility to stockholders who may be considering selling shares in ignorance of the likely advantages of holding on for the time being, and to the employees whose future may be at stake for better or for worse. But in case negotiations should break down, it may be better in the event not to tell anyone outside the boardroom, thus avoiding a sudden rise and subsequent fall in share prices. Yet the press will always seek to ferret out even secret talks, supposedly with the best intentions for the community in general. With large-scale protracted discussions, in particular, it is almost impossible to maintain a wall of secrecy for very long—mainly because there are usually too many opportunities for leaks, whether accidental or inspired. In this context the undercover aggressive takeover has considerable surprise advantage when making a first announcement.

On occasion, the tables have been turned on a takeover bid by a so-called reverse bid, where the hunter becomes the hunted, but by and large the quantitative odds are heavily in favor of the original bidder.

Most bids begin as a general offer to all stockholders, usually subject to the proviso that the bidders will receive sufficient acceptances to gain the desired control. At some subsequent stage the offer may become unconditional. Payment, too, may be (and often is) in the form of shares in the bidder company being given in exchange for shares in the company sought to be taken over. These are usually called "paper-for-paper transactions." Alternatively, there may be an offer of cash or a mixture of shares and cash. The situation needs careful handling, however, in view of the possibility of attracting capital-gains tax.

OVERRIDING CONSTRAINTS

Any mention of monopoly growth, aggressive bidders and takeovers, suggests a need for some control in the best interests of all concerned. For there is always the inherent danger of undesirable financial practices, even within the strict letter of the law, and of short-term exploitation, not long-term economic strength.

Public Policy on Mergers and Acquisitions

More fundamental, however, is the concern of the federal government over the fact that the control of American industry is tending to become more and more concentrated into fewer hands. This attitude, of course, has been underscored even more firmly since the 1950s in the light of the rapid growth of governmental efforts to assist small business and industry.

Inquiries into the main objectives motivating mergers and acquisitions are consistent with public policy. For these suggest, first, the seeking of wider control of particular markets, through an increased market share, and secondly, the building up of corporate strength to oppose any similar attacks by other firms. For a good many decades, it has been the government's intent to restrict the development of budding monopolies by blocking any combinations and mergers that might conceivably prove injurious to healthy and free competition. Such laws as the Sherman Antitrust Act, the Federal Trade Commission Act, and the Celler-Kefauver Act (all already discussed under "Marketing") bear witness to this stand on free enterprise. In recent years, both the Antitrust Division of the Department of Justice and the Federal Trade Commission have been exceedingly active in their pursuit of combinations in restraint of trade. Their investigations have resulted in actions against a variety of industrial giants, ranging from oil companies through producers of soap products to cereal manufacturers and manufacturers of computers. Generally, today, it would be advisable for any corporation to seek a ruling from the Federal Trade Commission before proceeding with an acquisition of substantial size.

In general, there are three types of mergers, as identified below:

(a) *Horizontal integration,* where mergers take place between compatible companies of similar kind. This type of integration constitutes the bulk and the rationale of mergers.

(b) *Vertical integration,* where companies join up with other companies able to supply them with raw materials, etc., or with companies having suitable customer outlets.

(c) *Conglomerates,* where the companies linking up their resources appear to have little or nothing in common and thereby tend to evoke controversial comment in the process.

Problems of Conglomerates

The systematic acquisition of companies extended over a wide range of industries may appear to offer advantages of diversification and of spreading risks, but in practice difficulties have been seen to arise, and the conglomerate image is currently subject to second thoughts. Part of the controversy can be ascribed to the stock market, which has expressed doubts about the ability of the companies concerned to demonstrate comprehensive expertise over a variety of totally different businesses all at the same time. Conglomerate ambition may start from a surplus of managerial capacity, but sooner or later it will outrun itself by the sheer weight of growth. Furthermore, it has become clear that the real economies of scale can only arise from the merging of companies within the same industry having features in common such as marketing, production, and research and development.

Other arguments against conglomerates center on the adverse effect they produce on the general competitive situation. Having financial interests in many completely different fields, for example, they can easily become indifferent to competitive trends in any one of them. Whatever the reasons, conglomerates today tend to attract a variety of critical comment, officially and otherwise.

There are, however, examples of successful conglomerates, usually with holding companies exercising tight central financial control, lopping off all unprofitable assets ruthlessly. Whether these are to be considered as desirable integrations or not is another matter.

Records suggest that more conglomerates fail, in the light of post-takeover experience, than any other type of merger. This confirms the insistence on industrial compatibility stressed earlier as being a decisive factor in the determination of whether any bid should in fact be made at all. Although it must be conceded that there are successful conglomerates, these are the usual outstanding exceptions to a given rule.

Multinational Corporations

Mergers within the same industry, linking two or more countries together, have clear advantages of scale. In fact, with some large national concerns, the only way to obtain any further substantial economies of scale is to go international. Generally speaking, the attractions of multinational corporations include the cross-fertilization of management ideas, expertise, and technical know-how, the encouragement of increased industrial investment to meet new challenges, and the visible/invisible export advantages reflected in the balance of payments.

Just how effectively multinational corporations are going to become truly international over the years ahead, is currently a matter for conjecture. Among the many problems to be dealt with are the setting up of proper channels of communication and understanding, as between different countries, and between different nationals; the granting of local autonomy irrespective of race or creed; objective international promotion policies, with no imposed national bias; and so on, particularly when any one country in a given situation happens to hold the reins of power.

In the international merger field there are many additional problems to be overcome, starting with the cost and difficulty of obtaining and understanding pre-merger information. Legal and accounting practices vary from country to country, as do language and philosophy, and taxation aspects add to the other complexities. Nevertheless, management problems exist to be overcome and the way ahead may well be increasingly in the direction of multinational merger, with all its opportunities as well as risks.

PRACTICAL PROCESSES OF INTEGRATION

Having looked at the general background to mergers and acquisitions, it is appropriate now to give some attention to the managerial problems to be faced in practice. Although full emphasis is usually placed on the strategic benefits of any given merger, often only partly justified by subsequent events, there are many cases where the directors concerned fail to appreciate the full extent of the practical problems involved. Nor do they sufficiently realize the considerable time and energy that it will take to rationalize the operations of the combined enterprise, as theoretically and hopefully planned.

Preparing the Way for Merger

Proof of inadequate planning and faulty anticipation of the benefits of merger is often forthcoming, evidenced by the calling in of management consultants to sort out the aftermath. Insufficient attention to detail and superficial prior investigation of all relevant aspects appear to be the main causes of potential failure.

In taking a brief look at the main functions involved, it is convenient to observe the usual order adopted previously in this book.

This method seems obvious and comprehensive, but all too often in practice there is undue concentration on, say, the financial implications to the neglect of other equally critical areas.

As usual, strengths and weaknesses should be listed, with as much information as possible, including such quantification as could reasonably be expected. This could be compared with the more subjective approach to the general advantages estimated to come from the proposed merger. All the functional areas would need to be investigated, but in doing so it is important not to arouse premature suspicions. Where there is likely to be a voluntary union, however, the search for fundamental information devolves into asking the right kind of searching questions, management to management, and checking the answers received with whatever other facts are known at the time. The following aspects are included by way of illustration:

(a) Marketing. It should not be too difficult to assess the effectiveness of advertising, sales literature, salesmen, dealer networks, and other such factors by collective observation and careful inquiry, or as a special market-research operation, gradually building up a comprehensive picture of product range, innovation policy, distribution methods, and geographical spread.

(b) Production. Similarly, it would be essential to make an assessment of the production skills, techniques, etc., of the company concerned, whether basic manufacturing processes or assembly, being aware of factory locations, plant and machinery used, raw-material sources, transportation facilities and so on, as appropriate to the industry concerned.

(c) Finance. This position is helped by the availability of published information, albeit historical information. Any assessment of potential would take note of trends with respect to profitability, liquidity, capital structure, share price performance, whether fixed assets have been revalued recently, and so on through the usual range of financial investigation. Such an assessment should preferably be carried out by an expert in merger finance, for example a merchant banker, bearing in mind, too, the fixing of a realistic figure for the initial bid.

(d) Management and Personnel. The effectiveness of management may be inferred from past performance, or by known reputation, but without direct personal contact it is not easy to discover how compatible a union of two different groups of people is likely to be. Yet this

factor is vital to the eventual success of any attempt at integration; such human considerations are elaborated on later, being important enough to justify a section on their own.

Companies seeking to find suitable partners for merger or acquisitions to facilitate their growth have access to a variety of professional advice. There are different kinds of merger promoters, with some emphasis on bankers, merger brokers, or management consultants who will usually assist in evaluating the terms for merger, based on alternative plans; in initiating and carrying out the negotiations; and in helping, as required, after a merger has finally taken place.

Human Considerations

In dealing with surplus employment it is relatively easy to start with any personnel who happen to be near the age of normal retirement; the younger employees, who unfortunately cannot be found suitable jobs in the new organization, may need to be looked after instead by some form of monetary compensation. The payment of so-called golden handshakes to directors and top executives is a well-known fact of life, coupled with any existing pension rights to which they are entitled.

Senior staff and staff generally, if not actually losing their jobs, may find themselves having to continue their employment under less favorable conditions. They may not, for instance, like the new management philosophy or climate of work, so that they will tend to seek other employment or at least lose their motivation and sense of loyalty. In such cases it should be made possible for them to leave without suffering any financial hardship while looking for fresh employment.

There are practical problems, however, such as existing pension rights that it may not be possible to transfer to a particular new firm. Incidentally, looking at the situation as a whole, there may be unexpected financial strains on a pension fund, by premature retirements, including some loss of future contributions. Mergers being with us, for better or worse, the old tradition of a single firm providing individuals with a life career must inevitably give way to progressive mobility of employment. On this theme, it could be argued in equity that service contracts, etc. should not be binding with respect to a merged organization, and furthermore that any workers not wishing to continue under the new management should at least be entitled to receive termination pay. The legal position, however, is more inflexible.

Whatever the proposed scheme of integration, and however much it may seem to be in the public interest, there will still be natural feelings of insecurity and fears of layoffs on the part of labor. Quite apart from layoffs, adjustments may well have to be made to meet changes in the character of jobs; there may be transfers to different areas, factory and departmental changes, all of which can be highly disturbing, in addition to inevitable clashes of personality and initial feelings of "them" and "us."

Dealing with Administrative Indigestion

At any normal time administrative work can be heavy, but this is minimal compared with the overwhelming problems of post-merger integration. Given a union between relatively equal corporate bodies, one of the first tasks is to produce a state of domestic harmony for the combined organization, which is a searching responsibility for the new top management. On the more practical side, it may be considered advisable to appoint a merger manager, with temporary authority, to control the whole operation of integration.

Reference to the points listed earlier demonstrates the magnitude of the physical task to be performed. In the process it is hoped that the synergy will emerge as planned; all too often the final value of the whole proves to be less (not greater) than the sum of the two separate parts. For the history of mergers is strewn with examples of failure; few corporate bodies, in fact, succeed in achieving *all* their merger objectives, even in cases of amicable consent to union.

The crucial period is the merger aftermath, when the plans made during negotiations have to be carried out quickly and effectively. The following list, by no means complete, illustrates the range of problems to be faced. As indicated earlier, these should have been identified, evaluated, and planned for right from the start of merger negotiations. Even so, it is seldom realized just how difficult such digestion can be, in physical and human terms, and just how long it can take to achieve effectively. However, the list includes:

(a) Determination of the board structure and the composition of the top-executive team. This may involve political struggles for power, possible temporary duplication of top jobs, clashes of personality between senior personnel, and a difficult shaking-down process generally. The same repercussions may be felt right through the hierarchy. A new order will gradually emerge, but there are usually casualties on the way through to uneasy peace. Ideally, there should be a completely new board and top-executive team.

(b) Reorganizing the marketing side, from publicizing a new company image and logotype, possibly related to a new company name, right through to an augmented, streamlined, or revitalized sales force as applicable to the combined geographical territory to be covered and the products or services to be sold.

(c) Integrating and concentrating the manufacturing/service processes, possibly closing surplus factories, offices, branches, shops, etc., where duplication appears uneconomic. This is often easy to plan on paper but fraught with problems in practice. The combined R. and D. programs, patents, copyrights, etc. should be integrated at the same time. Throughout these operations normal marketing and production activities must be maintained in proper balance.

(d) The problems of bringing together and reorganizing all the financial aspects is the province of the accountants, as reflected ultimately in the combined published balance sheets.

(e) On the personnel side the human problems range from the determination of layoffs, in liaison with the trade unions concerned, to the fixing of new salary structures and wage rates, pension terms, and fringe benefits. This is a vital area already dealt with above, but it must be emphasized that the corporate loyalties and friendships may well continue indefinitely on the basis of two quite separate groups of people. The balance of power as between them may be held precariously on one side or the other at any given time.

Enough has been suggested to demonstrate that this is a vast operation not to be undertaken lightly. In the case of a takeover, whether by willing consent or the result of a contested bid, the absorption of a smaller company into the larger organization is a less difficult operation, but the process and personalities involved still produce much the same kind of problems. With growth by conglomerate, the holding company adds yet another subsidiary needing to be indoctrinated into the group's way of corporate life.

The success of merger policy may be judged by various criteria. Basically, the furtherance of long-range growth objectives is the starting-point, coupled with more specific regard for the outcome of a particular merger as compared with the original plans for that merger. If it is hoped to have a series of takeovers, then each success will add strength to future negotiations. As an overriding factor, stockholders will expect to see a steady increase in profits and distributions.

The Ultimate Rationalization

Large-scale size is not necessarily the same thing as large-scale efficiency and profitability. Mergers and acquisitions being the practical means to desired ends of accelerated growth objectives, it is salutary to keep this sobering thought in mind. The alleged inertia of size has long been blamed for the inability of large corporate bodies to be able to respond quickly enough to the changes inherent in any dynamic environment. Such changes are abundantly illustrated by new marketing situations; new materials, products, and processes; new sources of supply and distribution outlets; and so on through a long list of vital factors to be wrestled with continuously. Part of the reason for inflexibility is the time it takes for board decisions to be reached, at least on major issues of policy, as compared with a small concern virtually dominated by one man's entrepreneurial flair. The lessons of quick decision-making in response to sudden change have yet to be fully learned by the large corporate body. In a merger situation these problems of unwieldy reaction are therefore likely to become even more difficult than they were before.

In Chapter Four stress was laid on the problem of breaking down administrative bulk, by various means, in an attempt to alleviate the heavy burden on the home office; reference was made, for example, to decentralization and divisionalization. Throughout this chapter the emphasis has been on a speeding up of growth, thus presumably adding substantially to the administrative bulk. Hence the ultimate rationalization may well be to find practical ways and means of achieving all the benefits now sought by merger, by the reverse process of creating many small independent units held together by a sophisticated but flexible system of corporate federalization. To achieve such a system, however, necessarily invokes a new philosophy of managerial life and the solving of innumerable problems starting with the law.

But, as stressed throughout this book, the difficult problems are the essence and challenge of management and, in today's scene, the challenge and opportunity of youth. For today's youth is tomorrow's top management.

Summary

1. Definition
   a. A merger implies comparable bargaining strength.
   b. An acquisition suggests a takeover by a stronger unit.
   c. These two terms are often used synonymously.
2. Current Trend
   a. Throughout the late 1960s, several thousands of mergers took place each year.
   b. The merger rate has been slowing down in the 1970s.
3. Developing Growth Objectives
   a. Growth rate is speeded up by merger or acquisition.
   b. A positive merger plan should fit into the corporate plan.
   c. Normally a merger or acquisition will be considered only if it can add to strengths and overcome weaknesses; there may, however, be other attractions.
   d. Issues of public policy need to be considered.
4. Implications of Takeovers
   a. Most mergers are by mutual agreement, but takeovers can be aggressive.
   b. Small firms should ensure that they are not financially vulnerable, as otherwise the bidder can exploit weaknesses.
   c. The chief attraction is the extra profit an efficient management can achieve by using existing resources.
   d. Negotiations and tactics should be seen in various forms.
   e. The takeover is finally settled by the stockholders accepting the bidder's offer of shares and/or cash.
5. Overriding Constraints
   a. The legal aspects are set out in a variety of legislative acts that extended from the Sherman Antitrust Act (1890) through the Celler-Kefauver Act (1950).
   b. Both the Federal Trade Commission and the Antitrust Division of the Department of Justice have been monitoring merger activity with increasing vigilance.

   c. Special problems arise with conglomerates and multinational corporations.
6. *Final Integration*
   a. Preparation for merger must be comprehensive.
   b. The full extent of practical problems should be studied well in advance.
   c. Special consideration must be given to human aspects.
   d. Administrative indigestion can be severe.
   e. Ultimate rationalization aims to achieve the benefits sought by merger.

Suggested Further Reading

ALBERTS, W.W., AND J.E. SEGALL, eds. *The Corporate Merger.* Chicago: University of Chicago Press, 1974.

HARVEY, J.L., AND A. NEWGARDEN, eds. *Management Guides to Mergers and Acquisitions.* New York: Wiley, 1969.

HUTCHISON, G.S., ed. *The Business of Acquisitions and Mergers.* New York: Presidents Publishing House, 1968.

LINOWES, D.V. *Managing Growth Through Acquisition.* New York: American Management Association, 1968.

PARSONS, R.Q., AND J.S. BAUMGARTNER. *Anatomy of a Merger: How to Sell Your Company.* Englewood Cliffs, N.J.: Prentice-Hall, 1970.

SHORT, R.A. *Business Mergers: How and When to Transact Them.* Englewood Cliffs, N.J.: Prentice-Hall, 1967.

SHUCKETT, D.H., ET AL. *Financing for Growth: Internal Expansion and Merger Techniques.* New York: American Management Association, 1971.

STEINER, P.O. *Mergers: Motives, Effects, Policies.* Ann Arbor, Mich.: University of Michigan Press, 1975.

WYATT, A.R., AND D.E. KIESO. *Business Combinations: Planning and Action.* Scranton, Pa.: International Textbook, 1969.

Index